When FOOTBALL
Went to WAR

When FOOTBALL *Went to* WAR

TODD ANTON and BILL NOWLIN

TRIUMPH
BOOKS

Library of Congress Cataloging-in-Publication Data
has been applied for.

This book is available in quantity at special discounts
for your group or organization. For further information,
contact:

Triumph Books
814 North Franklin Street
Chicago, Illinois 60610
(312) 337-0747
Fax (312) 280-5470
www.triumphbooks.com

Printed in U.S.A.
ISBN: 978-1-60078-845-1
Production by Patricia Frey

Honoring those who served and remembering those who paid the last full measure

Contents

Foreword

◆

Ibecame enthralled and deeply moved when I read the captivating stories in this book about the men who put all else aside in order to serve in the cause to which our whole nation at the time was dedicated.

On December 7, 1941, the day that Pearl Harbor was bombed and World War II began, I was a 16 year-old junior student and member of the football team at South Shore High School in Chicago. Even then, I was enamored by the game of football. So many of the NFL players of that time, whose names evoked hallowed memories for me as I read this entrancing account, were my gridiron heroes. Then they became much more than that as I, and the whole country, watched them march off to war on behalf of a cause that meant even more than gridiron glory.

They contributed in helping to inspire our nation during a desperate time. They also contributed to inspiring me along with 21 of my high school teammates and classmates, when in June 1943, on the day after we graduated from high school, we all enlisted in the Army Air Corps.

These revered NFL players, of course, were not the only ones who rallied to face this challenge, but it was an honor for them, too, to have been among the 16 million Americans who answered the call.

There is nothing "glorious" about war, despite how it is sometimes depicted. I can recall, just

a few years ago during a Pro Football Hall of Fame ceremony, sitting next to Artie Donovan, a great former NFL defensive lineman and a decorated veteran of several World War II battles in the Pacific. We were all viewing a big-screen presentation of a pregame "pep talk" being delivered by a fired-up player along the sideline to his teammates just prior to the kickoff of the previous season's AFC Championship Game.

That player was screaming, "This is war! This is war!" Artie turned to me and said, "Marv, I've played football, and I've been to war. Football is not war." I concur.

No, war is not "glorious." It is about sacrifice when it is most needed in circumstances that are dire, and I do believe that among the many who did make that sacrifice we can count those NFLers who stepped away from their coveted careers for such a vital purpose. After the war many of them came sprinting joyfully out onto the field of play once again. We remember them, but we must never forget those who would never play the game again. They are the ones who made the ultimate sacrifice—that of their lives.

We will not forget them, and this book serves as a wonderful tribute to them all and to the game of football, as well. So, go get your ankles taped and enjoy reading it.

—Marv Levy

Acknowledgments

I've long believed that victory in World War II, and all of our nation's conflicts, comes on the backs of the common man, the common soldier often depicted by Bill Mauldin's classic Willie and Joe cartoons. Some of those common men were extraordinary athletes who walked away from a game they loved to serve a nation they loved more. *When Football Went to War* grew out of that belief. There was a noted WWII adage: "We're all in this together." That is truer now than it was then. Our 2008 book, *When Baseball Went to War*, grew out of that belief, and here once again, a team assembled to look at the athlete as contributor to the war effort. For me, this team begins and ends with my wife, Susan, and two great kids, Jamie and Jason. We have a home divided at times, with half rooting for the Saints and the other half rooting for the Packers. Thanks for catching the fever. Also, what can I say about my right-hand partner/writer for so long, Bill Nowlin? His dedication, work ethic, and art in telling and writing a good story always inspire me. None of this would have happened without you, Bill. Your kindness is immeasurable. You are the best.

Also this project could not have happened without the National World War II Museum led by Dr. Gordon "Nick" Mueller, Stephen Watson, and the Board of Trustees who were patient, generous, and helpful in funding the research for this effort. Thank you to the Pro Football Hall of Fame in Canton, Ohio. Football is America, and spending any time in Canton will teach you that.

I would like to thank The Sons of the American Legion Pelham, New York Post #50 for your help and advice. I am proud to be a member!

Thank you to Triumph Books and Tom Bast for believing in this concept and supporting it. It doesn't get much better, and your passion, professionalism, and vision are truly appreciated.

There are others too who have moved this story along to its completion and whose vision and renaissance-like talent will take this story even further—Colin Hanks, Sean Stuart, Chuck Dalaklis, and all who all came aboard after a chance encounter with Steve Fuhrman, my brother, on a warm Southern California afternoon at the beach. Also thank you to American Military University for their support and assistance to me.

Lastly, thank you to my mom and dad who both served America and raised five children to do the same. Although you have both left us now, your spirit carries on as we grow into the people you wanted us to be.

It's amazing the journey life takes you on and the people you meet. I've learned a lot about people on this journey, and in the end kindness repays kindness, and we still see an endless road of freedom ahead of us—a gift from all of those who have gone before.

God bless all of you my friends,
Todd Anton

After returning from combat with the army in Europe, Chaffey Junior College tackle Wally Anton (Todd Anton's father) poses for the upcoming Junior College Rose Bowl Game in Pasadena, California, 1947. (Photo courtesy of Todd Anton)

I remain inspired by Todd Anton and his lifelong dedication to honoring our veterans. He is author of the book, *No Greater Love*, which I was pleased to edit and publish, and we have now collaborated on two "team effort" publications, one on professional baseball and *When Football Went to War*, which focuses on pro football but acknowledges the college game as well. Todd does community-based work as well. For many years now he, along with his eighth-grade history students, has presented a Veteran's Day dinner in his home community which has honored thousands of veterans while giving the students the opportunity to learn about their commitments and sacrifices and become involved in public appreciation of their service. Todd's dedication and enthusiasm are and remain inspirational to me, too.

Thanks to Tom Bast of Triumph Books, who first got me started in writing books back in the middle 1990s. Thanks for help with research to Saleem Choudhry of the Pro Football Hall of Fame. And thanks to Nick Mueller and Stephen Watson of the National World War II Museum, who agreed to sponsor the idea Todd and I had presented for a conference on baseball and World War II that was held at the Museum in New Orleans and led to the book, *When Baseball Went to War*. The Museum provided most of the funding for the research of this companion book.

The Professional Football Researchers Association was a source of a good amount of information, and we would particularly like to thank its executive director Ken Crippen and assistant executive director Andy Piascik.

I would also like to thank Triumph Books editor Karen O'Brien, who labored behind the scenes to make this a book in which we can all take pride.

—Bill Nowlin

The authors would like to thank the following individuals and institutions: Matthew Algeo; Bill Ames of Triumph Books; Jamie Anton; Sue Anton; Gary Bedingfield; Chuck Bednarik; Jay Blackman of the University of Tennessee–Chattanooga; Marv Levy; Art Donovan; Joe Foss; Steve Fuhrman; Col. Gregory Gadson; John Gunn; Ken Harbour; Paul Helgren of the University of Toledo; Joe Horrigan of the Pro Football Hall of Fame; Jeff Keag, Alison Reynolds, and Carrie Lynn Schwier from Indiana University; Bill Johnston of the San Diego Chargers; Charlie Joiner; Gregory J. Kocken of the University of Wyoming; Ken Kraetzer; Tod Maher; ProFootballArchives.com; Gino Marchetti; Frederic Allen Maxwell; Linda McCarthy; Gerald Parnell of the University of North Carolina–Wilmington; Andrea Pelose of Triumph Books; Melissa Pihos; Morgan Reed; Eamonn Reynolds of the Detroit Lions; Stew Salowitz of Illinois Wesleyan University; The Snowline School District; Mark Cohen, Brenda Barnes, Karen Tjarks, and Roger Rainwater from Texas Christian University; Charley Trippi; Brian Gunning, Suzanne Christoff, and Casey Madrick of the United States Military Academy; David and Ray Wemple; and Debi Whiting.

Section 1

When Football Went to War

THE LAST DAY OF INNOCENCE

In the orange haze of another Pacific sunrise, Japanese fighter planes, bombers, and torpedo planes rendezvoused at their rally point off the Hawaiian Island of Oahu. At 7:55 AM local time, the serenity of the tranquil Hawaiian morning was shattered by the roar of engines, the staccato patter of bullets, and the cacophonous reverberation of exploding shells. Japan's unexpected and brutal attack on the naval base at Pearl Harbor, Hawaii, had begun. Meanwhile, the people living in the contiguous 48 states of the United States of America were going about their weekly Sunday rituals. For them, Sunday, December 7, 1941, had begun like any other typical late-fall Sunday. Americans from California to Maine had no sense of how much their lives were about to change as they went about their routine of attending church and family gatherings and, of course, watching football.

Back in 1941, the National Football League consisted of 10 teams and two divisions, and every year the winner of the East Division played the winner of the West Division in a winner-take-all NFL Championship Game. As it happens, December 7, 1941, was the last day of the 1941 regular season, and only three games were scheduled to be played—one in New York City, one in Washington, D.C., and one in Chicago, which was the only game with playoff implications. The Cleveland Rams, Pittsburgh Steelers, Detroit Lions, and Green Bay Packers had already concluded their 11-game regular season, the New York Giants had won the Eastern Division, and all but the players on the Bears and the 10–1 Packers had begun their off-season.[1]

The Packers and their fans were anxiously awaiting the outcome of that day's intra-city rivalry game between the Chicago Bears and Chicago Cardinals at Comiskey Park to determine whether or not they would have to play a one-game playoff the following Sunday in order to represent the West Division in the NFL Championship Game. A Bears win that day would mean that the NFL would have its first-ever NFL divisional playoff game, with the winner earning the right to play the New York Giants in the championship game on December 21. A Bears loss would drop their record to 9–2 and propel the Green Bay squad directly into the NFL Championship Game against the Giants on Sunday, December 14. The games to be played at New York's Polo Grounds and Washington, D.C.'s Griffith Stadium on December 7 were for bragging rights and pride. The only people who had access to these NFL contests were the fans who passed through the turnstiles of the three home teams or who were fortunate enough to catch one of the radio broadcasts that day. Meanwhile, few Americans had any notion of what was taking place in the Pacific Ocean around the Hawaiian Island of Oahu.

It was 1:55 PM EST when the attack on Pearl Harbor began. At Comiskey Park in Chicago, the Bears and Cardinals were already embroiled in a hard-hitting affair that saw the Cardinals jump out to an early 14-point lead; they led the Bears 17–14 at halftime. It was during the first half that the public address announcer at Comiskey Park interrupted the game to tell all military personnel in attendance to report to their units; the fans and players were left to wonder what was going on. Unbeknownst to the men on the field at the time, many of them would soon be engaged in vastly different but significantly more important contests than this game. Even the iconic head coach, George Halas—whose Bears mounted a second-half rally that propelled them into the divisional playoff and ultimately to their second consecutive NFL championship—would answer the call to service in World War II. Halas left his undefeated Bears (5–0) halfway through the 1942 season in order to serve as a lieutenant commander in the United States Navy.[2]

Back in New York City, the New York Giants were hosting their inter-borough rival, the Brooklyn Dodgers, at the Polo Grounds—in the early days of the NFL, the football squad sometimes adopted the same moniker as the Major League Baseball team that shared the venue. Upon cursory inspection, the contest between the Giants and the Dodgers appeared to be anti-climatic; the Giants were already going to the NFL Championship Game while the Dodgers were playing out the string. But for the franchise-record 55,051 people who crammed into the Polo Grounds that day, as well as the millions of other Giants and Dodgers fans, this was a rivalry game. And because the Dodgers had beaten the Giants 16–13 at Ebbets Field in Week 8 of the season, the Dodgers and their faithful were not convinced the Giants were the city's best NFL team.[3]

In addition to the rivalry, fans were drawn to the Polo Grounds that day to pay tribute to their star running back, Alphonse "Tuffy" Emil Leemans, who the Giants wanted to honor for his contributions to the team. Their second-round pick in the NFL's first-ever college draft in 1936 played fullback and halfback—and even excelled on defense—and he consistently kept the Giants in championship contention through the years. For this and more, he had earned his own day. The Giants players quietly assembled on the field for the ceremony and watched as Tuffy Leemans was presented with a silver tray, a watch, and $1,500 in defense bonds.[4] The ceremony began at 1:30 PM EST, and the players on the field and the fans in the stands had no inkling that at 1:55 PM EST, shortly before the speeches honoring Tuffy Leemans had begun, the first Japanese planes were dropping their bombs on Pearl Harbor.

Those who didn't have a ticket to the Polo Grounds that day could still listen to the game over the radio. One such person was a red-headed teen who went on to become a Hall of Fame broadcaster for the Brooklyn, and then Los

Angeles, Dodgers baseball club. Eight days after his 14th birthday, Edward "Vin" Scully settled under his radio at his home in the Washington Heights section of Manhattan to take in the Giants-Dodgers broadcast on station WOR. The young Scully liked to lay under the stand upon which the family radio sat and hold on to the legs so that he could "feel the sounds of the game."[5] Like many other football fans, he was tuned into the Tuffy Leemans Day proceedings and had no hint that his life was about to change; there was no immediate report inside the stadium, or over the radio, regarding the surprise attack thousands of miles away. As the young Scully listened to the description of the intense action taking place on the field that day, the stadium's public address announcer could be heard paging the army intelligence chief, Col. William J. Donovan, with the directive to call "operator 19 in Washington."[6] The announcer also told all military personnel that they needed to report to their units. Suddenly, the radio broadcast itself was interrupted by the news of the Japanese attack; it, too, instructed all servicemen to report for duty.

The typical late-fall American Sunday afternoon had abruptly changed. As the news of the attack on Pearl Harbor poured out of the speaker and into the Scully home, young Vin sat there stunned by what he was hearing. It was shocking and scary. A bewildered Vin asked his parents, "What is going on?" The only words they could muster in reply were, "My God! This means war."[7]

Millions of other Americans reacted similarly to the Scullys when they heard the news of the attack on Pearl Harbor. Back at the Polo Grounds, the players on the field and the spectators in the stands had no awareness of what had just taken place in the Pacific Ocean; they did not find out about the attack until after the Dodgers' 21–7 victory. Two Sundays later, the Giants lost to the Chicago Bears 37–9 in the NFL Championship Game.

It was 7:55 AM Hawaii time that December day when military personnel at the base in Pearl Harbor were awakened by gunfire and explosions. Five time zones to the east, in Washington, D.C., the Washington Redskins and Philadelphia Eagles were preparing for a 2:00 PM EST start at Griffith Stadium. It was cold in Washington that day as 27,102 spectators made their way into the stands, reporters made their way to the press box, and the players on the field tried to stay warm. By game time thousands of Americans had been killed or wounded, but most of those inside Griffith Stadium had no clue that this was happening. The game was their sole focus; they were there to see "Slingin'" Sammy Baugh lead the Redskins to a respectable 6–5 record.[8] Soon after Philadelphia had taken an early 7–0 lead on their first drive, the PA announcer began a string of announcements: "Admiral Bland is asked to report to his office…. Captain H.X. Fenn is asked to report…. The resident commissioner of the Philippines is urged to report…." Baugh stated later, "We didn't know what the hell was going on. I had never heard that many announcements one right after another. We felt something was up, but we just kept playing."[9]

The only people in the stadium who had any hint of what was going on in the Pacific were the occupants of the press box. Associated Press reporter Pat O'Brien received a message instructing him to keep his report of the game brief; only in a follow-up second message did he get the news after he complained and asked the reason.[10] The spectators still had no idea. Feeling that it would distract the fans, Redskins owner George Preston Marshall wouldn't allow an announcement of the Japanese attack on Pearl Harbor during the game. As he later said, "I didn't want to divert the fans' attention from the game."[11] Oblivious to the world-changing event taking place outside, the fans inside the stadium loudly cheered as the Redskins were led to a 20–14 victory on the strength of two fourth-quarter touchdown passes thrown by their hero, Sammy Baugh. While a few hundred fans rushed the goalposts, the rest of the fans exited Griffith Stadium. It wasn't until they cleared the turnstiles that they heard the news. They were shocked to hear newsboys outside the stadium shouting, "Extra papers!"[12] and brandishing newspapers that declared "U.S. at War." The game was made inconsequential by this transformative national event, so much so that some have even referred to the Eagles/Redskins game played that day as "the most forgotten game ever played."[13]

Many Redskins and Eagles players and other football personnel would soon be going to war as they answered their country's call to arms. In fact, almost a thousand players and team personnel from the National Football League's 10 franchises would participate in history's bloodiest conflict in the ensuing four years. Sammy Baugh, the hero of the Eagles/Redskins game, went home to Texas expecting to receive a call from the draft board, but the call never came; Baugh worked on his ranch doing the essential work of raising beef cattle for the war effort. During the war he flew in on the weekends to play football games.[14]

For Americans, World War II began in a place most of them had never heard of, but what took place on that Sunday morning in the Pacific Ocean impacted all of them—immediately and completely. The world had suddenly become a more dangerous place. Americans would have to adopt an ethos of sacrifice. Americans from every corner of the nation and from every walk of life were called upon to do all they could for the cause. Some made the ultimate sacrifice, giving their lives for the cause of stopping totalitarianism. And the NFL was not immune. Both players and team personnel from the National Football League were among those who served and sacrificed. Many served with distinction, several were commissioned as officers, and some gave their lives. The attack on Pearl Harbor had shattered America's innocence. The United States government and all Americans were in for the battle of their lives as they sought to preserve the world for democracy.

Unnecessary Distraction or Morale-Builder?

As people throughout the United States tried to process what had taken place on December 7, they turned to President Franklin D.

Roosevelt for guidance. Naturally, the call for war was immediate, and on December 8, 1941, the United States Congress voted (almost unanimously) for a declaration of war on the Empire of Japan. War was declared on Germany three days later. Buoyed by the words of FDR's "Infamy Speech," Americans began to determine how they could help. Millions of young men, including thousands of college and professional football players, flocked to the nearest enlistment office. Civilians were asked to make sacrifices on the home front.

The attack on Pearl Harbor had an enormous impact on almost all areas of American life, and this included professional sports. Many wondered aloud about the propriety of playing sports in wartime. The political and public conversation fostered by the attack on Pearl Harbor centered on this question: "Is playing baseball or football during a time of national emergency appropriate?" Americans again turned to their leader at 1600 Pennsylvania Avenue. President Roosevelt's response was a resounding, "Yes!" In FDR's mind, professional sports would serve as a welcome diversion for the millions of civilians working in war-related industries. Even before the attack, millions of Americans were back working as the United States government carried out FDR's Lend-Lease edict; even before the United States' direct participation in the war, President Roosevelt had promised that the United States would provide its allies with war-making hardware such as tanks, planes, and guns "in ever increasing numbers." Millions more civilians swelled the ranks of the

homefront workforce as the nation geared up for war. It was President Roosevelt's contention that in the grim times ahead, the American people could benefit from the distraction and that it would boost morale. Thus, he encouraged the major sports to continue. The NFL did.

On March 24, 1942, NFL Commissioner Elmer Layden issued a news release stating that the United States government supported the continuation of the NFL seasons. Commissioner Layden's release read in part:

> From Aristotle's time on down we have been told, and it has been demonstrated, that sports is necessary for the relaxation of the people in times of stress and worry. The National Football League will strive to help meet this need with the men the government has not yet called for combat service, either because of dependents, disabilities, or the luck of the draw in the army draft.[15]

The NFL responded to the government's support by offering to create monetary and morale-boosting programs targeted at supporting the final objective—victory. Part of the reality of achieving total victory was that the league would see many of its stars as well as everyday players depart for military service. Players eligible for the service were leaving in droves, and those who were left to play in the ensuing wartime seasons were aptly described in the popular World War II–era song, "Too Young or Too Old." But the seasons went on.

Program from an August 1942 benefit game. (Photo courtesy of the John Gunn Sports Collection, MS 316, William M. Randall Library Special Collections, University of North Carolina–Wilmington, Wilmington, North Carolina.)

During the 1942–45 NFL seasons, the players played and the spectators cheered. The quality of the play was not as good, but the enthusiasm was there. Many of the league's best players were serving in theaters of war, battling for their lives. The National Football League paid a dear price for total victory. It had the highest casualty rates of any professional sports organization in America, and 22 men—20 players and two other NFL personnel—paid the ultimate price. One of those men killed—NFL legend Jack Lummus—earned the Congressional Medal of Honor.

Maurice Britt served with distinction, survived his injuries, and was also honored with the Medal of Honor. A third Medal of Honor recipient—Joe Foss—would come back home and play an instrumental role in the creation of the American Football League, as well as the Super Bowl.

THE SEASONS, 1941–45

The mobilization for war did not compel the NFL to discontinue the rest of the 1941 season. On December 14, the country was treated to a divisional playoff game between the Packers and the Bears, who went on to beat the New York Giants in the championship game a week later. Commissioner Elmer Layden had been named the first Commissioner of the NFL on March 1, 1941, but the war years took a toll on him as well as the National Football League itself. In his five years as the commissioner, Layden had to see teams through economically lean times as well as roster shortages, encouraging them to use creative approaches to ensure their economic survival—however, there were no Bill Veecks among NFL owners. Additionally, because most of the best professional and college players were off fighting the war, the 10 NFL clubs had to rely upon groups of ragtag replacement players. The paucity of talent and manpower forced some teams to merge into hybrid teams such as the Steagles. The Cleveland Rams were even forced to cease operations for a year, and the Brooklyn Dodgers franchise disappeared entirely. When the war ended, Elmer Layden was exhausted. His contract as commissioner was not renewed, and on January 11, 1946, Bert Bell (co-owner of the Steelers) replaced him.[16]

While the war years had exacted a heavy price on Commissioner Layden, the new commissioner would face his own unique challenges in 1946, including the formation of the rival eight-team All-America Football Conference.[17] Despite the decline in the quality of play and the eventual decrease in revenues, the National Football League did survive the war, though the wartime seasons were not without their share of drama and intrigue.

1941

President Franklin Roosevelt began an unprecedented third term of office on January 20, 1941. While the United States was not directly involved in the war taking place in Europe and Asia at that time, the so-called "Arsenal of Democracy," or American industry was ramping up production of military hardware under the Lend-Lease program. In Detroit, automobile manufacturers were asked to re-tool their assembly lines in order to make planes and tanks. Still, the Detroit auto industry had hopes of producing and selling approximately 5,000,000 automobiles. This optimism was understandable given the rise in numbers of laborers who were working in the factories. This burgeoning workforce suddenly had more disposable income, income that could be spent on cars, houses—and football. Americans were awakening from the Great Depression and receiving paychecks for more money than they had ever seen in their lives. After receiving a paycheck for $200, one factory worker in a weapons mill in Ohio quipped, "Thank God for Hitler!"[18]

The National Football League began its 22nd regular season in 1941. In the spirit of a rebirth in American economic optimism, Elmer Layden had become the first commissioner of the National Football League on March 1, 1941, and was contracted to be paid the gaudy and controversial sum of $20,000 per annum. Prior to the start of the season, the league bylaws were revised to provide for playoffs in case there were ties in division races and sudden-death overtimes in case of a tie during regulation.[19] But perhaps the most bizarre occurrence prior to the 1941 NFL season involved the swap of the two Pennsylvania-based franchises and the renaming of the Pittsburgh franchise.

Art Rooney Sr. had originally purchased the Pittsburgh Pirates football club in 1933. He ran the franchise at a small profit but was understandably worried that the impending war could inhibit his ability to keep the franchise afloat. In 1940, Alexis Thompson, a young man who inherited a large fortune, offered Rooney Sr. more than $160,000 for the Pirates. Rooney sold the franchise and hoped that Thompson could fulfill his wish to move the Pirates to Boston (the closest city to his New York City home that did not have an NFL franchise). Rooney then used the proceeds from the sale to buy at least half ownership of the Philadelphia Eagles, a club owned by his good friend, Bert Bell; it was Rooney's goal to split the Eagles' home games between Philadelphia and Pittsburgh. But things went sideways for the owners of both teams. Thompson was denied permission to move the Pirates to Boston, and Rooney soon became overwhelmed with regret at selling his hometown team. The ownership groups basically traded teams (players and all) in a swap of city and NFL rights. The players who played for the Pittsburgh club in 1940 were now Eagles, and the Philadelphia Eagles players were now members of the renamed Pittsburgh Steelers.[20] In a bit of irony, the Eagles had the first pick in all 22 rounds of the NFL draft, but because of the swap, all of their draft picks ended up playing for Pittsburgh, and the players Pittsburgh selected in the 1941 college draft ended up playing in Philadelphia during the 1941 season.

In 1941, the National Football League consisted of two five-team divisions called the East Division and West Division. Courtesy of the recent uptick in their finances, Americans attended more NFL games than ever. While baseball remained America's national pastime, NFL football was fast becoming a national passion. The turnstiles were spinning in record numbers during the 1941 football season. As the season progressed, millions of Americans across the nation tuned in as radio reports followed the intensifying West Division race between the Green Bay Packers and the Chicago Bears. They were equally enthralled by the East Division battle taking place among the Washington Redskins, New York Giants, and Brooklyn Dodgers. The Packers and Bears ultimately played the first-ever NFL divisional playoff to decide the West Division. The Giants clinched the East Division on Sunday, November 23, 1941, by defeating the Washington Redskins 20–13 at the Polo Grounds, thus removing the playoff drama

from two of the three contests scheduled to be played on the final day of the regular season—Sunday, December 7, 1941.

The New York Giants played their crosstown rivals, the Brooklyn Dodgers, in a game that was preceded by the Tuffy Leemans Day celebration. Five minutes before the ceremony honoring Leemans started, the act of Japanese aggression against the U.S. naval base at Pearl Harbor started. At 2:00 PM EST, Ward Cuff kicked off to the Dodgers and managed to slice the ball out of bounds—not a good start for the home team.[21] The Dodgers were tenacious all afternoon and bested the Giants 21–7, thus ruining Tuffy Leemans' day and claiming city supremacy by winning both games against their inter-borough rivals during the season.

On December 8, 1941, Franklin Roosevelt, leaning heavily on the arm of his son, James, a Marine captain, walked haltingly into the House chamber and addressed a joint session of Congress for six minutes and thirty seconds, asking for a declaration of war. The Congress declared war against Japan—and three days later, against Germany. Immediately, there rose the question of whether or not the playoff game to be played at Wrigley Field in Chicago on December 14 and the championship game scheduled for December 21 would continue as scheduled. In a December 9 *New York Times* article, Giants coach Steve Owen was quoted regarding his concern about the probability of losing some of his players to military service before December 21: "Last night, for instance, Jack Lummus, our freshman end from Baylor, who recently signed up for the navy, was called for an interview…. He was sent back, but there is no way of telling when they will call him again." Jack Lummus joined the U.S. Naval Reserve on December 17, 1941, and apparently he was considering active duty.[22]

Two other NFL games were played on December 7. At Comiskey Park in Chicago, the Bears had to battle their crosstown rivals before rallying for a 34–24 victory to earn a one-game divisional playoff date with the Green Bay Packers the following Sunday. The other game played that day, a 20–14 come-from-behind victory by the Washington Redskins over the Philadelphia Eagles in Washington, D.C.'s Griffith Stadium, has been referred to by some observers as the the "Most Forgotten Game Ever Played"—the weather was cold, the Eagles were a dismal 2–7–1 coming into the game, and the 'Skins had been knocked out of contention on November 23 because of their 20–14 loss to the New York Giants. And of course, the events that took place thousands of miles west at Pearl Harbor overshadowed the game.

The Bears and Packers, bitter rivals even today, carried identical 10–1 records into the NFL's first divisional playoff game held on December 14 (exactly one week after the attack on Pearl Harbor). In a game that took place in the "friendly confines" of Wrigley Field in Chicago, the Bears dominated the Packers. The Packers got on the board first with a one-yard rush by Clarke Hinkle in the first quarter, but the Bears countered with a rally of their own; Hugh Gallarneau returned a punt 81 yards to score and simultaneously energize the Bears. Despite the failed point-after attempt, the Bears had stolen the momentum. The Bears secured victory with 24 unanswered points in the second quarter on the strength of two Norm Standlee touchdowns and an additional score by Bob Swisher. The Bears won 33–14 and were crowned West Division champs, thus earning the right to play the 8–3 New York Giants with their star Tuffy Leemans and prized rookie Jack Lummus in the NFL Championship Game. Many observers actually considered the divisional game to be the true championship game of 1941.

On Saturday, December 20, gamblers had the Bears favored 4-to-1 to beat the Giants in the next day's NFL championship tilt. As a result of the anticipated blowout, tens of thousands of fans chose not to buy tickets. There was good football weather in Chicago that day, but the NFL Championship Game of 1941 was played at Wrigley Field on December 21, 1941, in front of the smallest crowd (13,341) for a championship game in the league's history. The paltry attendance actually hurt the players as their playoff share was based on attendance— each winning player received $430.94, and each losing player got $288.70. This was much less than the players had anticipated.

The game began well for the Giants as they jumped out to a 6–3 lead on a touchdown pass from Leemans to George Franck. Bob Snyder had kicked a field goal for Chicago's first three points. The Bears moved ahead on two more Snyder field goals and went to the locker room with a 9–6 halftime lead. The Giants tied the game on a Ward Cuff field goal early in the third quarter. It might have been either team's game. But the 1941 Chicago Bears—who were dubbed the "Monsters of the Midway" and are considered by some football insiders to be the best NFL team from the 1922–43 era—scored 28 unanswered points, highlighted by a 42-yard fumble return by Chicago's Ken Kavanaugh, to win going away. The Bears dominated in total yardage (389 to 157), the turnover battle (Bears 1, Giants 5), and the final score, 37–9. In a poignant reminder of the cost football paid during World War II, two players in that December 21 Championship Game would be killed in action before the war ended—the Bears' Young Bussey and the Giants' Jack Lummus.

After Kavanaugh's fumble recovery for a touchdown, Ray "Scooter" McClean utilized a strange and non-traditional style of kicking for the PAT (point after touchdown). He successfully executed a "drop kick" for an extra point. This wasn't seen again until 2005, when New England Patriots reserve quarterback Doug Flutie kicked one during the Patriots' regular season finale.

The 1941 NFL season began like many other seasons, but its conclusion was anything but ordinary. In the end, the Most Valuable Player for the 1941 NFL season was Don Hutson, the Green Bay Packers' star wide receiver. The fourth annual NFL All-Star Game between the champion Bears and a collection of NFL All-Stars was played on January 4, 1942, at the Polo Grounds in New York City. The Bears won 35–24 in front of a crowd of 17,725; the crowd was small because of the cold, snowy weather. The game was supposed to be played in Los Angeles, but travel restrictions brought on by World War II prompted the NFL to move the game to New York City rather than go all the way to the West Coast; it was the first January game ever held in New York.

As more and more young men from all over America joined the ranks of the United States military, the future of professional sports leagues in the United States seemed to be a bit tenuous. There was definite uncertainty among NFL owners to the quality of their product on the field. Commissioner Layden had the unenviable task of leading the National Football League through the war years.

The final standings for the 1941 regular season were as follows:

West Division		East Division	
Chicago Bears	10–1–0	New York Giants	8–3–0
Green Bay Packers	10–1–0	Brooklyn Dodgers	7–4–0
Detroit Lions	4–6–1	Washington Redskins	6–5–0
Chicago Cardinals	3–7–1	Philadelphia Eagles	2–8–1
Cleveland Rams	3–9–0	Pittsburgh Steelers	1–9–1

1942

The year 1942 became synonymous with "loss"—devastating loss on the battlefield. Despite all of the hope, optimism, and wide-eyed enthusiasm millions of young American men carried into battle, the United States' armed forces began 1942 unceremoniously by suffering a tremendous defeat at the hands of the Japanese in the Philippines. The defeat turned to humiliation when captured Filipino and American soldiers were brutalized and dehumanized by Japanese soldiers during a forced march known as the Bataan Death March. At this point, the Japanese seemed to be invincible. Like a harvester threshing a field of grain, the Japanese were conquering territory after territory. Mobilization in America was in full swing as 3,033,361 men were inducted into the armed services in 1942, but creativity, leadership, and sublime sacrifice were going to be necessary to topple a seemingly unbeatable foe. These attributes would also be essential for those leading the National Football League during the war years.[23]

The portside of the USS Yorktown *is hit by a Japanese torpedo during the Battle of Midway.* (Photo courtesy of the National World War II Museum)

As 1942 progressed, the Allies—the United States, Great Britain, and the Soviet Union—began to blunt German and Japanese expansion. In April 1942, the overconfident Japanese had the war taken to them in their homeland during the Doolittle Raid, which was carried out to boost American morale and exact a measure of U.S. retribution for the Japanese attack on Pearl Harbor. While the raid caused minimal material damage to Japan, it achieved its goal of bolstering American morale and causing the Japanese to begin to doubt their leadership; the Japanese civilians experienced the ravages of total war firsthand, and it was hoped that they would lose faith in their military leaders.[24] American morale was further buoyed by the U.S. naval victory over the Japanese fleet during the Battle of Midway in June 1942. This was a turning point of the war because now the United States showed itself able to become the aggressor, to take the offensive after being on the defensive.

This new offensive mentality was embodied in the Guadalcanal Campaign, which saw the

The grave of a U.S. Marine on Guadalcanal. (Photo courtesy of the National World War II Museum)

Allied forces take the fight to the Empire of Japan on and around the island of Guadalcanal in the Pacific Theater. From August 7, 1942, to February 9, 1943, the Allied forces relentlessly attacked the Japanese defenders and repelled Japanese counterattacks.[25] At the same time, Allied forces took on German and Italian forces in North Africa in an effort to fend off their expansionist claims. The Japanese eventually conceded the island to the Allies, but it was a Pyrrhic victory—the cost in American lives was steep. During the course of World War II, the United States suffered an average of approximately 415 deaths per day. This high fatality count compelled a need for greater manpower as the war progressed, which impacted the rosters of professional sports teams.

This need for able-bodied men had a profound effect on the National Football League. Nearly all of the teams endured a loss of between 20 and 30 percent of their original rosters.[26] Teams began filling rosters with college players not yet drafted by Uncle Sam and veteran active players and former players deemed too old for service; these NFL teams had to rely upon this diluted pool of talent in order to fill their rosters for the 1942 through 1945 football seasons. Some of the older players on the rosters did not practice during the week; rather, they worked in defense-related jobs and played NFL football on weekends.

Commissioner Layden had to walk a fine line between putting an attractive product on the field and not getting in the way of total victory in the war. The level of play suffered as the talent of the players declined, but fans did attend the games. It helped keep up morale for the millions of Americans on the home front, and news of the season offered a bit of home for the servicemen overseas. President Roosevelt proved to be both prophetic and wise in encouraging the continuation of both professional baseball and football during the war years.

The 1942 season, the 23rd regular season of the National Football League, was defined by depleted rosters and the dominance of two teams. While there were some rule changes, these were not as significant as some of the

Harvard vs. North Carolina Navy Pre-Flight. (Photo courtesy of the John Gunn Sports Collection, MS 316, William M. Randall Library Special Collections, University of North Carolina–Wilmington, Wilmington, North Carolina)

rule changes made the previous year, especially the one that precipitated the first-ever NFL divisional playoff game. Also, there was no late-season drama in 1942. As they had in 1941, the Monsters of the Midway reigned supreme in the West Division; the Chicago Bears "ran the table" to go a perfect 11–0. The Packers went 8–2–1, but their rivals to the south had no equal in 1942; there would be no tie-breaking playoff game this time around. Meanwhile, the Washington Redskins dominated the East Division with a near-perfect 10–1; their only loss was a 14–7 defeat at the hands of the New York Giants in Week 2 (September 27). The Pittsburgh Steelers went a respectable 7–4 to finish in second place, three games back.

Most of the drama in the 1942 season was reserved for the NFL Championship Game. The Chicago Bears had a perfect season and a third consecutive NFL title in their sights. Their final obstacle was a Washington Redskins squad that had suffered abject humiliation when the Bears walloped them 73–0—the largest margin of victory in NFL history—in the 1940 NFL Championship Game. Like the sailors, Marines, and airmen who were out avenging the attack on Pearl Harbor, Redskins players perhaps had their own more modest sense of vengeance in mind as they headed into their rematch with Coach Halas' juggernaut from Chi-town. George Halas was no longer coaching the Monsters of the Midway because he left the team mid-season in order to serve in the U.S. Navy. The Bears were being co-coached by Hunk Anderson and Luke Johnson.

When the Bears and Redskins took the field at Griffith Stadium on December 13, the Redskins were 20-point underdogs to the heavily favored Bears, a team touted by some to be even better than the 1940 squad. The Bears had given up more than 14 points only once all year, in Week 1 against the Packers, had four shutouts, and had won every game with a margin of 14 points or greater. Most impressively, they had a 292-point differential in total. In a word, they were dominant. The Redskins players didn't care about the odds; revenge and redemption were foremost on their minds and in their hearts—this was a vendetta. The 36,006 spectators in the stands, the servicemen overseas who were tuned into Armed Forces Network, and the national audience listening to Harry Wismer's and Russ Hodges' radio broadcast on Mutual Radio all needed a diversion from a war that was now more than a year old. Analogies to the real war in earnest may seem forced, but many servicemen in particular may have identified with the Redskins as they fought to overcome their 1941 defeat.

The Redskins were definitely emboldened by the lack of respect from the oddsmakers as well as by a need for vengeance. It also probably didn't hurt the Washington squad's chances that it was playing at home and hadn't played the Bears head-to-head during the regular season in 1942. Whatever the cause, the crowd of 36,006 saw and the millions of fans listening to the broadcast heard the description of a low-scoring, hard-fought contest dominated by the Redskins' defense. The Bears, led by their star quarterback Sid Luckman, failed to score any points on offense but did score first when tackle Lee Artoe returned a fumble 52 yards in the second quarter. The PAT failed, making the score 6–0. That was the last point the Bears scored. Appearing a bit rattled by the turnover, the Redskins players were calmed down by their head coach, Ray Flaherty, and inspired by Sammy Baugh, both of whom reminded the team that the 'Skins were almost undefeated themselves and that they had been in close situations before. This pep talk seemed to have the desired effect.

Baugh's experience and leadership began to prevail as the Redskins took the lead for good when Baugh connected with receiver Wilbur Moore on a 39-yard pass in the second quarter. Bob Masterson's kick put the Redskins up 7–6. For the rest of the game, the Redskins' defense was the story. The Bears, who had the league's best offense, struggled to move the ball. The Redskins then extended the lead in the third quarter. Baugh engineered a 12-play, 80-yard drive that was highlighted by running back Andy Farkas' 10 carries and capped off by a

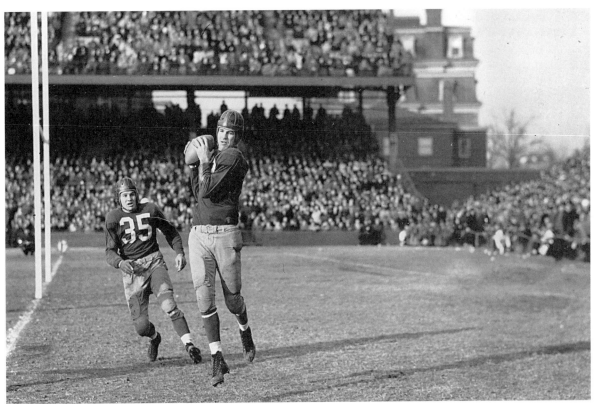

Sammy Baugh, quarterback for the Washington Redskins, intercepts a pass from the Chicago Bears in his own end zone to break up a Bears scoring threat in the fourth quarter of the NFL Championship Game in Washington, D.C., on December 13, 1942. The Chicago Bears tackle in the background is Lee Artoe (35). (AP Photo)

one-yard Farkas run—again, Masterson's PAT try was good. The drive burned precious time off the clock and served to magnify the Bears' frustration—they began sniping at one another in desperation.

When the final gun sounded, the jubilant Redskins fans savored a 14–6 'Skins victory, and revenge never tasted so sweet. The 73–0 massacre was avenged. Besides the nature of the huge upset, there were two other significant things to come from the 1942 NFL Championship Game. First, there was a good deal of discussion about suspending the league until the war's end. Obviously, this didn't happen because the 1943 season took place as scheduled, but a few teams did suspend their participation. Second, this was the last championship game in which helmets were not required; the following year, the league issued a mandate stating that all players must wear helmets.[27]

Unlike today, when the season ends with the Super Bowl as the concluding game, starting in 1938 the NFL champions had to play a game against a team of All-Stars two weeks after the NFL Championship Game. The 1942 NFL season concluded when the Redskins matched up against a team of NFL All-Stars on December 27, 1942, at Shibe Park in Philadelphia. They lost the fifth installment of the NFL All-Star Game 17–14 in front of 18,671 fans. The Bears' Hunk Anderson, who was the All-Star team's head coach, received a small measure of revenge for the December 13 loss, but it was of little comfort.[28] The NFL's Joe F. Carr (MVP) Award again went to the Green Bay Packers' wide receiver Don Hutson—the MVP of the 1941 campaign.

Americans on the home front as well as on the war front were treated to an epic clash between two great NFL teams as 1942 drew to a close—it was a welcome respite from thoughts of war. While the tide seemed to be turning toward the U.S. and its allies, victory in both the European and Pacific theaters was far from certain. The same could be said about the future of the NFL as it forged ahead into the 1943 season certain of few things. There would be a season, but what would be the quality of play if more star players left to serve, and would fans continue to show up?

The final standings for the 1942 regular season were as follows:

West Division		East Division	
Chicago Bears	11–0–0	Washington Redskins	10–1–0
Green Bay Packers	8–2–1	Pittsburgh Steelers	7–4–0
Cleveland Rams	5–6–0	New York Giants	5–5–1
Chicago Cardinals	3–8–0	Brooklyn Dodgers	3–8–0
Detroit Lions	0–11–0	Philadelphia Eagles	2–9–0

1943

This year was portending to be a turning point on the battlefronts of World War II and on the fields of the National Football League as future success was at a critical phase.

As the calendar turned over to 1943, millions of Americans were becoming citizen soldiers. Regardless of their social standing, wealth, profession, or level of fame, men from all corners of America continued to be inducted into the United States armed services.

In January 1943, President Franklin Roosevelt and Britain's Prime Minister Winston Churchill met in the North African city of Casablanca, where they affirmed the need for nothing short of "unconditional surrender" from Hitler and Germany. Soon thereafter, U.S. forces completed the capture of Guadalcanal and North Africa and were looking to invade Sicily and Italy. On the Eastern Front of the European Theater, the Soviets had prevailed in the Battle of Stalingrad, forcing the Nazis to initiate a retreat. The brutal battle marked a turning point for the Allies in Europe. In the Pacific, American forces tried to overcome determined Japanese resistance in the Solomon and Gilbert Islands.

For the 10 NFL franchises, the war forced owners to look for options to survive throughout the war's duration. Some clubs had to seriously consider halting operations because of the impact of the wartime draft. Hundreds of NFL players did not wait to be drafted—they enlisted. The mounting loss of players made 1943 a pivotal year for the National Football League. Could it endure

DANIEL FIELD vs. GEORGIA PRE-FLIGHT TWENTY-FIVE CENTS

Georgia Pre-Flight School vs. Daniel Field on October 2, 1943. (Photo courtesy of the John Gunn Sports Collection, MS 316, William M. Randall Library Special Collections, University of North Carolina–Wilmington, Wilmington, North Carolina)

the continuous talent drain and put a saleable product on the field?

Adversity loomed even before the 1943 season began when the Cleveland Rams, a mediocre franchise at best, asked Commissioner Layden and the league office for permission to suspend operations for the season. The club owners voted and approved the contraction; it was at the same league meeting that club rosters were slashed from 35 to 25 (eventually three more players would be added to each club's roster). The Rams did "loan" out their players for the 1943 season, but with their war-depleted roster, there was no guarantee that the Rams would even be around in 1944.

Seeing the demise of the Rams and anticipating trouble ahead for other NFL clubs inspired creative responses from some teams bent on survival. For example, the Philadelphia Eagles and Pittsburgh Steelers, who had swapped rosters the year before, now merged. They wore the Eagles' uniforms and played four home games in Philadelphia and two in Pittsburgh with "Phil/Pitt" as their official listing. However, the fans hybridized the two teams' names into the "Steagles," the name by which they are most commonly known today. Suffice it to say, the Eagles and Steelers players didn't much like one another and were a dysfunctional aggregation at best. The two head coaches—Earle "Greasy" Neale of the Eagles and Walt Kiesling of the Steelers—split coaching duties, but because they had contrasting personalities and coaching styles, they rarely spoke to each other.[29] Yet the Steagles gave the Keystone State something to cheer about all season long as they remained in contention for the East Division title most of the 1943 NFL campaign.

By February 1943, a total of 330 NFL players were serving in the armed forces. Teams made do with players who had medical deferments, or in some cases retired players like the Bears' Bronko Nagurski returned to the gridiron. Naturally, many clubs were struggling. The Rams had lost $100,000 during the 1942 season and had received permission to suspend operations.[30] The Brooklyn Dodgers, whose name would be changed to the Tigers in 1944, continued to fall short of expectations and experienced declining attendance. The argument for keeping the NFL alive became increasingly difficult. Daily reports described America losing boys in the defense of freedom, and one can understand the reluctance to continue professional sports. Was it appropriate to keep the NFL alive while American boys were dying on the battlefield? Wartime travel restrictions further complicated the decision to play the 1943 season.

Despite the shadows of doubt cast over the NFL as the 1943 season opened, play did begin. Of course, with the Cleveland Rams having suspended operations and because of the merger between the Eagles and Steelers, the 1943 season now consisted of two four-team divisions. The West Division was comprised of the Chicago Bears and Cardinals, Green Bay Packers, and Detroit Lions, while the East Division featured the Washington Redskins, New York Giants, Brooklyn Dodgers, and newly formed Phil-Pitt "Steagles." As a result of the loss of players, coaches, and teams, the NFL played a shorter 10-game schedule.

Remarkably, the 24th regular NFL season saw a growth in the league's popularity. The league drew a total of 1,072,462 fans in 1943. This was just 7,000 less than the previous year's record despite having 15 fewer scheduled games. The per-game average was actually greater in 1943.[31] Many have credited increased competitiveness among the weaker rosters for the jump in the average attendance from the previous year.

One of the major rule changes impelled by the depleted rosters significantly changed the game—the new substitution rule. Previously, a player could only enter the game once a quarter for the first three quarters, and in the fourth quarter, two players on each squad could be substituted twice. These restrictions forced players to play both ways, thus having to play offense and defense as well as special teams. The new rule change allowed for the creation of separate offensive and defensive units and special teams. The other major rule change made it mandatory for all players to wear helmets.[32]

The 1943 NFL season kicked off on September 19 with the Detroit Lions hosting the Chicago Cardinals. The rest of the teams began the season on September 26 with a marquee match-up between West Division rivals the Chicago Bears and the Green Bay Packers at City Stadium in Green Bay, Wisconsin. It resulted in a tie. The Bears and the Packers would once again dominate the West Division. The Packers' tie with the Bears in their opener would come back to haunt them later, especially since the Packers had effectively given the game away by committing five turnovers, three of which were interceptions that changed the momentum of the game. The Packers did come back in the fourth quarter to salvage a 21–21 tie, but the tie wound up being costly; the Green Bay boys finished one game back in the standings—the Bears finished 8–1–1 while the Packers finished 7–2–1. The Bears, whose only loss was to the Washington Redskins in their ninth game, would once again play the Redskins for the NFL championship.

The East Division was much more competitive. The dysfunctional Steagles won their first two games and actually led the division until they ran up against the Monsters of the Midway. The Bears laid waste to the Steagles, 48–21. Meanwhile, in another October 17 contest, the Washington Redskins thrashed the Green Bay Packers 33–7 to vault over the Steagles and into first place.[33] After their 21–7 defeat of the Bears on November 21, the 6–0–1 'Skins appeared to have the East Division race well in hand, but as they say, "That's why you play the games." One week later, perhaps because of overconfidence or because of a letdown after their decisive victory over the Bears, the Redskins began a three-game losing skid that saw them drop into a first-place tie with their rivals, the New York Giants, by season's end. Their opponent following their victory over the Bears? Those pesky Steagles.

The Steagles—despite all of the drama and friction between the leftover members from the '42 Eagles and '42 Steelers and their respective head coaches—were a different team, a better team than either the Eagles and Steelers had been separately the year before. Led by halfback Jack Hinkle and quarterback Roy Zimmerman, the Steagles took the fight to the Redskins at Griffith Stadium, the 'Skins home field, winning the November 28 game by a convincing 27–14 score. On the roster that day for the Steagles was a player who was something of a celebrity—Future Hall of Fame end Bill Hewitt. Hewitt, who had retired in 1939 and was now 34 years old, was the last NFL player to play without a helmet in the 1930s. While he did contribute to the Steagles' success, he was probably more remembered for his resistance to being forced to wear a helmet during his comeback season of 1943—he was definitely annoyed by the mandatory helmet rule.[34]

Had the Steagles beaten the Packers in their final regular season game (they lost 38–28), they would have forced a three-way tie for first place in the East Division. The Redskins, who were 6–1–1 heading into their last two games, dropped back-to-back games to the New York Giants, thus forcing a one-game playoff between the same two teams the following week, December 19, at New York's Polo Grounds. The Redskins recovered from their losing streak and shut out the Giants, 28–0. This set up a championship rematch with the Redskins' 1942 NFL Championship Game opponent, the Chicago Bears.

The 1943 NFL Championship Game was played the day after Christmas—the latest an NFL Championship Game had been played—in front of 34,320 Bears partisans at Wrigley Field in Chicago. Early on, the game was a scoreless defensive struggle. In the second quarter, the Redskins struck first on a one-yard touchdown run by running back Andy Farkas. The Bears answered when legendary quarterback Sid Luckman threw a 32-yard touchdown strike to All-Pro running back Harry Clarke. The Bears took a 14–7 lead just before halftime on Bronko Nagurski's touchdown run. While the Redskins gave it a valiant effort, they couldn't stop Luckman in the second half. He threw four more touchdown passes on the way to a 41–21 drubbing of the Redskins,

Bronko Nagurski, who came out of retirement to help the Chicago Bears win the Western title of the National Football League, works out for the title game at Wrigley Field, in Chicago, Illinois, on December 26, 1943. (AP Photo)

thus squaring accounts for the Bears' 1942 Championship Game loss.[35] Luckman had what was considered to be one of the greatest games in NFL history. He connected on 15-of-26 passes for 286 yards and five touchdowns, outrushed the entire Redskins team by carrying eight times for 64 yards, intercepted two of Baugh's passes and returned them for 39 yards, returned two punts for 32 yards, and booted three punts for 74 yards. For the 1943 season,

Luckman was named League MVP. He had completed 110-of-202 passes for 2,194 yards, 28 touchdowns, and 12 interceptions, and had a passer rating of 107.5.[36]

Luckman volunteered to serve with the U.S. Merchant Marines after the 1943 season. While he couldn't practice with the team, Ensign Luckman joined up with the Bears on game days during the 1944 and 1945 seasons and returned as the full-time starter in 1946. Luckman then led the Bears to a fourth NFL championship. Luckman hung up his cleats in 1950 after an illustrious 12-year career. Fifteen years later he was inducted into the Pro Football Hall of Fame. Many consider Luckman to be the greatest quarterback in Chicago Bears history, one of the top 10 all-time quarterbacks, and for one season (1943), the best quarterback in NFL history. For one day, December 26, 1943, he was the considered the greatest football player who ever lived.

The 1943 NFL season was definitely memorable. Among the football-related events that took place that season, a new phenomenon called the "Fans Forum" was born. A predecessor to today's studio sports talk shows, like ESPN's *Sports Nation*, the Fans Forum was the brainchild of smaller, local newspapers seeking to sell more subscriptions. During the week, these newspapers would invite fans to buy advanced tickets at the newspaper office for admission to an event that allowed fans to congregate, drink some alcohol, and discuss their local NFL team in the basement of the publication office on game day. Then the attendees would listen to Mutual Radio's broadcasts of the game. The newspapers not only made money via ticket sales, but they also would attempt to convince attendees, who were usually well-lubricated by a fair amount of drink, to buy subscriptions to the newspaper. This weekly community listen-in became so popular that the forums moved out of the local news office basement to a local watering hole. Whether the home game was sold out or the local team was out on the road, fans could still gather, drink, and enjoy the shared experience of talking football and listening to the game. Even the teams pitched in to make these forums successful. Newspapers sold more subscriptions,

The final standings for the 1943 regular season were as follows:

West Division		East Division	
Chicago Bears	8–1–2	Washington Redskins	6–3–1
Green Bay Packers	7–2–1	New York Giants	6–3–1
Detroit Lions	3–6–1	Phil-Pitt Steagles	5–4–1
Chicago Cardinals	0–10–0	Brooklyn Dodgers	2–8–0[37]

local bars sold more booze, and fans in NFL cities got to enjoy the NFL experience within a community of fellow football aficionados.

The year ended with a lot of unanswered questions about the future of the war and the NFL. When would the war end? Would there be football in 1944? Would the Rams come back? Would the Bears continue to dominate in future seasons? Would other teams survive or would they become a victim of the only true constant—change? For America, 1944 proved the most crucial year of the war. General Dwight D. Eisenhower was the commander

North Carolina Navy Pre-Flight School vs. Camp Lejeune Marines, November 13, 1943. (Photo courtesy of the John Gunn Sports Collection, MS 316, William M. Randall Library Special Collections, University of North Carolina–Wilmington, Wilmington, North Carolina)

of the Allied Forces in Europe, and he would lead the most complex military operation the world had ever seen, Operation Overlord. The D-Day invasion, as it is more commonly known, changed the course of the war in the European Theater.

1944

The year 1944 saw that turning point in the world war against tyranny. If there was a theme to the events of that year, Vaughn Monroe's 1942 popular hit, "When the Lights Go on Again," embodied it. Three years prior to the release of Monroe's song, the Nazi military surprised the world when it invaded Poland on September 1, 1939. In response to the invasion, British Prime Minister Neville Chamberlain, announced from 10 Downing Street that, "This country [Britain] is at war." A London broadcaster later proclaimed, "Tonight the lights are going out all over Europe and no one knows when they'll ever come back on." The answer was 1944.[38]

Yes, the lights were coming back on in 1944. Lights adorned the ships heading toward France to carry out what General Dwight D. Eisenhower referred to as "The Great Crusade" in Normandy. The lights of Paris would once again shine on the tri-color flag flying majestically over the Eiffel Tower; the red and white banner bearing the malevolent black swastika no longer adorned the tower. And in New York Harbor, the lights of the Statue of Liberty were turned on again to lift the hearts and spirits of Americans from sea to shining sea. Lights illuminated the skies above the

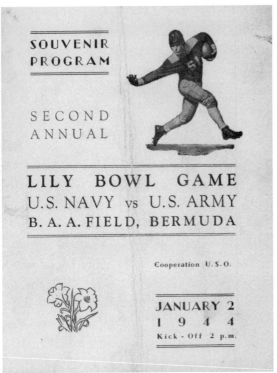

SOUVENIR
PROGRAM

SECOND
ANNUAL

LILY BOWL GAME
U.S. NAVY vs U.S. ARMY
B. A. A. FIELD, BERMUDA

Cooperation U.S.O.

JANUARY 2
1 9 4 4
Kick - Off 2 p.m.

Kicking off 1944 in Bermuda: Army vs. Navy in the Lily Bowl on January 2, 1944. (Photo courtesy of the John Gunn Sports Collection, MS 316, William M. Randall Library Special Collections, University of North Carolina–Wilmington, Wilmington, North Carolina)

battlefields of Saipan and Guam as well as the waters of the Philippine Sea and the Leyte Gulf. On Christmas 1944, artillery fire and flares cast an eerie glow over the besieged Belgian city of Bastogne. While the lights that came back on during 1944 served as a symbol of hope that democracy would triumph over totalitarianism, they alternately served as a reminder of the very high cost of victory.

The 1944 NFL season was the third full campaign to be played under the cloud of war. Some NFL clubs were still struggling to survive, largely because players continued to be drafted or voluntarily enlisted, and teams endured the continued depletion of their rosters. The Steelers, whose roster was decimated, were facing extinction. Their merger arrangement with the Eagles was terminated at the conclusion of the 1943 season, thus bringing the Steagles experiment to an end. The Eagles' owners felt confident that they could stand on their own— and they weren't wrong. The Eagles improved upon their initial success as the Steagles over the course of the next few seasons. The Eagles captured back-to-back NFL championships in 1948 and 1949 with contributions from several players who filled the 1943 Steagles' roster.

The Steelers' future was very uncertain now that the Phil-Pitt hybrid squad was history. The continued attrition of their roster compelled them to look for a new merger candidate for the 1944 season. They found a willing partner in the Chicago Cardinals, another team with a depleted roster coupled with shaky finances. But the Cardinals were awful; they concluded their 1943 campaign with a 0–10 record. When the two clubs merged, the official name of the team was Card-Pitt, and they played half of their home games in each city. Unofficially, this dismal squad was sardonically labeled the "Carpets" because they "laid down for anybody."[39] Out of contention for the West Division title by October 29, 1944, the Carpets added to their ignominy by setting a record that still stands for the worst overall punting average of 32.7 yards per punt.

It was a year of change in the NFL. The Cleveland Rams returned from a one-year

One of the hybrid teams, Card-Pitt, against the Green Bay Packers on November 26, 1944. (Photo courtesy of the John Gunn Sports Collection, MS 316, William M. Randall Library Special Collections, University of North Carolina–Wilmington, Wilmington, North Carolina)

hiatus. And like the millions of women who rushed to the marriage altar during the war years (many women tied the knot before they went off to factories and their husbands went off to war), NFL teams were changing their names. The Brooklyn Dodgers became the Brooklyn Tigers, dropping its connection with baseball. While the name changed, the results did not. The Tigers were winless (0–10) in a season that would be their last as an independent franchise. Brooklyn and the 0–10 Carpets combined to set

an NFL record for futility; it was the only time in NFL history that the league had two winless teams during the same season. At least the Tigers were competitive. The Brooklyn club lost seven of its 10 games by a touchdown or less and let wins get away from them at the end of two of those games.

The 1944 season also witnessed a return to a 10-team league. With the Eagles flying solo again and the Rams back in the fold, the league needed a 10th team. Enter the expansion Boston Yanks, the latest addition to the East Division. Given the bitterness of the modern-day Yankees–Red Sox rivalry, it's hard to fathom that fans in either city would accept a team in Boston being called the Yanks—it seems blasphemous. This naming *faux pas* reflected the lack of identity that plagued the NFL during the war years.

It was a clear sign of the improvement in the U.S. economy and consumer confidence that the U.S. government felt it necessary to tackle the airwaves to implore laborers working in war-related industries to remain at their jobs instead of being enticed to take better-paying jobs in the non-war-related private sector. This confidence in the improving economic climate seemed to spread to the NFL. The Rams and Eagles, both of whom took radical measures to stay solvent the year before, returned to normal operations and performed well enough to give their fans reasons to hope. But that optimism was not universal. Fans of the Brooklyn Tigers and Card-Pitt franchises had little to cheer about and little reason to pass through the turnstiles.

The Boston Yanks visit Wrigley Field to take on the Chicago Bears on November 12, 1944. (Photo courtesy of the John Gunn Sports Collection, MS 316, William M. Randall Library Special Collections, University of North Carolina–Wilmington, Wilmington, North Carolina)

Although the NFL again fielded a 10-team league in 1944, the league retained a 10-game schedule. As the 1944 NFL season unfolded, it became evident that the two divisions were very different. In the West Division, the Green Bay Packers dominated, exploding to a 6–0 record and coasting the rest of the way to the division title; their 8–2 record catapulted them into the championship game. The identity of their opponent, however, wouldn't be known until the last minute of the 1944 season. The East Division was much more competitive.

The parity among the Redskins, Eagles, and Giants created late-season drama. Washington and Philadelphia were both unbeaten two months into the season—the Redskins' record stood at 5–0–1, the Eagles were 4–0–2, and the New York Giants were lurking in the shadows at 5–1–1, just a half-game back. On November 19, there was high drama as the Eagles and Redskins went head to head. The Eagles thumped the Redskins 37–7 to lead the 'Skins and the Giants by a half-game. The following week the East Division standings flipped because the Eagles struggled at home against the Chicago Bears, suffering their only loss of the season by a 28–7 score. The Giants and Redskins, who were now tied at 6–1–1 after winning their games, moved ahead of the Eagles by a half-game; the Eagles' two ties, one each with the Giants and Redskins, were now looming larger and larger as the season came to a close. The Giants and 'Skins were slated to meet the next two weeks—the December 3 game was on the schedule but the game the following week was a makeup game. Thus, the Washington and New York football squads controlled their own destiny—"win and you're in."

On the first Sunday of December, some 47,457 fans flocked to the Polo Grounds in New York to witness the clash between the East Division's first-place teams. In a taut contest, the Giants came back to defeat the Redskins 16–13. Now sandwiched between the first-place Giants and the third-place Redskins, the Eagles had to win their final game the following Sunday and hope that the Washington team could recover from its setback and take down the Giants on its home field in D.C. The Eagles did their part by defeating the Rams 26–13 and pushing their record to 7–1–2. Now all they could do was wait. Alas, the Redskins could not propel the Eagles to the East Division title. It was all Giants in a 31–0 rout of the Redskins. The Giants took the division flag and earned the right to host the Green Bay Packers for the 1944 NFL championship the following Sunday.[40]

The NFL's 12th title game took place on December 17, 1944, at New York's Polo Grounds. On hand to watch the Giants do battle with the West Division champs, the 8–2 Green Bay Packers were 46,016 spectators. While the game taking place at the Polo Grounds wasn't insignificant, its importance paled in comparison to the pitched battle taking place across the Atlantic Ocean. In far away Belgium and Luxembourg, American troops including the 99th Infantry Division were engaged in a brutal life-or-death struggle known as the Battle of the Bulge. Because this was Hitler's last attempt to break through and turn the tide of the war back in his favor, the Nazi leadership pulled out all of the stops with one last desperate operation to save the Third Reich. The Germans hit the American troops hard and overran them. Numerous American troops were taken prisoner, and it appeared that the Allies were in serious trouble.

The Packers-Giants title tilt was broadcast on the Blue Radio Network with Harry Wismer calling the action.[41] Millions of listeners tuned in to hear Wismer describe the play-by-play action. What radio listeners heard and fans at the stadium saw was largely a defensive struggle. It was not so surprising that the Giants' dominant defense came to play; the Giants had only given up 75 points, or 7.5 points a game, during the entire 1944 season. The talented Giants defense had shut out the Packers on November 19, 24–0. The Packers defense was not as stout—they gave up more than two touchdowns per game during the '44 campaign—as the Giants' "D" was on paper, but they outplayed their opponent's defense on this day. Packers' head coach Curly Lambeau saw his offense surge ahead by scoring two second-quarter touchdowns. Running back Ted Fritsch put Green Bay up 7–0 with a one-yard scamper and followed it up with a 28-yard pass reception from quarterback Irv Comp (Don

The final standings for the 1944 regular season were as follows:

West Division		East Division	
Green Bay Packers	8–2–0	New York Giants	8–1–1
Chicago Bears	6–3–1	Philadelphia Eagles	7–1–2
Detroit Lions	6–3–1	Washington Redskins	6–3–1
Cleveland Rams	4–6–0	Boston Yanks	2–8–0
Card-Pitt	0–10–0	Brooklyn Tigers	0–10–0

The Green Bay Packers' Don Hutson (left) and Irv Comp (right) received instructions from Coach Curly Lambeau during training at Bear Mountain, New York, on November 15, 1944. (AP Photo/John Lindsay)

Hutson nailed both PATs); the Pack led 14–0 at halftime.

The defensive struggle continued in the second half. The Packers were held scoreless, but the Giants scored in the fourth quarter, a one-yard run by wingback Ward Cuff. Head coach Steve Owen's offense produced just that one score. At the final gun, the Green Bay Packers had won their sixth NFL championship, 14–7.

The 1944 NFL season itself gave witness to some of the best—and some of the worst—football played in league history up to that point. The tight East Division race was one the season's highlights. The dismal play of two winless teams was the lowlight. Another highlight was the improvement of one of the league's perennially weak teams, the Detroit Lions; they attained a 6–3–1 record, and one of their own, halfback Frank Sinkwich, won the Joe F. Carr Award as the league's Most Valuable Player.

The year 1944 ended with more uncertainty for both the United States and the NFL. Overseas, the Germans were clinging to waning hopes of winning the Battle of the Bulge, and the war's outcome was far from certain. Back home, several football teams had precarious futures.

1945

As the calendar turned over from 1944 to 1945, there was cause for optimism. Most Americans were celebrating the re-election of their President Franklin D. Roosevelt to an unprecedented fourth term of office—for many younger Americans, he was the only president they had ever known. Prior to his recent electoral victory, Roosevelt had already been president for one term longer than any other president before him, but now he was hoping to preside over a country that was neither mired in war nor an economic depression. As he officially began his fourth term in office, American morale was buoyed by the Allied victory at the Battle of the Bulge. Now under the command of

General Eisenhower, Allied forces were pushing the German forces back to the Rhine River. Meanwhile, out in the Pacific, Fleet Admiral Chester Nimitz and the army's General Douglas MacArthur were taking the fight to the Japanese in the so-called "island hopping" campaign and driving them back toward their home islands.

While Allied forces were seizing the upper hand in both the European and Pacific Theaters of the war, American intelligence (known as the O.S.S.) discovered that the Germans had badly mismanaged their atomic program.[42] American researchers were already on the cusp of testing the bomb. When word of how far behind the Germans were in developing atomic weapons reached them, many of the American scientists felt that the U.S. atomic program should be halted.[43] Albert Einstein, father of American atomic research, wrote to President Roosevelt, imploring him to abandon the program. Despite pleas to the contrary, construction of the atomic bomb continued as the Manhattan Project.

In 1945, Americans experienced a resurgence of optimism and hope, which was largely inspired by Allied victory and the ultimate return home of American boys. This *esprit de corps* extended to the NFL, as well. Many of the players who had left to go fight in the war overseas were now returning to their teams. Much had changed in America as well as the NFL since Tuffy Leemans Day on Sunday, December 7, 1941. The world and the NFL were indeed on the verge of a new epoch.

Despite the prospect of getting their players back and returning to normal operations, the NFL teams faced new challenges, especially the creation of the fledgling All-America Football Conference, which existed from 1946–49 and whose eight teams competed with the 10 NFL squads for the available talent. This foreshadowed changes that ultimately revolutionized the NFL.

The 1945 season would be the NFL's first in peacetime since Pearl Harbor Day. While the boys were coming home, there were still causes for concern among NFL teams as they made preparations. This would be Commissioner Layden's last year as commissioner; his contract was not renewed for the 1946 season, and Pittsburgh Steelers co-owner Bert Bell was appointed as the new commissioner.[44] In 1945, Bell's Steelers were getting back some of the talent lost to the war and were finally returning to form. The Chicago Cardinals also returned to normal operations in 1945 as the Card-Pitt merger—which produced perhaps the most hapless football team in league history—dissolved after one year, much to the delight of football fans in their home cities. Not all was cause for rejoicing, however. In Brooklyn, the Tigers (formerly the Dodgers), who were dismal in the 1944 campaign, merged with the Boston Yanks for one season. This newly formed hybrid squad went by the name "Yanks" and split its home games between Boston and Brooklyn. It played four games in Boston and one game in New York.

During the next off-season, Tigers owner Dan Topping shocked the NFL when he announced that he intended to join the newly established All-America Football Conference. Topping had wanted to move his Tigers from Ebbets Field in Brooklyn to Yankee Stadium in the Bronx. Recognizing this as a threat to the NFL as well as his own business interests, New York Giants owner Tim Mara used his territorial rights to block the move. The league revoked Topping's ownership and assigned all of the Tigers' players to the Boston Yanks. However, in response, Topping bought into the baseball New York Yankees and transferred his football club to the newly formed All-America Football Conference. Topping's renamed New York Yankees football club was given $100,000 by each of the other seven AAFC franchises as a reward for defecting, and most of his players defected with him. Topping was finished as an NFL owner, but he would become successful beyond his wildest dreams as an owner of America's pre-eminent sports franchise—the baseball Yankees.[45] In a bit of cosmic irony, Topping's New York Yankees baseball club became a team that consistently broke the hearts of the Brooklyn Dodgers and New York Giants baseball fans for many years to come.

The 1945 NFL season began in peacetime for the first time since 1941, but due to a controversial call in its culminating game, the ending was anything but peaceful. It was a season that saw the emergence of new powers, albeit temporarily, in the West Division. The Cleveland Rams and Detroit Lions finished at the top of the division—meaning that, for the first time in years, neither the Bears nor the Packers won the division. The East Division was once again won by the Washington Redskins—their fourth division title in six years, but they were challenged all season long by the

Philadelphia Eagles. The New York Giants, who adroitly played the role of spoiler by affecting the outcome of both division races, and the Chicago Bears were below average for the first time in years; both teams finished with only three victories apiece.

The story of the 1945 season had to be the Cleveland Rams. The West Division standings, with the exception of the lowly Chicago Cardinals, were a bit topsy-turvy when compared to years past. While the Detroit Lions, who finished 6–3–1 in 1944 and 7–3 in 1945, were something of a surprise to many who followed the NFL, it was the success of the 1945 Cleveland Rams that left most people stunned. The Rams, who had suspended operations during the 1943 season and had been a mediocre 4–6–0 in 1944, shocked most of the football world by winning the West Division with a 9–1 campaign and securing a place in the 1945 NFL Championship Game. A few months later the Rams would once again shock the football world and their fan base when they announced that they were moving out west to Los Angeles, California, for the 1946 season, thus initiating the NFL's conquest of the West.

When the NFL's 26th regular season began on Sunday, September 23, 1945, teams like the Chicago Cardinals and Pittsburgh Steelers had abandoned the practice of merging with other clubs and resumed normal football operations. The lone hybrid squad in 1945 was an amalgamation of the expansion Boston Yanks and the Brooklyn Tigers (formerly Dodgers). While the Tigers had been competitive yet not victorious during their 0–10 1944 season, the Yanks went a lowly 2–8 during their inaugural campaign. As a result, the two rosters comprising the 1945 Boston Yanks' football club were a pathetic 2–18–0 combined during the 1944 season.

This incongruous bunch began 1945 with so much more promise. The Yanks jumped out to a 2–0–1 record in the first month of the season, including a 28–20 victory over the eventual East Division champions, the Washington Redskins. A demoralizing 13–13 tie with those pesky New York Giants, who came back from a 13–10 deficit late in the October 14 game at Yankee Stadium to force the stalemate, was the only early blemish on the Yanks' first-month record. But it foreshadowed the Yanks' collapse later that season. Out of frustration, some members of the mixed-franchise squad began pointing fingers at one another over the tie. The unity of the two squads was fragile, and later in the season, things would really unravel. That frustration was on display a week after the tie with the Giants when the Green Bay Packers easily handled the Yanks 38–14. The Yanks were on the brink. Yet a 10–6 victory over the Pittsburgh Steelers on October 28 found the 3–1–1 Yanks sitting near the top of the East Division at the season's halfway point. This was to be the apogee of the Yanks' season. A 10–9 home loss to Detroit began a five-game losing streak; the team's confidence and tenuous team chemistry eroded badly as the Yanks staggered to the finish line with a 3–6–1 record.

The Washington Redskins were 3–0–1 at the halfway point of the 1945 season. Because of early season byes—during Weeks 1 and 2 on the schedule—the Redskins had played only four games by the season's mid-point; this meant that they had to play 10 consecutive weeks (11 if they won the division). The Yanks' second-half collapse turned the East Division into a head-to-head clash between the 'Skins and their rivals from the City of Brotherly Love, the Philadelphia Eagles. After a 16–0 shutout of the Redskins, the Eagles found themselves in a flat-footed tie with two games to go; both teams were 6–2. The New York Giants had the opportunity to spoil the East Division championship hopes of both clubs as they were slated to play the Eagles on December 2 and the Redskins in the final game of the season on December 9. While the Redskins dispatched the lowly Pittsburgh Steelers 24–0, the Eagles suffered a demoralizing 28–21 loss at the hands of those hated Giants. Yet the Eagles were still alive to perhaps attain a tie for the division if they could win their final game and the Giants could continue playing the role of spoiler by beating the Redskins. The Eagles put it to the Boston Yanks at home by a score of 35–7. But the Redskins, playing in front of their sixth consecutive sell-out crowd of 34,788 at Griffith Stadium, blanked their bitter division rivals 17–0. The Eagles, who were now in their 13th NFL season, failed to make the playoffs for the 13th consecutive year. Meanwhile, the Redskins were on their way to playing in their fourth NFL championship in six years.

In the West Division, which had been dominated by the Chicago Bears and Green Bay Packers over the years, two usually desultory teams arose from the ashes of oblivion to challenge the Packers for West Division supremacy. Over the course of the first half of the 1945 season, the Detroit Lions and the Cleveland Rams kept even with the Packers as all three sprinted out to a 4–1 record by the season's midway point. The Rams won their first four games, including a 41–21 drubbing of the Chicago Bears in Week 5, before losing to the Philadelphia Eagles 28–14 at Shibe Park in Philadelphia. The three-team race became a two-team race when the Packers went on to drop three of their last five games.

Meanwhile, the Rams and Lions stood at 5–1 following wins on November 4, 1945. The Rams avoided falling prey to the Giants' spoiler spell and defeated them by a score of 21–17 in front of 46,219 at New York's Polo Grounds on November 4, 1945. The Lions kept pace on that day by narrowly edging the Boston Yanks 10–9 on the strength of a blocked extra point attempt. This loss began the Yanks' five-game slide to a 3–6–1 season record. Both the Rams and Lions won again the following week to set up a three-game race to the title. In Week 9, the Rams cruised to a 35–21 win over the Chicago Cardinals. The Lions had to travel to New York's Polo Grounds and face the spoilers who donned the red, white, and blue. The Giants laid a beating on the Lions by a 35–14 tally. This set up a must-win scenario for the Lions in the following week's Thanksgiving Day showdown with the Rams. The Giants would reprise their role as spoiler against the Eagles two weeks later.

For the Detroit Lions, the 1945 edition of the annual Detroit Thanksgiving Day Game was a do-or-die contest for playoff survival. A win would put them even with the Rams at 7–2 with one game to play. A loss would drop the Lions' record to 6–3 and give the Rams an 8–1 record and the West Division title. In a playoff atmosphere on a brisk afternoon in Detroit's Briggs Stadium, the Lions dropped the game and the division. The game, and season, was highlighted by receiver Jim Benton's record day; he made 10 catches for 303 yards. The Rams, now 8–1, would complete their most successful, and last, season in Cleveland with a 9–1 record when they defeated the Boston Yanks on December 2 in front of a paltry crowd of 18,470 at Cleveland's League Park. Sadly, during the Rams' championship run, they only drew 77,878 spectators in four home games. This did not augur well for the Rams' future in Cleveland. The Rams would have to wait another week to see who their East Division foe would be in the NFL Championship Game to be held in Cleveland's Municipal Stadium on December 16, 1945. When the last week drama in the East Division concluded, the Cleveland Rams learned that their opponent would be the Sammy Baugh–led Washington Redskins.

The 1945 NFL Championship Game was held on December 16, which was exactly one year after the Battle of the Bulge, Hitler's last major campaign in Europe, had begun. On a day the men who fought in the Battle of the Bulge could definitely relate to, the visiting Redskins took on the Cleveland Rams in front of 32,178 observers at Municipal Stadium, a venue that later was derisively referred to as the Mistake by the Lake. The game-time temperature of minus-8 degrees set an NFL

Championship Game record. The game would not be best known for being the Rams' first and last championship in Cleveland nor would it be most remembered for the freezing temperatures. The game would be most memorable because of one controversial first-quarter call that would be rule-changing if not game-altering.[46] One thing that escaped most people's attention on that frigid Sunday afternoon on December 16 was the game-time temperature in southern California—it was sunny and 72 degrees.

Early in the first quarter, the Redskins were pinned deep in their own territory. With the ball on the 5-yard line, legendary 'Skins quarterback Sammy Baugh took the snap and faded back into the end zone. As he released the ball, it hit the H-shaped goalpost—which at that time was placed on the goal line rather than 10 yards behind the goal line as it is today. According to rule, when Baugh's pass made contact with goalpost and dropped to the turf in the end zone not the playing field, the play was declared dead and a 2-point safety was awarded to the Rams. While the weather was bitingly cold, the Redskins were hot and none more so than the owner, George Preston Marshall. But rules are rules, and the call stood. The Rams had an early 2–0 lead, and the Redskins' frustrations were just beginning.

In the second quarter, the Redskins lost their leader, Baugh, when he was knocked out of the game with bruised ribs. He was replaced by backup QB Frank Filchock, who stepped in admirably. Fitchcock led the 'Skins on a drive that culminated with his 38-yard scoring toss to receiver Steve Bagarus, and the successful

PAT gave Washington a 7–2 lead. The Rams answered back on the last play of the half when league MVP and Rams star quarterback Bob Waterfield connected with Jim Benton on a 38-yard pass late in the half. When Waterfield—who was a rookie out of UCLA and had been discharged from the army in 1944—lined up for the extra-point try, there were no seconds left on the game clock. Waterfield's kick was partially blocked but because there was only about a 10-yard distance between the spot from which he kicked the ball and that "accursed" goalpost, the football managed to land on the crossbar and hang there for a moment before it tumbled over and landed triumphantly on the frozen tundra of the end zone—the Rams now led the very frustrated Redskins at halftime, 10–9. The Redskins were feeling a little snake-bit.

When the Rams and Redskins resumed their tightly contested gridiron battle in the second half, the Rams padded their lead when right halfback Jim Gillette scored on a 44-yard pass from Waterfield. This time the PAT failed. The Rams now led, 15–7. For a moment, the Redskins set aside the angst that was provoked by the fluke occurrences of the day and played some good offensive football behind the resilient Frank Filchock, who rallied the 'Skins in the fourth quarter by orchestrating a drive that resulted in six points when he tossed an eight-yard pass to running back Bob Seymour. Because there was no two-point conversion option available then, the Redskins had to settle for a successful PAT try by place-kicker Joe Aguirre—Rams 15, Redskins 14. Later in the fourth quarter, Filchock would lead the 'Skins

on two more drives, both of which resulted in missed field goal tries by Aguirre. When the final gun sounded, the Rams, victorious by the final score of 15–14, left the field and celebrated their first and only title as the Cleveland Rams in the warmth of their locker room.

Yet most of the heat was coming from the field in the person of one George Preston Marshall. A more reasonable, rational person could argue that the Washington Redskins could have, and should have, won the game on the basis that the team had ample opportunities to do so. While the Rams offense stalled in the fourth quarter, the Redskins moved the ball and scored a touchdown but had two missed field-goal attempts—on tries of 46 and 31 yards—by kicker Joe Aguirre. But Marshall was anything but rational and reasonable. Believing that the obscure, first-quarter ruling was the primary reason for his team's NFL Championship Game loss, after the final gun he stormed the field to confront the game officials about the obstruction call; he wanted to know how such a rule could decide the outcome of such an important game. An indignant Marshall argued that the rule needed to be changed. With a decision that became known as the Baugh/Marshall Rule and is still in effect today, the NFL altered the rulebook. Now, any forward pass that strikes the goalposts is ruled incomplete, and the play is ruled dead.

So the 1945 NFL season did not end peacefully even though the year itself did. The controversial play that precipitated the Baugh/Marshall Rule somewhat marred the Cleveland

Joe Aguirre (19), a Washington Redskins end, attempts a field goal from the 25-yard line in the closing minutes of play of the 1945 Championship Game held in Cleveland on December 16, 1945. The ball fell inches short of the goal posts, and the Cleveland Rams won 15–14. (AP Photo)

Rams' best season. Two years removed from having suspended operations, they had reached the pinnacle of NFL success by earning the title of NFL champs. As they basked in the reflected glory of their home team's great season, the Rams' fans were probably not aware that this would be the team's final year in Cleveland; in 1946, the Rams would be playing their home games in the Los Angeles Coliseum in sunny southern California.

The sting of losing its team was tempered and then all but disappeared when the city was blessed with Paul Brown's All-America Football Conference franchise, the Cleveland Browns. In the four short years of the All-America Football Conference's existence, the Browns were a juggernaut, winning the league title all four of those years. Not lost on some football observers was the fact that the Browns opened the 1946 season with a 44–0 defeat of the Miami Seahawks in front of 60,000 plus fans at Cleveland's Municipal Stadium—the Rams didn't draw much more than that in four home games during their 9–1 regular season in 1945. Despite the dissolution of the AAFC in 1949, three teams from the now-defunct league—the Browns, Baltimore Colts, and San Francisco 49ers—joined the NFL in the 1950 season.

In 1945, the Rams' Bob Waterfield became the first rookie to win the Joe F. Carr Trophy as the league's Most Valuable Player. Waterfield headed back to California with the Rams, thus playing an important role in the NFL's westward

expansion. Rams owner Daniel F. Reeves pressured the NFL into permitting his team to move to the Los Angeles Coliseum, which had a seating capacity of 105,000. In order to get their consent to sign the deal, the Coliseum commissioners demanded that the team be racially integrated. In their new city, the Rams became a team of firsts. They were the first NFL team to be racially integrated, the first NFL team to be featured on television every game of the regular season (in 1950) because of their wide-open big-play offense, the first NFL team to surpass the one million mark for attendance in a season, and the first professional team to have a modern helmet in pro football (this occurred in 1948 when halfback Fred Gehrke painted horns on the Rams' helmets).

This was a year of both great triumph and great tragedy. Victory was achieved both in Europe and the Pacific, and the world was made "safe for democracy," though at great cost. There remained a threat to democracy in the form of the Soviet Union's Joseph Stalin, a brutal and cruel Communist dictator. Sadly, too, just five days after the NFL title game, the United

The final standings for the 1945 regular season were as follows:

West Division		East Division	
Cleveland Rams	9–1–0	Washington Redskins	8–2–0
Detroit Lions	7-3-0	Philadelphia Eagles	7-3-0
Green Bay Packers	6-4-0	New York Giants	3–6–1
Chicago Bears	3–7–0	Boston Yanks	3–6–1
Chicago Cardinals	1–9–0	Pittsburgh Steelers	2–8–0

States lost a military icon when General George S. Patton succumbed to injuries sustained as the result of a common traffic accident while traveling in Europe. The legendary general had managed to survive the entire war but died in an inglorious manner.

Felix (Doc) Blanchard, one of the U.S. Military Academy's greatest football players, is shown during a practice session at the U.S. Military Academy, West Point, New York, on September 28, 1945. Blanchard was an All-American in 1944. (AP Photo/John Lindsay)

Yet there were many triumphs in 1945. At the conclusion of the war, millions of American boys made their return from the war front and arrived in a country with a booming economy and a profound sense of optimism for a highly anticipated period of peace and prosperity.

The U.S. Army football team, the Black Knights, also gave people much to cheer in 1945. The Black Knights, who won their third national championship in 1945, were led by that year's Heisman Trophy winner, fullback Doc Blanchard. In 1942, Blanchard had enlisted in the U.S. Army out of the University of North Carolina. On July 2, 1944, he received an appointment to the United States Military Academy at West Point. In his three years on the Academy's football team, the Black Knights amassed an overall record of 27–0–1. Their 1945 season was highlighted by a 48–0 thrashing of the mighty Notre Dame Fighting Irish at Yankee Stadium on November 9, 1945; Blanchard's play impelled Notre Dame's 1944 head coach Ed McKeever to comment, "I've just seen Superman in the flesh."[47] In a move that revealed his character and heroism, Blanchard, who was drafted third overall by the Pittsburgh Steelers in 1946, eschewed the money and glory of the NFL in order to become a pilot in the newly formed United States Air Force.[48]

From college gridiron greats who participated in the Great War to the twenty-first century's Pat Tillman, footballers have embodied the sacrifice demonstrated by the likes of Doc Blanchard, a man who gave up fame and fortune to serve in both the Korean and Vietnam wars.

FOOTBALL AND WARTIME FROM WORLD WAR I TO THE GLOBAL WAR ON TERRORISM

While the World War II era represents the National Football League's period of greatest sacrifice, many football players before and since have traded the gridiron for the battlefield. World War I, which occurred prior to the formation of the NFL, saw numerous young men leave their college's playing fields to serve in the Great War and subsequently suffer horrors inflicted upon them in Flanders Field and the skies above it. One courageous young man who gave all in this horrific conflict was from Oberlin College.

Henry Burt Hudson developed a profound sense of duty and patriotism at a young age. Hudson's father, who fought for the Union during the Civil War, regaled young Henry with tales of American sacrifice. These stories and the lessons they conveyed were not lost on young Henry. He matriculated to Oberlin College and according to Oberlin University archives:

> The good humored Hudson, who was called 'Red' by his friends, was one of the most liked and respected men on campus. In 1916 the College awarded 'Red' the Varsity 'O' and his teammates elected him captain of the Oberlin College football team. During the summer of 1917 and before the fall collegiate football season, however, he enlisted in the Aviation Section, Signal Corps. Following his aviation training, he was assigned to a unit in France. He died in France on October

5, 1918, at the tender age of 24, when his single-seater, open cockpit Spad was gunned down in a dogfight by German Fokker planes behind enemy lines. He is buried in the Argonne Cemetery in France.[49]

College football players were the era's football heroes in those days, and many of them, like "Red" Hudson, sacrificed gridiron glory for what they thought would be glory on the battlefield.

There is no doubt that college football was king in those days. The passion of the American people for the sport had more to do with celebrating one's university and/or hometown than it did with the actual game. People arranged activities, gatherings, and parties that led up to the game. Football gave the working class an identity. Eventually, that passion for the game resulted in the development of a professional football league—the National Football League—on August 20, 1920, in Canton, Ohio. The college game would now have to share the limelight.

After World War II ended, Americans were looking forward to an extended period of peace and prosperity. Most Americans wanted to put war behind them, but the country was soon engaged in another bloody conflict, the Korean War that went from 1950–53. After the cessation of hostilities, many quickly put that war behind them, with some historians calling it the "Forgotten War." Many American men served. Some were veterans of World War II, but others were young men who were drafted—at the time, the United States had a peacetime draft, and most high schools had ROTC programs full of future soldiers.

As the war grew in intensity, many men who were playing for the NFL or their college answered their nation's call. Since old and young alike were being taken into combat, it seemed only natural for football players to serve once again. One example was Eddie LeBaron. Following college graduation, LeBaron served as a United States Marine Corps lieutenant. He was twice wounded and decorated with the Purple Heart. LeBaron was also awarded the Bronze Star for heroic actions. Much later, his actions were summarized as follows:

In a hard-fought battle at Korea's Heartbreak Ridge, Eddie LeBaron, a NFL QB for both the Cowboys and Redskins, left cover under heavy fire to contact the forward observation post of a mortar platoon, in sight of the enemy. After an assaulting rifle position in his area lost its commander, he took charge and resumed the attack. For his efforts, he was awarded the Bronze Star.[50]

Due to his diminutive size and the leadership skills he exhibited in combat, LeBaron was sometimes known as the "Littlest General." He returned to play 12 seasons in the NFL.[51]

The Vietnam War was probably the United States' most controversial war. While the reasons for fighting the conflict were hotly debated, there should be no debate about the men who served in it. They upheld the traditions, character, and honor of service, and this demands respect. Once again, among the men who honorably served in a branch of the U.S. military during the Vietnam War, there were

football players. In fact, only seven active pro athletes served in Vietnam, and six of them were football players (the other was a bowler).

Some of those players distinguished themselves in the service and then went on to have Hall of Fame careers in the game they loved yet set aside to serve their country. Others remind us of what could have been, those men who didn't come back to the game or, sadder still, at all. Men who came back to star in the NFL included the likes of Roger Staubach and Rocky Bleier. Staubach was a graduate of the United States Naval Academy and a Vietnam veteran who played for legendary Dallas Cowboys coach Tom Landry, who was also a veteran—Landry was a pilot during World War II. Rocky Bleier survived serious wounds to his legs and managed to rehabilitate himself and salvage his NFL career. It took a lot of determination and faith as well as an owner who believed in him in order for Bleier to become a feared player for the Pittsburgh Steelers and a passionate advocate for all wounded warriors.

While we don't have to wistfully wonder about "what could have been" for players like Staubach and Bleier, the same can't be said for Bob Kalsu. Adjudged to be among the best tackles to ever play for the University of Oklahoma, Kalsu was drafted by the Buffalo Bills in the eighth round of the 1968 NFL Draft. Other teams, including the Dallas Cowboys and the AFL's Denver Broncos, were interested in Kalsu but were leery of his military commitment. Kalsu had completed ROTC and was going to be commissioned as a second lieutenant after he graduated in May.

He made a promise upon joining the ROTC at the University of Oklahoma that he would serve on active duty. Friends and family pleaded with him to serve in the reserves like most of the other draft-able professional athletes had done, to which Kalsu responded, "I'm no better than anybody else."[52] He was not immediately called to active duty, so he was able to attend the Bills' camp and crack the roster. Eventually, Kalsu cracked the starting lineup and played right guard for the Bills during the 1968 season. He had an outstanding rookie year. In September 1969, Kalsu announced to his wife, Jan, that he was being shipped off to Vietnam.[53]

Jill Kalsu-Horning (left) and Bob Kalsu Jr. (right) pose with their mother, Jan Kalsu McLaughlin, and pictures of Bob Kalsu Sr. and his medals on Friday, April 30, 2004, in Edmond, Oklahoma. Kalsu Sr., an All-American lineman at the University of Oklahoma and a Buffalo Bills player, was one of three NFL players to serve in Vietnam. (AP Photo/Jeffrey Haderthauer)

Bob Kalsu left for Vietnam and didn't see his wife or daughter until he met up with them for a week of R-and-R in Hawaii in May 1970—Jan was seven months pregnant with their son. Jan flew back to Oklahoma while Bob flew back to Vietnam—they would never see each other again.

On July 21, 1970, Bob Kalsu became the only pro athlete to die in Vietnam. The Bills lost a great player, a wife lost a husband, and two kids lost their father. Despite having opportunities and the resources to get him out of active duty, Kalsu served nobly because as he said, "It was the right thing to do." This legacy of service and selfless sacrifice is reflected in the young men and women who served and continue to serve in today's conflicts in places like Iraq and Afghanistan.

Even in the recent Global War on Terrorism, America has witnessed athletes, including NFL players, express a willingness to serve and sacrifice. Given the amount of money and "hero" status that is conferred upon most modern athletes, it is refreshing to know that some athletes are willing to put their country above their own interests—some of them were football players. Some served in reserve units and came home to play in the NFL, like Tennessee Titans fullback Ahmard Hall, who served in Kosovo and Afghanistan in 2003. Other players lost a family member in combat, like Rams' center Jason Brown, whose brother, Lunsford, was killed in 2003. Of course, then there was the man who gave all—Pat Tillman. The Arizona State and Arizona Cardinals star traded in an NFL uniform for an Army Ranger uniform and paid the ultimate price. Pat Tillman lost his life and once again demonstrated that the cost of freedom can be very high.

Like the U.S. military, the NFL has attempted to mold men, investing long, hard yards and years of service into building a team that reflects the uniquely American ethic that the power of likeminded individuals in the pursuit of excellence can inspire those individuals to achieve great things, especially in the name of freedom.

Section 2

The Last Full Measure:
The KIA of the NFL

◆

Football lost more men in wartime than any other professional sport. We present here the honor roll of pro football players killed in World War II, followed by a look at college players killed in action dating back to 1896. We then look at pro football players killed in later wars.

Dates and locations of birth and death throughout are as presented on the website profootballarchives.com.

Nick Basca

Philadelphia Eagles / United States Army

Born: December 4, 1916, in Phoenixville, Pennsylvania

Died: November 11, 1944, in Obreck, France

Position: HB

Nick Basca played football for the Philadelphia Eagles on December 7, 1941—the day Japanese warplanes attacked Pearl Harbor. Three days later, he enlisted in the United States Army and was sent to Fort Bragg for basic training. He was assigned to the Tank Corps and became a member of Gen. George S. Patton's Third Army, fighting in France. He was killed on November 11, 1944—a date that was designated Armistice Day at the time in recognition of the date that World War I came to its close.

Both of Basca's parents came from what was once Austria-Hungary, but by the time of the 1930 Census, it was considered Czechoslovakia. His father, Michael, arrived in the late nineteenth century and worked as a steelworker at the Phoenixville steel plant. His mother, Mary, arrived in 1903. Nick himself was born on December 4, 1916. Both of Nick's parents spoke Slovak as their native tongue. Nick's given name was Michael Martin Basca Jr., but he was known as Nick because as a young boy he went door to door in the Phoenixville, Pennsylvania, neighborhood where he and his three brothers and sister were raised, asking to do odd jobs for a nickel. "Nickels" Basca soon became Nick.

Nick started football in grade school, playing for Sacred Heart where his father had coached football in 1920–21. He played for the Phoenixville High Phantoms. In 1938, he began college with Villanova where he was a triple threat under coach Clipper Smith. Don Wambold explained that he'd passed, punted, and drop-kicked, winning a place on the All-State team and several All-Eastern teams. On December 28, 1940, Basca was the starting left halfback for the North Team for the North-South game at Montgomery, Alabama, a 14–12 win for the North. The Associated Press dispatch from the game stated, "The Yankees, led by fleet halfback Nick Basca of Villanova and linedriving Joe Hoague of Colgate, were never threatened."[54] Basca's 22-yard first-quarter touchdown pass started the scoring. In the fourth quarter, Nick intercepted a pass and returned it to the 15; then he ran it to the 2, setting up a second touchdown by Joe Hoague.

Though he was short of stature, standing 5'8" and a stocky 170 lbs., at least seven NFL teams sought to sign Basca after graduation in 1941, including the New York Giants, Chicago Cardinals, Pittsburgh Steelers, Green Bay Packers, Washington Redskins, and Cleveland Rams—but it was Bert Bell of the Philadelphia Eagles who succeeded in signing his fellow Pennsylvanian.

As a rookie, Basca appeared in every one of the Eagles' 11 games in 1941. His one touchdown was on a two-yard run in the ninth game. In 15 rushing attempts, Nick ran 44 yards, his longest a 19-yard run. Three times he intercepted opposition passes. The team finished 2–8–1, and in fourth place in the East under coach Greasy Neale.

The December 7 game was the last game of the 1941 season. Slinging Sammy Baugh's three touchdown passes won the Griffith Stadium game for Washington, 20–14. Jack Banta started at left halfback and scored one touchdown; Basca came in and kicked the extra point. The Eagles scored again in the third quarter, and Nick adding an extra point. He finished the season 9-for-9 in extra-point attempts and was 1-for-2 in field goals attempted. The Eagles had a 14–7 lead heading into the fourth quarter, but Baugh hit for two TDs in eight minutes and the Redskins prevailed. He scored 18 points in his season for the Eagles.

During the course of the game, the Japanese air attack commenced. Three days later, Basca enlisted at Fort Meade, Maryland, on December 10, 1941. His interest in serving was not prompted by Pearl Harbor. He'd been accepted for selective service induction just two weeks earlier, on November 24.[55] He was told he could report after the season—after the game that happened to fall on December 7.

After basic at Fort Bragg, Basca was stationed at Pine Camp (Camp Drum) in New York. While still in the eastern United States, he was asked to play football for the Eastern Army All-Stars team to help raise money for the Army Emergency Relief Fund. The team "trained at Yale, during their brief six-week season, they played eight games in eight different cities, (in one case three games in eight days) playing professional teams such as the Brooklyn Dodgers and the New York Giants."[56] The *Boston Globe* noted that 25 of the men on Col. Bob Neyland's All-Army team that played a September 20, 1942, benefit game at Fenway Park against the Chicago Bears were former professional football players, five of them from the Philadelphia Eagles.[57]

After this interlude, Basca was transferred to Camp Bowie near Brownwood, Texas, where he "participated in maneuvers in the southwestern desert area."[58]

In December 1943, Basca was shipped to England as Allied forces began the buildup to D-Day. He was assigned to the Fourth Armored Division in Gen. Patton's Third Army. Knowing that German intelligence had its eyes on Patton, the Third Army played the part of decoys rather than participate in the actual invasion at Normandy. The Third Army arrived, via Utah Beach, on July 11. By August 1, Patton was on the attack and pushed his men relentlessly with the Tank Corps (supplied by the Red Ball Express) leading the way in a fast-moving assault that kept the German defenders off-guard and discombobulated. Allied command thought the Third was moving too quickly and slowed them down before finally giving them a second green light on November 8. Patton attacked Metz. Three days later, Corporal Basca was killed in action in Obreck, not far from Nancy, when his tank was hit by a German 88mm shell.[59]

Both of Nick's brothers, Paul and Steve, served in Europe during the war. At the time Nick was killed, Steve was only 60 miles away, recovering from wounds for which he was awarded one of the three Purple Hearts he had earned by war's end.

Charlie Behan

Detroit Lions / United States Marine Corps
Born: August 4, 1920, in Crystal Lake, Illinois
Died: May 18, 1945, in Okinawa, Japan
Position: E

It was Christmas Eve in 1944 on Guadalcanal. The six-month battle to take the island (August 7, 1942–February 21, 1943) had been over for a year and a half and cost more than 6,000 American casualties on land, sea, and in the air. It was the first major defeat for the Japanese and marked the end of their expansion. Their rollback was well underway by the end of 1944,

and Guadalcanal and the Solomon Islands were secure. However, the war itself was far from over.

Some of the Marines staged a touch football game, dubbed the Mosquito Bowl, involving men from the Sixth Marine Division, 4th and 29th Regiments. Thousands of men enjoyed the game, which ended in a scoreless tie. Behan was player/coach for the 29th Marines.

Most of those present were sent to Okinawa a little more than three months later, and Terry Frei of the *Denver Post* wrote that 12 of the troops who played in the game were killed in combat before the war was done.[60] He listed them:

- Dave Schreiner, Wisconsin's two-time All-American end and the Big Ten's most valuable player in 1942.
- Wisconsin tackle Bob Baumann, who served in the same platoon as Schreiner and died 15 days before his former Badgers teammate.
- Tony Butkovich, who first played at Illinois and then was the nation's leading rusher in 1943 for Purdue while on the campus in a Marine training program.
- Former Notre Dame end and captain George Murphy.
- Michigan center Bob Fowler.
- Lehigh tackle John Hebrank.
- Southern Methodist tackle Hubbard Hinde.
- Marquette halfback Rusty Johnston.
- Wake Forest and Duke halfback Johnny Perry.
- Amherst end Jim Quinn.
- Cornell tackle Ed Van Order.

The 12th man was Charlie Behan. A native and still resident of Crystal Lake, Illinois, up to the time of his death, Charles Edward Behan had been born there on August 4, 1920, the son of carpenter Charles Behan and his wife, Louise. He was sizable for the day at 6'3", with a playing weight of 195 lbs. He'd played end at Northern Illinois State Teachers College and had been signed by the Detroit Lions as a rookie in 1942. Behan appeared in nine games, with four receptions totaling 63 yards—fourth on the team. Though the Lions had annihilated the Philadelphia Eagles 42–7 in a September 6 preseason game held at night in Erie, Pennsylvania, Detroit failed to win a regular season game all year long and finished 0–11 for last place in the NFL West, scoring only 38 points all season long while being scored upon for 263 points. Bill Edwards and Bull Karcis coached the team. Under normal circumstances, Behan would have liked nothing better than to have come back the following year to fight for a better record. But war had intervened, and he found himself in the Pacific Theater.

Some six weeks into the battle for Okinawa (April 1, 1945—July 2, 1945), Lt. Behan was struck in the mouth by shrapnel on the morning of May 18 during the final day of the 10-day battle for Sugar Loaf Hill. Behan was still ambulatory and could have sought medical attention, but instead, said his "runner" Bill Hulek, "He kept changing cotton in his mouth."

"We went up Sugar Loaf and got up there all right," Hulek told Frei. According to Lt. Bill Osmanski, a former fullback for the Chicago Bears and a fellow Marine, Behan tossed three grenades at a Japanese machine gun nest. Next, Hulek said, "Lieutenant Behan kneeled there with a little carbine. That jammed, so he took my rifle and started shooting again."

Behan was hit by machine gun fire. "The bullets came right out of his back," Hulek said, "and you could see his jacket raised—plink, plink, plink."[61] Behan's family was informed of his death on May 26, and *The New York Times* ran a brief obituary on June 1.

The battle itself is detailed in the 1996 book, *Killing Ground on Okinawa: The Battle for Sugar Loaf Hill* by James H. Hallas. Behan was posthumously awarded the Navy Cross, and he was one of 1,656 Americans killed in the battle for this piece of prized Pacific real estate.

Navy Cross Citation:
The President of the United States takes pride in presenting the Navy Cross (Posthumously) to Charles Edwin Behan (0–22667), Second Lieutenant, U.S. Marine Corps (Reserve), for extraordinary heroism as a Platoon Leader attached to Company F, Second Battalion, Twenty-Ninth Marines, SIXTH Marine Division, during action against enemy Japanese forces on Okinawa, Ryukyu Islands, 18 May 1945. Refusing evacuation after first-aid treatment for a shrapnel wound in the mouth received while he was moving into position for an assault on Sugar Loaf Hill, first Lieutenant Behan remained steadfast with his platoon and, despite his inability to talk, directed

the movements of his platoon by arm and hand signals. Risking his life by taking an exposed position well in front of the platoon so that his men could see his signals, he led the attack through withering enemy fire and, although hit again and mortally wounded, dragged himself behind a rock and continued to convey his instructions to his men and direct the attack until he lost consciousness. By his daring initiative, staunch leadership, extreme fortitude, and perseverance in the face of overwhelming odds, First Lieutenant Behan contributed immeasurably to the successful completion of the company's mission. His courageous and unfaltering devotion to duty was in keeping with the highest traditions of the United States Naval Service. He gallantly gave his life for his country.

Commander in Chief, Pacific Forces: Serial 52787 (January 19, 1946)

Keith Birlem

Chicago Cardinals and Washington Redskins / United States Army Air Corps

Born: May 4, 1915, in San Jose, California
Died: May 7, 1943, in Polebrook, United Kingdom
Position: B-E

Keith Birlem went to San Mateo High School. His father, Frederick, worked as an insurance broker. Born in San Jose on May 4, 1915, Birlem played football as a quarterback with the San Jose State Spartans, and in 1939 he debuted with the NFL's Chicago Cardinals even before

finishing college. He's in the San Jose State Hall of Fame.

With the Cardinals, Birlem appeared in six games, converted from quarterback to end by Coach Ernie Nevers. Birlem started three of the six games, though he didn't play much. He had two receptions for 17 yards with no yards rushing. On November 8, he was placed on waivers and selected by the Washington Redskins. He appeared briefly in three games as a blocking back but recorded no yardage.

Birlem chose not to continue in football, instead notifying the Redskins in May 1940 that he would be enlisting in the Air Corps. It wasn't a spur-of-the-moment decision. Flying was what Birlem had long wanted to do—even while at San Jose State, he'd tried on seven separate occasions to enlist in the Flying Cadet Corps but had been rejected each time due to an inability to pass the eyesight examination. Only after completing college, when Keith was no longer on the swimming team, was he finally able to pass. The conclusion was that the chlorine in the pool had negatively affected his vision. After returning to wrap up his degree, he found himself able to pass the test.

Primary training was at the Ryan School of Aeronautics in California with basic training at Randolph Field in Texas. He told the *Washington Post* that his only regret in not returning to the Redskins was missing the team's fans who had impressed him mightily with their spontaneous turnout after their return from playing the last game of the year against the Giants, a 9–7 loss.[62] But Birlem was well on his way to winning his wings.

He advanced to the rank of captain, and by the end of 1942 he was stationed at Geiger Field at Spokane where he was tapped to lead a squadron of Flying Fortresses that he named the Redskins. Each aircraft would be named after a Native American tribe. It was the same squadron with which Clark Gable served as a gunner, the 508th Squadron of the 351st Bombardment Group (Eighth Air Force).

Birlem, now a major, flew his first combat mission on his birthday, May 4, as a co-pilot with the 303rd Bomb Group in a mission to bomb a plant in Antwerp, Belgium. Three days later, Maj. Birlem was killed in England on May 7, 1943, while trying to land his crippled B-17. Otto Vasak, the squadron's Engineering Officer, wrote that, "Keith was killed in a flight formation training exercise before the 351st Bomb Group started flying combat missions.

His B-17 dropped down and cut the tail off of the plane below. Both planes crashed near the Polebrook Airfield perimeter, and all 20 aircrew perished."[63] The other plane was commanded by Lt. Roy O. Snipes. The two aircraft were among 10 planes lost that one day.

Al Blozis

New York Giants / United States Army
Born: January 5, 1919, in Garfield, New Jersey
Died: January 31, 1945, in Colmar, France
Position: T

There are variations in the stories about how Al Blozis died, but the detailed account from Paul Lambert carries conviction. It was during the Battle of the Bulge, and Blozis was serving with A Company, 110th Infantry Regiment, 28th Infantry Division in the Vosges Mountains (France) on January 31, 1945, near Le Cras mountain and the village of La Baroche and the town of Orbey. It all began on what was reportedly Al's first day of combat, and it was Lambert's birthday.

"I was one of the four he went looking for," Lambert wrote. "There were 12 of us, but a German sniper wounded one of the men just before we reached the little village. I was a Machine Gunner. Al sent me and three others to the furthest outpost. I don't know where he sent the other seven, but evidently they all got out of there safely. As soon as we got to the place where we were to set up the machine gun, a big old farmhouse at the end of the valley, a German sniper got one of my three buddies and killed him. That left only three of us to manage that gun 24 hours a day for five days. We were pretty much exhausted and just about out of ammo and food.

"On that last day, I knew I had to get back to the command post that Al had set up in the little schoolhouse at the bottom of the mountain where we entered the village. It was snowing, and visibility was next to zero. I left my two buddies to man the gun and took off very cautiously toward the Command post about a quarter mile away. In the dense snow, as I got about half way, I saw a huge form advancing toward me. I stopped with my pistol ready and then suddenly realized it was Lt. Blozis. And he recognized me. I was about to say something, but he motioned to me to be quiet. Just then there was a blast from a German machine gun, and Lt. Blozis fell backwards to

Al Blozis, Georgetown tackle, is shown airborne in 1941. (AP Photo)

the ground. I carefully crawled on my stomach to him, but he was dead. He had several bullet holes in his body. I could do nothing except get back to my outpost.

"When I got back, I told my two surviving buddies what had happened. We didn't know what to do because we had no orders or any communications. We knew that we just couldn't desert our post. If we didn't get help very soon, we were goners because the Germans were not taking any prisoners. Just toward evening, an old man from the village came to us and told us that we had to get out of there because our comrades had all left. He told us we were surrounded by

During the Battle of the Bulge, an infantryman of the 1st Division comes out of a tree line near Bullingen, Belgium. (Photo courtesy of the National World War II Museum)

Germans and he pointed out the only chance we had of getting out of there. He showed us the direction to go and where to start climbing back over the mountain that was the least German-infested route. It took us four nights of climbing in waist-high snow to get over the mountaintop and over to the American side."[64]

A 1991 *New York Times* story quotes soldier Joe McCluskey as saying Blozis had been hit 38 times.[65] Blozis was officially declared as missing in action. In April he was finally declared dead;

the telegram from the War Department gave his date of death as January 31.

Blozis was one of those who had to really put up a fight to be allowed to serve. His problem was that he was too tall. At 6'6" (with a playing weight of 250 lbs.), he was fast, an exceptional tackle for Georgetown, but too tall for the navy, which set height restrictions based on the space in army transport ships. Blozis' parents had immigrated from Lithuania, and he was born in Garfield, New Jersey, on January 5, 1919. His father, Anthony, was a laborer for an electric company. Al went to high school in Jersey City and then to St. Luke's in Manhattan. Blozis appreciated all that America stood for and wanted to fight, preferably in Europe to help liberate Lithuania.

In a February 2003 profile in the *New York Daily News*, David Hinckley explained that Blozis set the world indoor shot-put record and would have been well-positioned to win the gold medal in the 1940 Olympics had they not been canceled due to the war engulfing Europe. He also ranked as one of the top discus throwers in the world.[66]

Though not a starting player until his senior year, he became an All-American tackle for Georgetown and was a fifth-round pick of the New York Giants in the 1942 draft. He appeared in all 11 games that year as an offensive left and right tackle and was a first-time Pro Bowler. In 1943, he played in all 10 games and was voted first-team All-Pro, "showing how quickly he was recognized as the kind of granite block around which a team could anchor an interior line for years."[67] He even scored a touchdown in the October 24 game against the Steagles when he pounced on a blocked kick and ran in the ball.

Blozis wanted to serve and wouldn't take no for an answer. "The branches of the armed forces, one by one, turned him down because of his size. But Blozis refused to give up. After two seasons playing professional football for the New York Giants, he obtained a size waiver and reported for duty. Then, like many well-known athletes and personalities of the day, Blozis was disappointingly assigned to Special Services, the recreation branch of the military. But military sports were not how PFC Blozis intended to spend the remainder of the war. He found a way into the infantry, earned his lieutenant bars, and along the way smashed the army grenade-throwing record with a toss of more than 94 yards [35 yards was considered respectable.]"[68]

There were opportunities in the army that didn't require shipment overseas, and in December 1943 he was allowed to enlist in the chemical warfare service and was given a job stateside as a physical instructor at Walter Reed—though he had to wait three weeks for specially sized uniforms to be issued to him.[69] Once in the army, he put himself forward for Officers Candidate School and was accepted. After completing his training at Fort Benning in November 1944 (where he set the army's hand grenade throwing record with a toss of 94 yards, 2', 6½"), he had missed most of the NFL season but had a brief furlough before being sent overseas.

He switched uniforms again, playing on weekend passes, and appeared in the last two games of the 1944 season for the Giants and was declared eligible for the NFL Championship Game with Green Bay. The Packers won 14–7, but Blozis was named one of three "defensive standouts" by *The New York Times*.[70] Two days after the Championship Game, he shipped overseas where just six weeks later, he met his fate.

His No. 32 was retired by the Giants, and he was even featured in the April 1946 issue of *True Comics* with a story titled, "The Human Howitzer."

Chuck Braidwood

Portsmouth Spartans, Cleveland Indians, Chicago
Cardinals, Cincinnati Reds / American Red Cross

Born: October 15, 1903, at an unknown location
Died: January 8, 1945, in the South Pacific
Position: E

As the Second World War reached its peak in 1945, the American Red Cross was extremely active, with more than 39,000 paid staff and some 7½ million volunteers. Throughout the war years, the Red Cross is said to have helped treat 1 million combat casualties. Much of this work was done on the front lines, and it should not be surprising that a number of Red Cross workers were themselves injured or killed. The Red Cross reports that, "Over the course of the war years, 86 Red Cross workers—52 women and 34 men—lost their lives as the result of their wartime service."[71]

One fatality was Chuck Braidwood on January 8, 1945, killed in action in the South Pacific. Charles G. Braidwood had been born at an unknown location on October 15, 1903, one of four children born to James and Cornelia Braidwood. James was a Canadian native working as a molder in a brass works at the time of the 1910 census. Twenty years later, Charles debuted as a pro football player with the Portsmouth Spartans. He was living at the time in Chattanooga with his wife, Wilma Lee. The couple had adopted a daughter, Betsy Ruth. His work was as a collector for the electric power company. But he was good at football, an end, who had attended both Loyola University Chicago and the University

of Tennessee–Chattanooga, from 1926–29.[72] It was in the fall of 1930 when he debuted with the Spartans. He was an even 6' and listed with a playing weight of 199 lbs. Portsmouth had a 5–6–3 season and finished tied for seventh place in the 11-team NFL.

They won their first two games and tied the third, but then the team began to slip downhill. Braidwood appeared in 10 games, starting two of them. He apparently saw little activity, however, as he is not credited with any scoring. In 1931, he started in eight of the 10 games played by the Cleveland Indians (2–8, eighth of 10 teams), but again was not involved with any scoring. He was, however, named to the second team All-NFL by United Press International. Playing for his third team in three years, the 1932 Chicago Cardinals, Braidwood was again on one of the less-distinguished teams in the league. The 2–6–2 Cardinals placed sixth. Braidwood's coach at Chicago was Jack Chevigny, who is profiled elsewhere in this book; Chevigny was killed on Iwo Jima on the second day of the invasion of the island. Braidwood only appeared in one game for the Cardinals. His contract was sold to the Brooklyn Dodgers in October 1932, but he never appeared in a game for them.

His team finished fourth in 1933, which sounds like an improvement, but the 1933 NFL season saw the league form two divisions of five teams each, and Braidwood found himself on his fourth team in four seasons—the Cincinnati Reds (actually, the fifth team, counting Brooklyn). Finishing fourth meant they were next to last in the NFL West (3–6–1), with only the 1–9–1 Cardinals (no longer coached by Chevigny) below them in the standings. Chuck was in six of their games, starting in the team's 27–0 loss to Brooklyn. This time, he shows up in the record books with two receptions for a total of 29 yards. When the Reds changed coaches in midseason, Braidwood was one of two players released. His football career had come to an end.

What he did in the succeeding dozen years remains unknown. He was reportedly an American Red Cross program director working overseas to help the war effort and is said to have died of a heart attack on Biak Island. He is buried in Fort William McKinley at Manila.[73]

Young Bussey

Chicago Bears / United States Navy

Born: October 4, 1917, in Timpson, Texas

Died: January 7, 1945, in Lingayen Gulf, Phillipines

Position: QB

Young Bussey was a brash, overly confident athlete who grew up in Houston and seemed to excel at anything he attempted. "In death," wrote biographer Ralph Cushman, "Young showed the only crack in his otherwise unconquerable spirit. You had to kill him to stop him!"[74]

He was the youngest of seven boys and three girls ("all of whom idolized him") born to Thomas and Katie Lee Bussey, on October 4, 1917, in his grandmother's house in Timpson, Texas, as Ruey Young Bussey. The Busseys had lived in the farm and ranch town in Shelby County for three generations, and Young was

the 13th child born to the couple. His father was a fiddler, accordionist, singer, and square dance caller in addition to working on oil leases and making a little moonshine on the side.[75] Thomas died while Young was still in school, and his widow had to farm out some of her children to make ends meet. Young's varied and accomplished athletic talents, and a scholarship arranged by none other than Louisiana's Huey Long, brought Bussey to Louisiana State University from which he graduated with top grades and a degree in petroleum engineering. This despite waking at 3:00 AM each morning for his milk delivery route.

Basketball was his favorite sport in high school, though he excelled at boxing, track, softball, and football. Among his classmates at San Jacinto High in Houston were Walter Cronkite and Dr. Denton Cooley, but Young was the big sports figure on campus—and often quite a challenge to coaches along the way because he always appeared to have his own way of doing things. He also was a bit of an organizer, leading a strike of his high school's football players to try to hold onto their coach.

Once in college, he led LSU in passing two years in a row (1937 and 1938), and had led the team in rushing in 1937. He was named captain, and both he and teammate Ken Kavanaugh were invited to try out for the Chicago Bears. Even after being drafted (in the 20th round of the 1940 NFL Draft) by George Halas and the Bears, Bussey was a little irrepressible, striding right into the sanctum of the coach's dressing room and telling Coach Halas he'd come to be a winner and the coach needed to either trade established quarterback Sid Luckman or keep him on as Bussey's backup.[76] Halas assigned him to Newark and after crushing Luckman and the Bears in a scrimmage against the varsity, Bussey went on to play the season with Newark, becoming the American Association's leader in passing yardage.

Bussey made the Bears in 1941, albeit as Luckman's backup at quarterback. And he won a championship watch in his first season.

His first scoring came with two second-quarter completions for touchdowns in the October 5 game against the Cleveland Rams, a 48–21 win in Cleveland. Luckman also completed two TD passes in the game. Each replicated the feat in the 53–7 October 12 home win against the Chicago Cardinals. By season's end, Bussey had appeared in 10 games, passing for 353 yards (tying him for tenth with Bob Snyder). Luckman was third with 1,181 yards, completing 68-of-119 with three interceptions. Bussey's completion percentage was much lower, 13-of-40 with three interceptions. And when asked to rush the ball, he was thrown for a net loss of 27 yards on the year. The one time he returned a punt, he did so for 40 yards. The two times he was asked to punt, he averaged 37 yards—his jersey number. He also intercepted two passes on defense. It was a good first-year effort for a backup, and his future looked bright.

But the last day of the season was December 7, 1941. Even after war was declared against Japan, the playoffs went on with a 33–14 win for the Division over the Green Bay Packers on December 14 and a 37–9 humbling of the New York Giants on December 21. Both games were at Soldier Field, Chicago. Bussey was successful moving the ball forward eight yards in the one pass he threw in the Championship Game. He hadn't figured at all in the game against Green Bay, the only team which had beaten the 10–1–0 Bears that year. But Bussey had become a crowd pleaser. Ralph Cushman wrote, "He had become the Bears' instant offense. The crowd quickly recognized his potential for electric action and screamed approval when he trotted into the arena. Actual records fail to define just how prolific Young was from the standpoint of points per minute of play…[he] often was sent in for a quick score and then was held in reserve as the Bears' defense dug in to preserve the lead."[77]

A member of the championship team, Pearl Harbor had more or less assured he wouldn't be back in 1942. While awaiting callup in the military draft, Bussey took a job early that year helping build Liberty ships at the Houston Shipbuilding Corporation. He did join the Bears at training camp before the 1942 season, but it became clear that Halas intended to stick with Luckman, who'd helped him win back-to-back championships in 1940 and 1941. Bussey played in the 1942 College All-Star Game in Chicago on August 28 before a record-breaking crowd of 101,103 spectators. He entered the game for Luckman in the second quarter and threw a touchdown pass, part of the 21–0 defeat of the college players.

As soon as the game was over, Bussey told Coach Halas that he was going to enlist in the United States Naval Reserve the very next day. He did, and was sent to Officer Candidate

School for training. Bussey was ultimately assigned to the USS *Warren*, an attack transport ship that was active in the South Pacific.[78] Lt. (Junior Grade) Bussey received his first commendation from the Commander of the Fifth Fleet for his work as assistant beachmaster during the late July 1944 invasion of Guam.

The *Warren* was very active at Kwajalein, Peleliu, Guam, Leyte, and Luzon. In all, Bussey took part in a full 10 landing assaults and was named as head beachmaster for the forthcoming January 1945 landing planned on the beaches of Lingayen Gulf, The Philippines. He had expressed his feelings that his luck was running out.

Katie Lee Bussey had six sons serving in the armed forces. Young's older brother, Keefer, was an army engineer and had been the sole survivor when a Japanese mortar shell wiped out everyone else in his bunker. But during a visit a bit earlier, Young had told Keefer that he would not come out of his next landing alive, and pressed his NFL championship watch on his brother. And the night before the invasion, he handed over all his accumulated letters and items he'd collected to the ship's chaplain, saying, "Tomorrow I make my ascension. Will you see that my mother gets these?"[79]

The *Warren* was transporting troops from Gen. Walter Krueger's Sixth Army and faced increasingly desperate Japanese resistance, including hastily constructed explosives-laden kamikaze bamboo plywood boats. After two days of unrelenting Naval bombardment meant to soften the enemy, the landing vessels set out on January 7, 1945—and in the heavy smoke,

Bussey's craft went astray and then hit a coral reef a little more than 75 yards off a beach that had not been weakened. Japanese fire opened up, and a direct mortar hit threw Bussey and most of the crew into the sea. Lt. Cmdr. Lawrence Beall, Bussey's friend on board, said that he'd been struck in the left shoulder and chest, the arm possibly completely blown off. As the smoke and dense ground fog offered some protection, Bussey was last seen signaling his men to get back behind its cover, using his right arm. Beall wrote, "I was in the water trying to swim without my life belt as it had been blown off. I leaned down to cut off my shoes, and when I looked up the two men I had seen swimming away from the wreckage had disappeared."[80] Most of the men survived, but Bussey was never seen again.

Other bodies washed ashore and were recovered. Bussey's was never found. Interviewed by the *Houston Chronicle* on Veteran's Day 11 years later, Katie Lee Bussey still held out hope that her youngest son was still alive. She had all his medals, trophies, and scrapbooks awaiting him at her home on East 12th Street. But her hopes were in vain.[81]

Jack Chevigny

Chicago Cardinals / United States Marine Corps
Born: August 14, 1906, in Dyer, Indiana
Died: February 19, 1945, in Iwo Jima, Japan
Position: coach

One of the more famous football quotations of all time came from the mouth of Jack Chevigny, according to Notre Dame lore. It was on November 10, 1928, when Coach Knute Rockne's "Fighting Irish" team faced what looked to be an overwhelmingly dominant Army team in a game played at Yankee Stadium before 85,000 fans. The team from West Point was unbeaten up to that point in the season; Notre Dame was struggling. But the game was scoreless through the first half. Army had made only one first down and Notre Dame only five. During halftime, Rockne gave a highly emotional speech, evoking the memory of star player George Gipp from several years earlier, who had died of pneumonia at the end of the 1920 season. From his deathbed, he'd reportedly urged, "Some time, Rock, when the team is up against it, when things are wrong and the breaks are beating the boys, tell them to go in there with all they've got and win just one for the Gipper."

The coach's speech inspired the team, but on the very first drive of the third quarter, Army scored. Notre Dame responded against a tough Army defense but brought the ball to the 1-yard line. Chevigny was driven back three yards, then fought to recover two of them and teammate Fred Collins recovered the third. From the 1-yard line, halfback Chevigny carried the ball again and pushed it across, tying the score and declaring, "That's one for the Gipper!" A later score by Johnny O'Brien won the game for Notre Dame, prompting Chevigny to burst out, "That's one for the Gipper, too!" The film *Knute Rockne—All American* starred Ronald Reagan as Gipp. Numerous sources cite Rockne as calling Chevigny the greatest blocking back he'd ever coached.

U.S. Marine Corps captain Jack Chevigny, former football coach at Notre Dame and the University of Texas, was reported to have been killed on February 19, 1945, while leading a Marine charge on Iwo Jima. Chevigny is shown here in a 1944 photo. (AP Photo)

John Edward Chevigny was born in Dyer, Indiana, on August 14, 1906. His parents, J.A. and Rose Ann Chevigny, both came to the United States from their native Canada in 1895 and were both nationalized in 1902. The family relocated to Hammond. Jack's father was a medical doctor. He had three older siblings—Graziella, Julius, and Marie. Julius was a doctor in Gary, Indiana, in 1945.

Jack played for Notre Dame from 1926 through 1928 and later worked as backfield coach for Rockne in 1929 and 1930. Chevigny considered taking a position at Navy in early 1931 but decided to put in another year at Notre Dame. A couple of months later, Rockne died. Hunk Anderson was appointed in his stead, and Chevigny took the job as junior coach. On January 30, 1932, however, he resigned his post in South Bend. On July 9, he signed on to coach the NFL's Chicago Cardinals.

It was a disappointing year, leading an injury-riddled Cardinals team to a disappointing 2–6–2 record, finishing seventh in what was then an eight-team league. Things didn't get better the year after he left to take a position as athletic director and head football coach in Austin, Texas, at St. Edwards; the Cardinals were 1–9–1 in 1933. Just 12 months after signing on with St. Edwards and leading them to a Texas Conference championship, the University of Texas Longhorns hired him as coach for three years, 1934–36 and a 7–2–1 first season that included a win over Notre Dame in his second game. His former teammate, Johnny O'Brien, took the coaching job at St. Edwards. Chevigny's record after three years with U.T., however, was 13–14–2, and he suggested the university find another coach, announcing his decision to retire at a banquet. He's the only coach in Longhorns history not to hold a winning record. Two months later, he accepted a position as an attorney in the State of Texas tax department. He then went into the oil business in Illinois, working with oil lease contracts and living with his sister in Hammond—Chevigny never married—when war was declared. Though without question old enough to be exempt from military service, he signed up on March

Chevigny's Camp Lejeune Marines took on Fort Monroe on October 16, 1943. (Photo courtesy of John Gunn Sports Collection, MS 316, William M. Randall Library Special Collections, University of North Carolina–Wilmington, Wilmington, North Carolina)

17, 1943, with the United States Marine Corps at Fort Benjamin Harrison in Indiana, and on June 12 he made lieutenant. Perhaps somewhat predictably, he was named football coach at Fort Lejeune.

First Lt. Chevigny was assigned to a desk job but told columnist Bill Henry that he was "sick of being a desk officer."[82] He requested a transfer to a combat unit in the Pacific and was granted his request.[83] He found the opportunity to see action and was serving as liaison officer with the 27th Marines when the invasion of Iwo Jima commenced. It was only the second day of the invasion, with the outcome still in doubt. It was just before noon on February 19. Chevigny was crouched in a foxhole with another former football pro turned Marine, Capt. George Franck, when he decided to try and make it to the command post. A direct hit by a Japanese shell killed him instantly, just before he reached the post.[84] There is no doubt that Franck survived, but Jeff Walker's research says that Franck decided to leave the relative safety of the foxhole—and the Japanese mortar round dropped right into the foxhole, killing all within.[85]

All sports and nations have legends—stories really—that have developed over time. Legends serve to tell in part a larger truth or something deeper using a story. George Washington never chopped down a cherry tree as a kid and never said, "I cannot tell a lie." In sports, other legends exist, too. In baseball we have the story of Babe Ruth's "called shot" where he pointed to the fence in Wrigley Field before digging in to the batter's box and then sent the next pitch over that fence for a World Series home run. Some say he predicted his home run; others say that story is pure nonsense. There is nobody left anymore to dispute it either way, so perhaps it comes down to faith. Ruth did hit a home run, however.

Football also has its share of legends, and legend has it that during the signing of the articles of surrender aboard the USS *Missouri*, one of the Japanese envoys was found holding a fountain pen presented to Chevigny inscribed, "To Jack Chevigny, a Notre Damer who beat Notre Dame." The pen was reportedly later re-inscribed, "To Jack Chevigny, a Notre Dame boy who gave his life for his country in the spirit of old Notre Dame." Legend is all it was, however, as Jeff Walker points out in the August 2008 issue of *Leatherneck*, terming the story a "complete fabrication."

Jack Chevigny's death was heroic enough that it needs no embellishment.

Eddie Doyle

Frankford Yellow Jackets, Pottsville Maroons / United States Army

Born: August 17, 1898, in New York, New York
Died: November 8, 1942, in Algiers, Algeria
Position: E

Eddie Doyle started six games as left end for an NFL team that remains a bit of a legend: the 1925 Pottsville Maroons was considered that year's NFL championship team until an "overly officious league" revoked the title because the Maroons had played an exhibition game on December 13 at what was said to be an unauthorized location.[86] It was Doyle's second year in the NFL; he'd played in 10 games for Pottsville's rival, the Frankford Yellow Jackets, in 1924. For those unfamiliar with the geography, Pottsville and Frankford are Pennsylvania cities that boasted an NFL franchise in the middle 1920s. The heir to Frankford today is the Pittsburgh Steelers; the Pottsville Maroons moved to New England in 1929 and became the Boston Bulldogs.

Pottsville at the time had a population of about 25,000. Today, it's not much more than

15,000. But from 1925–28, it was host to an NFL franchise—and at least briefly seemed to be the league champion. The only other contender was the Chicago Cardinals. On December 6 the 9–2–0 Maroons traveled to Chicago to play a postseason game against the 9–1–1 Cardinals at Comiskey Park, handily defeating their hosts, 21–7. Pottsville thus became 10–2, and Chicago became 9–2–1. There was no Championship Game in those days, but the Cardinals were the only other team that had been in position to claim the honor of being best in the league—and Pottsville had beaten them fair and square. There's no question how the game was seen. The *Chicago Tribune* that morning had headlined, "Cardinals Play Pottsville for Pro Title Today," and it followed up the morning after with "Pottsville Wins Over Cards and Takes Pro Title, 21–7." The headlines in papers such as *The New York Times* were typically succinct: "Pottsville Wins Title." The Associated Press wrote that "the postseason game was ordered to clear any doubt as to supremacy."

Notre Dame wanted to play a game against the top team, so it scheduled an exhibition game for the following week. No problem there, but interest in the game was so high that holding it in Philadelphia rather than the Maroons' home field, Minersfield Ballpark (capacity 9,000), was bound to be more lucrative.

It's worth recalling something almost buried in the *Chicago Tribune* story granting Coach Dick Rauch's Maroons the title over the Cardinals. Although the headline proclaimed that "Pottsville…Takes Pro Title," sportswriter Frank Schreiber realized that the NFL league office was a little unpredictable in those early days. He wrote, "The Cards owned the championship of the western half of the league, while Pottsville held claim to the eastern sectional crown, and the Pottsville eleven now has a clear road to the title—at least until the annual meeting of the league moguls is held. Last year the Chicago Bears claimed the title and apparently had it clinched until the league meeting was held and then the flag was awarded to Cleveland, just why no one seemed to know."[87]

The Cardinals made a move in hopes of padding their win total. Even though the season was over, they decided on their own to extend it and scheduled a game against the Hammond Reds, which they won. Two days after that, they quickly added another game, against Milwaukee, and won that one, too, giving them 11 wins. In the December 11 exhibition game in Philadelphia, Pottsville beat Knute Rockne's All-Star Notre Dame team and its renowned Four Horsemen, 9–7. The decision to play in Philly cost them, however. Although they had telephoned the league office for permission and believed they had been granted it—Philadelphia was in the territory claimed by Frankford. On December 29, the league suspended Pottsville as a member of the league. To their credit, the Chicago Cardinals consistently declined to accept the title until the team changed ownership in 1933. Although the Pottsville franchise was reinstated in time for the 1926 season (because of the NFL's fear it would join the AFL), the title was left with the

Cardinals—even after the Pittsburgh Steelers (78 years later, in 2003) formally withdrew Frankford's protest. David Fleming's 2007 book, *Breaker Boys: The NFL's Greatest Team and the Stolen 1925 Championship*, tells the story in more detail. A motion picture based on the book is reportedly in production.

Eddie Doyle, who'd started six of Pottsville's games and could boast one touchdown reception, remained without the honor of being on a league championship team.

Doyle was killed in North Africa during World War II. He'd come from humble beginnings, like many football players of the day. The 1900 Census shows his father as Edward J. Doyle Jr., a coachman living in Syracuse, born in New York of two Irish immigrant parents. His mother was Julia Doyle, born in New York of two New York parents. By 1910, he had a sister, Florence, born around 1901. His father worked then as a "chauffeur, police patrol." By 1920 Doyle's father was a city policeman in Syracuse. Doyle himself was born on August 17, 1898, in New York City.

An ambitious youth, Eddie was accepted to the United States Military Academy at West Point. He completed three years there and lettered in football in 1923. He was lured away to play professional football and never graduated. He started six games with the 1924 Frankford Yellow Jackets, playing right end. He appeared in four other games and is credited with two touchdown receptions. Frankford was Pottsville's rival, and Doyle found himself on the other side of the rivalry in 1925 with a similar record—starting in six of his nine games, this

time as left end, with one touchdown reception. He was 5'9" and weighed 175 lbs.

Unfortunately, we know little about Doyle and his career path from 1925 until his death in World War II. Eddie Doyle was a lieutenant colonel and commander of the 168th Regiment of the 34th Infantry Division. He helped lead the landing forces of Operation Torch in Algeria during which he landed at Apples Beach near Castiglione on the coast road to Oran, north of Blida Airfield.[88] After landing, he reportedly led 25 of his men on a mission straight toward Algiers. The December 12, 1942, issue of the *Pottsville Journal* said:

"Word has been received in Pottsville of the death of Edward J. Doyle…killed in action in Algiers. This was confirmed in an announcement which Mrs. Doyle received from the War Department. According to the War Department, Doyle was killed leading a charge into Algiers, and fell mortally wounded by a sniper…He is believed to have been the first American killed in North Africa during the war."[89]

J.W. "Grassy" Hinton

Staten Island Stapletons / United States Army Air Corps
Born: June 30, 1907, in Cleburne, Texas
Died: December 10, 1944, in Halmahera Island, Indonesia
Position: QB-TB

Grassy Hinton was a graduate of Texas Christian University, like Sammy Baugh and Davey O'Brien, and a quarterback for TCU. An older student who graduated at age 23, he was also a star on the school's baseball team in 1932. TCU's Athletics Media Relations Director Mark Cohen reports, "Grassy Hinton was a three-year letterman (1929–31) for the Horned Frogs. He passed for a team-high 206 yards in 1931, completing 13-of-17 passes (76.5 percent) for three touchdowns. Hinton was also an exceptional punter. He led TCU with averages of 36.0 and 39.2 yards in the 1930 and 1931 campaigns, respectively. The Horned Frogs were 27–4–3 during the three years he lettered, including a 1929 Southwest Conference championship."[90]

A native of Cleburne, Texas (some sources report him as born on the first day of 1907, though census records suggest a 1909 birthdate), his given name was apparently J.W., as his two older brothers, his older sister, and younger brother all have full names, while his remains the two initials. His father, Willie B. Hinton, came from Tennessee and was a farmer in Bosque, Texas, in 1900, moving with his wife, Sarah, to Cleburne by 1910 where he took up work as a bridge foreman for the steam railroad.

Soon after graduation that year, J.W. joined the NFL's Staten Island Stapletons and played tailback in all 12 of the team's 1932 games, starting in six of them. The Stapletons tied more games than they won, 2–7–3. Hinton completed 5-of-19 passes for a total of 46 yards; he bore two interceptions. He added 64 yards rushing (sixth on the team), including one touchdown. Hinton was 6' and weighed 185 lbs.

At some point after the season was done, J.W. Hinton enlisted in the Air Corps, receiving his wings at Randolph Field in 1934. He made a career of it, and early in World War II he was serving as a lieutenant colonel and director of training at Fort Worth Army Air Field. He'd previously served at Randolph, Barksdale, and Smyrna. Hinton was sent overseas to serve in the South Pacific and was apparently involved in American bombing raids in the Moluccas in 1944, attacking Japanese installations in the East Indies not too far from New Guinea.

On the night of December 10, 1944, Hinton was co-pilot of a B–24 Liberator that had been assigned to the 13th Air Force, 307th Bombardment Group, 372nd Bombardment Squadron. The plane had no nickname or special nose art. There were nine other crew members on board. His was one of two B–24s that took off from Pitu Airfield (Pitoe) on a strafing mission against Miri Airfield and Miri on Borneo. Loaded were 15 x 250 lbs. bombs, 10,000 rounds of ammunition, and 3,100 gallons of fuel. Weather was 12-mile visibility with high clouds above 10,000' with a few scattered clouds. No radio contact was made after takeoff. Last sighted by Captain Lex E. Souter, the exact cause of the crash was unknown.

Based on two mission reports filed after the plane went missing, an acquaintance of the men wrote that they were "killed in action taking off on an early morning shipping strike from Morotai with Colonel Hinton, our deputy group commander. I think Colonel Hinton was flying the plane with Pat [2nd Lt. Herbert N.F. Patrick] in the co-pilot seat. George [Asst. Engineer S/Sgt George H. Westlund] was attempting to make up a mission probably missed because of a cold or some other circumstance. The plane crashed into a hillside on Halmahera Island. The crash explosions could be seen from the runway on Morotai. A concentrated air-to-ground search was conducted for a period of six to ten days to no avail. We could not locate the plane or the crash site."[91]

The men were officially declared dead the day of the mission, but their remains were not recovered for some time. When they were finally recovered, the remains were transported to Manila and eventually interred in a group burial at Zachary Taylor National Cemetery in Louisville.

Hinton's father, living in Eagle Lake, Texas, at the time, was notified in mid-January according to an announcement on January 13, 1945, issued by the War Department. Somewhat surprisingly, in December 2009, a U.S. Army Air Corps Advanced Flying School ring of J.W. Hinton was discovered and offered for sale at an antique shop in Bali.

Howard "Smiley" Johnson

Green Bay Packers / United States Marine Corps

Born: September 22, 1916, in Murfreesboro, Tennessee

Died: February 19, 1945, in Iwo Jima, Japan

Position: G-LB

One of three former NFL players killed on Iwo Jima, Howard "Smiley" Johnson is remembered with at least a half-dozen athletic fields scattered across the South Pacific, and each year at the Peach Bowl, the Smiley Johnson Trophy is given to the game's outstanding defensive player. He's not been forgotten. The other two players killed on Iwo Jima were Jack Chevigny and Jack Lummus.

Born September 22, 1916, in Murfreesboro, Tennessee, and orphaned at age 10 (his father had been a farmer), Johnson was an accomplished multi-sport athlete at Clarksville High School, and he played football in 1937–39 as a guard for the University of Georgia despite weighing in at just 160 lbs. He packed on weight and is listed with a 198-lb. playing weight for his two years with the Green Bay Packers in 1940 and 1941. He stood 5'9".

Smiley was an undrafted free agent who came to Green Bay and finally got his chance in the fourth quarter of a preseason exhibition game when coach Earl "Curly" Lambeau put him in—and then left him in. He made the team, and Johnson played in every regular season game in 1940 for the defending NFL champs, as he did the next year in 1941. The Packers finished second in '40 but were first again in '41, losing the division playoff to the Chicago Bears.

After the season, Johnson enlisted and became a Marine. He went through basic training in San Diego, then shipped out to Hawaii where he was recommended to go to Officer Candidate School and sent to Quantico, Virginia. Fellow Corps officer Dan Magill knew Johnson at Georgia and came across him again at OCS in Quantico. He wrote, "Smiley was an unusual Marine. He was a teetotaler, who didn't cuss and who read the Bible every night. I recall one evening at Quantico we went to an off-base cafe for a milkshake. In walked an enlisted Marine whom I recognized as the movie star Tyrone Power. This cafe was headquarters for taxis taking Marines on weekend liberty to nearby Washington, and Power was there to reserve a cab to visit his wife, French actress Annabella. When the taxi manager informed Power that he needed to place a $10 deposit to reserve a cab, Power said he didn't have his wallet. Smiley overheard and told Power, a perfect stranger to him, 'I'll loan you $10, buddy.' To which Power snapped to attention when he saw 2nd Lt. Johnson, saluted him, accepted the $10 bill, obtained Smiley's barracks' address, and returned the money that

very night. That was the last time I saw my wonderful friend."[92]

It hadn't been easy to earn his commission, Magill explained, because of his shortcomings in math. The Commandant himself had to intervene. Lt. Gen. Thomas Holcomb saw PFC Johnson in exercises at Quantico and said, "That young man will make a fine platoon leader." He was told that Johnson was on the verge of flunking out. "The hell he will," declared the Commandant. "When his class graduates, I will be here to pin the bars on him."[93] And he was. By July 1943, Magill was at Camp Pendleton, and in

On the beachhead at Iwo Jima, PFCs Joseph De Blanc (Union, Maine) and Frank W. Hall (Reed, West Virginia) awaiting order in a shell hole. (Photo courtesy of the National World War II Museum)

mid-January he boarded the USS *Calvert*. As part of Operation Flintlock, the 4th Marine Division secured the islands of Roi and Namur in the Kwajalein Atoll on February 1–2, 1944, becoming the first division to go directly into combat from the United States, wrote Jeffrey S. Williams for the University of Georgia's Sports Communications office. The 4th Marines returned to Maui to resupply and prepare for the invasion of Saipan. In the meantime, the Maui Marines team benefited from Johnson's defense. Playing in six games, the Maui team scored 164 total points but the combined opposition scored a total of just six.

Johnson's Third Batallion, 23rd Marines led the July invasion of Saipan, landing on Blue Beach I and fighting for 24 days to take the island. Johnson was awarded the Silver Star and promoted to first lieutenant. His citation, written after Saipan and before the 4th Division moved on to Tinian, reads, in part, "When the enemy counterattacked the flank position held by his platoon, First Lieutenant Johnson daringly directed the defense, exposing himself to heavy fire and helping annihilate in hand-to-hand conflict the Japanese who penetrated the position."[94] The Marines then returned to Maui to prepare for the assault on Iwo Jima.

Johnson's battalion landed late in the afternoon on February 19. As they were digging in, with Johnson supervising, a Japanese mortar shell landed and seriously injured him and four enlisted Marines. Williams wrote, "It is said that Johnson refused medical attention until the enlisted Marines were treated first."[95] He died of his wounds, the only Packer to ever be killed in combat—but the third football captain

of the University of Georgia Bulldogs to die in the war. Johnson was posthumously awarded a second Silver Star. Initially buried in the division's cemetery, he was later re-buried at the National Memorial Cemetery of the Pacific in Honolulu, Hawaii, on February 2, 1949.

Eddie "King Kong" Kahn
Boston Redskins, Washington Redskins / United States Army

Born: November 9, 1911, in New York, New York
Died: February 17, 1945, in Leyte, Philippines
Position: G

Kahn was born in New York City on November 9, 1911. Lieutenant Kahn died on February 17, 1945, of wounds suffered during the Leyte invasion. He played football in college with the Tar Heels of the University of North Carolina and earned an honorable mention as an All-Southern guard. Kahn signed with the NFL's Boston Redskins after graduating in 1935 and played in nine games that year. In 1936 he played in just six games but helped them achieve their first winning season, making the playoffs for the first time in franchise history. A recovered fumble gave that year's championship to the Green Bay Packers. Kahn was named a second-team All-NFL guard.

The Redskins moved to Washington, and Kahn did, too, though only after some work. After the 1936 season, he'd been traded to the Chicago Bears, and it took some effort for Flaherty to buy him back—for cash. In 1937, he played in 10 games, scoring his only points as he returned a fumble for a touchdown. Coach

Ray Flaherty's Washington Redskins and quarterback Slingin' Sammy Baugh beat the Chicago Bears for the NFL championship.

Kahn was 5'9" but weighed 194 lbs., his stature helped him to earn his nickname. It was Robert Ruark who wrote, "The best guard I ever saw was a fellow with a perpetually bloody nose named Eddie Kahn. They called him King Kong."

After the 1937 championship season, he retired from the game and went into business, living in Roxbury, Massachusetts—though Flaherty lured him back one more time, the next year, hiring him as player/coach with the Hazleton (Pennsylvania) Indians farm club for the 1938 season.

With the outbreak of World War II, Kahn perhaps could have held back. He was, after all, in his thirties. Instead, he volunteered right after Pearl Harbor and chose to join the infantry, rising through the ranks. Kahn's sister, Edna, joined the Women's Air Corps, becoming a corporal in the WACs. Kahn himself advanced to lieutenant and suffered his first injuries at Kwajalein in the spring of 1944. He received a Purple Heart and a Presidential Citation, but he recovered in time to join the invasion of The Philippines. Leading a landing party onto the beach during the invasion of Leyte, Kahn was badly hurt in late October 1944 and succumbed to his injuries several months later.[96]

After he had learned of Kahn's death, his former coach from North Carolina, Carl Snavely, wrote to Eddie's father, Thomas, who had been a carpenter born in Russia, "…I cannot express my dismay at receiving such terrible news. I can truthfully say that I know how you feel, and I also know that no words from me or anyone else can make the loss much easier to bear. Of all the fine boys that I have coached… there is not one for whom I have greater respect than I have had and always will have for Eddie. He is just the type of boy who would enter the ranks and win his commission the hard way, and never stop fighting until he gave his life."[97]

In a postscript, Snavely explained how it was that he could truly say he knew the feeling that Eddie's father was experiencing, simply adding, "Our boy, our only child, was also lost a few months ago."

Alex Ketzko

Detroit Lions / United States Army
Born: November 19, 1919, in Illinois
Died: December 23, 1944, in Vosges, France
Position: T

Alexander Gregorieff Ketzko was a tackle for the Michigan State Spartans, who was born November 19, 1919. He was an inch less than 6' and weighed a solid 215 lbs. Born in Illinois, he was raised in Van Buren, Michigan, by his Russian immigrant parents, Harry and Anna Ketzko. Harry Ketzko was a farmer who grew fruit. Alex ultimately graduated from Mattawan High School in the small Michigan village not far from Portage and Kalamazoo.

After playing for Michigan State in 1938 and 1939, Ketzko signed in July 1940 with the Paterson Panthers of the American Football Alliance. He played as a guard or tackle for Paterson through 1942.

Though signed by the New York Giants, he never appeared with them. He spent one full year in the NFL with the 1943 Detroit Lions, appearing as a tackle in nine of the 10 games of the 3–6–1 third-place Lions. Ketzko started in three of the nine games.

Ketzko joined the military, and he served in France beginning in May 1944. He was assigned to the 15th Infantry Regiment, 3rd Infantry Division in Lt. Gen. Alexander Patch's Seventh Army. Patch had led American forces during the successful capture of Guadalcanal from the Japanese and was transferred to the European Theater to lead the invasion of Southern France in August 1944. Patch lost his own son in mid-October as Allied forces pressed north. Two days before Christmas 1944, on December 23, Private First Class Alex Ketzko was killed in action in the Vosges during the Battle of the Bulge. It was the very day after the German commander had demanded surrender from Gen. Anthony McAuliffe of the 101st Airborne during the siege of Bastogne, only to receive McAuliffe's famous reply: "To the German Commander: NUTS! The American Commander."

Ketzko was the third former Lion to lose his life in the war effort, Chet Wetterlund having met his end in September and Lee Kizzire in December 1943. Alex was survived by his widow, Helen Ketzko, of Teaneck, New Jersey.

Ketzko is buried in France at the Epinal American Cemetery in the village of Dinoze-Quèquement, Dinoze lies above the Moselle River and in the foothills of the Vosges Mountains, and he is one of 5,255 Americans interred there.

Lee Kizzire

Detroit Lions / United States Army Air Corps

Born: November 21, 1915, in Wyoming

Died: January 22, 1946, in New Guinea (actual date of death probably on November 27, 1943, or very soon afterward)

Position: FB

Captain Lee Kizzire came from Wyoming and played as a running back for the University of Wyoming Cowboys. He'd been born on November 21 or 23, 1915, somewhere in the state, the son of transplanted Iowans Viola Kizzire and her husband, William, head foreman at Mid-West Refining Co. in Greybull, Wyoming, in 1930.[98] Even by the time Lee (though sharing the first name with his father, he was always called Lee) was five years old, the state's total population was around 194,000, some 12,000 or so from Big Horn County. He graduated from Greybull High School.

William Lee "Kizzy" Kizzire was a four-sport letterman at the University of Wyoming in football, wrestling, track, and basketball, with football and wrestling his two best sports. He was named an All-American in football from 1933–37 and also became the Rocky Mountain Wrestling Champion. A 6', 200-lb. fullback, he played professionally for the Detroit Lions as Coach Dutch Clark's fullback in the 1937 season, appearing in seven games. The Lions finished second in the NFL West with a 7–4 record. Kizzire didn't play much, rushing for a total of 20 yards in seven attempts. After the season, he graduated in 1938 and left the game to coach at Riverton High School.

Six days after Pearl Harbor, Kizzire enlisted in the United States Army Air Corps. In 1942, after training at Visalia and Merced, he was commissioned as an officer at Stockton Field in California. His goal was to fly fighter planes, but he had difficulty folding his large frame into the smaller cockpits. He transferred to a squadron where he could fly larger aircraft. "Kazook"—one of his nicknames—was fortunate to survive the September 2, 1942, crash of a plane he piloted when it went down with motor trouble and crashed and burned in a patch of woods near a cornfield about three miles from Columbia, South Carolina, during a routine flight. All five aboard survived. His skill was said to have helped save their lives, only two of the five suffered bruises or lacerations. Kizzire expressed his desire to get into action because he had two younger brothers, Clarence and Leonard, who were both fighting in the European Theater.

Kizzire's own son, John Roger, had been born on July 4, 1943. Lee never saw his son. He'd been overseas leading bombing missions near Salamaua, New Guinea, as early as June, flying with the Fifth Air Force. He told war correspondents that he'd let his wife name their child and only hoped it wouldn't be too many months before he learned their child's name.

On September 21 that year, a dispatch from "Somewhere in New Guinea" reported the air assault on a Japanese airfield near Wewak as B–24 Liberators and B–25 Mitchell medium bombers attacked bridges in an effort to disrupt enemy communication lines south of Madang. Kizzire flew a Mitchell that "daringly hedgehopped mountains to strafe a road from Madang to Bogadjim."[99]

Several days later, a force of some 200 aircraft attacked Wewak airfields. Laramie's Kizzire was quoted as saying, "I don't see how we could help having done lots of damage.… Half the planes on the ground looked serviceable when we came in. I am sure we hit almost all of those." Kizzire's was one of two Mitchells that strafed and bombed antiaircraft positions on the seaward side of the Boram airstrip near Wewak. The formations of Kizzire and Maj. Ezra Best of Hollywood were "credited with the possible destruction of as many as 35 enemy planes on the ground."[100]

In October, he talked about shooting down a Japanese plane during a raid on Rabaul. "The trip probably was the finest ever planned. The take-off and rendezvous was perfectly planned so that we got off with little delay. The entire group made the trip over the water and just before we cleared the last ridge before the runway, we saw Betty bomber flying in the field traffic pattern. All I had to do was raise my nose a little and open fire on him. I saw my tracers enter him. Someone following saw him go into the ground. We flew along the runaway and revetments where all the planes were. We dropped our bombs and strafed all along. Japs and natives were walking along the runway when we swooped over the ridge, they never had a chance. The raid was a complete surprise and the most successful raid that I've ever been on. A lot more fun than the Wewak raid."[101]

On November 27, 1943, Captain Kizzire was reported leading a flight formation for the 498th

Bomber Squadron of the 345th Bomber Group of the U.S. Army Air Force when he was shot down on a mission to bomb Boram and ships in the harbor of Wewak Island, New Guinea, in the Pacific and was never found. He was declared missing as of that date. His flight commander wrote Kizzire's wife, the former Rita Elizabeth Campbell of Laramie, a grade school teacher, telling her, "Kizzy had his engine shot away and couldn't get enough power to get back so he had to land in the wrong territory."[102] The plane had been ditched, reported PacificWrecks.com, "in the shallow water of Murik Lagoon with the tail and rear fuselage visible. The crew were observed to get to shore safely. Supplies and an escape map were dropped to them and observed until the next day."[103] Searches were conducted by air, but the crew was never found.

He was initially thought to be a prisoner of war, and a Japanese propaganda broadcast was heard to give his name and address with a message that he had been treated by Japanese medics and was now a prisoner of war.[104]

Lee Kizzire was awarded the Air Medal and a Purple Heart, but he was finally declared dead on January 22, 1946.

Jack Lummus

New York Giants / United States Marine Corps
Born: October 22, 1915, in Ennis, Texas
Died: March 8, 1945, in Iwo Jima, Japan
Position: E

From a cotton farm in Texas to the NFL to earning a Congressional Medal of Honor for his heroic actions as a Marine on Iwo Jima that cost him his life—it was quite a path for Jack Lummus.

Andrew Jackson Lummus Jr. was born on October 22, 1915, in Ennis, Texas, on a cotton farm in Ellis County about 35 miles southeast of Dallas—which was at the time a fast-growing city of between 100,000 and 150,000. His father, of course, had the same name. His mother was Laura Francis Lummus. Jack was the youngest of their four children and their only son.

Lummus attended schools in both Alma and Ennis, attending Ennis High School for three years and earning All-District recognition in both football and track. He fell ill during his senior year and was unable to complete his studies, but in the summer of 1935 he was offered an athletic scholarship to Texas Military College in Terrell, Texas. After two years at TMC, he had completed high school and earned junior college credits and had earned All-Conference honors in football. He graduated on May 28, 1937, and made plans to attend Baylor that fall, declining a similar scholarship offer from Tulane. Lummus excelled at baseball for Baylor, winning All–Southwest Conference honors in 1939, 1940, and 1941.[105]

He signed two professional sports contracts after graduation in 1941, a minor league baseball contract with the Class D West Texas–New Mexico League's Wichita Falls Spudders, a Cincinnati Reds farm team, and an NFL contract with the New York Giants. Lummus is said to have been one of only two professional baseball players to have earned the Medal of Honor. The other was minor league

Jack Lummus of Baylor University in November 1939. (AP Photo)

pitcher Joe Pinder, who was killed on D-Day at Normandy.

He just had time to get his feet wet in each sport when war broke out. In the summer, he appeared in 26 games as an outfielder for Wichita Falls, batting .257 with two home runs, three triples, and six doubles among his 26 hits. His defensive play was not as good, as he committed five errors for a fielding percentage of .904.

After reporting to training camp and putting on the shoulder pads, the 6'3",

200-lb. Lummus made the Giants, appearing as backup in nine games as an end. He was credited with one reception for five yards. The team won its first five games and finished 8–3–0, good enough for first place in the NFL East. In the Western Division, both the Chicago Bears and Green Bay Packers finished 10–1–0, necessitating a division playoff on December 14. The Bears hosted and won that game on December 14 (33–14) then hosted the Championship Game, easily beating the Giants, 37–9. By the time of the game, everyone's mind was on the war against Japan declared just two weeks earlier. No one could know it at the time, but one player from each team made the ultimate sacrifice. Playing for Chicago had been Young Bussey, another Texan, who lost his life fighting in The Philippines.

Jack Lummus joined the Marine Corps Reserve in Dallas on January 30, 1942, and was immediately activated and sent to San Diego for training, which he completed first at Camp Elliott and then—when he joined the Marine Raiders in June 1943—at Camp Pendleton. In January 1944, Jack became the commanding officer of Company G, 2nd Battalion, 27th Marines, 5th Marine Division. Company G was re-designated Company F, and Lt. Lummus became its executive officer. On August 12, the Liberty ship USS *Henry Clay* shipped out of San Diego Harbor for Camp Tarawa, Hilo, Hawaii. In October, Lummus joined Headquarters Company as battalion liaison officer and was asked to form a baseball team, which won the honors

in the 5th Division, winning every game but one. On January 27, 1945, he shipped out of Pearl Harbor headed to Saipan on the USS *Highlands*. He arrived on February 11. Four days later, he was headed north to Iwo Jima.

A website set up by the Lummus family says, "Jack was in the first wave of assault troops that landed on Red Two a few minutes after H-hour."[106] Working as liaison officer for 2nd Battalion, he counted himself a key part of the effort that captured the airfield from Japanese defenders, and he no doubt enjoyed seeing the American flag raised atop Mount Suribachi. There was stiff and ongoing Japanese resistance even on D plus 17 (March 8). Lummus and his men had been fighting around the clock for more than 48 hours, trying to dislodge a well-entrenched body of some 3,000 troops. He helped lead his 3rd Platoon in clearing a way for some U.S. tanks to reposition themselves. What happened next has been told in dramatic detail, over the signature of President Harry S. Truman, in the citation for the Congressional Medal of Honor:

Citation:

For conspicuous gallantry and intrepidity at the risk of his life above and beyond the call of duty as leader of a Rifle Platoon attached to the 2nd Battalion, 27th Marines, 5th Marine Division, in action against enemy Japanese forces on Iwo Jima in the Volcano Islands, 8 March 1945. Resuming his assault tactics with bold decision after fighting without respite for 2 days and nights, 1st Lt. Lummus slowly advanced his platoon against an enemy deeply entrenched in a network of mutually supporting positions. Suddenly halted by a terrific concentration of hostile fire, he unhesitatingly moved forward of his front lines in an effort to neutralize the Japanese position. Although knocked to the ground when an enemy grenade exploded close by, he immediately recovered himself and, again moving forward despite the intensified barrage, quickly located, attacked, and destroyed the occupied emplacement. Instantly taken under fire by the garrison of a supporting pillbox and further assailed by the slashing fury of hostile rifle fire, he fell under the impact of a second enemy grenade but, courageously disregarding painful shoulder wounds, staunchly continued his heroic 1-man assault and charged the second pillbox, annihilating all the occupants. Subsequently returning to his platoon position, he fearlessly traversed his lines under fire, encouraging his men to advance and directing the fire of supporting tanks against other stubbornly holding Japanese emplacements. Held up again by a devastating barrage, he again moved into the open, rushed a third heavily fortified installation, and killed the defending troops. Determined to crush all resistance, he led his men indomitably, personally attacking foxholes and spider traps with his carbine and systematically reducing the fanatic opposition until, stepping on a land mine, he sustained fatal wounds.

By his outstanding valor, skilled tactics, and tenacious perseverance in the face of overwhelming odds, 1st Lt. Lummus had inspired his stouthearted marines to continue the relentless drive northward, thereby contributing materially to the success of his regimental mission. His dauntless leadership and unwavering devotion to duty throughout sustain and enhance the highest traditions of the U.S. Naval Service. He gallantly gave his life in the service of his country. [107]

The blast of the mine had blown off both of his legs. In his book, *Iwo Jima*, author Richard Newcomb said that his men "watched in horror as he stood on the bloody stumps, calling them on. Several men, crying now, ran to him and for a moment, talked of shooting him to stop the agony. But he was still shouting at them to move out, move out, and the platoon scrambled forward. Their fears turned to rage, they swept an incredible 300 yards over the impossible ground, and at nightfall were on the ridge, overlooking the sea. There was no question that the dirty, tired men, cursing and crying and fighting, had done it for Jack Lummus."[108] Legend has him telling a Navy surgeon just before he expired at a field hospital, "Well, Doc, I guess the New York Giants have lost the services of a damned good end." He was buried that night at the base of Mount Suribachi.

In April 1948, his body was returned to Ennis. His name lives on in the ship christened in 1986, USNS *1st Lt. Jack Lummus*.

William McCaw

Racine Legion, Louisville Colonels / United States Army
Born: February 6, 1898, in St. Paul, Minnesota
Died: April 19, 1942, in Bloomington, Indiana
Position: G-E

An Associated Press dispatch provides us almost everything we knew about Bill McCaw. It was datelined Bloomington, Indiana, and read: "Capt. William C. McCaw, 41, university military instructor and a star guard on I.U. football teams of the early 1920s, died of a heart attack in a Sunday morning radio broadcast here but listeners were unaware of his death. He was discussing the relation of ROTC training to the war. Captain McCaw was a native of Chicago."[109]

Digging more deeply, with the help of Indiana University, we were able to learn a little more about McCaw.[110] Although the AP had him as a native of Chicago, he was born in St. Paul and moved to Chicago at an early age. He attended Englewood High School in Chicago. He also received his first military training at Englewood, graduating in 1917. He got the football bug during high school and, after serving in the navy with overseas duty in the Mediterranean, he returned to college and earned varsity letters at Indiana in 1920, 1921, and 1922, when he graduated with a B.S. in commerce. He was a cadet in ROTC at I.U. and received a commission in the army upon graduation.

He was named as a guard to the All-Conference first team all three years. He had begun to attract the interest of football scouts

William McCaw lettered in football for Indiana University from 1919–21. (Photo courtesy of Indiana University Athletics)

as early as his sophomore year. The *Arbutus* yearbook for 1920 reads, "McCaw's consistent work and his wonderful playing in the Northwestern game attracted the attention of all football critics in the Middle West." The game was a remarkably low-scoring 3–2 effort with Indiana coming up short. The 1920 team rose from the conference cellar to the first division.

McCaw was also on the track and intramural basketball teams.

The 1922 yearbook said of "Bud" McCaw, "For three years he has been a mighty defensive bastion in the Crimson line. This last season marked the passing of one of the most powerful and resourceful linemen who ever fought on Jordan field." His academic work was solid, as well, the combination of academics and athletics earning him the university's Big Ten medal in his senior year.[111]

In 1923, McCaw played in three games for the NFL Racine Legion, and in 1926 he played in four games for the Louisville Colonels. He also went to the University of Chicago and LaCrosse State Teachers College for a degree in education. In 1927, he was working as a coach and instructor in physical education at Kenosha High School in Wisconsin. After six years, he moved on briefly to a position with the Wisconsin Power and Light Company in Clintonville in 1933. He joined the United States Army in 1933 as a first lieutenant. That October and for the next six years until October 1939, he was on active duty in the army in connection with the Civilian Conservation Corps as a company commander and area inspector.

In 1940, he applied for a position in Bloomington. Since October 1939 he had served as CCC Area Inspector in a civilian status by the War Department at Ludington CCC District in Ludington, Michigan. He wrote I.U. President Wells on November 22, "I have turned down the CCC District Quartermaster position here, with the anticipation of being called to active duty at Indiana University. Duty at Indiana and this type of work is highly desired by me."[112] He was on the active list as a captain in the army infantry reserve.

He began work as an instructor in the Department of Military Science and Tactics. He was taking part in a round table broadcast from the university auditorium over radio station WIRE. The other participants were Major Fenwick T. Reed and Lt. Bernard O'Neal.

After his sudden and wholly unexpected death, special tribute was paid on campus with an honor guard, a four-volley salute, and Taps. His body was sent to Oshkosh, where he was buried alongside his daughter, Jane, who had died several years earlier. His widow, Dorothy, and son, Billy, accompanied the body.

Jim Mooney

Newark Tornadoes, Brooklyn Dodgers, Cincinnati Reds, Chicago Cardinals / United States Army
Born: September 16, 1907, in Chicago, Illinois
Died: August 12, 1944, in France
Position: E-T-G

There was a Jim Mooney in the NBA and one in MLB, the latter a pitcher in the same era as Big Jim Mooney. James L. Mooney Jr. was in the NFL. Mooney was born in Chicago on September 16, 1907. His father was a lieutenant in the Chicago Police Department who had become chief of detectives by 1920 and was deputy chief of the department in 1930.

Jim Jr. grew up in the area and obtained his secondary education at the city's Loyola Academy, where—the school says—he was "the outstanding member of a trio of athletic brothers at Loyola Academy. He captained the Chicago All-Catholic Football Team in 1923 and holds the record for the longest punt, 85 yards." Bill and Phil Mooney were the brothers in question. Jim lettered in football in 1924 and is recognized in the Loyola Academy Athletic Hall of Fame. At Loyola, he was known as "Big Jim"—large relative to the norms of the day; he weighed 200 lbs. and stood 5'11".

From Loyola, Mooney went on to Georgetown University where he became an All-American and was considered "one of the greatest punters in the country."[113]

Probably his most notable game was a 7–2 win over New York University on a very wet and muddy November 3, 1928. G.U. scored early in the first quarter and then played defense, a vital element being Mooney's long punts (including one of 55 and another of 65 yards) with a "soggy, water-soaked football," driving NYU back from the 4-yard line and the 1-yard line. "Superman Mooney" also intercepted two passes and recovered one fumble.[114] Sixteen years later, *The New York Times* still recalled it as "one of the most extraordinary punting exhibitions ever."[115]

From that day forward, Big Jim Mooney was considered a standard to which other players were compared. When Louis Effrat asked what makes an ideal football player, Columbia head coach Lou Little answered late in 1945, "Give me a fellow who could pass like Sid Luckman or Sammy Baugh; one who could run like Cliff Battles or Red Grange; one who could punt like Jim Mooney, Jim Thorpe, or

Ken Strong; one as destructive as Thorpe or Bronko Nagurski; one with the speed of Buddy Young; and one with the defensive abilities of Mel Hein or Wilbur Henry—give me all that in one man and I'll give you the ideal football player."[116]

After college, Mooney had offers to play football professionally and signed to begin his career in 1930 with the Newark Tornadoes. Over the course of five seasons, he played for four different teams. A versatile player, he was never a star for any one team or at any one position but served his teams as an end, tackle, and guard. He began with Newark in 1930, starting in 12 games as right tackle, but he wound up the season with the Brooklyn Dodgers, starting two of the three games he played for Brooklyn. Mooney remained with Brooklyn in 1931, and he started in eight of the 14 games in which he appeared. The only points he scored in his pro career were two extra points for Newark in 1930 and one for Brooklyn in 1931.

Mooney spent 1932 out of the NFL, playing for the independent league Chicago Shamrocks, a team that rolled up a 6–2–2 record against teams from Cleveland, St. Louis, South Bend, Grand Rapids, and more.

In 1933 and 1934, Jim played for the Cincinnati Reds as left end. He appeared in seven games the first year, scoring once on a safety. He had probably his best season in 1934, starting in eight games, completing 4-of-6 passes for 27 yards, and carrying for 36 yards on six receptions. He added another 27 yards on three rushing attempts. Much of his value rested in his punting, keeping the ball as deep in opposition territory as he could and prompting the *Chicago Tribune* to label him "one of the best kickers in the professional league," and, "the best punter in the league."[117]

In 1935, his final year in the NFL, he played for the Chicago Cardinals, appearing in just four games. In '36, Mooney moved to play for the New York Yankees in the American Professional Football League. He coached the Yankees in 1937 but put himself into the game in the third quarter as an end—and broke his ankle.

A November 1938 story saw Mooney working at Soldier Field again, but this time as a policeman. Noted and promoted a year later, Mooney was in charge of the police detail at the August 1939 game featuring an All-Star team against the New York Giants.[118] In 1940, Mooney was back in the game as assistant coach for the newly organized Chicago Gunners under Lou Gordon.[119]

He was sent to France during World War II, and Corporal Mooney was serving with the 110th Infantry, 28th Division when he was shot by a sniper and died on August 12, 1944. We know little of the circumstances of his death, but he was remembered by *The New York Times'* Arthur Daley who wrote, "And now the game is over for Jim Mooney. He was only a corporal at the age of 36, but so sound a man and so sound a leader was he that his younger officers came to him for advice. He probably went the way he'd have liked to go, fighting a good fight until the end."[120] Mooney is buried in Brittany.

John O'Keefe

Philadelphia Eagles / United States Navy Air Corps
Born: Not known
Died: Sometime in 1942 or 1943
Position: Vice President

The 1944 National Football League Record Book contained, as it customarily did during the World War II years, a "Service Roster" listing, team by team, of the people in the various branches of military service. On pages 6 and 7 of the 1944 book were listed the members of the Philadelphia Eagles who had joined the service—28 of them in 1941 (Nick Basca was killed later), 22 in 1942 (Len Supulski and O'Keefe were killed), and three in 1943. The entry for O'Keefe reads: "O'Keefe, J., V-Pres. Navy Air Corps Killed in crash on Canal Zone Patrol." That's all we know.

Searching military records, there is a listing of 21 fatalities for U.S. service personnel in the Canal Zone during the war, but none of them is named O'Keefe. Francis J. O'Keefe from Philadelphia was killed during the war, although not in battle and not until January 23, 1944. He was a technical sergeant in the Army Air Corps, 343rd Bomber Squadron, 98th Bomber, and he is buried in Nettuno, Italy. The authors were unable to find any John O'Keefe who was killed in the service during the war, either in military records or in web searches of newspapers of the day—but there he is, listed in a contemporary source. One would think a team vice president being killed in the service would have rated some form of notice, but we have as yet to learn more.

Gus Sonnenberg

Columbus Tigers, Buffalo All-Americans, Detroit Panthers, Providence Steam Roller / United States Navy

Born: March 6, 1898, in Ewen, Michigan
Died: September 13, 1944, in Bethesda, Maryland
Position: T-FB-TB

Gustave Adolph Sonnenberg died of leukemia at Bethesda Naval Hospital on September 12, 1944.[121] He'd played for five NFL teams between 1923 and 1930 (he didn't play in the NFL in 1924), and is honored in the Professional Wrestling Hall of Fame.

He wasn't a tall one, standing a modest 5'6", but he was stocky at 196 lbs. and powerful. Born in Ewen, Michigan, on March 6, 1898, to Fred and Caroline Sonnenberg, he grew up on the family farm in Green Garden, about 100 miles east on the Upper Peninsula. He went to a small country school, but when he reached high school age, he moved about 10 miles north to Marquette in 1912 and lived with an older sister. He put in two years at right guard and saw the 1915 team explode to become the undefeated U.P. champions with a combined score over six games of Marquette 211, Opponents 7. Despite his short stature, Gus was on the school's basketball team, which also won a U.P. title in 1915–16. He earned himself scholarship offers from the University of Michigan, University of Minnesota, and Dartmouth.

Dartmouth was his choice, and it wasn't long before he'd qualified as a tackle on the freshman team where he earned Eastern All-Frosh honors. He dropped out after his first year and bounced around a bit, playing for both the Northern State Teachers College football and basketball teams in 1917. He took a position as coach as Escanaba High School in January 1919. That fall, he was back at Dartmouth as a tackle and was chosen All-American by the Eastern sportswriters. Sonnenberg's tenure at Dartmouth lasted just one additional year, and he transferred to the University of Detroit. He played there in 1921 and 1922 and graduated with a degree in law.

He took up professional wrestling in 1927 and was given the nickname "Dynamite" for his aggressive style. The Associated Press reported that he had disposed of his first three opponents in a total time of four hours and 20 seconds with his "flying tackle," perhaps his most potent move. In 1929, he became the first man to win the National Wrestling Association championship. He'd already been playing football for several years by then.

Sonnenberg's first position was with the Buffalo All-Americans—for all of one game before being moved to the Columbus Tigers. He played left tackle in 10 games for Columbus and was named a first-team All-NFL player by the *Canton Daily News*, perhaps reflecting some regional sentiment. He even picked up one rushing touchdown, his only offensive statistic in football. He was out of the NFL in 1924, playing with the Pottsville Maroons on their way to the Anthracite League championship. Pottsville joined the NFL in 1925, and Gus returned to NFL play, starting in every game of two 12-game seasons for the Detroit Panthers in 1925 and 1926, and in 1927 and 1928 for the Providence Steam Roller that became NFL champion on the strength of their 8–1–2 record in 1928. Sonnenberg was also place kicker for Providence.

Wrestling began to consume most of his time by then, and he only appeared in one more pro football game, for Providence in 1930. As late as 1939 he became world wrestling champion once again—against "The Shadow," Marvin Westenberg, at the Boston Garden. Thirteen days later, he was dethroned by Steve "Crusher" Casey.

He wrestled until the fall of 1942 when—at age 44—he entered the United States Navy as a chief specialist. He was serving at the Great Lakes Naval Training Station as a physical instructor when he was diagnosed with leukemia, at the time almost an invariably fatal disease.

Len Supulski

Philadelphia Eagles / United States Army Air Corps
Born: December 15, 1920, in Kingston, Pennsylvania
Died: August 31, 1943, near Kearney, Nebraska
Position: E

Like Al Blozis of the New York Giants, who also lost his life in the war effort, Leonard Supulski was the son of a Lithuanian immigrant father— from an even larger family. Leonard was one of 12 children. He was born December 15, 1920, in Kingston, Pennsylvania. His father, Joe, worked as a coal miner there in Luzerne County; his mother, Eva, was native to Pennsylvania but of Lithuanian ancestry.

Len completed his studies at Kingston High School then went to Dickinson College in Carlisle. Although he attended for four years with the Class of 1942, the school's website says he "fell just short of the credits needed to graduate."[122] Nonetheless, Supulski was inducted into the Dickinson Hall of Fame in 1981.

A multi-sport athlete, Len starred as an end at football, and the record he set in 1941— catching 48 passes for 586 yards—stood as a school record until 1984. He was a UPI All-Eastern first team choice, and he joined the Philadelphia Eagles for the 1942 season. The 175-lb. Supulski stood exactly 6' and appeared as an end in nine games for the Eagles under coach Greasy Neale, the year after Nick Basca had played for Neale. The team finished 2–9, and the two wins were against Pittsburgh and Brooklyn. Len himself had eight receptions for 149 yards and one touchdown in the opener, catching a 20-yard pass and running 21 more yards to score. The only rushing attempt he made earned him one yard. He also intercepted a pass on defense.

After the season was over, Supulski entered the Army Air Corps. He completed flight navigation training at Selman Field in Louisiana and received his commission on July 24, 1943. It was on to Washington State for further training at Moses Lake, and then he reported to Kearney Army Air Field in Kearney, Nebraska, for advanced training with the 582nd Bomb Squadron. Supulski trained as a navigator on B-17s.

On August 31, just two weeks after he'd arrived at Kearney, the pilot, Lt. James A.

McRaven, and his crew of eight went out for a routine training flight of their Flying Fortress, #42–5451. It's uncertain what occurred, but eyewitnesses saw a fire of unknown origin coming from the plane as it flew near the field at about 3,500 feet. The plane appeared to begin to bank, to try to return to base, but it lost altitude and dove into the ground about two miles east of the base, exploding on impact and killing all on board. It was the first of three B-17s to crash on or near Kearney. The eight men on board Supulski's aircraft each came from a different state.

B-17s of the 301st Bomber Group. (Photo courtesy of the National World War II Museum)

Don Wemple

Brooklyn Dodgers / United States Army Air Corps

Born: October 14, 1917, in Gloversville, New York

Died: June 23, 1943, in India

Position: E

Much of what we know of Don Wemple comes from the work of a member of his extended family, George Jesse Wemple, dating back more than 35 years ago. Donald Lester Wemple was born in Gloversville, New York, on October 14, 1917, and raised in the area, graduating from Gloversville High School in 1935. His father, George, was a salesman in a leather store; his mother worked at home as a glove maker (in Gloversville). Don was the youngest of three children. His older siblings were George and Doris.

Don went on to Colgate University where he played end on the Colgate Raiders team. He graduated in 1939. Colgate had some excellent teams in that area, frequently running up lopsided scores, and Wemple was noted early on as a contributor, coming fully into his own in his junior year. *The New York Times* took note, declaring, "Wemple, a powerful end of 190 lbs. had made so much progress that he promises to eclipse his more spectacular running mate, Ritchko."[123]

He was named co-captain of the team in December 1937. A year later, he was named to the All-East team. At the game, participants were asked if they hoped to go on to play professionally. Only nine of the 44 players at the January 2, 1939, East-West Game in San Francisco indicated any inclination in that direction. Wemple said he hoped to go into college coaching.[124] The West won the game 14–0; Wemple saw no action in the game.

A leg injury looked to prevent Wemple from playing in a game of All-Stars against the New York Giants at Soldier Field, Chicago, in the late summer of 1939 before some 80,000 fans, but at nearly the last minute he was able to play and he caught a late fourth-quarter pass from Sid Luckman for a first down on the Giants' 22, but it was the next-to-last play of the game, and the All-Stars went down to defeat 9–0 on three field goals. His career plans may have changed—after that game, he was included in a list of men who said they planned to enter business.[125]

The 6'2" end was signed to the Brooklyn Dodgers and reported to training camp at Princeton, New Jersey, in August 1941, the first rookie to arrive. He had his eye on military service, though, and one story reported his absence from practice at Ebbets Field during an October 29 workout "because he had to report for examination for his entrance in the army air service."[126] This was, of course, several weeks before Pearl Harbor. Wemple enlisted and was placed on reserve. He returned to football in time to catch a pass and bull his way from the 2-yard line, wrapped up by a tackle but willing himself to fall across the goal line to score the winning touchdown in a 13–7 defeat of Sammy Baugh's Washington Redskins on November 9.[127] He appeared in 11 games, always as a substitute, and is credited with two receptions for a total of 37 yards and the one touchdown.

Wemple was called to active duty by the Army Air Corps on January 13, 1942, formally enlisting in Albany. He was then assigned to Maxwell

Field in Alabama. He was married at the time. He received his flight training in Georgia and Florida, but he was scheduled to play in one more game, in September 1942 as part of the All-Army team that would play a benefit game against the New York Giants. Waddy Young was designated for the same Army team. The exigencies of duty may have interfered with plans because neither Young nor Wemple were at the game.

Lt. Wemple was ordered overseas in April 1943. George Jesse Wemple writes in a typewritten family book, "At the time of his death, he held the rank of lieutenant and was stationed in India and flew between India and China, flying over the 'hump,' when his plane was struck by enemy fire and crashed. He was accorded full military honors during his burial at his assigned station in India."[128] It was June 1943 when he lost his life in India, "killed in action over India piloting a two-motored transport plane."[129] His widow, Doris Johnson, later remarried.

Chet Wetterlund

Detroit Lions / United States Navy
Born: March 19, 1918, in Chicago, Illinois
Died: September 5, 1944, offshore of New Jersey
Position: TB-DB

On November 15, 1941, Illinois Wesleyan University Titans halfback Chet Wetterlund was locked in a scoreless battle with the college's traditional rival, Illinois State Normal. There were less than three minutes remaining, and the Titans had the ball fourth-and-15 on their own 20-yard line. Wetterlund was the team's primary punter, but he was also "recognized as one of the best forward passers of the conference."[130] Wetterlund first faked the expected punt but then pulled a "Frank Merriwell play" and fired a 41-yard pass to receiver Bill Alkire, who then ran it to the Normal 39. Illinois Wesleyan scored soon afterward, adding the extra point and taking the game, 7–0.[131]

Wetterlund was president of the junior class at the time. He was born in Chicago on March 19, 1918, to John and Lena Wetterlund. His father was a mason and a foreman by 1930. Both of Chet's parents were natives of Sweden who came to the United States in 1890. Chet was the youngest of four in the family. He entered Illinois Wesleyan in September 1938 and was a star from his freshman year at the college. Chet was vice president of the freshman class and played varsity football the next three years, becoming team captain in his final year.

Upon graduation in 1942, he was selected in the ninth round of the draft by the Chicago Cardinals. He trained with the team at Waukesha, Wisconsin, and traveled with the team to Denver for a preseason game. He sat on the bench that game and was moved to the Detroit Lions before his debut and never did play for Chicago. The Cardinals were just 3–8 that year, but the Lions fared worse, never once winning, putting up an 0–11 record. The team scored 38 points in its 11 games, allowing their opponents to put up 263 points. Wetterlund appeared in six games, starting three of them. He made 23 rushing attempts but only netted a total of six yards. He threw ten interceptions and no touchdown passes.

After the season ended, Wetterlund enlisted in the United States Navy, receiving his commission at Corpus Christi on March 7, 1943. He received advanced training at Deland, Florida, and was stationed at Wildwood, New Jersey, beginning in May 1944. Ensign Chester J. Wetterlund was completing his training as a night flyer, working with the carrier-based Curtiss SB2C Helldiver, a dive-bombing plane. He took his Helldiver out on a routine training flight off the New Jersey coast on September 5, 1944. The Helldiver had replaced the Dauntless, and most pilots weren't pleased with the development as it was, by all accounts, a difficult plane to fly. Trouble developed with Wetterlund's plane over the Atlantic, and he was forced to attempt a landing at sea. The plane crashed into the waters, and the attempts of deep sea divers to recover his body were in vain. The search was discontinued after a few days, and his parents were notified by the navy on September 9. Grieving as well was his fiancee, Ensign Myra Jane Roberts of Bloomington, Illinois. The engagement had just been announced a few days before the fatal flight, and she was visiting Wildwood station at the time.

Walter "Waddy" Young

Brooklyn Dodgers / United States Army Air Corps
Born: September 4, 1916, in Ponca City, Oklahoma
Died: January 9, 1945, in Sea of Japan
Position: E

Waddy Young served heroically in both theatres in World War II. After completing his full complement of 25 missions as the pilot of a B-17 Liberator, wreaking havoc on the German armed forces, he requested a return to combat—this time in the Pacific. There he "earned command not only of a gigantic new B-29 Super Fortress, but of an entire squadron of them."[132]

Flying his own aircraft, with "Waddy's Wagon" depicted on the nose, Young was part of the very first bomb run over Tokyo, launched from Saipan in November 1944. By January 1945, he'd logged more than 9,000 combat hours. But his time had run out. On January 9, his B-29 was lost and initially thought to have been shot down near Tokyo.

Young came from Ponca City, Oklahoma, and was born on September 14, 1916. His parents were farmers, both natives of Arkansas. They had five sons. Waddy was a football star during his junior high school days when his team posted an unbelievable record—not only were they never beaten (and never tied), but no opponent ever scored against them. Ponca High School wasn't that dominant, but Young was accorded All-State honors as a senior. He went on to the University of Oklahoma where he excelled on defense. He was first team All-Conference in 1937 and 1938, and the Sooners were Big Six champions in 1938. He was named All-American after Oklahoma nearly replicated the achievement of Young's junior high school team—they only allowed 12 points during their entire undefeated season. He was also the university's boxing champion.

The Brooklyn Dodgers picked him in the third round (20th overall pick) of the 1939 NFL Draft, and he played for Brooklyn in 1939 and 1940 as a 6'3", 205-lb. right end. He appeared in

11 games each year, with 15 receptions for 185 yards. After the 1940 season, he decided to join the army. He entered flight training on the first day of 1941 and received his wings on August 15 that year at Kelly Field in San Antonio, Texas.

Flying a B-24 Liberator on anti-sub patrol in the North Atlantic was his first assignment; the plane attacked one Nazi submarine and shot down two Luftwaffe fighter planes. After his transfer to the Pacific, he became commander of the 869th Bomber Squadron. His plane may not have actually been shot down that fateful January 9. What is known is that he'd completed his run, delivering his payload in an attack on the Nakajima aircraft factory in Musashino, Japan, and was heading back to Saipan when he realized that another plane in the squadron—piloted by his close friend, Bennie Crowell—was under attack and losing altitude over the Sea of Japan. Young turned back to try and help Crowell. Some of the other servicemen, including Young's ground crew chief, believe the two planes collided and exploded; nothing of either aircraft was ever found. As the website for the Jim Thorpe Association declares, "Young gave his life, doing in combat what he had done on the football field—running interference for his teammates."

In 2007, Berry Tramel of NewsOK spoke with Cleta Niemann, 90, who still remembered the last time she saw her brother-in-law. Their last exchange was in Salina, Kansas, where Young was stationed before shipping out. "That morning I told him goodbye," Niemann said. "'Be sure and do this up right, so the children won't have to go.'" Young told her not to worry,

that he felt like the war was over but, "There were things to do before the world was right."[133]

PROFESSIONAL FOOTBALL PLAYERS KILLED IN LATER WARS / VIETNAM

Bob Kalsu

Buffalo Bills / United States Army
Born: April 13, 1945, in Oklahoma City, Oklahoma
Died: July 21, 1970, in Thua Thien Province, Vietnam
Position: G

James Robert Kalsu was only 25 years old when he lost his life in Vietnam. He is commemorated on the Vietnam Memorial in Washington, D.C., on panel 8W, line 38. In 1978, representatives of the Buffalo Bills presented the Pro Football Hall of Fame with a plaque honoring their 1968 rookie guard Bob Kalsu. Lieutenant Kalsu was serving as acting field artillery unit commander with the 101st Airborne, 11th Artillery, Second Battalion, when he was killed by mortar fire at Firebase Ripcord near the A Shau Valley. The prior commander had been helicoptered out of the base just four days earlier with a shrapnel wound to his neck. Bob's son, Bob Kalsu Jr., was born two days after his father was killed, the death still unknown at the time.

Bob Junior, his sister, Jill Anne Horning, and their mother, Jan Kalsu McLaughlin, all attended the presentation in Canton. General Colin Powell offered a video tribute, saying in part, "America owes a great debt to those who died to keep us free."

Kalsu was honored in a *Sports Illustrated* cover story on July 23, 2001. William Nack's feature is recommended to those who wish for a more complete understanding of Kalsu's background and the details of his service and death.

Bob was a graduate of the University of Oklahoma and a second team All-American offensive tackle drafted by the Buffalo Bills in the eighth round of the joint 1968 NFL/AFL Draft—three days after he and Jan Darrow had married. He learned of the draft when they returned from their honeymoon. Of Czech ancestry, Bob Kalsu was the son—the only child—of Frank Kalsu, a sheet-metal worker at Oklahoma's Tinker Air Force Base, and Leah Aguillard Kalsu. Bob grew up in Del City, Oklahoma, graduated high school there in 1963, and went on to O.U. While there, he joined the campus ROTC and became a cadet colonel as well as the captain of the Sooners football team.

After his rookie year with the Bills—where he was named their Rookie of the Year—he was drafted again, this time by the U.S. Army. Actually, he was not so much drafted as needing to serve his obligatory stint in the army occasioned by his participation in ROTC. He then faced what NFL Films called "a question of character few athletes of his era ever had to answer; he was called on to serve his country."[134] Overseas. In Vietnam. Although some urged him to let the Bills try and secure him a spot in the Reserves, particularly with a new wife and young daughter, he said that he was committed. "I gave my word to my country. Just because I play pro football doesn't make me any better of a man or any different of a man than the men

Buffalo Bills offensive guard Robert "Bob" Kalsu. (Pro Football Hall of Fame via AP)

already serving our country. I'm going to live up to that commitment and the word I gave."[135] Kalsu went through basic training at Fort Sill, and in November 1969 he received his orders for Vietnam.

He was stationed atop what *Sports Illustrated*'s Nack described as "a steep, balding shank of rock and dirt" that rose 656' above the floor of the jungle "on a space no bigger than two football fields" while providing artillery support to two infantry battalions of the 101st Airborne. They had the high ground, but they were within mortar range of as many as 5,000 soldiers of the North Vietnamese Army in the area. The NVA was pumping 600 or more rounds a day onto the base. It was one such round that took out both Kalsu and one of the men to whom he was closest, Spc. 4th Class David Earl Johnson, 24, an African American from Arkansas and a graduate of Little Rock's Philander Smith College.

Although he was an officer who could have remained under cover or deeper in a bunker, Kalsu was typically out with his men, helping lug the 97-lb. artillery shells. Just a few days before his death Kalsu had suffered a shoulder wound, but his battalion was in the thick of battle and he wasn't going to let himself be evacuated. Captain Philip Michaud, serving at Ripcord at the time, said, "Rounds were coming in, and he was out there. I told him a few times, 'It's good to run around and show what leadership is about, but when rounds are blowing up in your area, you ought to hunker down behind a gun wheel. Or a bunker.' The guy thought he was invincible."

PFC Nick Fotias recalls the moment the mortar round hit. "I remember this tremendous noise and darkness. And being blown off my feet and flying through the door of the bunker and landing at the bottom of the steps, six feet down, and this tremendous weight crushing me. I couldn't see. I couldn't hear. I had dirt in my eyes, and my eyes were tearing. I rubbed them, and then I could see again. I pushed off this weight that was on top of me, and I realized it was Bob."[136]

Two days later, Lt. Col. Andre Lucas was killed as he led the evacuation of the besieged firebase—for which Lucas received the Congressional Medal of Honor.

Kalsu was also honored with a 1999 production of NFL Films, *Remembering Bob Kalsu*, which won an Emmy Award. The film includes a recorded message Kalsu had sent home to his wife, expressing his love for her, their daughter, Jill, and the as-yet-unborn and unnamed "Baby K."

On the plaque that hangs in Ralph Wilson Stadium, the final sentence reads, "No one will ever know how great a football player Bob might have been, but we do know how great a man he was to give up his life for his country."

Don Steinbrunner

Cleveland Browns / United States Air Force
Born: April 5, 1932, in Bellingham, Washington
Died: July 20, 1967, in Kontum, Vietnam
Position: T

For many years, it was thought that Bob Kalsu had been the only NFL player since World War II to have been killed in action while serving in the U.S. armed forces. Major Don Steinbrunner's name is on the Vietnam Memorial wall in Washington, at panel 23E line 096. He was killed in action in Vietnam when he was shot down over Kontum. He played in eight games for the 1953 Cleveland Browns; the 11–1 Browns, under Coach Paul Brown, finished in first place in the NFL East but lost 17–16 to the Detroit Lions in the NFL Championship Game. A graduate of Washington State, Steinbrunner had been a sixth-round draft pick in the 1953 NFL Draft.

Steinbrunner was selected All-State out of Mount Baker High School, and he became the captain on Washington State's basketball and football teams where he earned All-Conference honors after his junior year. He'd enrolled in the ROTC program while in college and was summoned to active service after his 1953 rookie year with the Browns. It was a two-year commitment, and Steinbrunner served as a navigator in the United States Air Force. When his tour of duty was completed he contemplated returning to the Browns, but he found service in the Air Force rewarding so he re-upped.

"Coach Paul Brown kept him signed while he was doing his commitment," Steinbrunner's son, David, said. "Coach Brown liked Dad and wanted him to come back to the team, but Dad really enjoyed the military. I think he wanted to get into coaching."[137] Steinbrunner remained with the Air Force, and in 1961 he joined the football coaching staff at the Air Force Academy, working as an assistant coach.

He was still serving at the Academy when the Vietnam War broke out, and in 1966 he was sent there. His wife, Meredyth, said, "He loved his children very deeply and had some reservations about leaving them behind. But he also felt very strongly about going to Vietnam. He was going there to defend his country. At the time, communism was considered a great threat to the world. Don said it was his duty to go, and he wanted to go. He believed strongly in the cause."[138]

As the Pro Football Hall of Fame has noted, "Not long after his arrival, he was shot in the knee during an aerial mission and was offered an opportunity to accept a less dangerous assignment. He declined. According to his family, the 35-year-old Steinbrunner reasoned that he was better suited to serve his country than many of the younger, less seasoned soldiers he'd observed. It was a decision that cost him his life. On July 20, 1967, Steinbrunner's plane was shot down over Kontum, South Vietnam."[139]

Major Steinbrunner was the navigator aboard a C-123 from the 12th Air Commando Squadron, conducting a defoliation mission near Gia Vuc, about 30 miles southwest of Quang Ngai. There had been suspected light ground fire in the area, but as the aircraft made its run—at just 150'—it was "hit by a hail of small arms fire, crashed, and burned." All five crewmen were killed. In addition to Steinbrunner, the other losses were: Major Allan J. Stearns, Girard, Pennsylvania, pilot; Lt. Col. Everett E. Foster, Beacon, New York, copilot; SSgt. Irvin G. Weyandt, Claysburg, Pennsylvania, loadmaster; and Sgt. Le Tan Bo, RVN Air Force, observer.[140]

A forward air controller reportedly saw the crash near Pleiku Air Base. Steinbrunner "was scheduled to return to the states in December and was looking forward to a return to coaching duty at the Air Force Academy, where he spent five years as an assistant coach and recruiter."[141]

Steinbrunner was posthumously awarded the Purple Heart and the Distinguished Flying Cross. His citation read in part, "Disregarding the hazards of flying the difficult target terrain and the opposition presented by hostile ground forces, he led the formation through one attack and returned to make a second attack. The outstanding heroism and selfless devotion to duty displayed by Major Steinbrunner reflect great credit upon himself and the United States Air Force."

It was 30 years after his death that Steinbrunner was honored again and recognized at Canton. After seeing the 2001 *Sports Illustrated* article on Bob Kalsu, which said Kalsu was the "only pro athlete killed in Vietnam," Steinbrunner's daughter, Diane, contacted the Pro Football Hall of Fame to inform them of her own father's service. The Hall immediately made arrangements to invite the Steinbrunner family to its inaugural Veterans Day ceremony that very year. It is now an annual ceremony. Diane's brother, David, said of the Hall of Fame, "They were just wonderful. We took Dad's old Browns jacket and Purple Heart, and it is on display now."

In addition to children Diane and David, Steinbrunner was also survived by his wife, Meredyth, and daughter, Wendy.

PROFESSIONAL FOOTBALL PLAYERS KILLED IN LATER WARS / AFGHANISTAN

Pat Tillman
Arizona Cardinals / United States Army Rangers
Born: November 6, 1976, in Fremont, California
Died: April 22, 2004, in Afghanistan
Position: DB

Many players and even coaches served in World War II. Changing uniforms from one team to the military was common, and giving one's life in that service was not unexpected. In Major

League Baseball two men gave their lives, and in the NFL more than 20 did the same. Those are just statistics, numbers really. What needs to be remembered is that each statistic represented people with futures that ended much too soon. Also forgotten is that many, if not all, willingly joined.

The world changed on December 7, 1941, and again on September 11, 2001. The numbers show that 2,403 American servicemen were killed at Pearl Harbor—and nearly 3,000 mostly civilians were killed and almost that many were wounded. The nation's rage and passion for retribution were palpable. To many people today, December 7 is ancient history. In some aspects, sadly, so is 9/11.

Those dates of infamy do share something in common, however. Pat Tillman was killed as a result of 9/11; and his great-grandfather was killed at Pearl Harbor on December 7, 1941. His sacrifice wasn't lost on Pat.

America today views Pat Tillman's decision to forgo a career in the NFL as an honorable aberration in a society full of materialism. During WWII athletes putting the needs of others and the nation ahead of their professional sports careers was the norm. They willingly walked away.

Pat Tillman walked away from more than people know.

He walked away from a $9 million offer from the Rams to stay with the team that drafted him—the Arizona Cardinals. Tillman had played locally for Arizona State University, earning senior honors as the Pac-10 All Defensive Player of the Year, and he often rode

Cpl. Pat Tillman in 2003. (AP Photo/Photography Plus via Williamson Stealth Media Solutions, FILE)

to his NFL practices on his bike. That was his style. Unpretentious is an understatement when it comes to Pat Tillman. He was no jock. He was 3.8 GPA student and a brilliant mind—a philosopher always searching for meaning and a larger purpose. His mind never stopped. He was the perfect embodiment of the human spirit with the passion and force of a hurricane. When you met or saw Pat Tillman play, it was an experience.

Then he saw two planes fly in to the World Trade Center on September 11, 2001, and his life was changed forever. "I have not done a damn thing as far as laying my life on the line. So I have a lot of respect for those that have and what the flag stands for," Pat said on September 12, 2001. Don't mistake this for a moment of blind patriotism born out of "God and Country." Tillman would never stand for that. He believed the war in Iraq was illegal, while at the same time in his heart he was an idealist who respected the flag but didn't want it to be used as a propaganda tool.[142] Both he and his brother, Kevin, also a Ranger, were awarded the ESPY from ESPN but chose not to attend since they felt they were not better than anyone else, although both left the sports they loved to serve a greater cause.

He got married that spring of 2002, deeply in love, yet he still left to serve.

He walked away from a $3.6 million offer from the Arizona Cardinals, opting instead to eat bugs and survive Ranger training not for you and for me but because he believed it was the right thing for him to do.

What people forget is that his brother, Kevin, was a second baseman who walked away from professional baseball's minor league system and joined his brother in the Army Rangers. Both were attached to 2nd battalion, 75th Ranger Regiment and saw action in both Iraq and Afghanistan. He, too, was courageous. He, too, stepped into the fire.

Pat Tillman walked into the unknown with the same force as he hit his opponents on the field. He wanted to hit Osama bin Laden with the same force, too. After completion of Ranger training, he was sent to Iraq and there became disillusioned with the war and what he saw developing all around him. According to Tillman's biographer Jon Krakauer, "[Tillman] knew he was sort of a maverick and not a typical jock and football star, but I had no idea how complex he was, how sensitive or how liberal were his politics. God, I cannot imagine how Pat served in the war in Iraq that he thought was wrong…. And he could have gotten out of the army after two years and returned to the NFL…. But Pat wouldn't do it even though he loathed the war, was not happy in the army, and felt guilt about how miserable he was making Marie.

"[Tillman's] journals show what an amazing love story there was between Pat and Marie. Marie did not talk about that, but Pat wrote about it extensively. It was very powerful and heartbreaking to me. Pat Tillman was a special guy, not just some jock constructing a different persona. He was the real deal."[143]

Pat was then sent on to Afghanistan.

Pat Tillman was killed on April 22, 2004, and that is the only real fact we can determine regarding his death.

The story of how he died is an evolution in itself. There was the initial report that he was killed in combat while fighting the Taliban. He was awarded the Silver Star for heroism.

Anticipating his own death, Tillman had requested that there *not* be a military funeral. It just wasn't what he was all about. His body was flown home, and nearly 3,000 attended his memorial service. It was an event that Tillman himself would have avoided. He would probably have said, "His death was no different than those civilians on 9/11 or any others he saw

in Iraq. Where are their accolades and their parade?" There was obscene media coverage of the Tillman memorial service. Then whispers began to circulate that what the American public and the Tillman family were being told was not the truth.

Tillman was on a mission near the Pakistan border when Taliban forces ambushed his patrol vehicle. In the chaotic randomness of the ensuing firefight, another Ranger unit shot at Tillman's position by mistake. Tillman, Specialist Bryan O'Neil, and a member of the Afghanistan Military Force (AMF) all came under fire by mistake, even after multiple attempts to identify themselves as friendlies using smoke flares.[144] The attempt to identify themselves as friendly didn't work, although Tillman keep shouting with pain in his voice, "Stop firing. i'm Pat F-ing Tillman."[145] Tillman and the member of the AMF were both killed.

That story didn't fit the narrative being told about him by the government and media outlets, and the most horrible part was that many in leadership knew the day of the funeral that the cause of death was friendly fire.

Kevin Tillman's testimony in Congress says this was no "fog of war" at all. Simply, soldiers in his unit lost control in a year (2004) that was ripe with political/military disasters—such as Abu Ghraib. Kevin Tillman asserted that the real narrative was changed to take the focus off of those disasters and that his brother was betrayed by the "system" and had his virtue "hijacked."[146]

Even today, the full story has not been given to the family.

Pat's mother, Mary Tillman said, "By making up these false stories, you're diminishing their true heroism. [The truth] may not be pretty, but that's not what war is all about. It's ugly, it's bloody, and it's painful. And to write these glorious tales is really a disservice to the nation."[147]

If you really want to honor Pat Tillman, read some Nietzsche and Thoreau. Embrace the passions of your humanity. Be alive. Question, reason, and—most of all—think.

NOTE: The Pro Football Hall of Fame mistakenly lists two men as killed in action who were not. The Professional Football Researchers Association explains:

Bob Mackert appears on a few lists of player deaths. Those lists seem to confuse Bob Mackert with Roy Mackert. Roy played for the 1925 Rochester Jeffersons and served in the army until 1918. Roy died on February 12, 1942. Bob Mackert went missing in July 1944 and was later declared dead. Bob Mackert never played in the NFL.

Frank Maher appears on some lists as being killed during World War II. He'd played in 1941 for both the Cleveland Rams and Pittsburgh Steelers. Frank died April 11, 1992, in Toledo, Ohio.

NOTE: Please see Section 4 for information about college football players killed during wartime.

Section 3

Hall of Famers Who Served

PROFILES OF THE 55 PRO FOOTBALL HALL OF FAMERS WHO SERVED IN WORLD WAR II AND LATER WARS

Cliff Battles

Boston Braves, Boston Redskins, Washington Redskins / United States Marine Corps

Born: May 1, 1910, in Akron, Ohio

Died: April 28, 1981, in Clearwater, Florida

Position: TB-FB-WB-DB

Cliff Battles, a sensational running back from West Virginia Wesleyan College, won the NFL rushing title in 1932 as a rookie with the Boston Braves. The next year the Braves were renamed the Redskins, and Battles became the first player ever to rush for more than 200 yards in a game. He accomplished the feat on October 8, 1933, in a game against the New York Giants as he rushed 16 times for 215 yards and scored one touchdown.

In 1937, Redskins owner George Preston Marshall moved his team from Boston to Washington. He brought Battles, the NFL's premier running back, with him and quickly added a sensational rookie passer, Sammy Baugh. It didn't seem out of the question that the Battles-Baugh ground and air threat would make the Redskins championship contenders for years to come. For the 1937 season, Baugh and Battles combined their talents just as everyone had anticipated. On the season's final day, Battles scored three touchdowns to power the Redskins to a 49–14 win over the New York Giants for the Eastern Division title. Against the Chicago Bears a week later, Battles scored the first touchdown in a 28–21 victory that gave the Redskins their first NFL championship.

Battles was again the league's leading rusher, and he won All-League honors for the fifth time in six years. In just six seasons, Battles totaled 3,511 yards rushing—really big numbers for that era—and Redskins fans looked forward to more of the same in the upcoming seasons. With Battles carrying the ball and Baugh tossing it, championships seemed assured.

But it was not to be. Inexplicably, Marshall, who had paid Battles $3,000 a year starting with his rookie campaign, refused to consider a raise, even though Cliff clearly was a star player with good fan appeal. After the season, the exasperated Battles accepted a $4,000 job as an assistant coach at Columbia University. The Redskins won only one more championship during Baugh's long and storied career. Loyal Redskins fans were left to wonder what would have happened if Marshall had only given Battles a raise.

[Career capsule courtesy of the Pro Football Hall of Fame.]

Clifford (Cliff) Battles, one of the greatest football stars of all time, was sworn in the United States Marine Corps reserve on July 7, 1943, as first lieutenant. He was assigned to the Division of Recreation and Morale. (AP Photo)

Battles was the son of Frank and Della Battles and attended Kenmore High in Akron. Frank Battles worked as a clerk for the B.F. Goodrich and Firestone tire companies, and Della worked there, too.

Cliff was a Phi Beta Kappa student who scored 15 touchdowns in his senior year in college. He led the NFL in rushing yards (576) for the Boston Braves in his rookie season and again in his final season (874). A three-time All-Pro, Battles left football at the peak of his playing career, right after winning the world championship in 1937, the year the Redskins moved to Washington.

He remained at Columbia as an assistant to Coach Lou Little until he enlisted in the Marine Corps, but before he reported he had been asked to serve as backfield coach for the Army team that played against the Redskins in Los Angeles on August 30.[148] Battles' former teammate, Sammy Baugh, led the Redskins to a 26–7 victory. Battles also coached the Columbia basketball team for the 1942–43 season. On July 7, 1943, he was commissioned as a lieutenant in the Marine Corps Reserve and was assigned in August to the Division of Recreation and Morale.

Battles worked in Special Services for the Marines, setting up training programs during the war. He was the player/coach of the 1944 FMF Pacific Marine football team and worked as a coach with Dick Hanley at the Marine Corps Air Station El Toro team, near Irvine, California. He played in more than one game, notably running for a touchdown in El Toro's 52–0 defeat of the Army Raiders from Beaumont, Texas, in October.[149] In May 1945, he was appointed chief recreation officer of the MarFair West Marine Corps base in California and coached an All-Star team at Pearl Harbor.[150] He was promoted to captain before being mustered out of the Marines, and he coached the Brooklyn Dodgers of the All-America Football Conference in 1946 and 1947.

Professionally, Battles later worked for General Electric as Defense Division legislative representative in Washington, D.C.

He was inducted into the Pro Football Hall of Fame in 1968, and was the first small college player to be enshrined in the College Football Hall of Fame (1955).

Among the pallbearers at his funeral were Supreme Court Justice Byron (Whizzer) White, Redskins quarterbacks Sonny Jurgensen and Ralph Guglielmi, and former president of the Pro Football Hall of Fame, Earl Schreiber.[151]

Chuck Bednarik

Philadelphia Eagles / United States Army Air Corps
Born: May 1, 1925, in Bethlehem, Pennsylvania
Position: LB-C

No National Football League player in the 1950s was immune to bone-jarring contact with the Philadelphia Eagles' Chuck Bednarik because the 233-pounder played on both the offensive and defensive units long after the two-way player had largely faded from the scene.

Bednarik didn't really get into football until he returned from World War II (after a 30-mission tour as a B-24 waist gunner with the Army Air Corps that saw him win the Air Medal). He showed up unheralded at the University of Pennsylvania where he went on to win All-America honors as a center his last two seasons.

Chuck was selected first overall in the 1949 NFL Draft as the Eagles' bonus draft choice and earned a starter's spot as a center on offense and linebacker on defense. As the center, big Chuck was a bulldozing blocker, both on rushing and passing plays. On defense, he was a true scientist in his field and the kind of tackler who could literally stop even the finest opposing runners on a dime.

BEDNARIK IN WWII

Chuck Bednarik grew up in poverty during the Great Depression on the south side of Bethlehem by the mills. There was an Italian parish, a Hungarian parish, a Polish one, and the Slovak parish, Saints Cyril and Methodius, where he went. "All row houses," he remembered in an oral history for The National World War II Museum. "I went to a Catholic elementary school and those Slovak nuns were tough and they would beat you! One day I came home and my knuckles and face were red, and my father went right down to the school to confront the nun. She and him started running around the room and he said, 'You son of a bitch, next time you hit my boy, I'll kill you!' Dad could barely speak English and work in the mines. I fully expected to work in the mines, too, after high school, but the war changed all that. I went to Liberty High School and also a vocational school where I learned electronics, which was also called Bethlehem High School, and I played baseball, basketball, and football. I was good at all three. Then the war came and changed everything. The whole world changed."

Chuck continued, "I was already 18. I took so many tests and did well. They asked me if I wanted to be in the Air Corps, and I said yeah. Then it was like piston A goes this way and piston B goes this way. What the hell did I know? I was no mechanic. I did my basic training in the U.S. I was assigned to gunnery school and then at first in the top turret on the B-24—you know, the one that spins around? I was assigned to a crew and we learned how to fly, formation flying and all that stuff and then flew to England to a place called Rackheath, right off of the English Channel. The Germans were just across the way there. That was something—to go flying all over through the Nazis' antiaircraft fire. I was getting too big for the turret. I outgrew it. I got up to 200 lbs. So I got stuck in the waist.

"We were at usually at 23,000–24,000 feet we wore some heated flack vests with steel plates when we got close to the target but you took them right off when you left it.

"A round trip mission to Berlin took us seven hours! A long time…and on those missions, my God, the flak was unbelievable—but Berlin was really nasty. That's where all the big shots were.

"June 1944—Berlin! Quite a first mission, huh? When I turned 19, I already had 4 missions under me!

"Then we went to Kiel, Munich, and Saarbrucken and Bremen, Hamburg, Cologne, and many others. Dresden, too. My 25th mission was against Dresden. Later on in March we went to Berlin again. God, the bigger the city the tougher it was! They were all tough!

"All missions were scary. I thought I was going to die each time! The day before they would say, 'All following crews alert for flight tomorrow!' and we would see our crew number and we would try to go to sleep that night, but you don't sleep, really, 'cause they wake you up at 4:00 to 5:00 in the morning. Briefing. Breakfast. And takeoff!

"Every mission is the same. Berlin was just a longer trip, and the flak was 10 times as worse; you could almost walk on it. You can hear the damn thing coming through and it could go through your heart or guts. I just know God was with me. That was the secret to my life. You could see the planes fall down. Sometimes we had flat tires, and when we landed we just veered off the runway. Rough landings…sometimes we counted the bullet holes.

"We were a tight crew, very fortunate. Nobody got hurt. I never shot down a plane. To shoot down a plane was tough. It had to be fighter to fighter. I didn't see those Messerschmitt fighters too often—thanks to the GIs in France pushing the Germans back. That way we got more fighter cover. God Almighty, it was that flak—let me tell you—all that black shit coming at you. I wanted the war to be the hell over. It's tough to be in combat like that.

"You know, when you are 18–19 years old, you don't where you are or really what you're doing. You're just a guy in a plane. You don't think of nothing unless you have a three- or four-day pass to London. It was just a job to me. In London, all I did was drink. Never had any sex; it was a sin, and I didn't want to go to Hell. On base I didn't really do that much. It was tough going from all that violence and then be back in a bed in a Quonset hut, like nothing happened. It was weird, really. After every mission I went to church, Mass really. It made me very religious. I'm religious now. I go every morning. I was always with my Rosaries. Got 'em right now.

"I tell you that was something. I'll never forget right after the 30th and final mission, I got out, kissed the ground, and said I don't ever want to fly again…that is enough! It was terrible.

"I had that GI Bill of Rights and went back to my high school coach and asked him where I should go to school. He said University of Pennsylvania. He set up a trip, and when I showed up, the coach said, 'Sign him up.' He had a bunch of kids and here I was, a World War II veteran. God, we had 78,000 attend the games. I was the Eagles' bonus pick. Got $3,000 on top of my $10,000 salary. I never saw so much money and spent the next 14 years playing for the Eagles. So with my four years at Penn and my next 14 with the Eagles I played in Philadelphia 18 consecutive years. Ben Franklin and I are pretty popular!"

B-24 waist gunners man their weapons. (Photo courtesy of the National World War II Museum)

And Bednarik was tough. He played both offense and defense. "So many of these guys today, I bet, would want to play both ways, but in my opinion they are overpaid and underplayed."

Could today's 19-year-olds handle something like World War II? "Not really. The Depression made us tough. Family welfare for clothes and food. We played on the street. Just don't break no windows! Kids today have everything.

"The war was worth it. It was a good war. I'm lucky to be talking to you."

*[**Source**: from an oral history of Chuck Bednarik conducted by The National World War II Museum]*

In 1950, Bednarik received All-NFL recognition as a center. Although he frequently played both offense and defense right up through the 1956 season, it was as a bone-jarring linebacker that he drew the most attention. He was named All-NFL as a linebacker 1951–57 and again in 1960.

His athletic abilities and inspirational play was particularly evident in 1960 when injuries forced the Eagles to ask their 12-year veteran to again play both sides of the line. The 35-year-old was sensational. He finished the campaign with a 58-minute performance capped by a game-saving tackle in the Eagles' NFL Championship Game victory over Green Bay. With just seconds remaining, the Packers' Jim Taylor appeared to be heading for a winning touchdown until the last Eagle in his path, Bednarik, bear-hugged him to the ground as time ran out.

[Career capsule courtesy of the Pro Football Hall of Fame.]

Chuck "Concrete Charlie" Bednarik's father was a laborer who'd become a foreman in the steel mill at Bethlehem. Chuck was just 16 years old when Pearl Harbor was attacked and still a teenager when he enlisted in the Army Air Corps where he served 2½ years in the European Theater of Operations flying as a waist gunner in a Consolidated B-24 Liberator.

Staff Sergeant Bednarik flew with the 467th Bomb Group, 788th Bomb Squadron and flew the first of his missions in August 1944. The waist gunner fired out of an opening in the side of the aircraft, rather than from a ball turret or a tail turret, and "the waist gunners had the unfortunate distinction in being on the most dangerous spot on the plane…. The spent shells from the waist guns simply dropped at the feet of the gunners, creating a difficult place to work."[152] Two of his flights ended in crash landings, and it was said that the crew never returned from a mission without counting at least 100 flak holes in the fuselage.[153]

"I couldn't wait to go because all my friends were there," Bednarik told CBS Sportsline. "I didn't make it as a pilot, but I became a crew member and a waist gunner. I survived 30 missions over Germany. How we survived, I don't know. Just taking off with a plane full of bombs, my life could've been over before I turned 21. The war really stands out in my mind. From then on, great things happened for me."[154] Bednarik's 30 missions were completed before he turned 20 years old. He earned the Air Medal with four oak leaf clusters and five battle stars.

Chuck Bednarik was named to the Pro Football Hall of Fame in 1967.

Paul Brown

Cleveland Browns, Cincinnati Bengals / United States Navy

Born: September 7, 1908, in Norwalk, Ohio
Died: August 5, 1991, in Cincinnati, Ohio
Position: coach

Paul Brown, perhaps more than any other person, is responsible for making pro football coaching the exact science it is today. When he organized the Cleveland Browns in the new All-America Football Conference in 1946, he employed methods no other pro coach had attempted.

Brown had a background of exceptional success as a high school, college, and military service coach when he was given his first pro assignment with the new Cleveland team. Immediately, he hired a full-time staff on a year-round basis, and he instituted a system for scouting college talent on a scale never before imagined by other pro teams. In his handling of his team, he became the first to: (1) use intelligence tests as a hint to a player's learning potential; (2) use notebooks and classroom techniques extensively; (3) set up complete film clip statistical studies; (4) grade his own players based on film study. Brown, always a firm disciplinarian, was the first coach to keep his players together at a hotel the night before a home game as well as a road game.

From the strategic standpoint, he started the practice of calling plays from the sideline by utilizing alternating guards as messengers. He developed detailed pass patterns for the offense that were designed to pick holes in the defense, then he devoted his efforts to perfecting the kind of a defense that could counteract a pattern passing attack.

Brown built a pro football dynasty in Cleveland, posting a 167–53–8 record, four AAFC titles, three NFL crowns, and only one losing season in 17 years. In the four seasons the Browns operated in the AAFC, they lost just four games. When the Browns joined the NFL

in 1950, they continued their winning ways, playing in the next six championship games and winning the title in 1950, 1954, and 1955.

[Career capsule courtesy of the Pro Football Hall of Fame]

Kerry J. Byrne of Cold, Hard Football Facts wrote in 2007, "Students of the Paul Brown School have won 18-of-40 Super Bowls." He said that Brown is "the deeply rooted trunk of modern football's most important coaching tree" and reminds us that Brown was not only the central figure behind two NFL franchises— the Browns and the Bengals—but that his Browns years remain unparalleled—10 straight championship games in two different leagues, winning seven of the 10.

Brown was raised in modest circumstances, mostly in Massillon, Ohio. His father, Lester, worked as a telegraph operator on the railroad around the time of his birth and rose in rank to a train dispatcher for the Wheeling and Lake Erie at the time of the 1920 and 1930 Censuses.

Coach Brown had worked at Washington High School in Massillon, Ohio, from 1932 to 1940 and then took over the head coaching job in Columbus at the Ohio State University from 1941–43. The Buckeyes were Big Ten champions in 1942. Just months after starting his first season, the attack on Pearl Harbor occurred, and by March 1942, three of his assistant coaches were all in the navy.[155] Ohio State first played directly against what became a very powerful Great Lakes Naval Training Station (Great Lakes N.T.S.) team, the Bluejackets, on October 9, 1943, at Ross Field,

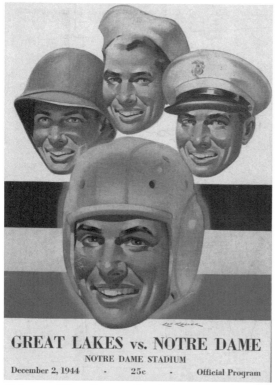

GREAT LAKES vs. NOTRE DAME
NOTRE DAME STADIUM
December 2, 1944 · 25c · Official Program

University of Notre Dame vs. Great Lakes U.S. Naval Training Station, December 2, 1944. (Photo courtesy of John Gunn Sports Collection, MS 316, William M. Randall Library Special Collections, University of North Carolina–Wilmington, Wilmington, North Carolina)

Chicago. Favored to win by three touchdowns, the Bluejackets were held scoreless by the Buckeyes for the entire first half of the game. The final score was 13–6, Bluejackets.

On April 13, 1944, Brown enlisted in the navy as Lt. (jg) Paul E. Brown and was scheduled to report for duty at the very same Great Lakes N.T.S. in Chicago. Though 45 years old, married, and the father of three boys, he was nonetheless declared 1-A by his draft board and entered the service, ready to do whatever

was asked of him. He served as assistant football coach to Lt. Tony Hinkle, giving Great Lakes football an even stronger foundation. The training station team was already tops in baseball, basketball, and swimming.

In October 1944, Hinkle was given orders to report for sea duty in the South Pacific, and Brown became football coach. On October 21, Brown worked from the visitors' clubhouse at Ohio State for the first time. Great Lakes lost 26–6 before more than 73,000 fans, the first loss of the season for the Bluejackets.

On February 8, 1945, Brown signed a five-year deal (effective whenever the war was over and he received his discharge) to become head coach of the as-yet-unnamed Cleveland team in the just-organizing All-America Football Conference. (Ultimately, the team was named the Browns after Coach Brown, though he tried to have it called the Panthers.) Brown's last game coaching the Bluejackets was in December 1945 when they beat Notre Dame 39–7. He was discharged from the navy on March 2, 1946.

Tony Canadeo

Green Bay Packers / United States Navy and United States Army

Born: May 5, 1919, in Chicago, Illinois
Died: November 29, 2003, in Green Bay, Wisconsin
Position: HB-TB-FB-DB

Tony Canadeo from little-known Gonzaga University was an unsung ninth-round choice of the Green Bay Packers in 1941, but it wasn't long before he earned the reputation of being a budding superstar who could—and would—do anything on a football field.

He played offense and defense, ran with the ball, threw passes, caught passes, returned punts and kickoffs, punted, and intercepted passes. In 11 years, he rushed for 4,197 yards, passed for 1,642 yards, recorded 69 receptions for 579 yards, gained 513 yards on punt returns, 1,736 yards on kickoff returns, and scored 186 points.

Altogether the versatile Canadeo gained 8,667 multi-purpose yards. Putting it another way, he accounted for almost 75 yards in each of the 116 games he played. He also intercepted nine passes and punted 45 times during his remarkable career. Green Bay from 1941–44 was one of pro football's premier teams. During that period, Tony initially served as an understudy to veteran quarterback Cecil Isbell. Then in 1943, he became the Packers' No. 1 passer. That year he was also named to the official All-NFL team. In 1945, World War II interrupted Canadeo's pro career.

When he returned from the army in 1946, the Packers were no longer contenders and Canadeo's role was significantly different. For his final seven seasons in the league, Tony became a heavy-duty running back and, predictably, came through with flying colors. In 1949, he became only the third player to rush for more than 1,000 yards in a season. He won All-NFL acclaim for a second time.

Small by pro standards, Canadeo was neither particularly fast nor elusive. Because he was prematurely gray, he was popularly known as "The Gray Ghost of Gonzaga." But Tony employed the attributes of most

great athletes—determination, courage, and tenacity—to attain Hall of Fame stature.
[Career capsule courtesy of the Pro Football Hall of Fame]

Canadeo's older brother, Savior Canadeo, was the Chicago Golden Gloves welterweight boxing champion in 1940. Their father, Antonio, worked as a motorman. Tony went to Steinmetz High School in Chicago but traveled to Spokane for college at Gonzaga because a number of his friends had gone there. He was of modest size—5'11" and 190 lbs.—but filled with determination and drive. He became an All-Pacific Coast player and a Little All American. He was signed on the recommendation of Gus Dorais, scooping the Redskins' Ray Flaherty, a Gonzaga alum who had perhaps thought he could take his time signing Tony because he'd have been unnoticed playing at such a small school.

In May 1943 Canadeo was enrolled as an aviation cadet at the DePauw University Naval Pre-Flight School, but he was honorably discharged later in the year. He then re-entered the service, sworn into the army in Milwaukee.[156] When serving in the army during wartime, he played in three 1944 games while on furlough but then missed the entire 1945 season while serving overseas. He'd been All-Pro in 1943 before his time in the army, and he was All-Pro again in 1949.

After Canadeo's playing career ended, he became a businessman in the steel industry in Green Bay and served on the team's board of directors and executive committee. For a while, he worked as a commentator on television games for the Packers and was active in the 1950s drive for a new City Stadium in Green Bay, saving the team for the city. City Stadium was re-named Lambeau Field in 1965. Tony's son, Robert, served in the Vietnam War and received the Bronze Star for heroism. Robert later donated one of his kidneys to his father.

Canadeo was inducted into the Pro Football Hall of Fame in 1974.

George Connor

Chicago Bears / United States Navy
Born: January 21, 1925, in Chicago, Illinois
Died: March 31, 2003, in Chicago, Illinois
Position: T-LB-DT-G

George Connor earned All-America honors three times—once at Holy Cross in 1943 and then at Notre Dame in 1946 and 1947. During his eight-year career (1948–55) with the Bears, he was named to the All-NFL team at three different positions—offensive tackle, defensive tackle, and linebacker. In 1952 and 1953, he was named All-League on both the offensive and defensive teams by different wire services.

Although George is remembered as one of the finest of the post–World War II tackles, it was as a linebacker that he made his biggest mark in the pro football world. And it was the sheer necessity of a desperate situation for the Chicago Bears that prompted George's switch to a linebacker position.

The Philadelphia Eagles were running roughshod over the NFL in 1949, and one end sweep with two guards and the fullback leading Steve Van Buren around the flank had been particularly successful. The Bears coaching staff hit upon the idea of moving a big, fast, and agile man like the 6'3", 240-lb. Connor into a linebacker's slot to try to stop the play. The move was made, the experiment was successful, the Eagles were beaten, and Connor became a linebacker for keeps.

That didn't mean, however, that he was a one-way specialist. He continued to play offensive tackle, winning All-NFL acclaim on both offense and defense. George was always one of the smartest men on the field. It seems he instinctively knew about keys—the tips that the movements of certain offensive players will provide to the alert defender as to which way the play is going—long before keys became vogue.

Connor always played the game hard and clean and with exceptional effectiveness. He might have continued in a starring role for many years had not a knee injury cut short his career after the 1955 season.

[Career capsule courtesy of the Pro Football Hall of Fame]

George Connor's college career may present a bit of a quandary to fans who root for Holy Cross against Notre Dame, or vice versa. After being named an All-State tackle at De La Salle Institute in Chicago, he went on to the College of the Holy Cross in his father's native Massachusetts. His uncle, Father George S.L. Connor, was president of the alumni association there (and himself a former end for the Crusaders.) George spent his first two years at Holy Cross, was selected as an All-American in 1943, and was named the outstanding football player in New England. He then spent the next two years in the United States Navy. After he had completed his V–12 training, he was assigned to active duty aboard a submarine chaser in the Pacific Theater.

He then played another pair of years, both for Notre Dame, on undefeated teams in 1946 and 1947. There was further parallel structure: At both Holy Cross and Notre Dame, Connor played tackle on offense and defense, and at both schools he was an All-American.

He might never have played football at all. He was born two months prematurely on January 21, 1925. Fortunately, his father, Charles Connor, was a physician and his mother, Mary, was a nurse. George weighed less than 3 lbs. and was given "less than a 10 percent chance to survive. He was placed on a diet of boiled cabbage juice, which his mother, a nurse, fed him hourly for a year with an eyedropper. He grew to 6'3" and 240 lbs."[157]

"He was indestructible," said his coach at Notre Dame, Frank Leahy. "Not quite," explained *The New York Times*, quoting Connor's wife, Suzanne, "He went through 32 surgeries on everything in his body except his head."[158]

Leahy of Notre Dame probably merits the most credit for molding Connor into becoming a professional, but Connor was far from his only success. As *Sports Illustrated* noted of those two great postwar teams in South Bend, "Forty-three Notre Dame players from either '46 or '47 [or both] played in the NFL or the rival AAFC."[159] This at a time when there were only 18 teams in the two leagues combined. And Leahy personally recruited Connor, the tackle

explained, when his ship had docked in Hawaii. "I was stationed at Pearl Harbor, and one day a command car pulled up and a guy said, 'Ensign Connor, Commander Leahy would like to see you at the Royal Hawaiian.' He talked me into coming to Notre Dame. He said we'd win the national championship, and I'd make All-America. It all came true."[160]

After his playing days, Connor worked as an assistant coach for the Bears and as a broadcaster for both Bears and Notre Dame football. He also worked in sales in the box industry.

Lou Creekmur

Detroit Lions / United States Army
Born: January 22, 1927, in Hopelawn, New Jersey
Died: July 5, 2009, in Tamarac, Florida
Position: T-G-DG-DT

Lou Creekmur, a 6'4", 246-lb. college star at William and Mary, joined the Detroit Lions in 1950 and quickly established himself as one of the most versatile and talented performers on a team loaded with outstanding stars.

During the 1950s decade when the Lions won NFL championships in 1952, 1953, and 1957, Creekmur was a perennial All-NFL selection. An outstanding blocker on both passing and rushing plays, Lou started his pro career as an offensive guard, winning All-League acclaim at that position in 1951 and 1952. He then was shifted to offensive left tackle where he remained, except for one season, the rest of his 10-year career. At that position, Lou was named All-NFL four times in 1953, 1954, 1956, and 1957. In 1953, he

Detroit Lions tackle Lou Creekmur (76) returns a kickoff during a game against the Green Bay Packers at Tiger Stadium in Detroit, Michigan, November 27, 1958. (AP Photo/NFL Photos)

earned All-League honors at both guard and tackle.

Then, in 1955, he spent most of the season filling in capably in an emergency situation at defensive middle guard. Throughout his Detroit tenure, the versatile Creekmur was used in critical short-yardage defensive situations.

Extremely durable, Creekmur played every preseason, regular season, and postseason game during his first nine campaigns, and going into his final season he owned a streak of more than 165 consecutive game appearances. Besides two divisional playoff games and four NFL championship contests he played in as a Lion, Lou was selected to eight consecutive Pro Bowl classics from 1950–57.

He joined Bobby Layne and Doak Walker as only the third offensive player from the Lions vintage years to earn Pro Football Hall of Fame membership. Defensive teammates already in the Hall included Joe Schmidt, Jack Christiansen, and Yale Lary.

[Career capsule courtesy of the Pro Football Hall of Fame]

James Creekmur, Lou's father, was a delivery service owner in Hopelawn. The family moved to Woodbridge, New Jersey, when Lou was young, and James took a position as a shoe salesman in a department store. Lou played football at Woodbridge High before joining the College of William and Mary and playing tackle on their football team. And then he fought in World War II. [161]

After two years in the army serving with occupation forces in Germany, Creekmur got back in the game while resuming his studies at William and Mary in 1947. He'd grown in the army in more ways than one; he'd added 4" of height (6'4") and as much as 60 or 70 lbs. (weighing as much as 270 lbs.) during those two years. William and Mary won the Southern Conference title in 1947.

While at the college, Creekmur also set the school record in the shot put. He played in the 1949 College All-Star Game, and then added another year in academia to earn his master's

degree in physical education. During the off-seasons, he'd worked as a taxi driver, in an iron works, and sold hot dogs. [162] In 1950, he was the second-round pick of the Lions taken from a special pool of players (including Y.A. Tittle) after the All-America Football Conference disbanded, and he debuted for the Lions that same year.

Creekmur put his education to work after finishing with football and began a 25-year career with Ryder Truck Lines of Jacksonville, beginning as director of labor relations and then serving both as director of lease development and director of public relations.

Art Donovan
Baltimore Colts, New York Yanks, Dallas Texans /
United States Marine Corps
Born: June 5, 1925, in Bronx, New York
Died: August 4, 2013, in Baltimore, Maryland
Position: DT-T

Art Donovan, the son of a famous boxing referee of the same name, first played football at Mount St. Michael High School in the Bronx. Somehow he was overlooked on the All-Metropolitan prep team, and when he played college football at Boston College, the best Art could do was second-team All-New England.

But in the professional ranks, it was a different story for Art, whose World War II service stint put off his college career so that he was a 25-year-old rookie when he joined the Baltimore Colts in 1950. The hapless Colts folded after one season, and Art moved to the

Art Donovan (second from right) with members of the Third Marines on Guam, July 1945. (Photo courtesy of Art Donovan)

New York Yanks in 1951 then played for the Dallas Texans in 1952.

In 1953, the well-traveled Donovan returned to Baltimore to play for the new Colts team, and as the Colts developed into a championship team, Donovan developed into one of the best defensive tackles in league history.

Artie was ready for stardom. Big, strong, fast, and smart, Donovan was also one of the most popular players in the league. He was an All-NFL selection in 1954, 1955, 1956, 1957, and 1958. In addition, he played in five straight Pro Bowls.

The Baltimore Colts' great title teams of 1958 and 1959 featured a terrific defensive line with future Hall of Fame defensive end Gino Marchetti, Don Joyce, "Big Daddy" Lipscomb, and Donovan, who by then had become the complete player. He was equally adept at rushing the passer, reading keys, closing off the middle, and splitting double-team blocks. He had the reputation of being almost impossible to trap.

As great of a contributor as he was on the field, many feel he was at least as valuable to the Colts as a morale builder with his sharp wit and contagious laughter. The first Colts player elected to the Pro Football Hall of Fame, Donovan played 12 seasons in the NFL.

[Career capsule courtesy of the Pro Football Hall of Fame]

IN HIS OWN WORDS

"Here is how small the world was. My unit was on Guam, getting ready to invade Japan—and I get a phone call from my father saying he was also on the island as part of a show for the troops. He was refereeing fights! Talk about amazing. Meeting up with my father halfway around the world! Incredible.

"It was a great experience for me. It made me grow up—made me a man. They talk about these guys in the NFL today as heroes? No way. They are just playing football—jumping around and all that show stuff. Let me tell you—the real heroes are those ones lying in the graves in Europe and the Pacific. I have two cousins buried in the Cemetery of the Pacific in Hawaii. Those are my heroes, not these guys in the NFL today. No way. You can quote me on that! The reason I can play above the grass [is] because of the men lying below it.

"Visiting Normandy, I sat there among all those white crosses, surrounded by those young boys who died for their country and I sat there and I cried thinking about all that we fought for. I saw those faces of kids I knew who were gone forever. They did that for me and for you."

[Art Donovan, speaking with Todd Anton on January 19, 2013]

Donovan took this photo of his gun crew on Saipan. (Photo courtesy of Art Donovan)

He was the son of Hall of Fame boxing referee Art Donovan and the grandson of "Professor" Mike Donovan, who had been middleweight champion of the world during a career than ran from 1866–91. Mike had sometimes fought with gloves and sometimes without them in the world of nineteenth century boxing. He'd been in the Union Army, marched through Georgia with General William Sherman, and had once boxed in a match refereed by Wyatt Earp. He'd boxed against both John L. Sullivan and Jack "Nonpareil" Dempsey, and he even sparred with his friend Theodore Roosevelt while Teddy was governor of New York and then President of the United States. Mike Donovan is in the International Boxing Hall of Fame, as is his son, Art, who was inducted into the Hall of Fame as a referee. That's three generations of Hall of Famers.

Art Senior's regular job was as an instructor for the YMCA. Art the younger had loved baseball most but was too slow. "The only way I could get past first base was to hit the ball out of the park," he said. After high school, his plans to study at Notre Dame were placed on hold until he completed 2½ years with the Third Marine Division in the Pacific. He served as an antiaircraft gunner on a light aircraft carrier, the USS *San Jacinto*, during the Battle of Leyte Gulf in October 1944 and then took part in the Battle of Okinawa. "We were only weeks away from the invasion of Japan," he recalled when the dropping of the A-bomb brought about an end to the war. "I was with a Marine Division at Okinawa, and

we had all our gear stenciled and ready to go. I hate to think how many casualties we would have suffered had we gone through with such a mission."[163]

When Donovan returned from the service and didn't feel sufficiently welcome at Notre Dame, he wanted to go to Fordham—where his childhood idol Alex Wojciechowicz had played football—but wound up going to Boston College instead.

After playing for three pro football teams in three years with a cumulative record of 3–31–2, he finally began to see some progress after the Dallas franchise moved to Baltimore for his second stint of playing for the Colts.

After football, Donovan continued to live outside Baltimore and owned a chain of retail carry-out stores there. He was inducted into the Football Hall of Fame in 1968, in the same class as Alex Wojciechowicz.

Bill Dudley

Pittsburgh Steelers, Detroit Lions, Washington Redskins / United States Army Air Corps

Born: December 24, 1919, in Bluefield, Virginia
Died: February 4, 2010, in Lynchburg, Virginia
Position: HB-TB-QB

Bill Dudley must have firmly believed that the ball belonged to him. He wanted it all the time. And it seemed there wasn't anything he couldn't do with it. The 5'10", 182-lb. halfback ran, passed, punted, and place-kicked. He returned punts and kickoffs, caught passes, and was a deadly defender.

Dudley, who was nicknamed "Bullet Bill" despite never being considered particularly fast, was a first-round draft pick of the Pittsburgh Steelers in 1942. He demonstrated from the start that his relatively small size and lack of blazing speed wasn't a detriment. In the first game of his pro career he ran for a 55-yard touchdown, and in his second game he scored on a kickoff return. He finished his rookie season as the league's leading rusher with 696 yards and earned All-League honors.

Dudley's nine-year NFL career was unique in that he played three seasons each with the Steelers (1942, 1945–46), Detroit Lions (1947–49), and Washington Redskins (1950–51, 1953). His career was interrupted in 1943 and 1944 when he served with the Army Air Corps during World War II.

He returned to the Steelers during the 1945 campaign. The 1946 season was, for Dudley, one for the record book—he led the league in rushing, punt returns, interceptions, and lateral passes attempted. Never before had an NFL player led the league in four distinctly different statistical categories, and it's not likely to happen again anytime soon.

Naturally, Bill was named the NFL's Most Valuable Player that year.

The following season, Bill again demonstrated his tremendous versatility when he scored 11 touchdowns for the Lions on one punt return, one interception return, seven pass receptions, and two rushes. Six times Dudley was named first- or second-team All-NFL. He was also named to three Pro Bowls, and more than likely would have been named to more

had the annual event not been temporarily discontinued.

[Career capsule courtesy of the Pro Football Hall of Fame]

By the time he graduated from the University of Virginia in June 1942, the war was on and Dudley's ambition was to fly for the navy. His father, Shelby, had worked as a commercial traveler for a packing house. Although the Steelers had made Bill their top draft pick, he really hadn't been thinking about football

The Los Angeles Coliseum hosted the Randolph Field Ramblers vs. March Field Flyers on December 10, 1944. (Photo courtesy of the John Gunn Sports Collection, MS 316, William M. Randall Library Special Collections, University of North Carolina–Wilmington, Wilmington, North Carolina)

professionally. "College football, and the bowl games, were the big thing," he said. "I was originally going to go in the Naval Air Corps. I was sworn in the Naval Air Corps in late May or early June 1942. But when they started checking my papers, this came out later, they found out I had to have my parents' consent because I wasn't 21. So in the meantime, I went out to play in the College All-Star Game in Chicago, and I signed a professional football contract. I played there with the Steelers mainly for the money," Dudley explained.[164]

He led the league in rushing in 1942, but in September, facing the draft, he enlisted in the Army Air Corps. Because there were so many people coming into the program at one time, he was informed it would be three months before he would be called.[165] This gave him enough time to play out his rookie season for the Steelers and be named to the First Team All-Pro squad.

He went through basic training and then was assigned to flight school at Randolph Field, Texas. "Ultimately, he was asked to join the army's football team. Dudley was told he was an 'essential' part of the war effort as a 'morale booster.' In the 1944 season, 'Bullet' helped his team triumph with a 12–0 record. That year he was named MVP and made the All-Service squad."[166]

He was sent to the Pacific and flew a couple of supply missions, serving as a B-25 and B-29 pilot.[167] Milton Gross wrote that he had taken part in the air offensive against Japan.[168]

After the war ended, the Army Air Corps asked him to play in three more football games against All-Star teams. This earned him a flight home rather than a sea voyage. He was able to return to Pittsburgh in time to play the final four games of the 1945 season for the Steelers. And he picked up right where he'd left off—after leading the league in rushing in 1942, he did so again in his next full season in 1946.

Bill Dudley was enshrined in the Pro Football Hall of Fame in 1966.

Weeb Ewbank

Baltimore Colts, New York Jets / United States Navy
Born: May 6, 1907, in Richmond, Indiana
Died: November 17, 1998, in Oxford, Ohio
Position: coach

When Weeb Ewbank started his NFL head coaching career with the 1954 Baltimore Colts, he was 47, not the age you ordinarily look for in a rookie coach. But the popular Ewbank stayed in command for the next 20 years, the first nine in Baltimore and the final 11 with the New York Jets. In so doing, he made an impact on pro football that has done much to ensure its emergence as America's most popular spectator sport.

He is the only coach to lead teams from both the National and American Football Leagues to world championships. His Colts won NFL crowns in both 1958 and 1959, and the 1968 Jets followed up their AFL championship with victory in Super Bowl III. Of even more importance than the victory is the effect that these Ewbank championships had on the growth of pro football.

Millions of fans watched on national television for the first time as the Colts defeated the New York Giants 23–17 in overtime in 1958. Many still call this game "the greatest ever played," and there is no doubt that the highly competitive nature of the contest did much to increase fan enthusiasm and anticipation in the years ahead.

A decade later, Weeb's old team, the Colts, was heavily favored to make it three straight Super Bowl victories for the supposedly superior NFL over the overmatched AFL. But spurred

Physical instruction programs initiated by Paul Brown continued even aboard ship, including the USS Monterey, *where navy pilots played basketball in the forward elevator.* (Photo courtesy of the National World War II Museum)

along by Weeb's careful prodding, the Jets pulled off one of the most stunning upsets in history. The competitive validity of the Super Bowl was never again in doubt.

In both Baltimore and New York, Weeb inherited young, disorganized teams. In both places, Ewbank instituted a patented building program that proved effective. In each place, his skill of judging and handling players was quickly apparent and became a predominant factor in his success.

[Career capsule courtesy of the Pro Football Hall of Fame]

Ewbank's father, Charles, ran a retail grocery store in Indiana. Charles and Stella Ewbanks' son, Wilbur, helped out with the family's two stores, even delivering groceries using a horse-drawn wagon.[169] The nickname "Weeb" came in childhood from his younger brother who struggled as an infant to say "Wilbur." Weeb graduated from Morton High School in Richmond, Indiana, in 1924 (he'd married his wife, Lucy Massey, while still in high school; they were married for 69 years.) After graduation, he continued on to college at Miami University of Ohio where he quarterbacked the football team, playing as a teammate of Paul Brown. He was captain of the baseball team, too, and led the Buckeye conference in batting two years in a row. Ewbank was a forward on the Miami Redskins' basketball team despite standing just 5'7", and he became a three-letter man in basketball. He graduated in 1928 and went into high school coaching at Van Wert, Ohio, while working toward his 1932 master's degree at Columbia

University. He also served as head football coach for Oxford, Ohio's McGuffey High School. He coached at McGuffey for 12 years and never had a losing season. His studies initially overlapped with 14 years serving as assistant coach at Miami, from 1930–43. His high school coaching overlapped most of that time.

Ewbank joined the navy in 1943 and was assigned to the Great Lakes Naval Training Center where he was reunited with Paul Brown, who was serving as the head coach of the Great Lakes football team. Lieutenant Ewbank became head basketball coach at Great Lakes at the end of November 1945.[170]

Before becoming head coach of the Colts in 1954, he worked as backfield coach (and head basketball coach) at Brown University beginning in 1946 and as head coach at Washington University in St. Louis for two years. He joined Paul Brown for a third time, working as tackle coach with the Cleveland Browns from 1949–53. After he secured his own head coach job in January 1954, and after his first few years with Baltimore, Ewbank was named NFL Coach of the Year in 1958. Kerry J. Byrne, publisher of Cold, Hard Football Facts wrote in May 2007, "[A]s much as any figure, he proved the AFL could compete with the NFL at any level. As much as any coach, he helped propel the NFL into its modern era of pop-culture dominance."[171]

Ewbank was a 1978 inductee of the Pro Football Hall of Fame.

Tom Fears

Los Angeles Rams / United States Army Air Corps

Born: December 3, 1922, in Guadalajara, Mexico

Died: January 4, 2000, in Palm Desert, California

Position: E

Tom Fears was a big-play receiver with the Los Angeles Rams from 1948–56. He first played football at Santa Clara, took three years out for military service during World War II, and then finished up with a pair of All-America seasons at UCLA.

Although originally drafted as a defensive back, Rams coaches realized his ball-hawking skills would be best utilized on offense. It was a wise decision. Fears went on to lead the league in receptions in each of his first three NFL seasons. He improved his total each year, setting a new league record with 77 catches in 1949 and then smashing his own mark with 84 in 1950.

In a game against the Green Bay Packers that year, Tom caught a then-league record 18 passes. One week later, the Rams defeated the Chicago Bears 24–14 to win the NFL Western Division title, and Fears scored all three touchdowns on sensational pass plays of 43, 68, and 27 yards.

Although the 6'2", 216-lb. Fears did not possess unusual speed, he ran extremely precise patterns, specializing in the buttonhook route, and was absolutely fearless when catching in a crowd. Time and again Tom demonstrated his big-play abilities, but no play was more memorable than his game-winning reception in the 1951 NFL Championship Game against the Cleveland Browns. In the fourth quarter, with the score tied at 17 apiece, Fears grabbed a short 13-yard toss from quarterback Norm Van Brocklin and raced an additional 60 yards for the tie-breaking touchdown and victory. It was the Rams' first title since moving from Cleveland following the 1945 season.

While one play doesn't make a successful career, in Fears' case, such heroics were standard achievements for nine seasons with the Rams. His career marks include 400 receptions for 5,397 yards and 38 touchdowns.

[Career capsule courtesy of the Pro Football Hall of Fame]

Contrary to most standard sources, Thomas Fears was born in Guadalajara, Mexico, as the son of American mining engineer Charles Williams Fears, a native of Milford, Texas, who worked for Amparo Mining, and a Mexican mother from Rosario, Sinaloa, Carmen Valdes.[172] The Fears family lived in Etzatlan, Jalisco. Thomas' birth was registered at the American Consulate in Guadalajara in 1922, not 1923.

His obituary in the *Los Angeles Times* called him "a tough, Depression-era kid growing up in South Central L.A. As a boy he worked at a downtown L.A. wholesale flower market, earning 25 cents an hour for unloading truckloads of flowers. When asked once if he had been a tough street kid in his teens, he replied, 'I suppose so. But I didn't get in many fights. Tough kids don't have to, right?' As a Manual Arts football star, he was a Coliseum usher for 50 cents a day, while he was being recruited by schools nationwide."[173] A lengthy profile in the August 28, 1975, *Times* discusses his youth in Mexican mining towns and then a largely Japanese neighborhood in Los Angeles.

Fears had been an All-Southern California end for Manual Arts High School in Los Angeles, and then played two years of football at Santa Clara in 1941 and 1942. His college career was interrupted by the Second World War. He joined the Army Air Corps and was stationed in Colorado Springs where he became a flight instructor and also captained the Second Air Force Superbombers team in 1944 and 1945. After the war, he returned to college, this time with UCLA in 1946 and 1947. "Pro scouts are positively drooling over Fears," wrote Al Wolf in the *Los Angeles Times*.[174] He picked up a few bit parts in Hollywood films at the time and is said to be visible for six seconds as a fighter pilot in Humphrey Bogart's *Action in the North Atlantic*.[175]

He was an 11th-round draft pick of the Rams. Although he was expected to excel on defense, he was shifted to offense and immediately made his mark as the first rookie to lead the league in pass receptions (51). He led the league in that category in 1949 and 1950, as well.

After his playing career ended, Fears went into coaching, first as an assistant coach with the Rams, and then with the Packers and Falcons. He was the first head coach of the New Orleans Saints and was with the team from 1967–70. He was offensive coordinator for the Philadelphia Eagles in 1971 and 1972. Fears was inducted into the Pro Football Hall of Fame in 1970. He had a number of business interests—he owned some restaurants and some avocado acreage, and he rented out numerous condominiums.[176]

Ray Flaherty

New York Yankees, New York Giants / United States Navy
Born: September 1, 1903, in Spokane, Washington
Died: July 19, 1994, in Coeur d'Alene, Idaho
Position: E-DE, coach

Ray Flaherty put himself squarely on the spot in one of his first public utterances after being named head coach of the Boston Redskins in 1936. On hearing of the signing of Wayne Millner, Ray wired his boss, George Preston Marshall: "With that big Yankee playing end, please accept my resignation if we do not win the championship this year!"

History shows, however, that while the Redskins did not win, neither did Flaherty resign. Instead, he stayed on with the Redskins, who moved to Washington in 1937, for six more years. In all, he led the team to two NFL championships and four divisional titles.

He guided the Redskins during a period when the Chicago Bears dominated pro football. Yet, Flaherty's Redskins defeated the Bears two out of three times in NFL title showdowns. Two important football innovations are credited to Flaherty, and each played an important role in achieving his NFL championships.

In 1937, Ray introduced the behind-the-line screen pass against the Bears. Redskins quarterback Sammy Baugh threw three touchdown passes against the unprepared Chicago defenses in a 28–21 victory for the NFL championship. Later, Ray developed a 1940s version of the two-platoon system. Both units played both ways, but one unit emphasized the passing offense while the second platoon featured the ground game. This substitution plan was particularly effective in the 1942 championship year, Ray's last season in Washington.

When Ray returned to civilian life after World War II, he opted to join the New York Yankees of the newly formed All-America Football Conference, and there he won two straight divisional crowns. Ray was also an outstanding end for eight seasons, most of them with the New York Giants, before he started coaching. He closed out his coaching career in 1949 with the AAFC's Chicago Hornets. For his entire coaching career, Ray's record shows 80 wins, 37 losses, and five ties for an excellent .676 lifetime winning percentage.

[Career capsule courtesy of the Pro Football Hall of Fame]

Flaherty came off the farm his father, Thomas, ran at Rock Creek, Washington, near Spokane and went to his hometown college, Gonzaga. Thomas Flaherty was born in England of two Irish parents; his wife, Alice, was born in Wisconsin of a Canadian father and an Irish mother. Ray first played professionally in the American Football League in 1926 for the Los Angeles Wildcats and then as left end for the 1927 NFL New York Yankees team. He transitioned to the New York Giants during the 1928 season, the year he was first named All-Pro. In 1929 and 1932, he also earned All-Pro honors. His 21 receptions for 350 yards led the league in receiving in 1932. He played for the Giants through 1935 and became the head coach of the Boston Redskins in 1936.

On November 27, 1942, the 39-year-old coach was sworn into the navy with the expectation that he would be on inactive status until after the December 13 playoff game brought the football season to its end.[177] He wasn't the only Redskin to go; at least 15 players and team trainer Don Mauro had all signed up for military service, four of them on the day before the Championship Game against the Chicago Bears, who were coming off a string of 18 consecutive victories.[178] The Redskins were considered big underdogs for the game, but newly commissioned naval lieutenant Flaherty told them after their 14–6 win over the previously undefeated Bears, "Half of us will soon be in the service. Let's hit the enemy half as hard as you hit the Bears today. It won't take long to finish the war and we can get right back here for some more football fun."[179]

Bears coach (and lieutenant commander) George Halas was due to return to his duties, getting navy pilots into good physical condition at Norman Naval Air Station in Oklahoma. With the win, the navy deferred Flaherty's activation until after the December 27 All-Star Game, which was to be a benefit for United Seaman's Service. A majority of the All-Stars were scheduled to report to service after the game, as were 15 of the Redskins. He'd been 54–21–3 with the Redskins, the most successful coach in franchise history.

Flaherty's assignment took him to the Farragut Training Station in Idaho where he was elevated in rank to lieutenant commander. At the end of January 1945, he was detached from duty at Farragut to be sent overseas but was discharged before June and was surprised to find he was not welcome back in Washington, as owner George P. Marshall had other plans. Instead, he was signed in August to coach the Brooklyn Tigers beginning in 1946. Team owner Dan Topping, who also owned part of the New York Yankees baseball team, arranged to shutter the Brooklyn franchise (which had merged with Boston in 1945) and instead develop a New York Yankees football team in the AAFC that would play at Yankee Stadium.[180] Flaherty became coach of the AAFC's New York Yankees team, winning the 1946 and 1947 division titles.

Ray Flaherty was inducted into the Pro Football Hall of Fame in 1976.

Len Ford

Los Angeles Dons, Cleveland Browns, Green Bay Packers / United States Navy

Born: February 18, 1926, in Washington, D.C.
Died: March 13, 1972, in Detroit, Michigan
Position: DE-E

Len Ford joined the Los Angeles Dons of the All-America Football Conference (AAFC) in 1948 as a two-way end. He was excellent on defense and a favorite on offense with leaping one-hand grabs that netted 67 receptions in two years.

When the AAFC disbanded after the 1949 season, Ford was placed in a special draft pool. The Cleveland Browns, who earmarked him for their defensive platoon, quickly grabbed him. It wasn't long before Ford was recognized as the very best of many stars on a unit that allowed the fewest points of any NFL team for 6-of-7 years during the 1951–57 period.

Ford developed into such a devastating pass rusher that the Browns changed their whole defensive alignment to take advantage of his rare talents. By using the linebackers behind the two ends and a pair of tackles, Cleveland in effect created the first 4-3 defense. This enabled Ford to line up closer to the ball-handling action and have a better shot at enemy quarterbacks.

A serious injury almost ended Ford's career in his first NFL season. When hit by the elbow of Cardinals fullback Pat Harder, Ford suffered a broken nose, two fractured cheekbones, and several lost teeth. Len was counted out for the season but plastic surgery, a strenuous rehabilitation program, and the use of a specially designed face mask made it possible for Ford to return for the 1950 title game with the Los Angeles Rams. Len responded with one of his finest games to help Cleveland to a razor-thin 30–28 victory. Ford, who recovered 20 opponents' fumbles in nine NFL seasons, was a first- or second-team All-NFL pick seven times. He also played in four consecutive Pro Bowls. In the 1954 NFL Championship Game against Detroit, he intercepted two passes as the Browns buried the Lions, 56–10.

[Career capsule courtesy of the Pro Football Hall of Fame]

The Washington Post called Len Ford Jr., "one of the first black stars in the NFL."[181] He grew up in the Anacostia area of Washington, the son of a "skilled laborer, U.S. Government" (according to the 1930 Census) and attended

Birney Elementary School and Shaw Junior High, and he was active in sports with the Police Boys Club. He majored in automobile mechanics at Armstrong Technical High School, and he earned nine letters in sports, captaining the basketball, baseball, and football teams. Ford was All-City in all three sports. The press release for his induction in the Pro Football Hall of Fame said that he "developed an interest in football by watching the Redskins practice a short distance from his home" but noted that the Redskins weren't using any African American players at the time. He'd initially wanted to become a major league pitcher in baseball. "Had someone like Jackie Robinson come along a few years earlier to open up Major League Baseball to blacks, Ford might well have opted for a pro baseball career. Since that avenue was still blocked to blacks in 1944, Len instead turned his attention toward football." He confidently said, "I can play for any team in the country if they will only give me the chance."[182]

Ford went to college at Morgan State in February 1944 and was All-League in football that fall. After a short stint in the U.S. Navy in 1944 and 1945, he transferred to the University of Michigan where he was an All-American in 1946 and 1947. Amusingly, he'd been named to the football team at Michigan within days of arriving, and his family and friends first learned that he'd made the team when they heard him mentioned in the broadcast of the game against Army. He played for a winning Michigan team in the Rose Bowl on January 1, 1948.

After his playing career, Ford worked as a recreation director and he sold real estate. He was a 1976 enshrinee of the Pro Football Hall of Fame, honored posthumously since he had died of coronary failure at age 46, four years earlier.

Dan Fortmann

Chicago Bears / United States Navy
Born: April 11, 1916, in Pearl River, New York
Died: May 23, 1995, in Pasadena, California
Position: G-LB

Legend has it that George Halas, the owner-founder of the Chicago Bears, selected Colgate guard Danny Fortmann as his team's ninth and final pick in the 1936 NFL Draft because he liked Fortmann's name. It was the league's first draft and not nearly as sophisticated as today's version.

On the surface, it appeared at first that Halas had made a mistake. At 6' and weighing 210 lbs., Fortmann was just 19 years old when he was drafted and appeared to be too small for line play in the NFL. A Phi Beta Kappa scholar, he definitely didn't possess the usual credentials for someone who was supposed to knock down enemy ball carriers or lead the interference.

By the time his rookie season started, Danny had turned 20 but was still the youngest starter in the NFL. He had determination and talent, however, and soon he was excelling as a little man in a big man's game.

On offense, he called signals for the linemen and was a battering-ram blocker. On defense, he was a genius at diagnosing enemy plays and a deadly tackler. For seven seasons, Fortmann and Chicago's No. 1 pick in the historic 1936 draft, tackle Joe Stydahar, were a formidable combination on the left side of the powerful Bears line.

The Bears were a dominant team during Fortmann's career. From 1936–43, the Monsters of the Midway won three NFL championships and took divisional titles on two other occasions, and Fortmann was the top man at his position in pro football. He earned first- or second-team All-NFL honors all eight years of his career.

Typical of his hard work and desire to excel, Fortmann continued his education while playing for the Bears and graduated in 1940 from the University of Chicago Medical School.

[Career capsule courtesy of the Pro Football Hall of Fame]

Dr. Fortmann was inducted into the Pro Football Hall of Fame in 1965. He was at the time "one of the most highly regarded surgeons in California." This son of German immigrants Bernhard and Emma Fortmann—Bernhard was a commission merchant dealing in butter and eggs in Rockland, New York—graduated Phi Beta Kappa from Colgate in 1936 at age 20. He was selected by the Chicago Bears in the first year the NFL held a college draft— that same 1936—and Fortmann was just 19 at the time of the draft. He began his rookie year having just turned 20 as the youngest player in the league.

Not ever expecting to be drafted, he'd applied to medical school at the University of Chicago. The university was on the quarter system, and he was able to manage both sets of responsibilities, thus earning his medical degree in the midst of his 1936–43 playing career while also earning All-League honors at football for five consecutive years, 1938–42. He captained the Bears in the August 28, 1942, benefit game at Soldier Field against the College All-Stars for army and navy relief.

About a year after Coach Halas left the Bears to become a lieutenant commander in the navy, Fortmann entered the United States Navy himself in 1943, bringing an end to his playing career and interrupting his residency. After the war, he completed that residency and became the team physician of the Los Angeles Rams from 1947–63. He practiced at the St. Joseph Medical Center in Burbank from 1948 until his retirement in 1984.

Frank Gatski

Cleveland Browns / United States Army

Born: March 18, 1921, in Farmington, West Virginia

Died: November 22, 2005, in Morgantown, West Virginia

Position: C-LB

During the period the Cleveland Browns were dominating first the All-America Football Conference from 1946–49 and then the NFL in the early 1950s, Frank Gatski anchored the offensive line that powered pro football's most potent attack. He concluded his 11-year tenure with the Browns in 1956 and then was traded to the Detroit Lions for a final season in 1957.

The 6'3", 233-lb. Gatski, who played three years at Marshall University before joining the U.S. Infantry in World War II, had to survive a grueling training camp tryout to earn a spot on the 1946 Browns roster. Then he had to serve a

D-Day gets underway. Here airborne troopers march toward their C-47 prior to the night jump into Normandy. (Photo courtesy of the National World War II Museum)

two-year apprenticeship behind the veteran Mo Scarry before taking over the regular center job for good in 1948.

Strong, consistent, blessed with a great attitude and exceptional pass blocking abilities, Frank was also durable. He never missed a game or a practice in high school, college, or the pros. He was named to the All-NFL honor roll in 1951, 1952, 1953, and 1955 and played as a starting center in the 1956 Pro Bowl. Perhaps because he played at a comparatively obscure position, Gatski was relatively unsung through most of his career.

Many of his more publicized teammates on both the Browns and the Lions preceded him into the Pro Football Hall of Fame. However, Frank can claim one single distinction—he played in 11 championship games in 12 seasons, and his team won eight times.

During his tenure, the Browns won all four AAFC championships and were in the title game their first six years in the NFL. The

Browns missed the playoffs in 1956, but Frank earned his eighth championship ring in 1957 when the Lions overwhelmed his old team 59–14 in Gatski's final game in the NFL.

[Career capsule courtesy of the Pro Football Hall of Fame]

Sam Huff once wrote in *Sports Illustrated*, "I was raised in a West Virginia coal mining camp called Number Nine, near Farmington. My dad worked in the mines, and so did the dads of every kid I went to school with. In those camps you rented your house from the mining company and bought your food and clothes at company stores.... My hero, besides my dad, was Frank Gatski, who also came from Number Nine. He went to Marshall, played offensive line for the Cleveland Browns, and is in the Pro Football Hall of Fame."[183] Gatski did indeed have to overcome economic disadvantage to make it. "When I first went out for football at Farmington High School, I got one shoe size 10½; the other was a 9," he told the audience at his induction in Canton, Ohio.[184]

The son of a coal miner, Frank worked a year in the mines himself after finishing high school, but it was football that gave him a way out when coach Cam Henderson helped him get a scholarship to attend Marshall in the fall of 1940. That may have been a lifesaver. Frank lost his father to the coal mines; he was killed in a mining accident.[185]

He earned the nickname "Gunner" before he ever entered the army "for his fierce blocking that blew away defenders."[186] When it came to the army, Gatski talked of his own experience in the infantry: "I didn't play my senior season because

Marshall dropped football in 1943 because of the war. Anyway, the army reserve unit I was in was activated.... After basic training, we were sent to England and later followed the troops through Normandy and into Europe." He added quickly, lest someone think he was bragging, "I wasn't in any heavy fighting."

After his discharge in 1945, he played part of the season with Auburn University. "Marshall hadn't started back up, and I hadn't played football for two years," he explained. "I didn't want to sit around and do nothing, so I went to Auburn."[187] Sitting around wasn't his thing. In his obituary, *The New York Times* wrote, "He said that he never missed a game, or even a practice, in his two decades playing high school, college, and pro football."[188]

A teammate from Marshall, Sam Clagg, introduced him to the newly organizing Cleveland Browns in the nascent All-America Football Conference and arranged a tryout for Gatski, who made the team after a survival of the fittest competition. After his playing career was over, he worked for a couple of years as a scout for the Boston Patriots before becoming head football coach and athletic director at the state reform school for boys at Pruntytown, West Virginia. He retired in 1982, hunting and fishing and living in a part of West Virginia that was so remote that the *Houston Chronicle* said he didn't even have a telephone in his house. He learned by reading a newspaper that he had been named to the Pro Football Hall of Fame in 1985.[189] Census and other records show him born in 1921, not 1922, as is commonly listed.

Otto Graham

**Cleveland Browns / United States Navy, United States
Coast Guard**

Born: December 6, 1921, in Waukegan, Illinois
Died: December 17, 2003, in Sarasota, Florida
Position: QB-DB, coach

When Paul Brown began organizing the Cleveland Browns team to play in the new All-America Football Conference (AAFC), the first player he signed was Otto Graham, a tailback from Northwestern University. Brown-eyed Graham was the perfect quarterback for Brown's new pro team.

Graham planned to concentrate on basketball at Northwestern. He was "discovered" playing intramural football as a freshman, and although he became a fine passer in three varsity seasons, he had no experience in the T formation. Brown never wavered in his decision. "Otto has the basic requirements of a T quarterback— poise, ball-handling, and distinct qualities of leadership."

The coach was right. Once Graham joined the Browns, he not only quickly mastered the mechanics of the T, but he became the heart of a dynamic football machine. With Graham at the controls, the Browns won four straight AAFC titles and compiled an awesome 52–4–3 record.

Still, pro football "experts" theorized Otto and the Browns would get their comeuppance once they faced the NFL in 1950, but both the quarterback and the team proved more than equal to the occasion. In the Browns' 30–28 victory over the Los Angeles Rams in the 1950

NFL Championship Game, Graham threw four touchdown passes.

His finest title-game performance came four years later when he scored three touchdowns and threw for a trio of scores in a 56–10 lacing of Detroit. Graham retired after that game but responded to Paul Brown's SOS early in 1955. In the final game of his career, the NFL championship against the Los Angeles Rams, he ran for two touchdowns and passed for two more in a 38–14 victory. For the ninth time in 10 seasons, Otto was named first-team All-League quarterback.

While Graham was guiding the Browns, Cleveland played in 10 straight title games and had four AAFC and three NFL championships.

[Career capsule courtesy of the Pro Football Hall of Fame]

Otto Graham had two stretches of work serving his country—first during wartime with the navy and then, after his pro football career, as athletic director of the Coast Guard Academy.

Graham's father, Otto Sr., was a high school music teacher; both he and his wife, Donna, came from Missouri but had moved to Waukegan where they raised their three sons, Eugene, Otto, and Victor. Otto Jr. became proficient on the French horn and at playing football. Indeed, he won statewide recognition at both talents in his senior year at high school; he was a member of Waukegan's National Champion brass sextet while also being selected to Wisconsin's All-State basketball and football squads.[190]

He later became the only athlete ever to win world championships in two different sports. He did so in back-to-back seasons.

Cleveland Browns coach Paul Brown talks with four of his players who will be playing for the third time against the Los Angeles Rams in an NFL Championship Game. Left to right: end Dante Lavelli, center Frank Gatski, Brown, quarterback Otto Graham, and tackle Lou Groza. This image was taken at a snow-covered league park where the Browns were training in Cleveland, Ohio, on December 22, 1955.
(AP Photo/Julian C. Wilson)

Graham went to Northwestern University on a full basketball scholarship, but he played football there, too. He made a name for himself on the national level, playing in the College All-Star game against the world champion Washington Redskins and returning an interception of a Slingin' Sammy Baugh pass for a 97-yard touchdown. He was third in Heisman voting in 1943, and he was drafted in the first round of the 1944 NFL Draft by the Detroit Lions. In his senior year, he was also named the MVP in basketball's College All-Star game, also against a Washington team, the reigning NBL champion Washington Bears.

On July 3, 1942, Graham enrolled in the navy's V–7 program that permitted him to continue his studies after which he would become a midshipman. He became cadet regimental commander. In 1944, he entered the navy itself, and by October he was playing and earning headlines for the North Carolina Preflight Cloudbusters team.

He received his commission and his wings as a naval aviator during his two years. In March 1945 while still in the navy, he signed on with Paul Brown's newly formed Cleveland Browns of the All America Football Conference (the first player Brown signed) and committed to join the team once he was discharged.[191] "I was getting a naval cadet's pay in World War II when Paul Brown came out to the station one day and offered me a two-year contract at $7,500 per," he said. "He also offered me a $1,000 bonus and $250 a month for the duration of the war. All I asked was, 'Where do I sign?' Old navy men say I rooted for the war to last forever."[192]

After he was mustered out, but before the football season started for the Browns, Graham signed to play pro basketball with the National Basketball League's Rochester Royals that won the 1946 NBL championship three years before the NBL merged with the NBA. And then later that same year, the Browns became AAFC champions, their first of four consecutive titles. He'd thus been on championship teams both in basketball and football.

After his football career, and recommended for the post by George Steinbrenner, Graham was commissioned in 1959 as a commander in the Coast Guard and became the head football coach and athletic director at the Coast Guard Academy in New London, Connecticut. "In 1963 Commander Graham produced the first undefeated, untied team in the Academy's history. In 1966 he became coach and general manager of the Washington Redskins. He was promoted to captain in the Coast Guard Reserve at that time. He returned to the Coast Guard as athletic director in 1970 and retired in 1985 with the rank of captain."[193]

Graham was the head coach of the Washington Redskins from 1966–68. He served on the President's Council on Physical Fitness and later as honorary national chairman of the National Cancer Society.

Bud Grant

Philadelphia Eagles, Minnesota Vikings / United States Navy

Born: May 20, 1927, in Superior, Wisconsin

Position: E-DE, coach

In Bud Grant's 18 years as head coach of the Minnesota Vikings from 1967–83 and a one-year final stint in 1985, his teams compiled a .622 winning percentage (158–96–5) in regular season play. His 168 coaching triumphs, counting 10 postseason wins, place him among the all-time greatest coaches.

At the time of his retirement, only George Halas, Don Shula, Tom Landry, Curly Lambeau, Chuck Noll, Chuck Knox, and Paul Brown had engineered more wins in pro football play. Grant, who had just completed a 10-year tenure as head coach of the highly successful Winnipeg Blue Bombers of the

Canadian Football League, took over the Vikings in 1967.

In just his second season, in 1968, he launched the Vikings on a string of championship seasons rarely equaled in sports competition. From 1968–78, the Vikings won the NFL/NFC Central Division 10 times in 11 seasons, missing only in 1972. During that span, the Vikings won the 1969 NFL championship and NFC titles in 1973, 1974, and 1976.

Grant's Minnesota teams appeared in four Super Bowls. An NFC Central title in 1980 gave Grant a total of 11 championship teams. Born May 20, 1927, in Superior, Wisconsin, Grant became a nine-letterman athlete at the University of Minnesota. He was a two-time All-Big Ten end in football, a two-year baseball star, and a three-year basketball regular.

Although a first-round draft choice of the Philadelphia Eagles in 1950, Grant postponed his NFL debut to play for the Minneapolis Lakers of the NBA. He played two years with the Lakers, who won the NBA title his first year. In 1951, Bud turned to pro football with the Eagles. He played on defense as a rookie and then became the No. 2 pass receiver in the NFL with 56 catches in 1952.

[Career capsule courtesy of the Pro Football Hall of Fame]

Harold Peter Grant Jr. played three sports at Superior High School—football, basketball, and baseball. His father was a fireman who "supplemented his income by running the ball park and handling the concession stands."[194] After high school graduation in 1945, he enlisted in the U.S. Navy and like so many others—particularly athletes—was assigned to the Great Lakes Naval Station near Chicago, Illinois. Great Lakes is still the largest training station in the navy.

Great Lakes processed about 1,000,000 people during the Second World War, supplying about one-third of all navy personnel. It was particularly well-known for its baseball and football programs. Paul Brown coached the football team, and Grant had been an All-State fullback in high school. He played right end in a number of games—for instance, he made the final touchdown in the 39–0 rout of Western Michigan on October 27, 1945, and scored two touchdowns for the Bluejackets in the November 17 game against the army soldiers of the Fort Warren, Wyoming, Broncos, a 47–14 win. The December 1 game at Ross Field was the final one ever played there, ending their World War II schedule. The Bluejackets beat Notre Dame, 39–7.

Grant entered college and played for the University of Minnesota Gophers after completing his navy duty, twice being named All-Big Ten.

Of Paul Brown, Grant later admitted, "He is the coach who got me interested in football as an organized activity. I played it in high school, of course, but it was just fun and games until I joined the navy. I was 18 years old and had no thought of going to college when I graduated and they sent me to Great Lakes. That's where I came across Paul Brown." He quickly came to appreciate the discipline involved in good football and the sense of accomplishment at playing well.[195] He played basketball at Great Lakes for Coach Weeb Ewbank.

Grant was named to the Canadian Football League Hall of Fame in 1983. Eleven years later, in 1994, he was inducted into the Pro Football Hall of Fame. There he joined Ewbank (a 1978 enshrinee), Brown (1967), and his Great Lakes teammate Marion Motley (1968).

Lou Groza

Cleveland Browns / United States Army
Born: January 25, 1924, in Martins Ferry, Ohio
Died: November 29, 2000, in Middleburg Heights, Ohio
Position: T-C-DT-K

When Lou Groza retired after the 1967 season, it was truly the end of an unforgettable era for the Cleveland Browns. The last remaining member of the original 1946 Browns team, the big offensive tackle and place-kicking artist played 21 years, more than any other pro player up to that time.

Many fans remember Groza primarily as a kicker, the first specialist who became so proficient that the Browns started thinking of making field goals, instead of touchdowns, when the going was rough and time was running short. Lou, who was one of pro football's finest offensive tackles, particularly in the middle years of his long tenure, preferred to think of himself first as a tackle who just happened to be the Browns' field-goal kicker because he "had the talent."

Groza was named first- or second-team All-League eight times during his career. In 1954, he was *The Sporting News'* NFL Player of the Year. Nine times he was named to the Pro Bowl. Six times he was a starting tackle. In 1946, 33-man rosters prevented any team from carrying a specialist, but Groza was almost that, doing all of the kicking and playing on the scrimmage line only occasionally.

Late in his second season, Lou made "the first team," and he didn't give up that cherished status until 1959. He sat out the entire 1960 season with a back injury and then returned in 1961 at the age of 37 for seven more campaigns as a kicker only.

In 21 years, "The Toe," as he quickly became known, tallied 1,608 points and for years ranked as the all-time top scorer. His most dramatic kick came in the 1950 NFL Championship Game when his 16-yard field goal in the final seconds gave the Browns a 30–28 victory over the Los Angeles Rams.

[Career capsule courtesy of the Pro Football Hall of Fame]

Groza's parents, John and Mary, were both immigrants from Hungary, with Mary arriving in 1898 and John in 1903. John worked as a coal miner. They had four sons. Louis, the third of the four, was born at Martins Ferry, Ohio. It was an athletically oriented town, and one of Lou's uncles, Julius Koteles, had played semipro football. His older brother, Frank, had excelled at place kicking in high school. While Lou was still in eighth grade, Frank taught him the fundamentals. Lou made the freshman team at high school and won a game for Martins Ferry with a field goal in his junior year. When not kicking, he worked as a tackle and was named All-State at tackle in his senior year. He not only captained the football team but the baseball and basketball teams, as well.[196]

He never played college football, except for freshman year on scholarship at Ohio State in 1941, after which he was drafted into the United States Army. He served as a surgeon technician, and was involved in the invasion of Leyte in The Philippines.

And he was a real specialist. As Red Smith of *The New York Times* wrote at one point in the early part of Lou's 21-year career (1946–59, 1961–67), "Groza is a football player, in the strictest sense. He goes through life without ever touching the ball with his hands. He could play with boxing gloves. He could play without arms. He plays football strictly by foot, and by foot he outscores practically everybody else…. In six seasons of professional play, he has never carried the ball from scrimmage, never run back a punt or a kickoff, never thrown a pass, although once in his life he did catch a pass and make a touchdown. Employing his big paws only that one time, he has scored 306 points—the equivalent of 44 touchdowns."[197]

Groza was one of the original Cleveland Browns. While at O.S.U., he had played his freshman year for Coach Paul Brown. And as Brown began to put together that first team, he reached out while Groza was still in the service. Groza was on Okinawa helping treat wounded soldiers when he received Brown's letter via military mail that said he wanted Lou to join the team after his discharge. "I signed it. I didn't know if I'd get back," he said.[198] Groza asked him to send some footballs for Lou to kick around. Groza took advantage of his time and those footballs. "In Okinawa and Hawaii and The Philippines, he set up goal posts and practiced field goals whenever the army gave him a spare hour."[199] Those makeshift crossbars on Leyte and Okinawa paid off. "Upon being discharged in early 1946, Lou went to Cleveland, a place he would never leave."[200]

Groza did complete his degree at Ohio State during the off-seasons and graduated with a degree in business administration. He later owned a couple of dry cleaning establishments and became an insurance salesman after working for a couple of years as an expeditor at a Cadillac plant in Cleveland.[201]

He was named to the Pro Football Hall of Fame in 1974.

George Halas

Chicago Bears / United States Navy
Born: February 2, 1895, in Chicago, Illinois
Died: October 31, 1983, in Chicago, Illinois
Position: E, coach

George Halas was associated with the Chicago Bears and the NFL from their inception in 1920 until his death in 1983. He represented the Bears, originally known as the Decatur Staleys, at the NFL's organizational meeting held in Canton, Ohio.

During his incredible career, he filled the shoes of owner, manager, player, and promoter, and he was an influential leader among the NFL's ownership. It was, however, as a coach that he excelled and was best known. Although Halas coached his Bears for 40 seasons, he stepped away from the coaching ranks three

Members of the armed forces seemed to predominate, as owners in the National Football League or their representatives got together at their annual meeting in Washington on December 14, 1942. The league voted to continue football during the war if possible. Left to right are: Lt. Comdr. George Halas, USNR, former Chicago Bears coach; Lt. Comdr. George M. Glenn, executive officer of naval pre-flight school at Norman, Oklahoma; Ray Flaherty, Redskins coach who was going into the navy as a lieutenant; and Lt. Dan Topping, U.S. Marines, owner of the Brooklyn Dodgers. (AP Photo)

times—1930–32, 1942–45 (to serve in the military), and 1956–57.

Each time a rejuvenated Halas returned to the sideline to coach and win an NFL championship. Twice, in 1934 and 1942, Halas' teams had undefeated regular season records.

His 318 regular season wins and 324 total victories were long-standing NFL records until broken by Don Shula in 1993.

His Chicago Bears teams won six NFL titles, the first coming in 1921 after the Staleys moved to Chicago. George's Bears won three other divisional titles and finished second 15 times. Only six of Halas' 40 teams finished below the .500 mark.

As a coach, Halas was first in many ways— the first to hold daily practice sessions, to utilize films of opponents' games for study, to schedule a barnstorming tour, and to have his team's games broadcast on radio. With his players, George maintained tight control. Disobedience and insubordination were not tolerated. Along with Ralph Jones, his coach from 1930–32, and consultant Clark Shaughnessy, Halas perfected the T-formation attack with the man in motion. It was this destructive force that propelled the Bears to their stunning 73–0 NFL title win over Washington in the 1940 NFL Championship Game and sent every other league team scurrying to copy the Halas system.

[Career capsule courtesy of the Pro Football Hall of Fame]

George Halas served in the United States Navy both in World War I and World War II. His parents, Frank and Barbara Halas, had both came to the United States from the Pilsen area of Bohemia, arriving in 1878 and 1867, respectively. Frank worked as a grocer and also as a tailor.[202] The couple had four sons, and George was the youngest.

Born in the waning years of the nineteenth century, Halas worked hard at school and got himself into the University of Illinois at Urbana-Champaign where he played football (under Bob Zuppke), baseball, and basketball. He was all but finished when the U.S. went to war and— lacking just one semester for graduation—he

enlisted in the United States Navy. In honor of his service, he was later granted his degree. Many members of the Hall of Fame either instructed at the Great Lakes Naval Training Station in North Chicago or passed through the program there during the Second World War; Halas was assigned there in World War I and worked to organize service teams both in football and basketball. Ensign Halas was the MVP in the 1919 Rose Bowl as the Great Lakes team beat the U.S. Marine Corps team from Mare Island, 17–0.

After his navy service, Halas played major league baseball briefly as an outfielder, appearing in 22 games for the 1919 New York Yankees. He hit .091 with two singles in 22 at-bats and without either an RBI or a run scored. A serious hip injury curtailed his career. The following year, he played football for the Chicago Bears (or, as they were known in 1920, their first season, the Decatur Staleys). Halas played right end—and coached the team— and he played with the Bears for nine seasons through 1928. Then he coached all the way through the 1967 season—save for the years 1943–45 when he re-enlisted in naval aviation.

When Halas announced in October 1942 that he had applied to join the navy, he was in line to become the sixth owner of an NFL team to join the military in World War II. Fred Levy and Dan Reeves, co-owners of the Cleveland Rams, both joined the Army Air Corps. Dan Topping of the Brooklyn Dodgers joined the Marines. Alexis Thompson of the Philadelphia Eagles was in the army. Wellington Mara of the Giants signed up for the navy.[203]

The Bears had won the NFL championship in 1940 and 1941. "During World War II, Halas spent three years in the South Pacific with the navy, mainly organizing R&R and entertainment for weary troops. While he was away the Bears, coached by Luke Johnson and Hunk Anderson, won another title in 1943. Halas returned at the end of the 1945 season and led his club to a final championship of the decade in 1946."[204] He began his second stint in the service as a lieutenant commander and served under Admiral Chester Nimitz in the Seventh Fleet working on welfare and recreation programs for 2,000,000 officers and men during his 20 months in the Pacific. He was awarded the Bronze Star by Adm. Nimitz.[205]

Halas actually served a third hitch—for one day—when he was re-enlisted in order to be promoted to captain.[206] After his service, he also received numerous citations for his peacetime contributions to navy welfare programs.[207]

Clarke Hinkle

Green Bay Packers / United States Coast Guard

Born: April 10, 1909, in Toronto, Ohio

Died: November 9, 1988, in Steubenville, Ohio

Position: FB-LB-HB-DB

Clarke Hinkle was a hard-nosed player who loved to challenge his opponents. He was a pile-driving runner, but he could turn the corner as well as hit the middle. Hinkle could catch the ball out of the backfield and was also the Packers' punter and place-kicker.

As brilliant as he was on offense, Hinkle may have been even deadlier on defense. Backing up the Packers line, he was a vicious tackler against the run and terrific on pass defense—Hinkle proudly claimed he let only one receiver get behind him during his decade of pro football.

During his 10 years with the Green Bay Packers, Hinkle was named first- or second-team All-League each year. He is perhaps best remembered for his head-to-head duels with another great fullback-linebacker—Bronko Nagurski of the Chicago Bears. Nagurski was the prototype power runner of the 1930s, but the rugged Hinkle, 30 lbs. lighter, was determined to hold his own with anyone on an NFL gridiron. Hinkle's creed was "get to the Bronk before he gets to me," a tactic he used to perfection one day in 1934. Trapped on the sideline by Nagurski, Clarke escaped his tackle by driving directly into and over him. The Bears' superstar was helped from the field with a broken nose and a fractured rib.

Hinkle, with his burning desire to compete and willingness to play in spite of painful injuries, always enjoyed the lasting respect of friend and foe alike. Nagurski himself turned out to be Clarke's staunchest press agent and even presented him for induction into the Pro Football Hall of Fame in 1964.

"They said I was hard to tackle, but here was a guy who didn't have too much trouble," Nagurski said of his Green Bay foe. When he retired after the 1941 season, Clarke Hinkle was the leading rusher in NFL history.

[Career capsule courtesy of the Pro Football Hall of Fame]

Clarke Hinkle's father, Charles, worked as a forger in a steel mill. He and his wife, Lillian, raised three sons. Clarke was the youngest. The eldest, Gordon, played major league baseball and was a catcher for the 1934 Boston Red Sox. Gordon's last game was at Fenway Park on September 30 against the Philadelphia Athletics. Clarke Hinkle played at Fenway Park a few weeks later, kicking a 42-yard field goal on November 4 to help the Packers to a 10–0 win over the Boston Redskins who used Fenway for their home field.

Clarke was a student at Bucknell, and he was named the outstanding player of the 1932 East-West Shrine Game held in San Francisco. His football career ran from 1932–41, all for the Green Bay Packers.

During World War II, Hinkle joined the United States Coast Guard and went through training, becoming a lieutenant (jg). In September 1942, he joined the football coaching staff at the Coast Guard Academy at New London, Connecticut. Hinkle worked under his superior officer, Gene Tunney, and made his way up to lieutenant commander in the Coast Guard, ultimately becoming commander of a destroyer escort. Though he was 32 at the time, he went into the Coast Guard after the 1941 season, ending his ten-year NFL career, and he went out on top, leading the league both in rushing attempts and field goals in 1941.

After his Coast Guard service, he pursued other paths, doing some coaching and even working for a while as a sports director for a broadcast station in Ohio. He had hoped to be interviewed for the head coach slot at Green Bay, but was not, and worked to try to hand a franchise in the United Football League. He turned to selling industrial supplies for the American Lubricants Company of Dayton.

Hinkle was honored with induction into the Pro Football Hall of Fame in 1964.

Elroy Hirsch

Chicago Rockets, Los Angeles Rams / United States Marine Corps
Born: June 17, 1923, in Wausau, Wisconsin
Died: January 28, 2004, in Madison, Wisconsin
Position: E-HB-DE

In a crucial game late in the 1951 NFL season, the Los Angeles Rams found themselves trailing the Chicago Bears 14–0 and deep in a hole on their own 9-yard line. Quarterback Bob Waterfield faked a handoff, stepped back a few paces, and threw far downfield. Elroy Hirsch took off at the snap and was running full-throttle at midfield. Waterfield's pass was over his head, but Elroy gathered in the ball by his fingertips and raced for a 91-yard touchdown. The Rams went on to an important 42–17 victory. It was a patented "Elroy Hirsch special," a sizzling shocker that was repeated 16 other times that year.

Besides his 91-yard bomb, Elroy had numerous other long-yardage touchdowns as he established a new league record at the time of 1,495 yards receiving. It wasn't just the number of long-gainers but the way he did the job that set Hirsch apart from all others. "Crazylegs" had a unique running style that made him famous. When running downfield, his muscular legs seemed to gyrate in six different directions at once.

Pro football success did not come easily to Hirsch, even though he was an All-American halfback at both Wisconsin and Michigan before he joined the Chicago Rockets of the new All-America Football Conference (AAFC) in 1946. Hirsch described his three seasons in Chicago as "frightful."

When his AAFC contract expired, Hirsch happily joined the Rams. After a year spent mostly on the bench in 1949, Elroy was shifted to end. Not familiar with playing end, he initially struggled. However, his hard work eventually paid off, and a year later he became a primary contributor to the Rams' impressive march to the NFL title. Many observers insisted Crazylegs was the best end ever, but Hirsch modestly downgraded his own case. "I'm just a busted-down, retreaded halfback who happened to get lucky."

He played for the 1942 Badgers as a triple-threat halfback. That club was 8–1–1, including a 17–7 win over No. 1-ranked Ohio State (Hirsch threw one touchdown pass and accounted for more than 200 yards of total offense against the Buckeyes) and finished the season ranked third nationally by the Associated Press. Hirsch rushed for 786 yards, passed for 226 yards, and had 390 yards receiving on the way to third-team All-America honors from *Look* magazine.

[Career capsule courtesy of the Pro Football Hall of Fame]

Both of Hirsch's parents were Wisconsinites. His father, Otto, was a foreman in an iron works whose parents had both come from Germany; Mayme was his mother, and her father was

from Sweden and her mother was from Norway. Elroy was a high school football and basketball star for Wausau High School—so good that he was inducted into the National High School Sports Hall of Fame in 1988. Hirsch entered the University of Wisconsin at Madison in the fall of 1941. He couldn't have known it at the time, but he was about to be transferred from one Big Ten school to another. He played for the nationally third-ranked 1942 Badgers.[208] He hadn't been at Wisconsin on an athletic scholarship, but rather, "in the fashion of the time, Wausau businessmen 'sponsored' him, paying his tuition, room, and board. For spending money, Hirsch worked as a radio station receptionist and in a dairy."[209]

One of his first games for Wisconsin was against the Great Lakes Naval Training Station at Soldier Field in Chicago; about half the 60,000 in attendance paid their admission. Service personnel were admitted free. One of the men playing for Great Lakes was Steve Belichick, father of New England Patriots head coach Bill Belichick. Hirsch scored the first touchdown after scampering 61 yards. Wisconsin won, 13–7. Sportswriter Francis Powers wrote in the *Chicago Daily News* game account that Hirsch "ran like a demented duck. His crazy legs were gyrating in six different directions all at the same time." It's probably fortunate that "Crazylegs" became his nickname rather than "Demented Duck."

Hirsch signed up for the Marine Corps after the season, enrolling in the V-12 program that transferred him to the erstwhile rival University of Michigan where the program was based. Nearly a dozen of his teammates joined him, approaching a wholesale transfer of Badgers to Wolverines. Michigan became Big Ten co-champion in 1943 and was ranked third. When the two teams met up, headlines acknowledged the oddity: "Michigan Downs Wisconsin, 27–0, With Help of 10 Former Badgers."[210] Hirsch, Michigan's leading scorer heading into the game, was out with an arm injury, but he did come off the bench "to convert after Michigan's final score."[211]

Hirsch earned four letters in varsity sports—football, basketball, baseball, and track and field. On one remarkable day in the spring of 1944, he broad-jumped 22'5" for third place in the Big Ten outdoor track championships at Illinois and then drove to Bloomington, Indiana, where he threw a four-hitter for the Michigan baseball team.

On June 8, 1944, Hirsch was transferred to Parris Island with 23 other Michigan athletes. By 1945, he was playing football for Marine Corps Air Station El Toro. In October 1945, he signed to play for 1946 with the Chicago Rockets—one of 14 of the El Toro Marines signed by the team.[212] He was the MVP of the 1946 *Chicago Tribune* College Football All-Star Game. He had been on track to take part in the invasion of Japan, but four of his Wisconsin teammates from 1942 were not as fortunate. Marines Dave Schreiner and Bob Baumann fought on Okinawa—Schreiner was killed and Baumann was wounded. Mark Hoskins was shot down over Hungary and survived a Nazi prison camp. Paul Hirsbrunner lost a finger and suffered other wounds during fighting on Saipan.

In 1953, Hirsch was the subject (and starred with Lloyd Nolan) in the Republic Pictures film, *Crazylegs*. When he left football, it was to go into radio and television as a broadcaster. His film career wasn't over, though. He had parts in *Unchained*, a 1955 prison movie, and *Zero Hour*, an airliner disaster film two years later.

Hirsch later returned to football to work as an assistant to Rams president Dan Reeves. Hirsch was inducted into the Pro Football Hall of Fame in 1968 and he finally returned to the University of Wisconsin in 1969, serving as Director of Athletics from 1969–87.

Frank "Bruiser" Kinard

Brooklyn Dodgers, New York Yankees / United States Navy
Born: October 23, 1914, in Pelahatchie, Mississippi
Died: September 7, 1985, in Jackson, Mississippi
Position: T

Today it is unlikely that a pro football lineman named "Bruiser" would weigh a mere 195 lbs. However, in 1938, when Hall of Fame tackle Frank "Bruiser" Kinard began his pro career, that's exactly how much he weighed. Even in his final season, and still playing the big man's position of tackle, he tipped the scales at just 216 lbs. But his play was as his name implies—bruising.

Kinard earned a host of accolades during the nine years he played pro football, including All-NFL recognition from 1938–44 as a member of the Brooklyn Dodgers/Tigers team. In 1946, after a one-year hiatus due to military service, Bruiser returned to pro football as a member of the New York Yankees of the newly formed All-America Football Conference. That same year, he became the first pro football player to earn All-League honors in both leagues.

Kinard was a two-time All-American at the University of Mississippi when he was drafted in the third round by the Dodgers in 1938. It was a year abounding with outstanding rookies but only two, Kinard and Byron "Whizzer" White, made the All-NFL team. Kinard had a burning desire to play, and he played for keeps.

He had outstanding speed for a tackle, and his admirers, of whom there were many, insist that he would have been outstanding at any position. On offensive plays, and particularly the Dodgers' patented "shovel pass," Kinard was the key blocker. On defense, he was a crushing tackler.

The Bruiser was tough and durable even in the rough-and-tumble competition of pro football. He rarely needed a rest and near-60-minute performances were the rule rather than the exception. He missed just one game due to injury, and even then it was doctor's orders, not a lack of willingness to play, that kept Bruiser on the sideline.

[Career capsule courtesy of the Pro Football Hall of Fame]

Frank Kinard had two brothers who played in the NFL, too. George Kinard was a couple of years younger, born in October 1916. He was a guard who played 11 games for the Brooklyn Dodgers in 1941 and seven games in 1942. After the war George played 11 games for the New York Yankees—all three years on the same team as Frank. Billy Kinard was quite a lot

Brooklyn Dodgers tackle Frank "Bruiser" Kinard (44) poses for a photo in 1938, location unknown. (AP Photo/Pro Football Hall of Fame)

younger, born in December 1933. Billy played for the Browns in 1956, the Packers in '57 and '58, and the Buffalo Bills in 1960.[213] All three brothers played college ball at the University of Mississippi (Ole Miss). Frank's first year in the pros was 1938, for Brooklyn. They were the sons of Mississippi farmer Mason H. Kinard and his wife, Pearl. Sometime between 1920 and 1930, Mason Kinard left farming to become the proprietor of a lunch room.

Another brother, Henry, played at Ole Miss but never turned pro. In 1939, Frank ran for the Mississippi State Senate.

Frank Kinard's last game before joining the service—he was co-captain of the Brooklyn Tigers (they'd changed from Dodgers in 1944)—was played against the Philadelphia Eagles on December 3, 1944. The season couldn't have been more discouraging; Brooklyn's record on the year was 0–10–0 after the 34–0 shutout. During the team's last four games, they had been shut out three times and had suffered a cumulative 64–6 point differential. Nonetheless, he'd done his job and was rewarded with his third All-Pro selection as second team tackle. He joined the navy on April 17, 1945, and served until March 17, 1946.

In the fall of 1945, Kinard played left tackle on Bill Reinhart's Fleet City Bluejackets team (Navy Bluejackets) of S.F., an integrated team which was the flip side of the Brooklyn team— it was undefeated. Back Buddy Young was the star of the final game against the El Toro Marines, scoring three touchdowns on runs of 20, 88, and 94 yards, and the *Pittsburgh Courier*, a leading "Negro newspaper" noted that most of Young's teammates were white and many came from the South—but "harmony was one of the greatest assets the Fleet City team had" and perhaps that would augur well for Jackie Robinson, the paper suggested. Young, Kinard, and Harry Hopp were said to be the three most popular players on the team.[214]

On February 10, Young led an All-Service team against the Pacific Coast Professional Football League's Hollywood Bears. Joining the All-Service team were Elroy Hirsch from the El Toro Marines and both Kinard brothers, George on guard and Frank at tackle. The All-Stars won, 14–13. Only Frank played in the game.

After the war was over and he was back in civilian life, Frank clearly hadn't lost a step. He was named All-Pro for a fourth time in 1946, his first season back.

Kinard was instrumental in bringing Buddy Young to the Yankees in 1947 and keeping him from signing with the Chicago Rockets; both Kinard and Nate Johnson were among Young's teammates in the navy and urged him to come to New York.[215]

Kinard worked as an assistant football coach at Ole Miss for 23 years. Early in 1971, an Associated Press story reported that brother Billy had been named head coach at Ole Miss, where all three brothers had played football as students. Frank Kinard was named athletic director on the same day. In the preceding semester, Billy's predecessor had suffered a mild heart attack, and it was Frank who served as the interim coach and "guided the Rebels through the last half of the season and took them to the Gator Bowl where they lost to Auburn."[216] His son, Frank Jr., also played at Ole Miss. He signed with the San Diego Chargers but was cut before making the team.[217]

Frank was enshrined in the Pro Football Hall of Fame in 1971.

In September 1973, both Billy and Frank were relieved of their positions as the university sought a new direction.

Frank died at the Veterans Administration Medical Center in Jackson on September 7, 1985.

Tom Landry

**New York Yankees, New York Giants, Dallas Cowboys /
United States Army Air Corps**

Born: September 11, 1924, in Mission, Texas

Died: February 12, 2000, in Dallas, Texas

Position: DB-HB-QB, coach

Tom Landry was selected as the head coach when the Dallas Cowboys started their first NFL season in 1960. He remained in that capacity for 29 seasons until new ownership opted for new field leadership after the 1988 campaign.

At the time of Landry's retirement, only George Halas, who coached the Chicago Bears for 40 years, surpassed his 29-year tenure with one club. It took Landry a few years to develop his young club into contender status, but once he did, the Cowboys enjoyed exceptional success for more than two decades.

The Cowboys under Landry had their first winning season and their first NFL Eastern Conference championship in 1966. They didn't fall below .500 again until 1986. During that period, Landry's teams had 20 straight winning seasons, 13 divisional championships, five NFC titles, and victories in Super Bowls VI and XII. The Cowboys also played in Super Bowls V, X, and XIII.

Landry's regular season career record is 250–162–6, and his record counting playoffs is 270–178–6. Only Halas and Don Shula top his 270 career wins. Landry gained a reputation as a great technical innovator, as well as an inspirational leader. He introduced the "flex defense" and "multiple offense" in the 1960s.

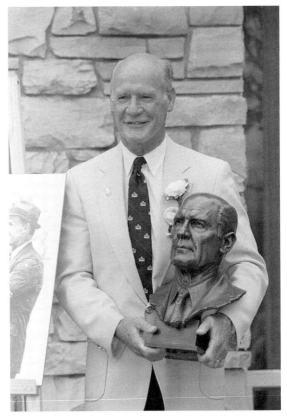

Tom Landry is inducted into the Pro Football Hall of Fame in Canton, Ohio, on Saturday, August 4, 1990. Landry coached the Cowboys for 29 seasons, appearing in a record five Super Bowls and winning two championships. (AP Photo/Jeff Glidden)

In the 1970s, he restructured the "shotgun" or "spread" offense, and in the 1980s, he embraced and helped develop the "situation substitution" concept of handling his player talent.

Landry was an excellent player in the pros. He was a defensive back, punter, and kick returner with the 1949 New York Yankees in the All-America Football Conference and with the New York Giants in the NFL between 1950 and

1955. He recorded 32 career interceptions and had a 40.9-yard punting average. He served the Giants as a player-coach in 1954 and 1955 before becoming a full-time defensive coach from 1956 to 1959.

[Career capsule courtesy of the Pro Football Hall of Fame]

Tom's father, Ray Landry, was the proprietor of a garage in Mission, Texas. Tom's mother, Ruth, gave birth to four children, and Tom was born second. In his senior year at Mission High, Tom led his team to an undefeated season. He was an All-Conference player with the University of Texas with the Longhorns— but that came after the war. He'd entered U.T. in 1942 but completed just one semester. The United States was at war, so joined the United States Army Air Corps. "Priorities," he said. "It was all a matter of priorities."[218]

Landry trained at Sheppard Field and had pre-flight at Kelly Field. He earned his wings at Lubbock Army Airfield (later Reese Air Force Base) in 1944 and was commissioned as a second lieutenant. He was assigned to fly B-17 Flying Fortress bombers as a pilot with the 860th Bomb Squadron of the 493rd Bombardment Group known as Helton's Hellcats stationed at the Royal Air Force base at Debach, England.

He minimized the dangers involved, speaking about as succinctly as possible. "I went over to England about six months before the war ended [November 1944]. I was a pilot in a B-17. We flew about 30 missions." Asked if his plane had ever been hit, he replied, "We'd get a few holes once in a while, but that was fairly normal."[219]

A 1986 exhibition game in England against the Chicago Bears enabled Skip Myslenski of the *Chicago Tribune* to get a little more out of Landry. "After you've been out of the war as long as I have, you don't think about war. You don't want to think about war.... I was so young. I hadn't been out of my hometown, but suddenly, here I was, dropping bombs on Germany.... I guess I was too young. I guess I didn't really know what fear was. And we were lucky we came over when we did. You didn't have much of the Luftwaffe then. Our biggest problem was the weather and landing in the fog in England."

He had every reason to be afraid. Tom's older brother, Robert, had been flying a B-17—ferrying it to England—when his plane went down somewhere near Iceland in the North Atlantic. It was some weeks later that he was declared dead.[220] The loss of his brother motivated Tom to join the Army Air Corps and to fly B-17s himself.

There was a time he crash-landed in England. He brought his aircraft in wheels-up, giving it a better chance to grind to a halt before hitting the trees around the camouflaged airstrip. He still hit the trees. "We sheared off both wings, and a tree was all the way up to the instrument panels by the time we stopped. But the whole crew walked away. I guess, to some extent, it was luck. We skipped right through and stopped right in time."[221] On another mission, his B-17 was over occupied Belgium and the engines cut out. The pilot gave the orders to bail out, but then, Landry recalled, "When I got out of my seat, I noticed that the fuel mixture was bad. So I just shoved the lever forward, and all four engines cut on again. The ack-ack planes were on our tail all the way to England, but they never got us. Again, I think it was a little bit of luck."[222]

What did he learn about the crash landing? "Your instruments are better than you are."[223]

After discharge as a first lieutenant in November 1945, Landry returned to the Longhorns and helped lead his team to back-to-back bowl game wins in 1948 (Sugar Bowl, over Alabama) and 1949 (Orange Bowl, over Georgia.) He turned pro and played for the New York Yankees and New York Giants, a first-team All-Pro in 1954. He worked as a player-coach for a couple of seasons, and then transitioned into becoming defensive backfield coach for the Giants until he was offered the job as head coach of the Cowboys.

He coached his final season in 1988. Tom Landry was enshrined in the Pro Football Hall of Fame in 1990.

Dante Lavelli

Cleveland Browns / United States Army

Born: February 23, 1923, in Hudson, Ohio

Died: January 20, 2009, in Cleveland, Ohio

Position: E-DE

Dante Lavelli, a quarterback in high school and a halfback as an Ohio State freshman, was switched to end by Buckeyes coach Paul Brown before his sophomore season. Yet, when Dante joined the newly formed Cleveland Browns in 1946, injuries and a long stint in the U.S. Army had limited his college experience to just three games.

To make the Browns, he had to beat out four more experienced and highly regarded candidates. But Dante not only prevailed, he led the league in receptions and won All-AAFC honors in his rookie season. He also caught the winning touchdown pass in the first AAFC championship game between the Browns and the New York Yankees.

There were many more high moments in Lavelli's career. He was All-AAFC again in 1947, and when the Browns moved to the NFL, he was All-League twice more and a starter in three of the first five Pro Bowl games. In the 1950 NFL Championship Game, Dante caught 11 passes—then a record—and scored two touchdowns as the Browns edged the Los Angeles Rams, 30–28.

Lavelli was a favorite target of the Browns' great quarterback, Otto Graham. All but 20 of Dante's 386 career receptions came while Otto was at the Cleveland helm. Like any great pass-catch team, the two spent long hours learning the other's every habit. Dante was a dedicated pattern-runner but once there was a hint things weren't going right, he preferred to take off down the field and yell for the ball. More than once, his penetrating voice provided a homing signal for Graham, and the combination clicked for a long touchdown. His great hands set Lavelli apart from all other receivers. When Dante went up for a pass in a crowd, you could be sure "Gluefingers" would come down with the ball.

[Career capsule courtesy of the Pro Football Hall of Fame]

One of the original Browns, Lavelli had joined a team that seemingly couldn't lose.

Cleveland won the AAFC championship in every one of the team's four years (1946–49) before it merged into the NFL and then won the league title for three seasons (1950, 1954, 1955). His parents, Angelo and Amelia, were immigrants from Italy who had come to America in 1902 and 1918, respectively. They must have been pleased to see him settle into Hudson High School as a quarterback who led the team to three straight state championships. Angelo Lavelli worked as an iron worker and by 1940 had his own shop specializing in ornamental iron work.

A multi-sport athlete, he might have played baseball instead; right after high school in 1941, Detroit Tigers scout Wish Egan tried to talk Dante into going with the Tigers as an infielder. He said Egan had taken him to the game that ended Joe DiMaggio's 56-game hitting streak and he was set to sign until he learned they wanted to farm out to the Carolinas.[224] Instead, Coach Paul Brown recruited him to play at Ohio State, where his college years were interrupted by World War II. He'd played just three games before getting injured against U.S.C.[225] He joined the U.S. Army in April 1943—about five months after his sister, Edith, joined the WACs at Fort Hayes in Columbus.

There was no football for Lavelli during his 2½ years in the army. Dante saw combat overseas, serving with the infantry in the Battle of the Bulge, and he was involved in fighting in Belgium, France, and Germany.[226] "We had a real tough go of it in the Battle of the Bulge," he said later. He was discharged on December 10, 1945.

"After the war, I was broke. Although I had two seasons of college eligibility remaining in football, I thought about pro baseball again. I planned to try to catch on again somewhere." Instead, Paul Brown—now recruiting for Cleveland's new pro team—reached out to him once more and brought him on board.[227] He did eventually get his degree, attending school part time even after turning pro.[228]

He retired in April 1956 but then showed up again three months later, ready to play for one final season. After his ultimate retirement, Lavelli worked as a scout for the Browns beginning in 1963, and he also ran a furniture business. He was one of the founders of the NFL's Alumni Association.[229]

Cousin Tony Lavelli was an All-American at Yale in basketball and later played as a forward in the NBA for the Boston Celtics (1949–50) and the New York Knicks (1950–51). Later, Tony forged a career as a songwriter and noted accordionist.

Dante Lavelli was named to the Pro Football Hall of Fame in 1975.

Marv Levy

Kansas City Chiefs, Buffalo Bills / United States Army Air Corps

Born: August 3, 1925, in Chicago, Illinois

Position: coach

In 1986, when Marv Levy was chosen to direct the fortunes of the Buffalo Bills, he brought with him more than 30 years of coaching experience. A graduate of Coe College, Levy began his pro coaching career in 1969 as kicking

Buffalo Bills Hall of Fame head coach Marv Levy during Super Bowl XXVIII, a 30–13 loss to the Dallas Cowboys on January 30, 1994, at the Georgia Dome in Atlanta, Georgia. (AP Photo/ NFL Photos/Ben Liebenberg)

teams coach for the Philadelphia Eagles before joining George Allen's staff as a special teams coach for the Los Angeles Rams in 1970.

He followed Allen to Washington in 1971, where he served as the Redskins special teams coach for two seasons. Levy then became the head coach of the Montreal Alouettes of the Canadian Football League for five seasons. After two CFL Grey Cup championships, Levy returned to the NFL in 1978 as head coach of the Kansas City Chiefs.

When he joined the Chiefs, the team was coming off a 2–12 season. Under his leadership, the team steadily improved, posting a 4–12 record in 1978, followed by a 7–9 season in 1979, 8–8 in 1980, and 9–7 in 1981. He left the Chiefs after a disappointing 3–6 in the strike-shortened 1982 season.

Midway through the 1986 season, following a two-year hiatus from coaching and one season as the head coach of the Chicago Blitz of the United States Football League, Levy returned to the NFL as head coach of the Buffalo Bills. He finished the season with a 2–5 record. In 1987, his first full season with the Bills, the team returned to respectability with a 7–8 record and were in the playoff hunt throughout most of the season.

The following season the team posted a 12–4 record and won the first of six AFC Eastern Division titles. With his high-powered "no-huddle" offense, Levy, who has a master's degree in English History from Harvard, went on to set a new standard for NFL coaches as he led his AFC championship team to four consecutive Super Bowl appearances.

From 1988–97, the Bills were first in the AFC in winning percentage and second only to the San Francisco 49ers in the NFL. Levy, the winningest coach in Bills' history, recorded a 112–70 regular season record and was 11–8 in the playoffs during his 11½ seasons with the Bills. He was named NFL Coach of the Year in 1988 and AFC Coach of the Year in 1988, 1993, and 1995.

[Career capsule courtesy of the Pro Football Hall of Fame]

The day after he graduated from Chicago's South Shore High School in 1943, Marv Levy enlisted in the United States Army Air Corps. He was very much following in the footsteps of his father, Sam Levy, who had come to the United States from his native England at age six—and had left home at age 16, lying about his age to sign up for the Marines during World War I. Sam Levy fought in the June 1918 Battle of Belleau Wood. Some 1,811 Americans were killed in the battle, out of a total of 9,777 casualties—one of whom was Sam Levy, who was wounded and gassed. He was awarded a Purple Heart. Sam worked as a "proprietor of fruits and vegetables" in Chicago, according to the 1930 Census. Sam's wife, Ida, was a 1910 immigrant from Russia. Sam had come to the U.S. in 1914; his parents were Polish.

Levy recalled the day he joined the army: "I remember my teammates at South Shore High School, and I remember with pride those 21 classmates whom I joined when we all enlisted in the Army Air Corps on the day after we graduated high school in 1943. Nineteen of us came home after the war. The other three remain forever young."[230]

In his first year of eligibility, Marv Levy was enshrined in the Pro Football Hall of Fame in 2001. In his speech, he remembered his father. "The greatest run I ever knew of was by my father, who during World War I, along with his comrades from the storied 4th Marine Brigade, raced several hundred yards into withering machine gun fire, across the wheat fields at Belleau Wood in France. Their valor on that June day in 1918 succeeded in halting the

German army advance just 25 miles from Paris.

"He was my hero even before I was born. One day many years later, I telephoned my father to tell him I was leaving Harvard Law School and that I wanted to be a football coach.

"Thirty seconds of painful silence followed, and then the old Marine said simply, 'Be a good one!'"

Levy served Stateside during the war, working as a meteorologist because of his nearsightedness.[231] While recuperating in an Army hospital from an injury, Marv rediscovered his love of English literature and after being discharged from duty in 1946, he enrolled at Coe College, from which he graduated Phi Beta Kappa.

Joe Horrigan wrote that Levy was once asked about a particular game and whether or not it was a "must win." Levy's response: "No. World War II was a must win."[232]

Sid Luckman

Chicago Bears / United States Merchant Marine
Born: November 21, 1916, in Brooklyn, New York
Died: July 5, 1998, in Aventura, Florida
Position: QB-HB-DB

Sid Luckman, in his 12 seasons with the Chicago Bears, became the first successful T-formation quarterback. One game in Luckman's second season, the 1940 NFL title game, saw the Bears defeat the Washington Redskins 73–0 and showcased the explosive possibilities of the T attack. Almost immediately, many other pro teams began to adopt the new formation.

Bears owner and coach, George Halas, first presented Sid with a Bears T-formation playbook when he was practicing for the College All-Star game in 1939. Astonished and somewhat alarmed by the complexities of the new system, Sid was not an instant success. He fumbled frequently, had trouble with handoffs, and in general flunked his first T test. Halas shifted Luckman to halfback for a while before making another effort that paid dividends on the second try.

Not all teams had the success with the T-formation that the Bears enjoyed. Chicago won four NFL championships, just missed a fifth, and Luckman was a major reason for the success. The crafty quarterback was named first- or second-team All-League from 1940 through 1948 and won the NFL's Most Valuable Player honors in 1943.

Sid may be best remembered for the 73–0 victory over the Redskins. Because the Bears went ahead so early in the game, he actually had to pass only six times, completing four passes for 102 yards and a touchdown.

Apparently, just the threat of Luckman and the T was enough to keep defenses off balance. Luckman had many more outstanding games but two, both in 1943, stand out above the rest. On November 14—Sid Luckman Day at the Polo Grounds—he passed for a record-tying seven touchdowns in a 56–7 win over the New York Giants. Later that year, in the Championship Game against the Redskins, he threw for 276 yards and five touchdowns in a 41–21 triumph.

[Career capsule courtesy of the Pro Football Hall of Fame]

Sid Luckman of the Chicago Bears, 1942. (AP Photo)

Sid's parents, Meyer and Ethel, both came to America from Russia and spoke Yiddish as their native language. Meyer became a truck driver, and Sid worked in the family trucking business during the off-seasons early in his football career. He was highly sought after as a high school player at Erasmus High in Brooklyn and reportedly turned down as many as 40 college offers to play for Columbia—one of the few schools that did not offer athletic scholarships. "As soon as I met [coach] Lou Little, I knew I wanted to play for him." Luckman worked his way through college.[233]

Luckman's playing record shows continuous time with the Chicago Bears from 1939 through 1950, but during the 1943 season he signed up to join the United States Maritime Service—the Merchant Marine, America's "Forgotten Service." His volunteering to join resulted in one incident in November 1943 just before the game on the 21st against the Washington Redskins. An anonymous person made several telephone calls on November 17, spreading word that Luckman had played his last game and that he had orders to report to New York. The call may have been a practical joke or a ruse by gamblers to gain an edge in the betting on the upcoming game. Bears management checked it out and were reassured that Ensign Luckman—who had been sworn in on November 15—could finish out the season and then report to the maritime service school at Brooklyn's Sheepshead Bay for training.[234] Luckman led the Bears to the NFL title and was awarded the Carr Memorial Trophy as the league's Most Valuable Player. He reported for duty on January 3, 1944, and it was understood at the time that Sid would not play in 1944.[235] His cousin, Robert, was serving in an anti-aircraft unit with the Marines in the South Pacific.[236]

He was given a 10-day leave to play with the Bears against the College All-Stars in August '44, and a month later he signed to play for the Bears under an arrangement approved by his commanding officer at Sheepshead Bay whereby he could use his regular weekend leaves to play until his sea duty orders arrived.[237] He did ship out on a tanker in very early October.[238] He returned safely and got over his sea legs in time to play his first game of the regular season (he'd missed the first four games on the schedule) on October 29, throwing one touchdown pass and orchestrating three others as the Bears beat the Cleveland Rams, 28–21.

There were one or two articles printed that suggested that he was proving that daily drills weren't necessary for success at football, but of course that's likely true only for people with exceptional talent and a team able to adapt. He did miss those first four games, and another, only appearing in seven Bears games and starting none of them. But he still made the All-Pro team that year, and the 11 passes he threw for touchdowns helped earn him second ranking in league passer rating. He was first in passing yards per game.

In early 1945, he shipped out yet again to England and France.[239] But by the time the 1945 season began, the war was over and Luckman was able to return to a regular schedule. He was voted into the Pro Football Hall of Fame in 1965.

Wellington Mara

New York Giants / United States Navy

Born: August 14, 1916, in New York, New York

Died: October 25, 2005, in Rye, New York

Position: team owner

Wellington Mara's family owned the New York Giants, and his entire life was dedicated to the NFL.

The son of the late Timothy J. Mara, who was the Giants' founder and a charter member of the Pro Football Hall of Fame, Wellington

During the attack on Pearl Harbor, the USS California *was hit by a Japanese torpedo and here lists to port.* (Photo courtesy of the National World War II Museum)

Mara joined the Giants in 1937 as a part-time assistant to the president. He began full-time work in 1938 as club secretary and later served as vice president before becoming the team's president after the death of his older brother, Jack, in 1965.

Mara's extensive experience in organization, player personnel, trading, and drafting helped produce 16 NFL/NFC divisional titles (two came after his induction into the Hall of Fame) and four NFL championships during

his 68-season tenure that began with his graduation from Fordham in 1937. Even as a college student, Mara made a significant contribution when he drafted and signed future Hall of Famer Tuffy Leemans in 1936. Mara-engineered trades that brought such stars as Y.A. Tittle, Andy Robustelli, and Del Shofner to the team were combined with his drafting of Frank Gifford and Roosevelt Brown, both future Hall of Famers, to mold the Giants into a dominant team in the late 1950s and early 1960s.

From 1956–63, the Giants won six divisional championships and the 1956 NFL title. In more recent years, Mara's Giants won Super Bowls XXI and XXV. Mara, who was born August 14, 1916, in New York City, was respected as one of the most knowledgeable executives in pro football.

From 1984 to 2005, he served as president of the National Football Conference. He had served on the Hall of Fame and realignment committees, as co-chairman of the long-range planning committee, and on the NFL Management Council's executive committee. In previous years, he was a member of the constitution, pro-college relations, and commissioner search committees.

[Career capsule courtesy of the Pro Football Hall of Fame]

Named after the Duke of Wellington, it's not surprising he himself bore the nickname "Duke." *The New York Times* called Wellington Mara "the patriarch of the NFL" and noted that he'd been around football since its leather-helmet days, serving as a nine-year-old ball boy for the 1925 Giants, the team owned by his father, when the team played its very first game.[240] Wellington went to Loyola High School in Manhattan and then to Fordham University, and he began working fulltime for the Giants after his graduation in 1937.

His father, Timothy Mara, had been a "salesman of books" according to the United States census in 1920. By 1930 he was the owner of the Giants. He was a charter member of the Pro Football Hall of Fame in 1963; Wellington Mara was inducted in 1997. The Maras became

the first father and son to be accorded pro football's highest honor. Well Mara met his future wife, Ann Mumm, in church. A couple of years after Well's death, Ann was profiled in a Mike Lupica piece in the *New York Daily News* and she remembered an old friend of his from Fordham, who worked for a while as an assistant coach for the Giants, as seen in the light of more recent lionization. "All this Lombardi around you, no matter where you turned, and all I could think was, *Vinny used to sleep on our couch!* We didn't know at the time we had an immortal sleeping on the hideaway."[241]

Tim Mara had come from more humble beginnings himself. His son once described himself as "an Irishman named Wellington whose father was a bookmaker."[242] Or, as presented to the census enumerator, a "salesman of books." Tim Mara was in turn the son of an immigrant Irish widow on the Lower East Side. He left school at 13 to run bets for bookmakers (as Joe Horrigan of the Pro Football Hall of Fame has pointed out, this was a legal profession at the time) and served as a "beard" for noted New York gambler Chicago O'Brien.[243] Tim Mara bought his interest in the Giants for the princely sum of $500.

Less than five weeks after Pearl Harbor, Mara was able to present the Navy Relief Society with a check from receipts of the Bears/Giants All-Pro game on January 5 at the Polo Grounds. And it wasn't long before he signed up for the navy himself. Within four months, he had entered and graduated—on May 13—from the naval reserve midshipman's school and was commissioned as an ensign.[244] In his three years of service in the navy, beginning as Ensign Mara in 1942, he served aboard aircraft carriers.[245] He became a lieutenant commander by the time he was discharged.

Wellington Mara was honored by remarks made in Congress by U.S. Rep. William Pascrell (D-NJ) after his passing: "During World War II, Mara briefly left his beloved Giants and joined the navy. He served in the Atlantic and the Pacific Theaters. He earned the rank of lieutenant commander. He returned to the Giants following the war."[246] His service in the navy was the only interruption in all his many years devoted to the New York Giants from his childhood to his death.

Gino Marchetti

Dallas Texans, Baltimore Colts / United States Army

Born: January 2, 1927, in Smithers, West Virginia

Position: DE-T-DT

Ernest Marchetti had the somewhat normal parental fear that his son, Gino, might get hurt playing football. The protective parent advised him to "stay out of the other boys' way so that they won't hurt you."

Although every quarterback who played in the NFL in the 1950s and early '60s wishes Gino had listened to his father, the 6'4", 244-lb. end chose the gridiron.

Gino wound up instead as one of the game's greatest and most feared defensive ends to play pro football. Marchetti, who played 13 brilliant seasons with the Baltimore Colts after one season with the Dallas Texans, was a talented all-around defender. He was adept at stopping

the running play but was best known for his vicious pass rushing techniques.

He was known for clean but very hard play, and he was a particular terror on third-down, obvious-passing situations. When opponents double-teamed him, or sometimes even triple-teamed him, that tactic only served to make the rest of the Colts rush line more effective.

Ironically, Gino suffered the most serious injury of his career—a broken leg—in the Colts' famous 1958 overtime Championship Game victory when his parents were watching him on television for the first time. Gino made a key stop that ended a New York Giants drive and gave the Colts a chance to tie the game in regulation time. Many thought this serious injury would prematurely end Gino's shining career.

As it turned out, all it really did was prevent him from playing in his fifth consecutive Pro Bowl. Gino had already been selected for the postseason classic, but he had to miss the game, the only gap in a string of 11 Pro Bowl appearances from 1955 through 1965, a record at the time. During the same period, Gino was named All-NFL nine times, 1956–64.

[Career capsule courtesy of the Pro Football Hall of Fame]

By October 1944, just a few months after graduating high school, Gino was serving in Europe with Company I, 273rd Regiment of the 69th Infantry Division. "When you enlist," he wrote in a piece for ESPN, "you don't realize how tough it's going to be. You don't realize that you're going to see some of your friends go down." He fought in the Battle of the Bulge. "When we first went over there, we were at the Siegfried Line, a defensive perimeter the German forces built along their border. I was in a machine gun section…. One day we were taking this town, and I was kind of looking around, until a buddy said, 'You better pull your head down.' I said, 'They're not close, they're cracking.' And he said, 'That's when they're close. When they zing, they're far away.' We took the town, but my friend didn't come back.

The next time I saw him, he was in a barn—which is where, after any combat, you'd kind of move the soldiers that didn't quite make it.

"But the army taught you to be strong. It taught you obedience. My training taught me about leadership.

"In football, when you're a leader of a team, when a team is having problems, people look for you to do something about it—and you do

Hall of Fame defensive end Gino Marchetti (89) of the Baltimore Colts with Hall of Fame head coach and fellow veteran Don Shula during the NFL West squad's 34–14 victory over the NFL East squad in the 1965 NFL Pro Bowl on January 10, 1965, at the Los Angeles Memorial Coliseum. (AP Photo/NFL Photos/Ben Liebenberg)

GINO MARCHETTI ON WWII

"I was in the 69th Division, a machine gunner on a Browning .30 cal, which fired 250 bullets a minute; the belt that fed it had some 500 bullets on it. Our gun had a five-man crew. A machine gunner, the belt man who fed the gun, and the rest were ammo carriers. God, they ran like Hell back and forth all the time.

"I fought in the Bulge, but I didn't really get in to the rough stuff as the guys in mid-December did. We were coming up in January and it seemed like we were just cleaning up, but it wasn't as easy as that sounds. Good men died doing that. God, was it cold!

"The German soldier was a well-trained soldier, and they did everything they possibly could against us. Trouble with them was—they were not like American soldiers. American soldiers could think and act for themselves in the field. In other words, if your lieutenant goes down, somebody in the ranks will jump in and lead you. If a German officer or a German NCO went down, there would be confusion and they would just stop.

"We went on into Germany through the Siegfried Line and then on to the Elbe River. My unit was the first to link up with the Russians at the Elbe. We were really going on toward to Berlin.

"When the war ended [in Europe], it wasn't all that important to us. You may think it is strange to say that, but the first week after the war was over we were ordered to pack up and prepare to go over to Japan and fight in the South Pacific."

—*Gino Marchetti,*
as told to Todd Anton on January 19, 2013

something about it by taking action, by just attacking the problem.… The army prepared me for that. I am so appreciative of everything the army did for me. It taught me discipline. It gave me direction. When I got home, the GI Bill gave me the opportunity to go the University of San Francisco and play football, and I ended up playing professional football for 14 years.

"Had I not gone into the army, none of that would have happened."[247] At the time of the 1930 Census, Gino's father, Marino Marchetti, was a road laborer who had come to America in 1920 from Italy; his mother, Josephine, had come the following year. In 1940, Josephine worked as a sewing machine operator in a furniture factory, apparently widowed.

After football, Marchetti launched Gino's Hamburgers (with former Colts teammates Alan Ameche and Joe Campanella), which spread to more than 300 outlets.[248]

Marchetti was a 1972 inductee into the Pro Football Hall of Fame.

George McAfee

Chicago Bears / United States Navy
Born: March 13, 1918, in Corbin, Kentucky
Died: March 4, 2009, in Snellville, North Carolina
Position: HB-DB

Halfback George McAfee at 6' and 178-lbs. did not have the physique of the average pro football player, even in the 1940s when he starred for

*Men of the 75th Infantry Division march along a snow-filled wooded path to reinforce the front during the Battle of the Bulge in December 1944. (*Photo courtesy of the National World War II Museum)

the Chicago Bears. Even Bears founder and Coach George Halas, who signed the Duke All-American after he was the No. 2 overall pick in the 1940 draft, wondered if he had made the right decision.

From the start, however, McAfee established himself as an explosive game breaker, the kind of back that was a threat to go all the way every time he had the ball. In his first exhibition game, George returned a punt 75 yards for a touchdown with just seconds remaining to defeat the Brooklyn Dodgers. In the 1940 regular season opener, he ran back a kickoff 93

yards and threw a touchdown pass in a 41–10 Bears victory over arch-rival Green Bay.

In the historic 73–0 rout of the Washington Redskins in the 1940 NFL Championship Game, McAfee contributed a 35-yard interception return for a touchdown. Eventually, to be compared to McAfee by Halas was considered the highest compliment.

McAfee's pro career was not particularly long—limited to just eight years before and after World War II service. While his career statistics are not overwhelming, they do show that he did just about everything a player could

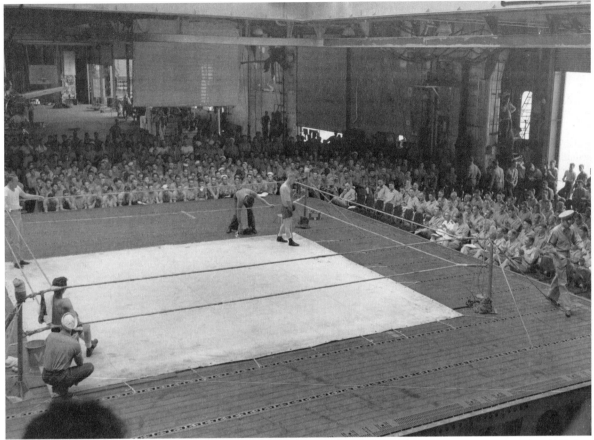

Another example of physical training continuing aboard ship, shown here on the USS Enterprise. (Photo courtesy of the National World War II Museum)

do with a football. He was a breakaway runner, a dangerous pass receiver, and one of history's best kick-return specialists as evidenced by his record-breaking 12.78-yard average on 112 punt returns.

George also played defense and recorded 25 interceptions during his career. George, whether running wide or up the middle, either as a pass receiver or a decoy, was known as "One-Play McAfee," and he was a constant headache to the opposition. McAfee also pioneered the use of low-cut shoes, which he believed improved his speed and elusiveness.

[Career capsule courtesy of the Pro Football Hall of Fame]

Rather than be subject to the draft, McAfee signed up for the navy not long after the 1941 Bears won the NFL championship. "I didn't want

Lt. Commander Edward W. Mahan (left), athletic officer at the naval air station in Jacksonville, Florida, and three-time All-American back at Harvard, watches George McAfee, former Duke backfield ace and later of the Chicago Bears, limber up with a practice bomb on May 8, 1942. A patrol bomber is seen in the background. (AP Photo/U.S. Navy)

to be drafted," George McAfee said. "I enlisted as did so many other young men at the time. I felt like it was my duty and the thing to do." His father, Clarence, worked as a secretary at the YMCA. Clarence and his wife, Lydia, had nine children; six of them were older than George.

McAfee had played on December 7, then won playoff games against the Packers (33–14) on December 14 and the Giants (37–9) on December 21. His 12 touchdowns led the NFL in 1941. His last game before donning a United States Navy uniform was when the Bears beat a team of NFL All-Stars 35–24 in a January 4, 1942, benefit at the Polo Grounds for the Naval Relief Fund. McAfee—the "wonder boy from Duke, scored one touchdown and further cemented his standing as "perhaps the most remarkable runner in football's annals."[249] McAfee enlisted in the navy on March 14 and served for most of the next four seasons.

Initially working as a physical education instructor under Gene Tunney, he played some football for the Jacksonville Naval Air Station team and then ran a similar program at the University of Michigan. In 1944, Ensign McAfee was assigned to run the V-12 physical training program at the University of Virginia and later the air base at Charlotte.

He was on a ship heading across the Pacific when the atomic bombs were dropped in early August 1945, ending the war.[250] McAfee was able to return in time to rejoin the Bears and get into three games in 1945, scoring three touchdowns in his first game back on November 25. He played five more seasons through 1950, helping the Bears to another title in 1946. Red Grange called him, "the most dangerous man with the football in the game."[251]

After football, he spent 31 years in the oil distribution business.

McAfee's grandson, Paul Stouffer, joined the navy himself and became recognized as a Tillman Scholar by the Pat Tillman Foundation in its Class of 2011. A part of Stouffer's profile on the foundation website, says, "Particularly influential was the story of Paul's maternal grandfather, George McAfee, who voluntarily joined the navy in 1942 at the peak of his NFL career after leading the league in rushing and winning two consecutive league championships. Hearing of this as a young man in a society overly focused on celebrities and material riches, Paul gravitated toward that patriotic spirit of service and devotion to causes greater than self."[252]

Reid Forgrave, writing for FoxSportsArizona, said, "Like Tillman, Stouffer's grandfather played in the NFL. George McAfee won two NFL championships as a speedy halfback for the Chicago Bears. And McAfee, like Tillman, was at the height of his NFL stardom when something terrible happened to his country: Japanese planes bombed Pearl Harbor. America joined the war against fascism, and McAfee decided there was more to fight for than just winning football games."[253]

The Pro Football Hall of Fame added McAfee to its list of inductees in 1966.

Johnny "Blood" McNally

Milwaukee Badgers, Duluth Eskimos, Pottsville Maroons, Green Bay Packers, Pittsburgh Pirates / United States Army Air Corps

Born: November 27, 1903, in New Richmond, Wisconsin
Died: November 28, 1985, in Palm Springs, California
Position: TB-HB-WB-BB-DB, coach

John McNally still had a year of college eligibility remaining when he decided to take a shot at pro football. To protect his eligibility, he needed an alias, a common practice in the 1920s. He and a friend passed a theater where the movie *Blood and Sand* was playing. Suddenly, McNally exclaimed to his friend,

Quarterback Johnny "Blood" McNally of the Green Bay Packers on November 14, 1935. (AP Photo)

"That's it. You be Sand. I'll be Blood." So "Johnny Blood" it was, through 14 seasons in the NFL.

At 6'1" and 188 lbs., Blood was unbelievably fast, a superb running back, and possibly the finest receiver in the NFL at that time. He could throw passes and punt with the best.

On defense he was a ball hawk and a deadly tackler. He played on five NFL teams in 14 seasons, but his best years came with the Green Bay Packers, with whom he was a major contributor to four championship teams in 1929, 1930, 1931, and 1936.

His off-the-field antics, however, constantly drew attention away from his exceptional playing skills. A talented youngster, Johnny graduated from high school at 14, an age when he was small and immature and could not compete athletically.

At Saint John's University, however, he began to grow and his natural athletic talents burst into full bloom. He was the basketball team captain and a letter winner in three other sports—football, baseball, and track—in his junior year.

Some say McNally clung so fiercely to boyhood that he never grew up, at least not until after his pro football days that ended when he was coach with the 1939 Pittsburgh Pirates. He didn't marry until he was in his mid-forties, and it was his wife, Marguerite, who described him most accurately. "'Even when Johnny does the expected," she said, "he does it in an unexpected way."

[Career capsule courtesy of the Pro Football Hall of Fame]

Johnny McNally played in the NFL from 1925 through 1938, working as player-coach in 1937 and 1938 and then as coach for the first three games of 1939. He'd grown up in Wisconsin, the son of John and Mary McNally—both Wisconsin natives themselves, but all four of Johnny's grandparents were born in Ireland. John worked as the manager in a milling company. His family later became part owners of the *Minneapolis Tribune*.[254]

McNally attended Saint John's University in Minnesota where he earned letters in football, baseball, and track and was captain of the basketball team. He began playing pro football for the 1925 Milwaukee Badgers under the assumed name of Johnny Blood in order to preserve his college eligibility.

After 14 years in pro football, he moved on to other things, but when World War II broke out, he tried repeatedly to get into the service. He finally entered the United States Army Air Corps in June 1942 and went through basic training at Fort Sheridan. He was sent overseas in March 1943 to work as a staff sergeant in the Signal Corps as a cryptographer in the China-Burma-India Theater, serving a year in India, three months in Burma, and 16 months in China.[255] And in February 1944, Arthur Daley of *The New York Times* quoted Curly Lambeau as saying he'd received a letter from Johnny Blood. "And where do you suppose he is? He's in India with the ground crew of a bombing squadron. In his letter he wrote, 'My immediate ambition is to learn how to operate a bomber and go for a ride some day.' Over in India they probably don't know what that means. But I do. From long experience I'm fully aware of how his mind works. Mark this well. Some day Johnny is going to borrow a bomber and bomb Tokyo all by himself. It would be typical of him. Years ago, when he was playing football for me on the Packers, he used to say, 'I want a sensational life and a sensational finish.'"[256]

The stories about McNally are legendary. He'd first gone to Notre Dame but only lasted a few weeks before he "borrowed" a motorcycle and wound up in Nebraska. In April 1945, Daley was forwarded a letter from him, from China, talking a bit about his time in Tibet and organizing a basketball team to play six games in Chungking.[257] The legend sometimes trumped reality. Daley once wrote in the *Times* that the first day Johnny worked as head coach of Pittsburgh, he'd returned the first kick on the first play of the season and run for exactly 100 yards for a touchdown.[258] He did indeed return a kickoff in that September 5, 1937, game for a long distance, but it was in the fourth quarter and it was for 92 yards.

This was the same Johnny Blood of whom even the Packers Hall of Fame website says "jumped across a narrow ledge six stories from the ground to gain access to a Los Angeles hotel room, fled a towel fight with Lavvie Dilweg by climbing on top of a fast-moving train and crawling across car tops until he reached the engine, and was rescued by teammates while he was hanging on a ship's stern flagpole on a Packers trip to Hawaii."[259]

After the war, McNally finally returned to St. John's to finish up his degree in economics and is said to have written a textbook on the Malthusian theory of economics.[260] He also turned to coaching football at St. John's from 1950–52 and even once ran (unsuccessfully) for sheriff in Wisconsin's St. Croix county. One of the most colorful players in the game, he didn't disappoint when asked what his principal reform would be were he to be elected to the post. His two-word answer, "Honest wrestling."[261]

Johnny "Blood" McNally was elected as one of the 17 charter members of the Pro Football Hall of Fame in 1963.

Wayne Millner

Boston Redskins, Washington Redskins / United States Navy

Born: January 31, 1913, in Boston, Massachusetts

Died: November 19, 1976, in Arlington, Virginia

Position: E-DE

When Wayne Millner joined the Boston Redskins in 1936, the news so excited the team's new coach, Ray Flaherty, that he promised to resign if "we don't win the championship with that big Yankee playing end."

The Redskins did win the Eastern Division title that year, and Millner, a star on both offense and defense, was a major contributor. During the next few seasons the Redskins, who moved to Washington in 1937, won two more divisional titles and one NFL championship, and Wayne became the favorite target of the brilliant passer, Sammy Baugh.

The two combined for many a blockbuster play during some of the Redskins' finest seasons. In the 1937 championship showdown with the Chicago Bears, Baugh threw touchdown passes of 55 and 78 yards to Millner, then used him as a decoy when he threw the game's winning pass to Ed Justice. Wayne wound up the day with nine catches for 160 yards.

Millner was among the last of the outstanding two-way ends. When he wasn't catching Baugh's passes, he was blocking for Sammy. He was competitive, determined, and known for his sure hands.

A "money player," he was always at his best when the stakes were the highest and the pressure was on full force. Millner, who entered the navy after the 1941 season, wound up his seven-year career in 1945 with 124 receptions for 1,578 yards and 12 touchdowns, which were the best ever for a Redskin up to that time.

Had he played for any other pro team, he might have captured more headlines, but the Redskins had Baugh, who gained most of the publicity. There may also have been one other factor—so often did Millner deliver under pressure, the press, fans, and even his own coaches came to take his clutch performances for granted.

[Career capsule courtesy of the Pro Football Hall of Fame]

The son of Mainers Charles and Lillian Millner, Wayne was raised in the Boston area where his father worked as a foreman in a leather company in 1920 but was apparently reduced to becoming a belt maker in a leather shop by 1930.

A college star and two-time All-American for Notre Dame, Wayne Millner put in six seasons for the Redskins before World War II broke out, and then he lost three prime years while serving in the United States Navy. He was on four divisional championship teams for the Redskins—in 1936, 1937, 1940, and after returning from those three seasons in the navy as a player/coach in 1945. In 1942, the navy had him work as the end coach of the V-12 football team at his alma mater, Notre Dame. He could only read about 1942's championship Redskins team. His 1943 and 1944 were spent aboard ships.[262] As a lieutenant, he was in charge of a gun crew on a merchant ship.[263]

After his playing career ended, he worked as a Redskins assistant coach from 1946–48 and worked briefly with the Chicago Hornets and Baltimore Colts. In 1951, he served a year as head coach of the Philadelphia Eagles, taking over in midseason for the ailing Bo McMillin. He was able to find additional work as the public relations director for a Ford dealer in Falls Church, Virginia. Millner returned to the Redskins and worked for 13 years as a scout for the team. He was scouting for the team at the time of his death.

Millner was named to the Pro Football Hall of Fame in 1968.

Marion Motley

Cleveland Browns, Pittsburgh Steelers / United States Navy

Born: June 5, 1920, in Leesburg, Georgia
Died: June 27, 1999, in Cleveland, Ohio
Position: FB-LB

In 1946, one year before Jackie Robinson signed with baseball's Brooklyn Dodgers, four players smashed pro football's race barrier. The trailblazers were Marion Motley and Bill Willis, who signed with the Cleveland Browns of the new All-America Football Conference, and Kenny Washington and Woody Strode, who signed with the National Football League's Los Angeles Rams. Injuries ended Washington's career after three seasons, while Strode played just the 1946 season.

Motley and Willis, however, went on to have Hall of Fame careers. Motley joined the Browns as a 26-year-old rookie. Browns coach Paul Brown was already familiar with Motley, having coached the big fullback at the Great Lakes

Naval Training Station during World War II.

He also knew Motley from his high school playing days in Canton, Ohio. Paul coached football at neighboring Massillon High School. Motley, with his powerful running on Cleveland's famed trap and draw series, made the Browns' ground game go, but he is also credited with vital contributions to the Cleveland passing attack because his blocking for quarterback Otto Graham was exceptional.

At 6'1" and 232 lbs., Motley was an imposing figure. The constant threat of him hurtling up the middle kept defenses honest. Marion was the AAFC's all-time rushing leader and also led the NFL in ground gaining in his initial season in the league in 1950. That year, in a game against the Pittsburgh Steelers, the powerful Motley rushed for 188 yards on just 11 carries for a 17.1 yards-per-carry average.

In his nine professional seasons, he amassed 4,720 yards on 828 carries for an amazing 5.7 yards-per-carry average. When he retired, Marion held a host of Browns club records. In addition to be elected to the Hall of Fame in 1968, Motley was named in 1994 to the NFL's 75th Anniversary All-Time Team.

[Career capsule courtesy of the Pro Football Hall of Fame]

Much of the credit for Marion Motley becoming one of the first two black players in the AAFC can be ascribed to Cleveland Browns coach Paul Brown. The coach first saw Motley play during Marion's high school days; his father found work in a local foundry and had moved the family to Canton when Marion was three. Brown was coaching Washington High School

Cleveland Browns Hall of Fame fullback Marion Motley (76) runs upfield during an AAFC game against the Buffalo Bills in Buffalo, New York, on November 2, 1947. The Browns defeated the Bills 28–7. (AP Photo/Pro Football Hall of Fame)

in Massillon, Ohio, and Motley was playing for Canton's McKinley High. In three years, the only three games McKinley lost were all won by Massillon—but Brown had a chance to see Motley in action. Motley attended South Carolina State and the University of Nevada at Reno, but he returned to Ohio to work in a Republic Steel mill.

He enlisted in the navy and played under Lt. (jg) Brown for the first time; Brown was the coach at the Great Lakes Naval Training Station. Later in the war, the *Chicago Tribune* declared that Motley "appears to be the best player on the 1945 Great Lakes football team."[264] The final win for the powerhouse Bluejackets team, before the program was shut down in the postwar era, was a 39–7 shellacking of Notre Dame on December 1.

As Andy Piascik wrote, "With the end of the war and with pro football's apartheid racial policies firmly in place, it seems as though Motley's football playing was at a premature end."[265] Change was in the air, however, as Piascik went on to explain. "Tens of thousands of people of color had fought for the United States against the racism of the Third Reich for four years and were all the more determined to resist the continuation of such policies domestically." Indeed, the Los Angeles Coliseum informed the Los Angeles Rams that they could not play in the facility unless the team integrated.

Paul Brown had been named the first coach of the new AAFC Cleveland Browns team, and he was GM and part owner of the team. Motley was brought on board—though perhaps initially just to be a roommate for African American back Bill Willis—and the Browns became AAFC champions in 1946. Indeed, Motley played for the Browns through 1953, and his team finished first in its division for every one of those years. From 1946–49, the team won four consecutive AAFC championships and won the NFL championship in 1950, its first year in the league. The Browns were division champs in 1951, '52, and '53, as well.

At the time of his 1968 induction into the Pro Football Hall of Fame, Motley was working in Cleveland as a placement officer for the Neighborhood Youth Corps. In 1982, he said, "I felt proud to be a black American. Just as Martin Luther King had a dream, let me tell you, without a dream, you can't accomplish anything."[266] After Motley's passing, Paul Brown's son said, "My dad always felt Marion was the greatest back he ever had."[267]

Ernie Nevers

Duluth Eskimos, Chicago Cardinals / United States Marine Corps
Born: June 11, 1903, in Willow River, Minnesota
Died: May 3, 1976, in San Rafael, California
Position: FB

Of all the records in the history of the NFL, the one that has survived the longest was set on November 28, 1929, when Chicago Cardinals fullback Ernie Nevers scored every one of his team's points (six touchdowns and four extra point conversions) in a 40–6 rout of the Chicago Bears.

The next week, the former Stanford University star again scored all his team's points for a two-game total of 59 solo points. At Stanford, Nevers had gained gridiron fame when he courageously led the Indians against Notre Dame in the 1925 Rose Bowl.

Playing on what amounted to two very sore ankles, both of which were broken earlier in the season, Nevers rushed for 114 yards as Stanford lost to the superior Irish, 27–10. Stanford coach Pop Warner once called him "the football player without a fault" and compared him favorably to another player he coached, the legendary Jim Thorpe. Like Thorpe, when it came to football, Nevers could do everything exceptionally well, including run, pass, kick, call signals, and play rock-hard defense.

After he finished his Stanford career, Nevers signed pro basketball and baseball contracts and was destined to throw two home run pitches to Babe Ruth during Ruth's historic 60–home run season in 1927. But pro football also beckoned.

In 1926, Nevers turned pro with the NFL's Duluth Eskimos.

The Eskimos were a traveling team. That season the team crossed the country, playing 29 games, 28 of them on the road, against league and non-league opponents. Nevers reportedly played all but 29 of a possible 1,740 minutes.

Injuries forced Ernie to sit out the entire 1928 season, but he returned as the do-everything man for the Cardinals in 1929. In both 1930 and 1931, he was also the playing coach of the Cardinals. Nevers earned All-NFL honors in each of his five pro seasons.

[Career capsule courtesy of the Pro Football Hall of Fame]

Ernie Nevers was the son of Canadian natives George and Marie Nevers. He played high school football in Superior, Wisconsin (and part of his senior year in Santa Rosa, California), and then he became a two-time all-American fullback at Stanford, winning 11 letters in college athletics. Baseball was his other main sport, and he pitched three seasons for the American League's St. Louis Browns from 1926–28. He was 6–12 with a 4.74 earned run average and notably gave up homers No. 8 and No. 41 in Babe Ruth's 60-homer season in 1927. "What ruined me in baseball was a football injury. I hurt my back, and this caused me to alter my pitching motion. I hurt my arm and that was the end."[268]

Lou Gehrig hit a pair of homers off him, too, and Nevers in the NFL was like an iron man himself in playing those 29 football games in 1926. Yet he never played for a team that won more than six games in a season—not even as a

coach—but his play was such that he was one of 17 charter members of the Pro Football Hall of Fame when it was founded in 1963.

It was quite an era. As Art Rosenbaum wrote of the Eskimos in the *San Francisco Chronicle*, "The team had no trainer as such. Players carried their own uniforms and duffle bags." And quotes Nevers on the minutes he'd missed in the one game: "I was told by the doctor to stay out because of an appendicitis attack, but we were trailing Milwaukee 6–0 in the mud, and I had to do something. I threw a 60-yard pass to Joe Rooney in the end zone. It's in the record book."[269]

Although 38 years old when the United States was plunged into World War II, he joined the Marines where the former captain of the Eskimos became a captain of Leathernecks—but he worked his way up to the rank, reportedly enlisting as a private despite being offered the opportunity to work Stateside in the navy's physical training program.

He was an ordnance officer in the 134th Torpedo Bomber Squadron on duty in the South Pacific in the Solomon Islands and worked on a torpedo boat squad for some months during the battle for Bougainville.[270] At one point, Nevers and his battalion "were reported missing for several months. When they were finally found on a deserted island, several had died, and Nevers, who suffered from beri beri, weighed only 110 lbs."[271]

After he left pro sports, Nevers worked as head coach at Lafayette and an assistant at Stanford and Iowa. He did color on some 49ers broadcasts and worked doing PR and sales promotions for a wholesale liquor company in San Francisco.

Leo Nomellini

San Francisco 49ers / United States Marine Corps

Born: June 19, 1924, in Lucca, Italy

Died: October 17, 2000, in Stanford, California

Position: DT-T

To many of his opponents, it must have seemed that Leo Nomellini was around an awfully long time—he was, too. Leo didn't miss a game for the San Francisco 49ers from the day the team first played in the NFL in 1950 until after the 1963 campaign, 14 long years later.

Leo played in 174 straight regular season games and, counting all appearances, including 10 Pro Bowl games, he played in 266 pro contests. Nomellini was an All-American tackle for two years at Minnesota and the number one draft choice of the 49ers in 1950.

A Marine sniper takes aim on Okinawa. (Photo courtesy of the National World War II Museum)

The choice of Nomellini proved to be a superb one. At 6'3" and 260 lbs., "The Lion" had everything needed to be a success—size, speed, agility, aggressiveness, dedication to the game, superb conditioning, and the willingness to go the full 60 minutes of any game.

Nomellini was one of the few players ever to win All-NFL recognition both on offense and defense. Leo was named All-League at offensive tackle in 1951 and 1952, and then he received All-NFL honors for his defensive line play in 1953, 1954, 1957, and 1959.

The status as an all-time pro grid great is a far cry from the impoverished days Leo knew as a youth. Born in Lucca, Italy, in 1924, Nomellini came to Chicago as an infant. Because he had to work to help support his family, Leo had to pass up high school football. So the first game he ever saw was one he played in as a member of the Cherry Point, North Carolina, Marines team.

Later at Minnesota, he was a starter in the first college game he ever saw. Freshmen were eligible then, and it was the start of a brilliant four-year college career. Like a fine old wine, Leo improved with age during his long term with the 49ers. When he finally retired at 39 after 14 years of battering the enemy, Nomellini had been tagged "indestructible." It was a tag he had truly earned and appreciated.

[Career capsule courtesy of the Pro Football Hall of Fame]

Leo came to America just before his first birthday and grew up on Chicago's West Side with his immigrant parents, Paul and Julia Nomellini. Paul had arrived in the U.S. in

University of Minnesota tackle Leo Nomellini is shown in 1948. (AP Photo)

1905 and worked as the proprietor of a candy kitchen. Leo worked at part-time jobs, sold newspapers, and throughout high school worked a full shift in a foundry to help bring income for the family. In the 1930s, Julia Nomellini lost Paul and married Fred Orsolini, who ran a tavern where Julia worked as a waitress. Shortly after Pearl Harbor, he enlisted in the United States Marine Corps and was introduced to competitive athletics for the first time when the team was short of members and Capt. Bill Hopp noticed Leo's size. A member of the Cherry

Point Leathernecks football team, he did go on to see combat in the Pacific, as a buck sergeant in the Marines who took part in the invasions of Saipan and Okinawa, there for "Opening Day."[272]

He became a dual pro—at football and professional wrestling as "Leo the Lion." After his time in the Marine Corps, Bernie Bierman, who had been a colonel in the Marines, and the GI Bill helped Nomellini receive a football scholarship from the University of Minnesota. There he played football and became the Big Ten heavyweight wrestling champion. He'd learned to wrestle in the Marines, too. Vern Gagne was a fellow wrestler with the Gophers. Leo claimed that wrestling was by far the physically rougher sport, though it was also one at which he made considerably more money.[273] He reportedly became one of the most popular wrestlers on the West Coast.[274]

After his pro careers ended (wrestling lasted about 10 years and football lasted 14), he started the Nomellini Macaroni Company in the Bay Area and later became an executive with the Northwestern Title Company of Oakland, California.[275]

Former 49ers quarterback Y.A. Tittle, who played with Nomellini from 1951–60, told the *San Francisco Chronicle*, "Leo was one of the kindest, gentlest, biggest tough men you'd ever want to meet. More than that, though, he was a great human being. He never had any bad things to say about anyone. He was a guy you could poke fun at, and he'd poke fun at you."[276]

Clarence "Ace" Parker

Brooklyn Dodgers, Boston Yanks, Brooklyn Yanks, Brooklyn Tigers, New York Yankees / United States Navy

Born: May 17, 1912, in Portsmouth, Virginia
Position: TB-DB-QB

Ace Parker never really intended to play pro football when he completed his career as an All-America tailback at Duke University in 1936. His ambition was to be a Major League Baseball player, and he signed a contract with the Philadelphia Athletics. After the 1937 baseball season, he obtained permission from Connie Mack of the Athletics to give pro football a try.

He joined the Brooklyn Dodgers of the NFL, still really expecting to play out just one pro football season and then call it a career. History now records that the 1937 season wasn't "the end of it" for the 5'10", 178-lb. fireball. Ace stayed with the Dodgers until World War II military service interrupted his career in 1942.

He returned to the pros in 1945 with the Boston Yanks and added a brilliant final campaign with the New York Yankees of the All-America Football Conference in 1946.

Interestingly, it was baseball and not the huge NFL linemen that Ace faced every weekend that proved to be the biggest stumbling block in his career. Broken ankles twice endangered his pro football career, and in 1940 he won Most Valuable Player honors in the NFL even though he had suffered a broken left ankle in a summer baseball game that year.

For the first three weeks of the season, he had to wear a 10-lb. brace that extended from his ankle to his knee.

Ace wasn't exceptionally fast anyway, but he continued doing just what he had always done—running, passing, catching passes, punting, place-kicking, returning punts and kickoffs, and playing defense. The Brooklyn Dodgers of the early 1940s were a constant threat to the New York Giants and Washington Redskins for supremacy in their division, and Parker was the guiding force of the Dodgers attack.

[Career capsule courtesy of the Pro Football Hall of Fame

Parker's list of fractures was impressive: 1932 (right hand), 1934 (right wrist), 1939 (left hand), 1940 (left ankle), and 1941 (right ankle.) Both of the ankles were broken while sliding into a base—and both times he was safe. But his playing career was cut short due to his service in the navy during World War II.

Parker had played baseball for Connie Mack, appearing as a utility man in 38 games in 1937 and 56 games in 1938. He hit for a combined .179 career batting average while playing second base, third base, shortstop, left field, and center field. He hit two homers—including a ninth-inning two-run homer off Wes Ferrell at Fenway Park in his first major-league at-bat—and drove in 25 runs. He spent 11 seasons playing minor league baseball from 1937 into 1952. From 1948 through 1952 he was a player/manager—for the Portsmouth Cubs in '48 and the Durham Bulls the next four years. Ace Parker's parents, Elmer and Maggie, both worked in a shoe factory in Portsmouth.

Parker took part in what was the first professional football game ever televised, as his NFL Dodgers defeated the Philadelphia Eagles at Ebbets Field, 23–14.[277] The next year, he was named MVP of the NFL (receiving the Joe F. Carr trophy) in 1940, but within a few weeks of Pearl Harbor he applied to enlist in the navy. In March 1942, he was accepted as a chief specialist in physical training. He went through the program at the Norfolk Naval Training Center with baseball's Bob Feller and Sam Chapman, and even joined Feller by playing at a number of benefit games.

Ace was discharged from the navy on October 2, 1945, and suited up for the Boston Yanks in time to appear in eight games that season. He'd gone in as a chief and was promoted to first lieutenant after 43 months of service. In 1946, he was signed again by Dan Topping of the New York Yankees, for whom he'd worked in 1941 as a member of Topping's Brooklyn team that beat the Giants on December 7, the day the announcement came of the attack on Pearl Harbor. Topping took a chance on a 34-year-old quarterback. A Pro Football Hall of Fame press release said he, "was the spearhead of the Yankees' surge. He played three games with three dislocated vertebrae, sat out three games while the pain eased, and then returned to spark the late-season rally that produced a division championship."[278]

He was named to the Pro Football Hall of Fame in 1972.

Joe Perry

San Francisco 49ers, Baltimore Colts / United States Navy

Born: January 22, 1927, in Stevens, Arkansas
Died: April 25, 2011, in Chandler, Arizona
Position: FB

Joe Perry put Compton Junior College on the football map when he scored 22 touchdowns in one season. However, before he completed his college football career, he was called into military service. He was playing football for the Alameda, California, Naval Training Station team when he was spotted by a player from the San Francisco 49ers of the new All-America Football Conference. The player reported his find to the 49ers' hierarchy who offered Joe a contract. Upon his discharge from the military in 1948, Perry accepted their proposal.

Although he had great speed, Perry was basically a straight-ahead runner when he turned pro. But as in everything he did on a football field, Joe quickly adjusted and promptly emerged as one of the premiere runners in the young league. His superior speed earned him the nickname "The Jet" during his second season.

In 1950, the 49ers and their star running back joined the NFL. Perry, at 6'0" and 200 lbs. was small for an NFL fullback. Unlike the typical fullback of the day, his forte was not as an inside power runner. Instead, he combined his power with his quickness and deceptive elusiveness to slash through opposing defenses.

It was an awesomely effective style, as he became the first player in NFL history to rush for 1,000 yards in consecutive seasons, a feat he accomplished in 1953 and 1954. A veteran of three Pro Bowls, Perry was All-AAFC in 1949 and All-NFL in 1953 and 1954.

The Jet played 13 seasons with the 49ers before being traded to the Baltimore Colts in 1961. After two seasons with the Colts he returned to San Francisco for one final season. In 16 seasons of outstanding play, Joe Perry amassed a total of 9,723 rushing yards and averaged an amazing 4.9 yards per carry.

[Career capsule courtesy of the Pro Football Hall of Fame]

Joe Perry's mother, Laura, encouraged him at track, basketball, and baseball at David Starr Jordan High School in Los Angeles, but she "strongly opposed his football desires."[279] His father, Fletcher Joe Perry Sr., had worked as a laborer in drain construction. Joe's wishes to play the game prevailed. ("I forged her name on the form giving permission. Then, wouldn't you know, I broke my ankle the first day.")[280] Realizing how much her son truly wanted to play football, his mother became his biggest booster. He entered Compton Junior College, looking forward to a career in electrical engineering, and he scored 22 touchdowns his first year.

It was when Perry was playing for the Alameda Naval Air Station Hell Cats that San Francisco 49ers tackle John Woudenberg saw the quality of his play and recommended him to team owner Tony Morabito and Coach Buck Shaw. "Shaw was practically camping out at our field," Perry later recalled, and he accepted Shaw's offer even though the Rams had offered him "almost twice as much," and 14 college offers were attractive, too.[281] He had also represented the navy in track at the West Coast Relays in 1947. Perry joined the 49ers right out of the navy in 1948 and stepped into a 16-year pro career.

"I was the first black to play football here," he said. "It was tough as hell…. It was probably worse playing football instead of baseball, like Jackie Robinson did, because football is such a physical game. The 49ers were great, though. If one person was in a fight, the whole team was in a fight. We were like a big family."[282]

After football, Perry worked as a DJ in Oakland and then did outreach for Greyhound. Perry was a 1969 enshrinee in the Pro Football Hall of Fame.

Pete Pihos

Philadelphia Eagles / United States Army

Born: October 22, 1923, in Orlando, Florida

Died: August 16, 2011, in Winston-Salem, North Carolina

Position: E-DE

Pete Pihos began his nine-year NFL career as a two-way end with the Philadelphia Eagles in 1947. When the platoon system was instituted, his coaches decided to have him concentrate on playing offense.

Then in 1952, the Eagles suddenly found themselves in need of a defensive end. Without a second thought they called on the versatile Pihos who not only stepped in at the position but earned All-NFL honors. For the remaining three years of his career, he switched back to offense and led the league in receiving all three seasons.

Pihos was the Eagles third-round draft choice in 1945, but two years of military service prevented him from joining the team until 1947. One of the truly great iron men of pro football, he missed just one game during his nine seasons of play.

Immediately after Pete joined the Eagles, the team marched to its first divisional championship. In the playoff game against the Pittsburgh Steelers for the Eastern Division crown, he blocked a punt to set up the first touchdown in the Eagles 21–0 win. Philadelphia won three straight divisional championships and then back-to-back NFL titles by shutout scores. In 1948, the Eagles defeated the Chicago Cardinals 7–0. One year later, Pihos caught a 31-yard touchdown pass in the Eagles 14–0 win over the Los Angeles Rams.

Although Pihos lacked great speed, he was a consistently outstanding pass receiver with sure hands, clever moves, and courage. Any defender who battled Pete for a pass was bound to get the worst of it physically. He played it clean but very hard, and after he caught a pass he ran like a bulldozing fullback. Pete led the NFL in receiving from 1953–55, earned first-team All-Pro or All-League honors six times, and was named to six Pro Bowls.

[Career capsule courtesy of the Pro Football Hall of Fame]

The son of Greek immigrants, Pete Pihos suffered tragedy early in life. His family was in the café business at the time of the 1930 United States Census. In the mid-1930s, when Pete was just 13 years old, his father was killed during a robbery at the restaurant where he worked, and

Pete ended up moving from Orlando to Chicago to complete his high school education.[283]

Pihos was an All-American for Indiana University as an end and as a fullback. He left college after 1943 to enter the United States Army and was inducted on January 8, 1944. He went through basic training and was sent overseas to France. Pihos served 14 months as a paratrooper in the European Theater of Operations, earning five battle stars.[284] He returned to Indiana on September 25, 1945, and was able to play most of the 1945 season at fullback. His first game back was four days later, and he scored the touchdown against Northwestern on a nine-yard pass that led to a 7–7 tie. After the 1945–46 campaign, Pihos was granted an extra year of eligibility because of his military service and was named team captain for the Hoosiers in 1946.

The Philadelphia Eagles' Greasy Neale had made him the team's fifth-round draft pick in the 1945 NFL Draft even though they knew he would be unable to play until 1947. "I can wait for a player like Pihos," Neale said.[285] But they put down their marker and saw him join the team for the first of nine seasons from 1947–55. After football, Pihos coached at Tulane University and later pursued a career in sales for a plastics company in Pennsylvania, becoming executive VP at the Regal Home Improvement Company of Richmond, Virginia.

Pete Pihos was inducted into the Pro Football Hall of Fame in 1970. After a lengthy struggle with Alzheimer's, likely attributable in good measure to the many hits he took playing football, he died in 2011, but not until after his daughter, Melissa, made a short film, *Dear Dad*, expressing her love for him as he fought the disease.[286]

Dan Reeves

Cleveland Rams, Los Angeles Rams / United States Army Air Corps

Born: June 30, 1912, in New York, New York
Died: April 15, 1971, in New York, New York
Position: team owner

On January 11, 1946, Dan Reeves announced he was moving his Cleveland Rams to Los Angeles. This was shocking news because the Rams had won the NFL championship less than a month earlier. In addition, air travel was still in its early stages, and Los Angeles was 2,000 miles away from the nearest NFL city.

Most importantly, Reeves' fellow NFL owners were dead set against the move. But Reeves was just as determined. It took a sometimes bitter fight and even a threat to withdraw from the NFL before Reeves could convince his colleagues that he meant business.

Once the move was made, the Rams had to fight a life-and-death struggle with the rival dons of the All-America Football Conference (AAFC). Reeves had lost money in trickles in Cleveland, but his initial losses in Los Angeles came in tidal waves. The AAFC folded in 1949 just as the Rams were embarking on a string of outstanding seasons on the field.

Boasting some of football's most glamorous stars, the Rams won four divisional titles in seven years and the NFL championship in 1951. The effect at the gate was astounding.

Topped by a crowd of 102,368 for a San Francisco 49ers game in 1957, turnouts in the Los Angeles Coliseum surpassed 80,000 on 22 occasions during the Rams' first two decades in California.

The innovative Reeves made several other significant contributions to pro football. He instituted the famed Free Football for Kids program that enabled youngsters to enjoy the game in their formative years and hopefully become ardent fans as adults. His signing of the ex-UCLA great, Kenny Washington, in the spring of 1946 marked the first time a black player had been hired in the NFL since 1933. Dan's experimentation in the early days of television provided the groundwork for pro football's current successful TV policies. He was also the first owner to employ a full-time scouting staff.

[Career capsule courtesy of the Pro Football Hall of Fame]

The son of an Irish immigrant who built up a chain of neighborhood grocery stores in New York and sold them to A&P, Dan Reeves became an investment banker in the Empire State. He used some of the proceeds and joined Fred Levy Jr. to buy the Cleveland Rams in 1941. Why a team in Cleveland? "Because it was the only one for sale."[287]

He couldn't have known that the world was about to change, and his team wouldn't even operate in 1943. After the attack on Pearl Harbor, it wasn't long before both Cleveland co-owners, Fred Levy and Dan Reeves, signed up to join the U.S. Army Air Corps and asked for permission to shut down the team. Levy

was a major and Reeves a lieutenant. "The Rams simply ceased operations in 1943. A dispersal draft was conducted under a one-year, war-time loan agreement. Thirty-six players were on the 1942 Cleveland roster. Of those, 16, most of whom went into the military, never played again. By 1945, only receiver Jim Benton, guard Riley Matheson, and end Steve Pritko from the 1942 Rams were even on the roster."[288]

Reeves was stationed at the Rome Air Station in Rome, New York. After Reeves bought out Levy's interest in the team in December 1943 and the team was reactivated for the 1944 campaign, he remained in the service and was able to get to most of the team's games. Attendance was, of course, down dramatically from prewar levels, though even before the war, the franchise had been losing money.

"Reeves was a man of reserved nature but wry wit. In four seasons, he had grown accustomed to the perennial financial losses—'Irish dividends,' as he called them—common to owning a pro football team. But the 1945 season had been uniquely rewarding and frustrating. Reeves had returned home just two months earlier, after a three-year tour of duty with the Army Air Corps, to what would become a season-long victory celebration. America's triumph in World War II had been officially consecrated during August two-a-days, and the long lines that greeted the end of gas rationing dissipated by the season-opening win over the Chicago Cardinals."[289] Reeves had served in the Army Air Corps as a second lieutenant, rising to the rank of captain.

On January 12, 1946, the NFL gave him permission to move the franchise to Los Angeles. He was the first to bring a major-league professional sports team to the West Coast. At one point, he also owned the Los Angeles Blades in the Western Hockey League. He died of cancer in his New York apartment at the age of 58 in 1971. He was inducted into the Pro Football Hall of Fame in 1967.

Andy Robustelli

Los Angeles Rams, New York Giants / United States Navy

Born: December 6, 1925, in Stamford, Connecticut

Died: May 31, 2011, in Stamford, Connecticut

Position: DE

The Los Angeles Rams drafted Andy Robustelli, an end from tiny Arnold College, in the 19th round of the 1951 NFL Draft. A long shot to make the team as an offensive end because the Rams already had stars such as Tom Fears and Elroy "Crazylegs" Hirsch, Robustelli responded in the only way he knew how—to go all out to make the defensive unit.

History records that Andy became one of the finest defensive ends in pro football history, playing five years with the Rams and then nine years with the New York Giants. He was a regular for the Rams' 1951 championship team, and the one game he missed that season was the only one he missed in 14 NFL seasons.

After five outstanding seasons in Los Angeles, the Rams dealt him to the Giants for a first-round draft pick. Andy performed even better in New York, and he is credited with

molding together the 1956 Giants team that won the NFL championship.

A natural leader as well as an outstanding player, Robustelli was a big factor in the Giants' on-field success. He stayed with the New York team for nine seasons, the last three as a player-coach. Robustelli was not big for a modern-day defensive end, weighing only 230 lbs., but he was clearly one of the finest pass rushers the game has seen.

He was named All-Pro seven times and was named to the Pro Bowl seven times. In 1962 the Maxwell Club selected Robustelli as the NFL's outstanding player, an honor that until then was generally reserved for an offensive player. The honor was indicative of the high regard that fans, teammates, and opponents all held for the future Hall of Fame defensive end.

[Career capsule courtesy of the Pro Football Hall of Fame]

Andy Robustelli didn't begin his pro football career until 1951 when he was 26 years old. His friend, Greg Michie, said, "Andy was four years older than most rookies. A lot of people forget he spent four years in the navy during World War II before going to college."[290] His father, Louis, was a barber who had immigrated from Italy; his mother, Catherine, was second-generation Italian.

Andy was a veteran, and older as a rookie, because he had seen combat as a watertender third class serving in the navy for 30 months before entering Arnold College in 1947. He earned eight letters at Arnold, playing on the baseball team as well as the football team. Andy graduated from Stamford High School and wanted to attend Manhattan College, but he needed some extra credits in science and chemistry, which he took at LaSalle Military Academy before quitting school to join the navy early in 1944. He served on the destroyer escort *William C. Cole*. After several escort missions across the South Pacific, the ship was involved in the battle of Okinawa in April and May 1945 and was the target of a number of kamikaze attacks. Robustelli's general quarters duty was as a gunner, and the *William C. Cole* did shoot down at least three attacking planes.

After football, Robustelli ran a sporting goods store and a travel agency in his home city of Stamford.

Pete Rozelle

Los Angeles Rams, NFL Commissioner / United States Navy

Born: March 1, 1926, in South Gate, California
Died: December 6, 1996, in Rancho Santa Fe, California
Position: Commissioner of the NFL

During his 30 years as commissioner of the NFL, Pete Rozelle was recognized as the premier commissioner of all professional sports. A charismatic leader, he guided the league through a period of unprecedented growth. Rozelle was the 33-year-old general manager of the Los Angeles Rams when he left for the annual NFL meetings in January 1960.

The principal business was to name a new commissioner to replace the popular Bert Bell, who had died three months earlier. After 23 ballots had failed to produce a new leader, two owners asked Rozelle to leave the meeting room while they and the other owners had a discussion. After a couple of hours, Pete was invited back to the meeting to hear the news that he was the NFL's new leader.

Rozelle's accomplishments are legendary, and the NFL's many challenges during his tenure are well documented. Such things as blockbuster television contracts, the war with the competing American Football League and the resulting merger, the development of the Super Bowl into America's premier sporting event, difficult player issues including strikes and threatened strikes, plus numerous court and legislative battles all dominated headlines during his stewardship.

Throughout it all, Rozelle remained a dominating factor. His leadership created the profound image of stability and integrity still associated with the NFL. He continually encouraged the club owners to work together despite numerous challenges while always demonstrating a calm, reassuring, and strong management style. It was Rozelle who convinced NFL owners to share equally their television revenues.

A former University of San Francisco sports information director, Rozelle first joined the Los Angeles Rams as public relations director. He later worked as a public relations specialist at the 1956 Summer Olympics in Melbourne, Australia, and then returned to the Rams for a three-year tenure as general manager before his election to the NFL commissioner's post.
[Career capsule courtesy of the Pro Football Hall of Fame]

Alvin Ray "Pete" Rozelle grew up in Southern California where his father managed a market and later worked for ALCOA. Pete graduated from Compton High School in 1944 where he played some tennis and basketball—but he never played football. He did demonstrate one particular talent, "an early knack for sports promotion. After watching a high school friend pitch a no-hitter, Rozelle called every newspaper in the area to tout the accomplishment. The friend: Duke Snider."[291] The two had known each other since age 12 and were both on the basketball team at Compton. Rozelle later said, "Overall, I was a sort of frustrated athlete." With 40 seconds to play, Snider threw a 64-yard pass that beat Long Beach Poly. Reporting that story earned Rozelle a nod as high school correspondent for the *Los Angeles Times*.[292] After high school, he was drafted into the navy and served as a yeoman 2nd class, working 18 months in the Pacific on an oil tanker. It was a "coastal tanker that," he said, "never went far from San Pedro, the Southern California port."[293]

After the war, he enrolled at Compton Junior College (where he also worked as sports information director) and then transferred to the University of San Francisco. There he worked as the sports publicity director and assistant athletic director. He graduated U.S.F. in 1950, and in 1952 he was hired as head of P.R. for the Los Angeles Rams. His career progressed from there.

As commissioner, he had a somewhat surreal experience as he explained in a 1991 interview for the Academy of Achievement. "I was in the navy during World War II, out in the Pacific on a tanker, and take that into account. But in the '60s, we have a visitor to this country. Came to New York and came to the New York Jets

game. Hirohito! And to me, it was so incredible, thinking of my background, and having been out there, and the way everything was during the war, and I was sitting with my family behind bullet-proof glass, covered, watching the game from a box." Emperor Hirohito's troops had fought the U.S. in World War II, but it fell to Rozelle to try to explain American football to the emperor. "It was just so...you know, what sports can do. It's just weird! Too much for my mind. So I attempted to explain the game through an interpreter as best I could.... I did the best I could, but I don't know if it was very good, though."[294]

An amusing story followed that meeting. His stepson, Robby, age six or seven, was at the game and coincidentally was asked in school to write a page on what he'd done the week before. A couple of months later, Pete's wife, Carrie, was at a PTA or school function and Robby's teacher said, "Robby has really got a very creative imagination, very vivid." Carrie asked what she meant and was shown his paper. He'd written, "I went to a football game and ate a hot dog, and sat with the Emperor." The teacher said, "Obviously, all fanciful," but Mrs. Rozelle said, "No, it wasn't."[295]

Tex Schramm

Los Angeles Rams, Dallas Cowboys / United States Army Air Corps

Born: June 2, 1920, in San Gabriel, California

Died: July 15, 2003, in Dallas, Texas

Position: team administrator

Tex Schramm, except for a three-year stint as the assistant director of sports for CBS television

The USS Arizona *lies smoking in the mud following the Japanese attack on Pearl Harbor.* (Photo courtesy of the National World War II Museum)

in the late 1950s, played a dynamic role in professional football throughout a 44-year span from 1947–90.

He began his NFL career as the publicity director of the Los Angeles Rams and finished as president and chief executive officer of the World League of American Football. In

between, he served with the Rams for 10 seasons and the Dallas Cowboys for 29 years.

Schramm earned his journalism degree at the University of Texas. After two years as a sportswriter with the *American-Statesman* in Austin, Texas, Schramm moved to Los Angeles to join the Rams. He advanced through the ranks and was general manager of the team when he joined CBS in 1957.

Tex joined the Cowboys at the time of the team's inception in 1960. In a 29-year tenure that ended after the 1988 season, Schramm fashioned the Cowboys into one of the showcase franchises of all professional sports. His Cowboys teams played in five Super Bowls and won two, had 20 consecutive winning seasons, and made 18 playoff appearances in those 20 years.

Schramm's contributions to pro football did not stop with the Cowboys, however. For 23 years, he was the chairman of the influential NFL competition committee. Along with Lamar Hunt, he was a leading force in the AFL-NFL merger that was culminated in 1970.

Schramm introduced the concept of three divisions in each of two conferences with wild-card playoff teams. He led the fight for instant replay as an officiating tool and a fan-interest enhancer. He was a leading advocate of such innovations as a referee's microphone, a 30-second clock between plays, extra-wide sideline borders, wind-direction strips on goal post uprights, and multicolor striping for 20- and 50-yard lines.

[Career capsule courtesy of the Pro Football Hall of Fame]

Texas Earnest Schramm Jr. bore the name Texas as his given name, as had his father before him. His father was fairly well-off, working as a securities broker in 1930 and earning $30,000 a year. Despite the Depression, he kept at his work and was still in the same trade a decade later. Tex Jr. attended the University of Texas at Austin and briefly tried to play football—enough to earn a letter—but opted instead for a career he envisioned in journalism.[296] He was at U.T. in 1941, working as the associate sports editor for *The Daily Texan*, the university newspaper. Less than two weeks after the attack on Pearl Harbor, however, he enlisted in the Army Air Corps, signing up at Randolph Field on December 18, 1941.

He completed officers' training school and was assigned to the air transport command at Hamilton Army Air Field in Novato, California. Captain Schramm was later transferred to Hawaii.

Discharged late in 1945, he returned to the University of Texas. In February 1947, the year he graduated, he became the sports editor of one of Austin's two major newspapers, the *Statesman*.[297] He had worked as a summer intern at the *Los Angeles Times* and parlayed his talent for the press and publicity into a career, working as publicity director for the Los Angeles Rams from 1947–56—during which time he was in a position that enabled him to hire Pete Rozelle as the public relations director for the team.

Other Schramm innovations included the use of a headset in the quarterback's helmet, and in 1972 he introduced the Dallas Cowboy Cheerleaders.[298] In 1967, the first Super Bowl came as a result of his 1966 efforts to merge the AFL and NFL.

Tex Schramm was named to the Hall of Fame in 1991.

Ernie Stautner

Pittsburgh Steelers / United States Marine Corps

Born: April 20, 1925, in Prinzing-by-Cham, Germany

Died: February 16, 2006, in Carbondale, Colorado

Position: DT-DE-G

At 6'1" and 230 lbs., Ernie Stautner was smaller than most defensive linemen of the 1950s. Still, the Pittsburgh Steelers were willing to take a chance on the undersized lineman and drafted him in the second round of the 1950 NFL Draft.

It turned out to be a sensational pick. Blessed with excellent mobility and burning desire, the Boston College star went on to excel in the game of giants. For the next 14 years, Stautner was a fixture at defensive tackle, a veritable folk hero with long-suffering Steelers fans and a major factor in the Pittsburgh defense, one of the most punishing in the NFL at the time.

His outstanding play earned him first- or second-team All-NFL honors nine times. Selected to nine Pro Bowls, Ernie had the unusual distinction for a defensive tackle of winding up not once but twice in the NFL record book. His three career safeties tied him for a then all time high, and his 23 fumble recoveries placed him third on that list.

However, Ernie's true worth on a football field could never be measured in lines in a record manual becaue statistics can't measure such assets as competitive nature, team spirit, grim determination, and the will to win. Extremely resilient, the native of Bavaria missed only six games during his entire NFL career. That's not to say he didn't suffer a number of

injuries. His maladies included broken ribs, shoulders, hands, and a nose broken too many times to count.

When Ernie finally retired, the Steelers honored him by retiring his No. 70 jersey. It was something the team didn't ordinarily do. But then, Ernie Stautner was hardly ordinary. A throwback to another time, Stautner was considered by teammates and opponents alike as one of the toughest competitors the game ever produced.

[Career capsule courtesy of the Pro Football Hall of Fame]

Joseph Stautner and his wife, Hedwig, brought their three children to America from Bavaria when Ernie was three years old. The family settled in Albany, New York, where Joseph worked as a machinist in a chemical annealing works.

Ernie overcame the objections of his father to play high school football, and then went straight into the Marine Corps after graduation. He served from 1943–46, playing football for the El Toro Marines and also seeing combat on Okinawa.[299]

He went to Notre Dame after the war was over, but Coach Frank Leahy told him he was "too small and too slow to play big-time college football"—so he went to Boston College, majored in psychology, and became a two-time All-American. While at B.C., he was honored by being named the winner of the Edward O'Melia trophy, awarded to the outstanding Eagle of the season in the name of a former Holy Cross player and Marine officer who had been killed during the war.[300] After graduation, he couldn't get a job playing football professionally. There followed a third attempt to dissuade him from pursuing a pro career, which came from New York Giants coach Steve Owen: "I don't think you have the size, son."[301]

The Pittsburgh Steelers selected him in the second round of the 1950 NFL Draft, and he played for Pittsburgh from 1950–63. He was elected to the Pro Football Hall of Fame in his first year of eligibility in 1969. After his playing career had ended, he continued to operate a drive-in movie theater in Saranac Lake, New York, while he worked for many years as an assistant coach for the Steelers, Redskins, Broncos, and from 1966–88 for the Dallas Cowboys.

Joe Stydahar

Chicago Bears / United States Navy

Born: March 16, 1912, in Kaylor, West Virginia
Died: March 23, 1977, in Beckley, West Virginia

Position: T

By 1936, Chicago Bears owner/coach George Halas was steadily building the powerful Chicago Bears team that would dominate the NFL during the 1940s. Halas sought only the finest talent, so it was somewhat of a surprise when the NFL staged its first college draft before the 1936 season and Halas selected a little-known tackle from West Virginia named Joe Stydahar. It was not that Stydahar didn't have the credentials to be a blue-chip pro.

He had earned various All-Eastern honors and played in the College All-Star Game before joining the Bears. It was just that the Bears

passed on several more publicized stars. As it turned out, a Bears end, West Virginia alumnus Bill Karr, tipped off the Bears' coach to the talents of Stydahar. History shows the choice was as good as any the Bears ever made.

In many ways, "Jumbo Joe" was the epitome of the Bears' overpowering strength at that time. Fearless and huge by the standards of the day, the 6'4", 233-lb. Stydahar possessed incredible power and remarkable speed.

Flaunting his disdain for superstition by wearing jersey No. 13, he was a 60-minute performer who often shunned the use of a helmet. His consistently outstanding play earned him All-NFL recognition from 1936–40 and second-team All-NFL acclaim in 1942.

Stydahar's tenure as an active player became synonymous with Chicago Bears championships. Starting with his rookie season, he was a fixture at the tackle spot for seven years until he was called into the U.S. Navy following the 1942 season. He returned in 1945 to play for two more years. During that period, the Bears won three NFL championships and five Western Division titles. In Joe's final game, the 1946 Bears defeated the New York Giants, 24–14. It was the last major triumph of the Bears' dynasty years.

[Career capsule courtesy of the Pro Football Hall of Fame]

Joe Stydahar's father, Pete, came to the United States from Dreznik, Yugoslavia (most likely the Dreznik in today's Serbia), and worked as a coal loader while Joe was growing up in the mining town of Kaylor. Joe had four younger sisters and two younger brothers. Mother Lucille

(Naglic) Stydahar was reported to have come from Austria, though the Austrian empire was such that she may well have come from Serbia, as well.

He played football and basketball at West Virginia University, excelled in hoops, and was captain of the basketball and football teams. He was a first-round draft pick of the Chicago Bears in 1936, and he played seven years for the Bears through the 1942 season. He was a Pro Bowl player for four consecutive years, 1938–41. Joe was invited to take part in the eighth annual Chicago All-Star football game between the Bears and the College All-Americans on August 28, 1941. The list of those who took part in the game is remarkable, ranging from future Hall of Famers Young Bussey, Dan Fortmann, Sid Luckman, and George McAfee, to Tom Harmon and UCLA halfback Jackie Robinson.[302]

On February 22, 1943, Stydahar entered the U.S. Navy, the 25th Chicago Bear to do so and the 10th since the end of the 1942 season.[303] Ensign Stydahar was ordered to report for seagoing training at Dartmouth on March 8. At 6'4" and 233 lbs., there were remarks made about not assigning "Jumbo Joe" and teammate Ed Kolman, a tackle of similar stature and another of the Monsters of the Midway, to service aboard the same PT boat. After he was commissioned as a lieutenant, Stydahar joined the Fleet City Naval Training Station Bluejackets team and was named Service All-America team by the Associated Press.[304] He did see sea duty, however, both in the Atlantic and Pacific theaters, as a gunnery officer.[305] By November 1945, he was in the process of being discharged and preparing to report back to Wrigley Field to rejoin the Bears. He got into three games that year.

An anecdote that ran in a couple of papers over the years had Stydahar in uniform, sitting in a restaurant when he overheard a father telling his son how important it was to pick his goal in life and then devote every effort to attaining that goal. The father then asked, "Tell me. What do you want to be when you grow up?" Stydahar, eavesdropping, couldn't resist the temptation. "Tell him, sonny, that you want to be a civilian."[306]

After the 1946 season, Stydahar joined the Los Angeles Rams as an assistant coach. He became head coach of the Rams from 1950–52 and of the Chicago Cardinals from 1953–54. After football, he became the assistant eastern regional manager for the container division of Chicago-based Southwest Forest Industries.[307]

In 1967, Joe Stydahar was enshrined in the Pro Football Hall of Fame.

Charley Trippi

Chicago Cardinals / United States Army Air Corps
Born: December 14, 1922, in Pittston, Pennsylvania
Position: HB-QB-DB

In 1946, Charley Trippi, a two-time All-American from the University of Georgia, was a key figure in the inter-league battling between the new All-America Football Conference (AAFC) and the National Football League.

The AAFC's New York Yankees were so sure they had signed him to a contract that

Charley Trippi (right), a 24-year-old All-American halfback, tries on a Chicago Cardinals uniform at Comiskey Park in Chicago on January 17, 1947. Trippi signed a four-season $100,000 contract with the NFL. Cardinals coach Jimmy Conzelman looks on. (AP Photo)

they called a press conference in New York to announce the happy news. But while the New York newsmen gathered, Chicago Cardinals owner Charles W. Bidwill Sr. announced in Chicago that he had signed Trippi to a four-year contract worth $100,000. For those days, the size of the contract was stunning news and a big breakthrough in the inter-league war.

Trippi's acquisition completed Bidwill's quest for a "dream backfield." Although Bidwill did not live to see it, Charley became the game breaker in a talented corps that included Paul Christman, Pat Harder, Marshall Goldberg, and later Elmer Angsman.

Never was Trippi more magnificent than in the 1947 NFL Championship Game when the Cardinals defeated the Philadelphia Eagles, 28–21. Playing on an icy field in Chicago, Charley wore basketball shoes for better traction and totaled 206 yards, including 102 yards on two punt returns. He scored touchdowns on a 44-yard run and a 75-yard punt return.

Trippi could and would do anything on a football field. He played as a left halfback for four seasons before switching to quarterback for two years. Charley then moved back to offensive halfback for one campaign before changing almost exclusively to the defensive unit in 1954 and 1955. He also was the Cardinals' punter, and he excelled on the punt and kickoff return teams.

Due to relaxed regulations during the war years, Charley played in five College All-Star classics, two while at Georgia, two while in the service, and a fifth as a Cardinal in 1948.

[Career capsule courtesy of the Pro Football Hall of Fame]

Charley Trippi's father, an immigrant grocer in the mining town of Pittston who also worked as a laborer for the W.P.A., was dead set against his son playing football. "I used to have to sneak out for football practice," Charley said. "He disliked the game with a passion."[308] But football got Charley into the University of Georgia, and his father and football eventually reconciled.

He played for the Bulldogs in the 1943 Rose Bowl when Georgia beat UCLA 9–0 and was retroactively named the Rose Bowl Player of the Game, running for 24 yards more than all the UCLA Bruins combined.[309] That April he was drafted into the army and Trippi's time at Georgia was interrupted by 2½ years serving in the Army Air Corps in Greensboro and Tampa, working as a physical instructor. He advanced to become a staff sergeant. But he was able to play two full seasons of service football for the Third Air Force Gremlins, thus keeping up his skills. In fact, Trippi was named to the 1944 All-Service team.[310] He was stationed in Tampa and was even able to play in a number of games for Georgia during the war years, including appearances in 1943, 1944, and 1945, thanks to

CHARLEY TRIPPI ON WWII

"After my high school graduation in 1940, the world was really falling apart. All you had to do was turn on the radio—you could hear the war coming.

"I was just part of a bigger team in the service, that is all. I am no different than the rest of us who went. It didn't matter if I played football or not. It didn't matter what any of us did. America needed us, so we went.

"I often wonder if people really remember all those lives so long ago. All those kids, so many of them just gone… I wonder if anyone still cares.

"A hero is one who didn't come home from the war. Those who came home are survivors, and there is a difference."

—*Charley Trippi,*
as told to Todd Anton on January 19, 2013

a relaxation of eligibility rules to accommodate having so many students in military service. After the war was over, he was deemed non-essential to the war effort and was discharged at Drew Field, Tampa, in what seemed to some a somewhat controversial early discharge at the behest of Georgia's two United States Senators.[311] He was too good at football to be treated like everyone else.

Indeed, even though he said he had requested overseas duty, he told reporter Joe Livingston of the *Atlanta Journal*, "My commanding officer couldn't send me overseas because attached to my file was a card which said: 'Frozen—hold for 1945 football project.'"[312]

War over, he declined offers to turn pro and played in the last six games for Georgia and was named the MVP of the final game, setting Southeast Conference records for passing yards and total yards in a single game.[313] He became the overall No. 1 draft pick by the Chicago Cardinals in the 1945 draft.

In his final year at Georgia before turning pro, he was awarded both the Maxwell and Walter Camp Trophies, and Georgia was ranked third in the country. Trippi had also been an All-American shortstop for the Georgia baseball team, and he thought about playing baseball. He hit .334 in 106 games in 1947 while playing Double A baseball for the Atlanta Crackers (Southern Association).

He'd been courted by the New York Yankees football team (and apparently even been offered "a fabulous football-baseball combination pact" by New York's Dan Topping, who owned both

teams).[314] In the end, he decided to focus on football and play just one sport.

Topping made the offer, but Chicago Cardinals owner Charles Bidwill had the inside track—he was Trippi's attorney. The Cardinals won the NFL championship in his first year, 1947, and Trippi was named All-Pro in 1948 when the Cardinals lost the championship game to the Philadelphia Eagles. After his career in football, Trippi was successful in commercial real estate.

Clyde Turner

Chicago Bears / United States Army Air Corps
Born: March 10, 1919, in Plains, Texas
Died: October 30, 1998, in Gatesville, Texas
Position: C-T-LB-G

Clyde "Bulldog" Turner excelled as a premier center and linebacker for the Chicago Bears for 13 seasons. Yet had it not been for a fortunate set of circumstances while he was still a college player at Hardin-Simmons University, he might never have had the chance to play in the NFL.

Pro football scouting was in its early stages in the late 1930s. Most teams relied on football magazines with their traditional preseason All-America selections. Players from little-known colleges simply weren't included. Yet not one but two NFL teams eagerly sought Turner.

A Hardin-Simmons fan tipped off Frank Korch, a Bears scout, about Turner's abilities during his junior season. After watching Turner, Korch convinced Coach George Halas that the Bears should draft him. Meanwhile, the Detroit

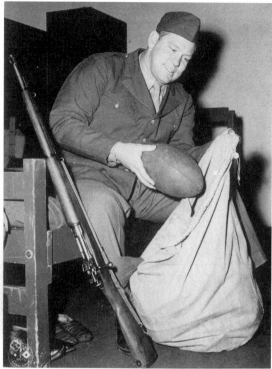

Private Clyde Turner, known to football fans as "Bulldog" Turner of the Chicago Bears, tucks away the pigskin and gets set to pick up his rifle at Fort Lewis, Washington, on February 14, 1945. (AP Photo/U.S. Army)

1942, led the league in interceptions with eight.

On offense, he was a flawless snapper and an exceptional blocker who could also play guard or tackle. Never was his versatility more evident than in 1944 when he was asked to fill in as a ball carrier in an emergency situation. He consistently ground out long gains, including a 48-yard touchdown romp. Three years later against Washington, Turner came up with what he called his favorite play of his career, a 96-yard interception return for a touchdown.

[Career capsule courtesy of the Pro Football Hall of Fame]

To look at Turner's record, one wouldn't know he served a hitch in World War II. His NFL career began in 1940 and ran through 1952, but in 1945 he only appeared in two games—though he said he was there for more of them. Turner spent most of the year in Colorado Springs with the U.S. Army Air Corps, and he played for the superb Second Air Force Superbombers team. The Chicago Bears explained, "Turner played with the 1945 Army Air Corps Superbombers team during World War II. He plugged his team's weakness by playing guard and won both AP and UPI All-Service acclaim."[315] He'd played guard on the Superbombers.

One of the advantages of being in the Air Corps was access to aircraft, and Turner said, "Tom Fears was a pilot in the outfit. I'd arrange passes and he'd check out a plane and we'd fly up to Chicago." Asked how he was able to play in the Bears games without the chain of command interceding, he simply answered, "They never knew I was playing pro. I'd play on

Lions were so sure they had convinced Turner to turn down offers from other NFL teams that they didn't even bother to draft him.

For the Bears, acquiring Turner in the first round of the 1940 draft proved to be a masterstroke. For both, the 1940 season marked the beginning of a period of dominance of their particular specialties, the Bears in winning championships and Turner in becoming the best all-around center in pro football. As a linebacker who was blessed with halfback speed, Turner, in the service team on Saturday, fly to the Bears game, then report back to base for Monday. The pros didn't get much publicity, and they never knew I was still playing."[316] He added, "It seems crazy now, but it just seemed like the thing to do at the time."[317] Turner was credited with shutting out the stultifyingly named Personnel Distribution Command Comets in an Army Air Forces game in Albuquerque 13–0 on October 21, 1945.[318] In March 1946, he signed again with the Bears.

Turner was selected All-League at center in the NFL from 1941–44, 1946, and 1948—and he was on the All-Service team in 1945. He took to wearing a face mask during games because he'd suffered a broken nose on at least six occasions. After football, he continued to work for the Bears as an assistant coach for four seasons and later was the head coach of the New York Titans for one year before returning to his ranch in Texas where he raised cattle, sheep, and horses. His father, William, had run a gas station in Texas and then turned to farming and raising stock with his wife, Ida. Bulldog Turner was enshrined in the Pro Football Hall of Fame in 1966.

Norm Van Brocklin

Los Angeles Rams, Philadelphia Eagles / United States Navy

Born: March 15, 1926, in Eagle Butte, South Dakota
Died: May 2, 1983, in Social Circle, Georgia
Position: QB

Norm Van Brocklin was a standout quarterback for 12 seasons in the National Football League, the first nine with the Los Angeles Rams. Then he was traded to the Philadelphia Eagles in 1958, and within three years the "Dutchman" had guided the Eagles to the NFL championship.

Without a doubt it was his finest performance in a brilliant career. One of the most colorful and competitive individuals that pro football has ever seen, Van Brocklin blazed a sometimes stormy but always eventful path in his dozen campaigns as an active player.

Norm left the University of Oregon, where he still had a year's eligibility remaining, to join the Rams in 1949. The only problem from Van Brocklin's standpoint was that the Rams already had one future Hall of Fame quarterback in Bob Waterfield.

The net result was that two great quarterbacks had to share passing duties for a few seasons, a situation that any great competitor, which Norm certainly was, couldn't be expected to accept with any enthusiasm. Still, Van Brocklin won the NFL passing title in both 1950 and 1952, although he was playing only half the time on offense. He added a third passing championship in 1954.

His greatest day as a passer came in 1951 when he threw for a record 554 yards against the New York Yanks. It was also in 1951 that Van Brocklin threw a 73-yard pass to Tom Fears that gave the Rams a 24–17 victory over the Browns and the only NFL title the Rams had won since moving to Los Angeles.

In Philadelphia he was given a free hand at running the offensive show, and behind his leadership the Eagles won the NFL title in

Quarterback Norm Van Brocklin of the Philadelphia Eagles tries his hand at firing an M-1 rifle at the Indian Gap, Pennsylvania, military installation on August 5, 1959. Van Brocklin and other members of the NFL team toured training facilities of the 28th infantry division. Person at left unidentified. (AP Photo/U.S. Signal Corps)

1960. Thus, the Dutchman was the only man to defeat a Lombardi-coached Green Bay team in championship game play.

[Career capsule courtesy of the Pro Football Hall of Fame]

Norm Van Brocklin came from a big family; his mother, Ethel, and father, Mack, had nine children and worked at farming. The Depression may have hit them hard; the 1940 Census shows Mack delivering papers and Ethel

working sorting and cutting in a cannery. The Van Brocklins had moved to California. "It was tough," Norm recalled. "We scratched for a living. We preceded [*Grapes of Wrath* author John] Steinbeck's characters. I can vouch that his account was very accurate. One never forgets the sight of tents pitched in almost every yard and every open field around the Walnut Creek area. It was beautiful country, but people didn't think of the beauty then. They were too busy following the basic human instinct of survival."[319] He worked from the age of 12, picking fruit, pumping gas, hauling bricks and cement, and wheeling tomatoes to the belt line in canneries. He was able to play football, baseball, and basketball at Union High and then Acalenes High School, but when he was old enough, he joined the United States Navy.

"I was in the navy three years. I went in and six weeks later I was gone to the South Pacific [1943–46]. I was in the engine room on a destroyer"—dangerous duty—"I believe they left us down there to die."[320] Van Brocklin served as machinist mate third class in the so-called "Black Gang." He held one memory of the time his destroyer had sunk a Japanese submarine. When they saw the oil slick appear on the ocean surface, "We stood around cheering as if we were a football team that had just scored a touchdown. It was pure relief to know we got the sub before it got us."[321] After the Japanese surrender, he stayed in the Pacific for another four months with ports of call in Korea, China, and the Philippines.

Thanks to the G.I. Bill, Norm was able to attend the University of Oregon. He'd aspired to pitch Major League Baseball, but at Oregon he eventually earned a berth on the football team. He became an All-American, and the offers started coming in.

He studied through the summers and graduated in three years. He left Oregon for the NFL with one remaining year of college eligibility, which might have prevented him from turning pro, but his service time in the navy was allowed to bridge the problem. He

joined the Los Angeles Rams and ultimately earned his way to the Pro Football Hall of Fame. Norm was inducted in 1971.

Bob Waterfield

Cleveland Rams, Los Angeles Rams / United States Army
Born: July 26, 1920, in Elmira, New York
Died: March 25, 1983, in Burbank, California
Position: QB

In the 1945 NFL Championship Game, Bob Waterfield threw 37- and 44-yard touchdown passes to lead the Cleveland Rams to a 15–14 victory over the Washington Redskins. That capped a season in which he was a unanimous All-NFL choice and became the first rookie ever to win the league's Most Valuable Player.

Early in 1946, the Rams moved to Los Angeles. As the Rams' quarterback—later splitting time with Norm Van Brocklin— Waterfield took the team to three straight title games, 1949–1951. The Rams won it all in 1951 with a 24–17 win over the Cleveland Browns in the title game.

As a passer, Waterfield was known for his ability to throw deep. He led the NFL in passing in 1946 and 1951, finishing with career totals of 814 completions, 11,849 yards gained, and 97 touchdown passes.

He was named first- or second-team All-NFL five times. One of the game's most versatile players, he was also an ace defensive back for his first four seasons, a top punter with a 42.4-yard average, and a deadly place kicker. In eight seasons he totaled 573 points on 13 touchdowns, 315 PATs, and 60 field goals.

Former pro football stars (left to right) Bob Waterfield, Guy Chamberlin, and Otto Graham posed together prior to ceremonies in Canton, Ohio, during which they were inducted into the Pro Football Hall of Fame on September 11, 1965. (AP Photo)

For the next seven seasons, the Rams were pro football's most feared offensive team, and Waterfield was the brilliant field general and precision passer who put points on the scoreboard. Always calm against even the greatest odds, he often led his team to come-from-behind victories.

In one 1948 game, the Rams fell behind to eventual league champion Philadelphia 28–0. Waterfield rallied his team to a tie on four late touchdown passes. Waterfield proved to be a determined competitor in the pros. In the 1950 divisional playoff, although he was unable to practice all week because of the flu, he came off the bench and threw three touchdown passes in a 24–14 win over the Chicago Bears.

[Career capsule courtesy of the Pro Football Hall of Fame]

"He was Captain America and the mighty Thor rolled into one," wrote Rob Fernas in the *Los Angeles Times*, "a real-life superhero who rewrote the record book, won the big game, and got the girl—a movie star, no less."[322]

Bob Waterfield graduated high school in Van Nuys, California, and went to work for three years to help earn money for himself and his mother, Frances, who was working in private nursing to try to get by. His mother urged him to go to college, and Bob enrolled at UCLA. He didn't play freshman football but caught some attention by fooling around punting the ball in his sophomore year. Added to the team as quarterback, he became an All-American in 1942 and led the Bruins to their first Rose Bowl in January 1943. He had been a first lieutenant in ROTC at the university and was expecting a callup in August.[323] In April 1943 Bob married the woman who was a legendary pinup in army barracks—movie actress Jane Russell, his high school sweetheart.[324]

He was inducted into the army on May 21, entering as a second lieutenant and tagged for Officer Candidate School at Fort Benning, Georgia, where he planned to become a paratrooper. He played some at Fort Benning, and on November 14 he threw three touchdown passes and scored a TD himself as his 176th Infantry team beat the 300th Infantry 27–20 in front of 20,000 soldiers.[325] Jane Russell had moved to Columbus, Georgia, to be with her husband.

Bob suffered a knee injury while playing basketball on an army team, and in June 1944 he was discharged for medical reasons and returned to UCLA.

The injury healed, and Bob played football again for the Bruins despite being a fifth-round draft pick of the Cleveland Rams in 1944. He was still "better known for his wife than for his play until a Most Valuable Player performance in the annual East-West Shrine game in San Francisco on New Year's Day 1945."[326] A combination of long punts, some quick kicks, and his passing and running (he scored the winning points on a lateral from Bob Kennedy), saw Waterfield as the headliner of the 13–7 game.

He signed with the Rams in June 1945 and began his pro career. He served as head coach of the Rams from 1960–62. He was named to the Pro Football Hall of Fame in 1965.

Arnie Weinmeister

New York Yankees, New York Giants / United States Army

Born: March 23, 1923, in Rhein, Saskatchewan, Canada
Died: June 28, 2000, in Seattle, Washington
Position: DT-T

Few players ever have been as dominant at their position in pro football as Arnie Weinmeister was in his six-year stint as a defensive tackle, which began with the New York Yankees of the All-America Football Conference in 1948 and ended with the New York Giants of the NFL in 1953.

He won second-team All-AAFC as a rookie followed by first-team All-AAFC in 1949. He was a unanimous All-NFL choice all four years with the Giants and he was selected to play in the NFL Pro Bowl each of his first four years in the league.

Arnie was one of the first defensive players to captivate the masses of fans the way an offensive ball-handler does. At 6'4" and 235 lbs., he was bigger than the average player of his day and he was widely considered to be the fastest lineman in pro football.

Blessed with a keen football instinct, he was a master at diagnosing opposition plays. He used his size and speed to stop whatever the opposition attempted, but it was as a pass rusher that he really caught the fans' attention. A natural team leader, he was the Giants' co-captain during his final season in New York.

In high school Arnie was a two-time All-City tackle. He played end, fullback, and tackle in his four-year tenure at the University of Washington, a tenure interrupted by a four-year army stint. New York Yankee coach Ray Flaherty first spotted Weinmeister as a fullback but wisely made him into a two-way tackle when he turned pro in 1948. When he moved to the Giants, Arnie was used almost exclusively on defense. With a six-year tenure in the AAFC and NFL, his career is one of the shortest of any Pro Football Hall of Fame member.

[Career capsule courtesy of the Pro Football Hall of Fame]

Arnie Weinmeister's parents both emigrated from Russia to Canada. His father, John, worked in 1940 as a pipe fitter for a plumbing contractor after moving to Portland, Oregon, when Arnie was still an infant. Arnie was an All-City tackle for Washington High. He received an athletic scholarship and played as a tackle and end for the University of Washington before having his career interrupted by wartime. He spent three years in the army, seeing action in France and Germany in a 155mm Long Tom field artillery unit with the 1st Army and with General Patton's Third Army.[327] After the war in Europe was over, Sergeant Weinmeister and his unit were asked to prepare to redeploy in the Pacific and were less than 48 hours out of arriving back in New York when V-J Day came. He was discharged in 1946 and returned to Washington to finish his studies.

It was at the January 1, 1948, East-West Game at Kezar Stadium in San Francisco where he truly drew national attention (and that of coach Ray Flaherty, which got him a tryout with the AAFC's New York Yankees.) He had never really been a standout at Washington, but his effort that day saw Flaherty dub him "the best-looking fullback prospect in the country." For his part, and referring to the new competition between the NFL and the young, aggressive AAFC, Arnie said, "Frankly, if it hadn't been for the two leagues and the 'war,' I wouldn't have played pro ball. The salaries they were paying before wouldn't have interested me. The 'war' was a good thing for the players and in a way, for pro football, too. It brought a lot of fellows into the game who wouldn't have considered it otherwise."[328]

Oddly, after his six-year NFL career had ended, he was approached to play Canadian football and signed with the British Columbia Lions. The New York Giants went to court to block his signing but lost their case, with the court ruling that the Giants had waived their option.[329] He played for the Lions in 1954 and again in 1955 before suffering a career-ending shoulder injury. Within six months, he had taken a position as an organizer with the Teamsters Union. His father and a brother had been active in labor affairs.

Weinmeister—who had majored in economic and labor courses in college—worked his way up to become the highest-ranking Teamsters official in the Pacific Northwest and an international vice president with the Teamsters. After the disappearance of Teamsters leader Jimmy Hoffa and ongoing government investigations, when the Justice Department filed suit in 1988 "to remove the Teamsters' senior leadership, charging that it had made a 'devil's pact' with organized crime, it accused Weinmeister and the 17 other members of the executive board of failing to root out corruption. Under a consent decree, scores of union officials were removed by overseers. Weinmeister remained in office. He said in a 1988 deposition that he had no knowledge of organized crime other than what he had read in the newspapers or had seen in the *Godfather* movies."[330]

When he was named to the Pro Football Hall of Fame in 1984, he said he'd heard from people he'd not heard from for 30 or 40 years.

"I met the owners of the Giants at a reception in Honolulu and told them that after 30 years it ought to be time to bury the hatchet."[331] It was a good feeling for someone who had been more or less given the cold shoulder after leaving to play in Canada.

Ralph Wilson Jr.

Buffalo Bills / United States Navy
Born: October 17, 1918, in Columbus, Ohio
Position: Team owner

Ralph Wilson Jr. was the man responsible for reintroducing pro football to western New York when, as one of the original owners in the American Football League, he formed the Buffalo Bills in 1959. As the undeniable leader of the Bills, Wilson continues to play a major role among NFL franchise owners as "the voice of reason" for his ability to tackle some of the league's toughest issues.

During his tenure as owner of the Bills, Wilson has watched two of his teams capture the AFL Championship (1964–65) and AFC titles in 1990, 1991, 1992, and 1993 on the way to an unprecedented four consecutive appearances in Super Bowls XXV, XXVI, XXVII, and XXVIII. The team also won AFL/AFC Eastern Division titles in 1966, 1980, 1988, 1989, and 1995. The Bills' 103 regular season wins in the 1990s were second best behind the San Francisco 49ers.

Always a football fan, Wilson first entered the pro football world when he purchased a minority share of the Detroit Lions. He later joined Lamar Hunt and the six other AFL originals who collectively became known as "The Foolish Club."

In the beginning, members of the NFL and the sports media regarded the AFL with considerable skepticism. Although the early years of the AFL were at best a struggle and Wilson was losing money, he "never once thought of throwing in the towel or selling the team." Determined to see the league succeed, Wilson even invested in another AFL team to prevent it from financial collapse. The Foolish Club did succeed, and following initial talks in January 1965 between Wilson and the late Carroll Rosenbloom, owner of the NFL's Baltimore Colts, a full merger plan between the two leagues was developed and implemented.

A former president of the AFL, Wilson served on the Expansion Committee of that league and the AFL-NFL Negotiations Committee. He was also prominent in the negotiations that resulted in a 1977 agreement between the NFL Management Council and the NFL Players Association.

Once described as the conscience of the NFL, Wilson has also served as the Chairman of the NFL Pension Committee and Labor Committee and currently serves on the Board of NFL Charities, the Super Bowl Site Selection Committee, and the NFL's Expansion Committee.

[Career capsule courtesy of the Pro Football Hall of Fame]

[Note: Some information about Wilson's service is contained in the section devoted to current NFL owners who served in World War II.]

NFL PERSONNEL WHO SERVED IN KOREA

Dick "Night Train" Lane

Los Angeles Rams, Chicago Cardinals, Detroit Lions / United States Army

Born: April 16, 1928, in Austin. Texas
Died: January 29, 2002, in Austin, Texas
Position: DB E

Dick Lane was an army veteran "looking for a good job" when he stopped in the offices of the Los Angeles Rams in 1952 and asked for a tryout. All he had for credentials was a battered scrapbook that chronicled his football experiences in high school, junior college, and the army.

The defending-champion Rams' coach Joe Stydahar saw just enough "good press" in the scrapbook to offer Lane a trial. At first Dick was tried at end, but with future Hall of Famers Tom Fears and Elroy "Crazylegs" Hirsch set as starters, his chances didn't look good. Lane did, however, spend a great deal of time consulting with Fears, who was continually playing the hit record, "Night Train," on his phonograph. One day, a teammate entered the room, saw Dick and blurted out, "Hey, there's 'Night Train,'" and "Night Train" Lane it was from then on.

Once Stydahar moved Lane to defense, he quickly made an impression. Blessed with outstanding speed, exceptional agility, reflex action, and a fierce determination to excel, Night Train set the NFL on fire as a rookie. He intercepted a record 14 passes in the 12-game season. Aside from being a constant threat to steal passes, Lane also became known as a devastating tackler.

Lane was also willing to take chances on the field in spite of the risks. Most, however, would agree that percentage-wise he was well ahead of the game. Lane played two years with the Rams before being traded to the Cardinals in 1954.

Six years later, he was sent to the Detroit Lions where he enjoyed his finest years. Dick was named first- or second-team All-NFL every year from 1954–63. Named to seven Pro Bowls, Night Train intercepted 68 passes for 1,207 yards and five touchdowns during his Hall of Fame career.

[Career capsule courtesy of the Pro Football Hall of Fame]

Today, we don't know what Richard Lane's real name is, and perhaps it's just as well. He was, as his official website, explains, "born to a mother who was a prostitute and a father who was a pimp…. At three months of age, he was adopted by Ella Lane, a widow with two children. She found the infant lying in a dumpster, left for dead."[332] Ms. Lane heard his cries from the dumpster and found him wrapped in old newspapers.[333] She rescued him from the dumpster and brought him home where she raised him. At the time of the 1930 Census, she worked as a laundress, working out of her own home. Records do seem uncertain as to Dick's actual age.

Numerous public records and his gravestone say he was born in 1928. The Social Security Death Index says he was born in 1929. When the 1940 Census was taken, Ella Lane was 67, working as a cook in a private home. Her son

L.B. lived with her, working as an insurance salesman; he was 29. "Richard, adopted son," was listed as ten years old. Her granddaughter, Elly May Edmondson, 13, was living in the house, too. Richard's mother was Johnny Mae, and his father was known as Texas Slim, but it was only when Lane was in high school that he learned that Johnny Mae had shot and killed his father (her pimp) in his sleep after he had beaten her. She spent several years in prison for the murder.[334]

Richard played a lot of football at Austin's L.C. Anderson High School, and then he spent one semester at Scottsbluff Junior College (now Western Nebraska Community College). He'd gone to Scottsbluff because that's where Johnny Mae had gone after prison, and when he visited her there, she agreed to pay for his education. "While playing in a pickup baseball game that summer at Scottsbluff, Lane was seen by a scout from the Kansas City Monarchs of the Negro National Baseball League. He agreed to play for one the team's minor league affiliates, the Omaha Rockets. He had to play under the name Richard King so he would remain eligible to play college football."[335] But he didn't play long because Ella Lane took ill and he rushed back to Austin to be with her. He was just in time; she died within days. Returning to Scottsbluff, he made the freshman football team and was named a Junior College All-American.

When he learned that Johnny Mae was turning tricks again, he was so angry he quit college and joined the army in 1948. Of all places to go, he was sent to Fort Knox for basic training. Lane rose to corporal and was stationed at Fort Ord where he had plenty of opportunity to play baseball, basketball, and football. He was second-team All-Army in 1949 and first team in 1951.[336]

After his February 7, 1952, discharge, he wasn't sure what he wanted to do next, but he started working in an aircraft factory "lifting large sheets of oil-covered metal into bins," according to the firm that represented him, CMG Worldwide. It was a job he despised. "Frustrated with his employment situation, Lane went out to seek other work. By happenstance, he found his way into the Los Angeles Rams office and asked for a tryout. With only his scrapbook of high school and junior college football clippings, the Rams decided to take a gamble on Lane." It was a gamble that paid off nicely for all concerned.

During his football years, he had met and married Dinah Washington, the famous entertainer, in 1963, but it was a short-lived marriage due to her death from an apparent overdose of drink and diet pills.

After football, he became a special assistant to Detroit Lions owner William Clay Ford, a position he held for seven years. Coaching came next, working as defensive coordinator at Baton Rouge's Southern University and Ohio's Central State University, but both were relatively short-term postings.

His post-football career took an unexpected turn when comedian Redd Foxx hired Lane to be Foxx's right-hand man, a combination road manager and bodyguard. Lane was enshrined in the Pro Football Hall of Fame in 1974 during this time.

After a year or so of work in the entertainment field, Detroit mayor Coleman Young named him in 1975 as head of the city's Police Athletic League, where he worked for a number of years.

Ollie Matson

Chicago Cardinals, Los Angeles Rams, Detroit Lions, Philadelphia Eagles / United States Army
Born: May 1, 1930, in Trinity, Texas
Died: February 19, 2011, in Los Angeles, California
Position: RB-FL

When Ollie Matson first signed to play with the Chicago Cardinals in 1952, he was hailed as the fleet-footed ball carrier who would hopefully lead the Cardinals out of pro football's basement.

Seven years later, when traded by the Cardinals to the Los Angeles Rams for an unprecedented nine players, he was tabbed as the star who could give the Rams a long awaited championship. Through no fault of his own, Ollie did neither. Yet little of the luster was lost from one of the most brilliant pro football careers ever.

Obviously, the greatness Matson achieved on NFL gridirons must be considered an individual accomplishment. He never enjoyed the winning team momentum to carry him along, and only two of the 14 teams on which he played finished over the .500 mark. Enemy defenses almost always concentrated on him alone. Yet his career record is exceptional.

Altogether, he gained 12,844 yards on rushing, receptions, and returns. He rushed for 5,173 yards and caught 222 passes for another

3,285 yards. He scored 40 touchdowns running, 23 on receptions, 9 on kick returns, and one on a fumble recovery.

Matson, an All-American college star at the University of San Francisco, was the Cardinals first-round draft choice in 1952. He delayed his pro signing so that he could compete as a member of the American track team in the 1952 Olympics. He won a bronze medal in the 400-meter race and a silver medal in the 1,600-meter relay. When he finally joined the Cardinals, he experienced a sensational rookie season.

Then military service interrupted his career for a year, but once back in a football uniform, he was an All-NFL performer year in and year out. During his 14 pro seasons, Ollie earned first- or second-team All-NFL honors six times and was selected to play in six Pro Bowls.

[Career capsule courtesy of the Pro Football Hall of Fame]

While a football player at the University of San Francisco, Ollie Matson bore some discrimination. The 1951 U.S.F. team had a perfect 9–0 season but received no invitations to bowl games in the South. *The New York Times* wrote, "It was later reported that the Orange, Sugar, and Gator Bowl committees that season did not consider inviting any teams that had black players." Hall of Famer Gino Marchetti confirmed that when his coach told his team they might get an invite to the Orange Bowl if they agreed to play without Ollie and Burl Toler, they declined. "We answered, 'No, we'd never do that.' And after we said no and removed ourselves from consideration, nobody ever had a second thought about it."[337]

It was quite a team. As Matson's obituary in the *Times* further noted, "Three of the players on that San Francisco team—Matson, Marchetti, and Bob St. Clair—were voted into the Pro Football Hall of Fame, a feat achieved by no other college team. Toler became the NFL's first black on-field official. The team's public relations director was Pete Rozelle, who was also voted into the Hall of Fame after a distinguished career as the NFL commissioner." The *San Francisco Chronicle* noted that the U.S.F. squad was destined forever to carry the slogan, "Unbeaten, Untied, and Uninvited."

The U.S.F. team had traveled to Tulsa, Oklahoma, in 1949 to play the University of Tulsa Golden Hurricanes. His reputation preceded him and there was anticipation of his Matson's arrival. He was dubbed the "Colored Comet" in the school's yearbook. Tulsa shut out U.S.F. in a 10–0 upset in November 1949, but when the Tulsa players traveled to San Francisco to play on September 23, 1950, "Ebony Ollie" (the phrase came from the Tulsa yearbook) scored two touchdowns in the first period and U.S.F. won the rematch 23–14.

Sports Illustrated noted, "Matson joined Jim Thorpe as the only athletes to earn an Olympic medal and induction into the college and pro football halls of fame."[338]

Toler had been born in Trinity, Texas, and the 1940 Census shows him living alone with his father, Ollie Matson Sr., a laborer in a sawmill. His mother, Gertrude, worked as a schoolteacher and lived elsewhere in Trinity with Ollie's twin sister Ocie. The 1930 Census shows Ollie Senior and Gertrude living together; Ollie Sr. was a track laborer for the steam railroad. Ollie Jr. moved with Gertie to San Francisco when he was still in his teens, completing Washington High School there. After a year at San Francisco City College, he went on to U.S.F.[339]

After college, and his Co-Rookie of the Year season with the Cardinals, Matson was beckoned into the army as an infantryman and—rather than being sent to Korea, where the war was winding down—was stationed at Fort Ord, where by May 1953 he was competing in the Sixth Army track meet for Fort Ord and won the 440.[340] He also played football for the Fort Ord Warriors. He was named All-Army in 1953 and named MVP by the *Army Times*.[341] In the Salad Bowl game of 1954, Maston scored three touchdowns, easily beating the Great Lakes Navy team and thereby winning the All-Service championship. Even though he was still in the service, Matson was offered a pro contract with the Cardinals intended to keep him with the team. He signed and returned to the NFL for a first workout on October 1, 1954—but not before a Congressional investigation regarding the armed forces "coddling" athletes in the service. Matson was one of 20 athletes named, including some from baseball, basketball, boxing, and golf.[342]

When Ollie had moved from the Cardinals to the Rams after the 1958 season, the Rams had to offer nine players to pry him loose. An image of the February 28, 1959, telegram in which Pete Rozelle announced the trade is offered on the Pro Football Hall of Fame website.[343]

After his pro career, Matson worked in athletic programs teaching phys ed and coaching football at Los Angeles High School, then coaching college running backs for San Diego State and doing some pro scouting for the Philadelphia Eagles. He worked for 11 years as special-events supervisor for Los Angeles Memorial Coliseum. Unfortunately, the rigors of the game may have taken its toll in later years, and at the time of his death he had been "mostly bedridden for several years due to a form of dementia. [His nephew Art Thompson] said Mr. Matson hadn't spoken in four years."[344] Noted neurosurgeon Robert Cantu has included Ollie Matson and fellow Hall of Famer John Mackey among the 33 deceased NFL players in his 2012 study of chronic traumatic encephalopathy (CTE).[345]

Thompson also remembered Ollie's mother, Gertrude, who had struck her own blow against discrimination. "In 1964, my grandmother was the first African American to have a float in the Rose Parade. She was watching the parade and wondered why there weren't any black people in it. She said, 'I'm going to get a float in the Rose Parade.' She solicited [Mr. Matson]. He funded the whole thing. It won a prize, too."[346]

He'd been a man of modesty and when he was named to the Pro Football Hall of Fame in 1972, his own children hadn't known how accomplished their father had been. "You mean they got a parade just for you, daddy?" asked his daughter, Barbara. Years later, Barbara said her father rarely mentioned his football career. "He wasn't the type of person who talks about himself or what he's done…. A lot of things about him I found out later in life, reading books and magazines."[347]

Mike McCormack

New York Yanks, Cleveland Browns / United States Army

Born: June 21, 1930, in Chicago, Illinois

Position: T-DG-OT

Mike McCormack, one of the game's greatest offensive tackles, began his pro football career in 1951 with the NFL's New York Yanks where as a rookie he earned the starting right tackle spot. That year he earned the first of six trips to the Pro Bowl before being called into military service.

The Baltimore Colts acquired his rights before the start of the 1953 season and traded him to the Cleveland Browns in a massive 15-player deal. Although the Browns knew Mike would not be available for a full year, he was the key man in the trade. Coach Paul Brown always considered it one of his wisest personnel moves.

During his first season in Cleveland, McCormack, a former University of Kansas star and Chicago native, was asked to fill the middle guard position that had been vacated by the retiring Bill Willis on the defensive unit. It was a tall order, considering Willis would be elected to the Pro Football Hall of Fame. McCormack, not surprisingly, was up to the challenge.

He quickly became an important factor on an excellent Cleveland defensive team. Mike enjoyed perhaps his most memorable individual moment there when, in the 1954 NFL Championship Game, he stole the ball from Detroit Lions quarterback Bobby Layne to set up one of the early touchdowns in a 56–10 Cleveland rout.

But it was as an offensive tackle that McCormack made his lasting mark in pro football. Mike was the Browns' offensive right tackle for eight years from 1955–62. During that period, the Browns' forward wall played a major role in assuring a balanced offensive approach and McCormack, equally adept as a blocker on rushing plays and as a quarterback protector, was a stabilizing factor throughout the period.

[Career capsule courtesy of the Pro Football Hall of Fame]

Mike McCormack had been captain of the University of Kansas Jayhawks and played in 12 games for the 1951 New York Yanks, who posted an unhappy 1–9–2 season. It was the last year for the franchise. With that NFL year under his belt, McCormack was expected to join the 1952 Dallas Texans, coached by Jimmy Phelan. It wasn't to be—and the 1–11 Texans only lasted one season before the franchise was moved to Baltimore to become the Colts. Instead, McCormack was called in the late summer of 1952 to serve two years in the United States Army.

He'd already passed a preliminary physical, and though there was some question, his induction was expected. "The healthy looking McCormack has a confused medical history because of a lifelong lung condition," explained the *Dallas Morning News*. "He once was turned down for ROTC membership on medical grounds, and was surprised when he was given approval by a draft board physician."[348] He was indeed inducted.

McCormack was actually still in the army when he was included in a large trade involving 15 players—the March 26, 1953, trade took him to the Browns. It was an unusual trade because of the five players the Browns received for the ten they sent to Baltimore, only one was someone they could count on getting—Don Colo. Both McCormack and Herschel Forester were in the service, John Petitbon was expecting a call to serve, and Oklahoma center Tom Catlin's "status with the armed forces won't be clarified until after his graduation."[349] McCormack had been posted to Fort Leonard Wood in Missouri. He and Hal Mitchell of UCLA and Fort Lee were named the All-Army tackles for 1953.

By August 1954, he was out of the service, in training camp with the Browns, and on his way to a superlative career. Paul Brown considered him the best offensive lineman that he had coached in his own Hall of Fame career.[350] Thirty years later, in 1984, Mike McCormack was enshrined in the Pro Football Hall of Fame.

After his playing career, McCormack coached the Philadelphia Eagles for three seasons (1973–75), the Baltimore Colts for two (1980–81), and the Seattle Seahawks for one (1982). His work as interim head coach for the Seahawks only lasted one year because he had actually been president and general manager of the team, a post to which he returned full time once Chuck Knox was hired for 1983. McCormack later became the first president and GM of the Carolina Panthers.

Les Richter

Los Angeles Rams / United States Army
Born: October 6, 1930, in Fresno, California
Died: June 12, 2010, in Riverside, California
Position: LB-MG

Linebacker Les Richter was the second player selected overall in the 1952 NFL Draft by the New York Yanks. Two days later, the franchise folded and was sold back to the NFL. Shortly thereafter the assets of the club, including the signing rights to Richter, were granted to the expansion Dallas Texans. The Los Angeles Rams then dealt 11 players to the Texans to obtain the All-American from California.

Los Angeles had to wait two years while Richter served in the military. When he returned he signed with the Rams and embarked on a nine-season career that earned him the reputation as one of the best linebackers of his era. He was especially known for his rugged and punishing style of play.

Richter was selected to eight straight Pro Bowls. The only time he did not receive the honor was in his final season in 1962. He was also named a first- or second-team All-NFL each season during a six-year span from 1955–60. Aside from his play at linebacker, Richter also saw some time at center and handled the Rams' place-kicking duties early in his career. He received much attention in 1955 for his play on defense and his clutch place-kicking that helped the Rams to an 8–3–1 record to win the NFL Western Division crown and a berth in the Championship Game.

Les Richter (right), University of California All-American and the No. 1 draft choice of the expansion Dallas Texans of the National Football League, talks over contract terms for the 1952 season with Jim Phelan, head coach and general manager of the team after Richter arrived in Dallas, Texas, on April 25, 1952. (AP Photo)

He led the Rams in scoring in 1955 and 1956. In all, he totaled 193 points off 29 field goals and 106 extra points during his career.

Richter recorded 16 career interceptions that he returned for 206 yards. Twice he had four picks in a season (1957 and 1961) and was the Rams leading interceptor in 1957. Richter battled through various injuries but never missed a game during his 112-game NFL career. In fact, early in the 1961 season he suffered a broken cheekbone during a game against the Pittsburgh Steelers. He played through the injury not initially knowing it was broken. He had a protective guard added to his helmet and completed the season even though he broke his cheekbone again five weeks later.

Richter passed away on June 12, 2010, at the age of 79.

[Career capsule courtesy of the Pro Football Hall of Fame]

Leslie Richter grew up in Fresno where his father, Clifford, worked as a cashier for an insurance company. Les was a star on both the Fresno High School football and baseball fields, and he was the president of his class. He was captain of the football team. He went on to the University of California at Berkeley where he became an All-American guard for the Golden State Bears under noted Cal coach Pappy Waldorf—and also set a Pacific Coast Conference record with 40 point after touchdown kicks in 1951. Indeed, he was All-American both on defense and offense. He was also a top student, the valedictorian of his 1952 graduating class at Berkeley. His degree was in business administration.

Although signed to the Yanks and then the Texans, the Los Angeles Rams really wanted to get him—enough so that they, in effect, traded an entire team to do so. The 11 players traded remains the largest deal in pro football history to get just one man. He signed his Rams contract on June 30, 1952. That the Rams would trade so many players for one man was particularly impressive because it was known that Richter had already been commissioned as a second lieutenant in the Army Reserves and expected to be called to serve since the Korean War was on in earnest.[351]

His last game before serving was an August 15 exhibition game in Chicago for the College All-Stars against the team with which he'd signed—the Rams. It was a close game, but the Rams won 10–7. Rams coach Joe Stydahar said the toughest player of all was Richter—as he'd expected, and why they had traded 11 players

to have him on hand a couple of years in the future.

After the game, Les reported to Camp Cooke for service in the United States Army, where he was assigned to the 44th Infantry and sent on to Fort Lewis, Washington. He played and helped coach football in the army, working in special services. He also hosted a weekly sports radio show in Tacoma.[352]

He played some football in the army, too, and injured his knee at one point in the fall of 1952. One of the doctors who examined it was Dr. Dan Fortmann, later a Hall of Famer himself.[353]

The recently discharged First Lieutenant Leslie Richter reported back to the Rams on June 6, 1954, after nearly two years in the army. In the era of 33-man rosters, he was as reliable as they come, never once missing a game.

After retiring from football, Richter began work that landed him in another hall of fame. He became a co-owner of Riverside International Raceway and also co-founded the International Race of Champions, ultimately becoming a vice president of NASCAR and playing a dominant role in the development of California Speedway. The interest in racing was one Richter had from childhood. As his obituary in the *Fresno Bee* noted, early on when he was "too small to play football, his passion was auto racing. Oh, how he loved seeing the local drivers pilot their cars around the track."[354] He was inducted into the Motorsports Hall of Fame of America in 2009.

Richter was a member of the Class of 2011 in the Pro Football Hall of Fame. His children, Jon and Annie, represented their late father at the enshrinement.

Don Shula

Cleveland Browns, Baltimore Colts, Washington
 Redskins, Miami Dolphins / United States Army

Born: January 4, 1930, in Grand River, Ohio

Position: DB, coach

Don Shula's record as head coach of the Baltimore Colts from 1963–69 and the Miami Dolphins from 1970–95 is unmatched in NFL history. In 1995, he concluded his 33rd season as the winningest NFL head coach ever with a career mark of 347–173–6 (.665).

Of all NFL coaches, only Shula and the immortal George Halas have attained 300 victories. The Colts under Shula enjoyed seven straight winning seasons, and in 26 years at Miami, Shula's Dolphins experienced only two seasons below .500. Shula's team reached the playoffs 20 times in 33 years, and his teams won at least 10 games in a season 21 times.

Shula holds the NFL record for having coached in six Super Bowls, but his teams won only twice. In Super Bowl VII, the 1972 Dolphins completed their historic 17–0–0 campaign—the only perfect complete season in NFL history—with a 14–7 win over the Washington Redskins. In 1973, Miami defeated the Minnesota Vikings in Super Bowl VIII to culminate a two-season span when the Dolphins won 32-of-34 games.

Shula, who was born January 4, 1930, in Grand River, Ohio, played college football at John Carroll University in Cleveland and then became one of two rookies on Coach Paul Brown's 1951 Cleveland Browns team. In 1953, Shula moved to the Baltimore Colts as part of a historic 15-player trade. He played cornerback for the Colts for four seasons and for the Washington Redskins in 1957 before turning to coaching as a college assistant.

He returned to pro football in 1960 as the Detroit Lions' defensive coordinator. In 1963, Shula was hired as head coach of the Baltimore Colts. And at just 33, he was the youngest head coach in NFL history.

In seven years, he led the Colts to a 73–26–4 record and playoff appearances in three seasons. In 1970, he made a major career move when he took over the Dolphins in only their fifth season. Almost immediately, he turned the Miami team into a perpetual winner.

[Career capsule courtesy of the Pro Football Hall of Fame]

Larry Csonka told *USA Today* in 2012, "Of the top five people I have met in my life, two of them—you know, in the Marines, the ones you land on the beach with—are Tom Coughlin and Don Shula."[355] In 2009, Shula had joined Admiral Mike Mullen, the chairman of the Joint Chiefs of Staff, and others (including NFL running back Warrick Dunn) on a morale-building USO tour visit to Iraq and Afghanistan. "There he was, at age 79, strapped into an army helmet and a 40-lb. bulletproof vest, squeezed into a Blackhawk combat helicopter slicing across the Afghan desert over enemy Taliban outposts."[356] One can never overestimate the benefits of such visits, but Shula wasn't in the Marines. Among the places the group visited was the Pat Tillman USO on Bagram Airfield, Afghanistan, on July 15.

Shula himself had served in the 145th Armored Regiment, Company C, of the Ohio National Guard and was activated with his unit in early 1952 and sent to Camp Polk, Louisiana, to undergo preparatory training for duty in Korea. Corporal Shula and former Browns Carl Taseff (who attended John Carroll College with Shula) arrived at Camp Polk together on January 25.[357] They were incorporated into the 37th Infantry Division. Shula's unit was officially deactivated in November, and by November 16 he was fresh out of the army and made a brief appearance in his first game after rejoining the team, a 29–28 win over the Pittsburgh Steelers. He started in the November 23 game against the Eagles but wound up having to leave the game due to a badly cut lower lip and with three teeth that had been loosened.

Shula was born in Grand River, Ohio, and grew up in Painesville, the son of Czech-born Donald Shula, a foreman in a local nursery, and Mary Shula, born in Ohio to two Czech parents. The fate of the nursery during the Depression is unknown, but at the time of the 1940 Census, there were six children in the family, and Don Sr. was working as a laborer in a tin factory. In 1944, Don Jr. wanted to go out for high school football, but to do so he had to forge his mother's signature on the form requesting parental consent. He considered entering the priesthood while at the Jesuit Catholic John Carroll College, but he was too enamored with the game of football. He graduated in 1951 and years later endowed the Don Shula Chair in Philosophy at what is now John Carroll University. The school also has a sports stadium and lecture series bearing the Shula name.

NFL Personnel Who Served In Vietnam

Charlie Joiner

Houston Oilers, Cincinnati Bengals, San Diego Chargers / United States Army
Born: October 14, 1947, in Many, Louisiana
Position: WR

Charlie Joiner played pro football for 18 years, longer than any other wide receiver in history at the time of his retirement. When he retired at the age of 39 after the 1986 season with the San Diego Chargers, he ranked as the leading receiver of all time with 750 catches.

Blessed with excellent speed and tantalizing moves, Joiner averaged 16.2 yards per catch and accounted for 12,146 yards and 65 touchdowns on his receptions. He ranked sixth in career reception yardage.

The Houston Oilers targeted Joiner for the defensive backfield when they picked the 5'11", 180-pounder from Grambling in the fourth round of the 1969 AFL-NFL Draft. Joiner played briefly on defense and the kickoff return team but soon became established as a premier pass catcher.

In his fourth season in 1972, Houston sent him to the Cincinnati Bengals in a four-player swap. Four years later in 1976, he was traded to San Diego. With the Chargers, Joiner blossomed into super-stardom. He and quarterback Dan Fouts formed a lethal pass-catch team that accounted for the preponderance of his 586 receptions as a Charger.

During his 11 years in San Diego, Joiner caught 50 or more passes seven times and had 70 or more receptions three seasons. Injuries cut into his playing time at the beginning, but in a 193-game span over his final 13 seasons, Joiner

missed only one game. He was an All-NFL pick in 1980 and a Pro Bowl choice three times. In the 1980 AFC title game, he led the Chargers with six receptions for 130 yards and two touchdowns.

Joiner, who was born October 14, 1947, in Many, Louisiana, was once described by San Francisco 49ers coaching great Bill Walsh as "the most intelligent, the smartest, the most calculating receiver the game has ever known."

[Career capsule courtesy of the Pro Football Hall of Fame]

The San Diego Chargers' Charlie Joiner catches a Dan Fouts pass for 20 yards in the third quarter to set an NFL career reception record with 11,843 yards on October 6, 1986. The play came in their game against Seattle. Joiner broke Don Maynard's record of 11,834 yards. (AP Photo)

Soon after being drafted by the Houston Oilers, Charlie had another obligation to fulfill. Thanks to good advice he received, the 1968 graduate of Grambling State University took the proactive step of joining the U.S. Army Reserve rather than await events and probably be drafted into the U.S. Army. He went through basic training and then was assigned to a unit in Houston—the 4005th Hospital Unit. It's a unit that was formed in July 1916 as the American Red Cross of St. Mary's. A number of changes both in the way the Reserves are organized and the hospital units incorporated followed over the years, but since May 1963 the 4005th has been organized in Houston. In 1952 this group became our present United States Army Reserves, and the 329th General Hospital in Houston continued as a Ready Reserve Unit and the Organized Reserves as the 11th General Hospital.

Someone associated with the Oilers had a connection with the medical unit, and Charlie was welcomed. After completing basic training, he was promoted to private first class and served as a nurse in the hospital unit. Though the unit was not mobilized during the Vietnam War, they stood ready to do so at any time, and Joiner recalled two times that the unit was asked to assemble on standby for two or three days "but we never got the order to go to Vietnam."[358] He served alongside some men who were conscientious objectors. "Some people did that because they had beliefs that they didn't want to carry a gun and that's why they were in the hospital unit. I just happened to be assigned to that unit." PFC Joiner fulfilled his Army Reserve obligation on weekends, permitting him time to continue to train during the rest of the week with the Oilers.

The 4005th was partially mobilized in Operations Desert Shield and Desert Storm and was also partially mobilized in Operation Determined Effort (Bosnia). It was actively mobilized during the Global War on Terror with deployments to Iraq and Afghanistan as well as to backfill at Landstuhl Regional Medical Center in Germany. Its first warzone deployment began in September 2009, and some 35 personnel were sent to Afghanistan to help train medics of the Afghan National Army.

At the time Joiner retired after the 1986 season, he held records for the most career receptions, most receiving yards, and most games played of any wide receiver in NFL history. Since 1987, he has worked as the receivers coach for the Kansas City Chiefs and the San Diego Chargers. He was elected into the Pro Football Hall of Fame in 1996.

Bob Kalsu

Buffalo Bills / United States Army

Please see the biography of Bob Kalsu in Section 2.

Ray Nitschke

Green Bay Packers / United States Army

Born: December 29, 1936, in Elmwood Park, Illinois
Died: March 8, 1998, in Venice, Florida
Position: LB

Ray Nitschke, according to Hall of Fame quarterback and teammate Bart Starr, was a "classic example of Dr. Jekyll and Mr. Hyde."

Off the field he was a thoughtful caring person. On the field, he was a ferocious middle linebacker who at times seemed to truly enjoy hitting people.

A fierce competitor, Ray was the heart of the great Packers defense of the 1960s. He was the first defensive player from the Packers' dynasty years to be elected to the Pro Football Hall of Fame.

In the mid-1960s, a national sports magazine asked a group of former NFL linebacking stars to rate the middle linebackers of the day. The panel first determined the skills it would seek in the ideal man—strength, quickness, speed, toughness, and leadership. Ray Nitschke, the choice as the all-around top man, ranked very high or absolutely tops in every category. "The core of the Packers"… "an inspiration on the field"…"gives 100 percent all the time"…"has an overwhelming desire to make the play"… "without a peer as a leader"…panel members remarked as they explained their consensus opinion.

Ray was born in Elmwood Park, Illinois, and grew up in a tough Chicago neighborhood. He was an All-State quarterback in high school and could have signed a professional baseball contract with the St. Louis Browns.

He opted for a football scholarship at Illinois, where he was shifted to a combined fullback on offense, linebacker on defense. The Packers drafted Ray No. 3 in 1958. Although he started eight games as a rookie, it wasn't until his third season that Nitschke got the job of middle linebacker for good. Ray was a complete player.

Ray earned either first- or second-team All-NFL honors seven times in eight years from 1962–69. In addition to being a hard-hitting tackler, he was excellent in pass coverage as his 25 lifetime interceptions attest.

[Career capsule courtesy of the Pro Football Hall of Fame]

It wasn't just that Nitschke grew up in a tough neighborhood. He had a rough childhood, too. His father, Robert, was killed in a car accident in 1940, and his mother died of a blood clot when Ray was in his early teens. "My father died when I was three, my mother when I was 14, so I took it out on all the kids in the neighborhood. What I like about this game is the contact, the man-to-man, the getting-it-out-of-your-system."[359]

His second call to the army came in 1961, when the Green Bay linebacker was ordered to report to Fort Lewis, Washington, that November, on the same day the army ordered Paul Hornung to Fort Riley, Kansas.[360] Ray had previously served a six-month stint in the service before joining the Army Reserve. "I took an oath of obligation when I joined the reserves and never considered applying for deferment," Nitschke said after he had reported to the 32nd Red Arrow Infantry Division.[361] Fortunately for the Packers, and his own professional standing, Pvt. Nitschke was given weekend liberty on a game-to-game basis, which allowed him to continue to play during the remainder of the season. On July 9, 1962, he was discharged from Fort Lewis.

Roger Staubach

Dallas Cowboys / United States Navy

Born: February 5, 1942, in Cincinnati, Ohio

Position: QB

Roger Staubach joined the Dallas Cowboys as a 27-year-old rookie in 1969 and didn't win the regular quarterbacking job until his third season in 1971. But for the nine seasons he was in command of the potent Cowboys attack, the Cowboys played in six NFC championship games, winning four of them, and also scored victories in Super Bowls VI and XII.

The 6'3", 200-lb. Staubach wound up his career after the 1979 season with an 83.4 passer rating, the best mark by an NFL passer up to that time. His career chart shows 1,685 completions in 2,958 passing attempts, which were good for 22,700 yards and 153 touchdowns.

Making Staubach particularly dangerous was his ability to scramble out of trouble—his 410 career rushes netted him 2,264 yards for a 5.5-yard average and 20 touchdowns. He led the NFL in passing four times. He was also an All-NFC choice five times and was selected to play in six Pro Bowls.

Staubach first starred as a quarterback at the U.S. Naval Academy, where he was a Heisman Trophy winner as a junior in 1963. Following his graduation, he spent a mandatory four years on active duty, including service in Vietnam, before he was able to turn his attention to pro football.

During his finest years with the Cowboys, Roger had the reputation for making the big play. He was the MVP of Super Bowl VI and provided the offensive spark in a defense-dominated Super Bowl XII victory.

In 1972, he missed most of the season with a separated shoulder, but he relieved Craig Morton in a divisional playoff against San Francisco and threw two touchdown passes in the last 90 seconds to defeat the 49ers 30–28. With that performance, he won back his regular job and did not relinquish it again during his career.

[Career capsule courtesy of the Pro Football Hall of Fame]

His coach at Annapolis called him "the greatest quarterback Navy ever had." With the Heisman and two wins in the Army-Navy Game, Staubach had become nationally famous. Virtually every American serving in Vietnam knew who he was.[362] He worked as a logistics and supply officer there, and he took some ribbing. "I learned a lot in the military, supporting those Marines in Vietnam, and those guys were unbelievable. They were out there fighting the fight. And I was in the rear, and they used to give me a hard time like, 'Hey Staubach, what are you doing?' They would be out on combat missions, but they were great. I lived at Camp Tinshaw with a bunch of Navy Seals for a while, and they used to go out on a mission and they would come back and say, 'Hey Staubach, where were you? Did you go to the O(fficers) Club tonight?' My respect is limitless for our Special Forces."[363]

He had a different take from some as to where one can find additional meaning in service work. "The teamwork is not people falling into step, but is rather people truly caring about someone other than themselves. In the military, you are watching the back of your brethren all the time, whether it is in combat—and I was not out there in combat. I was in Vietnam and supported the Marine Corps and the South Vietnamese troops, which was in northern South Vietnam. They were unbelievable.… In the military, and I also mean at the Naval Academy, you learn about the importance of someone other than yourself, to get that balance in life, not only to take out of life but to give back…all of us should be working on it every day because you cannot do it by yourself. When you start saying 'It's all about me,' and it's only about you and you are only trying to satisfy yourself, you have a problem. In the military, it is just the opposite. You are there to make sure you understand the importance of someone else and what they mean to you."[364]

He lost a classmate, Tommy Holden, in Vietnam. And he once was quoted in *The Stars and Stripes* saying that he'd felt guilty he wasn't doing enough there in Vietnam. "And I got hammered by an Admiral over there. He actually called me in and said, 'Roger, you are doing your job over here, and there are a lot of people like you doing your job.' He really chewed me out for that."

Color blindness had prevented him from more of a frontline role. His job was indeed an important one, as he served in-country for a year. For most of that time, he was stationed at Chu Lai, "in charge of the 'Sand Ramp,' an ugly curve of oil-stained beach where LSTs crunched ashore to disgorge vehicles, ammo, fuel, and crated supplies. I had 100 or more enlisted men under me and about 30 Vietnamese. I was in effect the beachmaster there, in the Freight Terminal Division…in charge of all the shipping and receiving where all the ammunition supplies came in, and we would get it off to the Marine bases. We would get these big forklifts to go in and offload these LSTs, and then we would send all the ammunition supplies out to the Marine bases.… We moved gear, all right. Fortunately, I never came under fire, and my 12-month tour of duty ended before the Tet Offensive of early '68."[365]

It wasn't that he was destined to become a Hall of Famer. He had only ever played quarterback in high school and wanted to play baseball as well as football. Getting into the Naval Academy was almost a bit unexpected, but when he did, it proved a perfect fit. He earned seven letters at Annapolis in football, baseball, and basketball. He had thought about making the navy a career despite having a pro contract in his back pocket. Even after pro football, and a very successful career in real estate, Staubach made time to attend numerous veterans events and has been a leading spokesman for the National Vietnam War Museum in Weatherford, Texas.

Don Steinbrunner

Cleveland Browns / United States Air Force

Please see the biography of Don Steinbrunner in Section 2.

[Note: The positions provided for each player are those as indicated on ProFootballReference.com.]

War Service and the Pro Football Hall of Fame

by Andy Piascik

World War II impacted pro football like no other event. After Pearl Harbor, things were so dire in the National Football League that for a while there was talk of shutting down the pro game. That did not happen, but the NFL season was shortened, attendance dwindled, and several franchises either merged or ceased operations.

Hundreds of players served in the military during the war. Hundreds of other future pro players went from high schools and colleges into the service and had their pro careers delayed. Many other potential careers were ended before they began by death, injuries, psychological trauma, and time away from the game. Twenty-one active or former players made the ultimate sacrifice.

But the game survived, and every franchise from 1941 was around to play again in 1946. In part because of the NFL's perseverance in the face of such adversity, pro football experienced a major surge in popularity after the war.

Some of the game's greatest players graced NFL fields during those difficult years. Many of them have been elected to the Pro Football Hall of Fame. Of the Hall of Famers who served during the war, there is a small group whose time in the military appears to have been factored into their selections. Those players are Ace Parker, George McAfee, Bill Dudley, Wayne Millner (all of whom missed three years), Charley Trippi (who missed two years), and Tony Canadeo (who missed one season).

Looking at what these players achieved without considering the interruption or delay to their careers, it could well be argued that only Dudley has credentials that are of Hall of Fame caliber. Yet with the exception of Millner—widely considered to be the Hall's biggest mistake—the selectors were absolutely justified in taking into account the unique circumstances when they voted in these men.

By no means is this meant to question the abilities of these players. All except Millner were selected as first-team All-Pros at least twice, several had MVP and MVP-like seasons, and all but Dudley played in at least one Championship Game. The point simply is that while these players had careers that were potentially of Hall of Fame caliber, that is perhaps different from a bona fide Hall of Fame career.

What complicates matters is that there is an equal number of players similarly impacted by the war with better credentials who have been bypassed by Hall of Fame selectors. In several cases, the bypassed players have vastly superior credentials to the ones mentioned above. Two of those players—Mac Speedie and Gene Brito—missed four seasons because of military service, while Dick Barwegan, Dick Stanfel, and Lou Rymkus missed two years.

Significantly, four of the five bypassed players were linemen. Canadeo, Dudley, McAfee, Parker, and Trippi, on the other hand, were all backs. Of probably even greater significance, three of the five bypassed players played substantial parts of their careers in the All-America Football Conference. Many modern-day fans and perhaps some Hall of Fame voters do not realize that the AAFC was a major league that many observers at the time regarded as approximately the equal to the NFL.

Mac Speedie

End, Cleveland Browns 1946–52

Mac Speedie is a bit of an anomaly to this discussion because he belongs in the Pro Football Hall of Fame irrespective of the time he lost to the military. Of the five great receivers from the decade after World War II—Pete Pihos, Elroy Hirsch, Tom Fears, Dante Lavelli, and Speedie—Speedie was the best, yet he is the only one not in the Hall of Fame. Speedie won more receiving titles (4) and was a first-team All-Pro as a receiver more times (6) than his great contemporaries even though his career was by far the shortest.

One of Speedie's most impressive credentials is being named to the first team on the combined All-AAFC/NFL teams in three different seasons. No other end who played in the 1946–49 period, not any of the four above or any among Jim Benton, Mal Kutner, Ken Kavanaugh, Alyn Beals, Jim Keane, and Billy Dewell was named even twice. In fact, of all the great players from that era, only five were named both All-League and All-AAFC/NFL in the same season three times: Otto Graham, Steve Van Buren, Bulldog Turner, Al Wistert, and Speedie.

It's all the more remarkable, then, that Speedie accomplished what he did despite missing four full seasons to military service. By the time he played his first pro game, he was

only four months shy of his 27th birthday. As short as his seven-year career may seem, he was already 33 years old because of the time he lost when he went to play in Canada in 1953. Even then, Speedie was still among the very best in the game as he led the league in receptions and was a first-team All-Pro in his last NFL season.

When he went to Canada, Speedie was second in career receptions and was first all-time in catches and yards per season, ahead even of Hutson. Those records stood until they were broken by Charley Hennigan of the Oilers, who played primarily in the early years of the American Football League when it was vastly inferior to the NFL. Setting the early AFL aside, Speedie's per-season records were the highest among receivers who played at least seven seasons for 20 and 25 years, respectively. When they were surpassed, it was by all-time greats Lance Alworth and Charley Taylor, both of whom had their best years during the 1960s passing revolution and both of whom were slam-dunk Hall of Famers.

The Browns made it to their league Championship Game in every one of Speedie's seven seasons, winning five times in succession. Of all players from every era who are not in the Hall of Fame, only Al Wistert and several others have Hall of Fame credentials that are the equal of Speedie's. Given that he spent 51 months in the U.S. Army, however, Speedie is probably the one player on the outside looking in who is most deserving of induction.

Note: The 1946 Cleveland Browns Media Guide *informs us that Speedie "entered the army in March, 1942 and was discharged as first lieutenant in June, 1946. Served in reconditioning work in the medical corps." He was stationed at Fort Warren, Wyoming, for most of his service time and played football for the base team, most notably against Paul Brown's Great Lakes team in 1945.*

Dick Barwegan

Guard, New York Yankees, Baltimore Colts, Chicago Bears 1947–54

While attending Purdue University, Dick Barwegan joined the Army Air Corps and served for two years. He then returned to Purdue in 1946 for a year before signing with the AAFC Yankees. By the time he played his first pro game, Barwegan was almost 26 years old.

He played for four different franchises in two leagues in his eight seasons, and at each stop he was one of the best guards in the game. Like Mac Speedie, Barwegan established that fact in his very first season while playing with a strong Yankees team. He played both ways early in his career, but it was on offense that Barwegan was one of the game's best linemen.

Also like Speedie, Barwegan did very well on the All-AAFC/NFL teams. He was a second-team choice as a rookie and then garnered first-team honors in 1948 and 1949. He was also a first-team All-AAFC choice in all three of those years.

Barwegan was one of the game's best guards even when he was playing for a weak Colts team in 1949. After the merger of the AAFC and NFL, he was traded to the Bears, one of the NFL's strongest teams with one of football's best lines. Although he played alongside two Hall of Fame linemates—Bulldog Turner and George Connor—it is Barwegan who was the best player on Chicago's line, and he was a unanimous first-team All-Pro in his first two NFL seasons.

Barwegan remained one of the game's best linemen through the end of his career. He was a second-team All-Pro in 1952 and was named to the Pro Bowl four times in a row after each of the 1950–53 seasons. Because of the delayed start to his career, he was 33 years old when he played his last game after just eight seasons.

And again like Speedie, Barwegan has unfairly suffered in Hall of Fame consideration because of the inaccurate perception that the AAFC was not a major league. Relative to the NFL, the AAFC was stronger than the AFL until at least 1968 and possibly for that league's entire history. The brevity of Barwegan's career when compared to players from more recent years is also likely to have caused some voters to bypass him.

Even setting aside the two years he lost to the military, however, closer examination reveals that Barwegan's career was not short at all for the times. That is evident when he is compared to a number of Hall of Famers from his era. Barwegan played eight seasons and 92 games in his career. By comparison, Doak Walker played six seasons and 67 games, Arnie Weinmeister played six seasons and 71 games, Ace Parker played seven seasons and 68 games, George McAfee played eight seasons and 75 games, Steve Van Buren played eight seasons and 83 games, Jack Christiansen played eight seasons and 89 games, George Connor played eight seasons and

90 games, Bob Waterfield played eight seasons and 91 games, Bill Willis played eight seasons and 99 games, Tom Fears played nine seasons and 87 games, and Charley Trippi played nine seasons and 99 games.

Note: Dick Barwegan played football for the 4th Air Force team during the war, competing against Lou Rymkus and the Navy team in the January 7, 1945, Army-Navy Pacific Ocean Championship game at Honolulu. He was discharged in May 1946.

Dick Stanfel

Guard, Detroit Lions, Washington Redskins 1952–58

Although he was not colorful in the manner of Bobby Layne or a national icon like Doak Walker, Dick Stanfel was one of the cornerstones of Detroit's outstanding teams of 1952–54. He stepped into a starting job as a rookie and was a unanimous first-team All-Pro in his second season. It is no coincidence that Stanfel's first year was Detroit's first championship season in 17 years and the beginning of the greatest era in Lions history.

Stanfel went into the military not long after turning 18 and served for almost two years. Upon being discharged, he enrolled at the University of San Francisco, graduating in 1951. By the time he arrived at training camp that summer, he was 24 years of age.

Stanfel's career was then delayed another whole year when he suffered a serious knee injury. In 1952, he became an integral part of an excellent Detroit line that included Vince Banonis and Lou Creekmur. Beginning with

his great 1953 season, Stanfel became a regular All-Pro and Pro Bowler.

Stanfel played so well that he was a first-team All-Pro in 1954 despite missing half the season because of another serious injury. When he was injured again in 1955, he considered retiring. However, Redskins head coach Joe Kuharich, Stanfel's coach at USF, engineered a trade and convinced Stanfel to join Washington.

Stanfel regained a spot as a first-team All-Pro in 1956 and then repeated in 1957 and 1958. He was also a Pro Bowler in all three of his seasons with Washington. After a tremendous seven-year career, Stanfel then retired when Kuharich, who had been fired by the Redskins and hired by Notre Dame, offered Stanfel a job as the Fighting Irish's line coach.

Having decided early on to pursue a second career as a coach, Stanfel walked away from the NFL while at the top of his game. His bad knees were a factor, but the opportunity to coach at Notre Dame was the main reason. Had that opportunity not come along, Stanfel has said he could have played several more years.

In games played, Stanfel's career was short by more recent standards. Still, he played more seasons and games than several Hall of Fame contemporaries. More importantly, he was probably the best player at his position in the 1950s. And his retirement at 31 after seven seasons raises an issue that is essential to understanding why careers were shorter 50 years ago.

When he retired, Stanfel's salary as an assistant coach was not much less than what he had earned as a five-time All-Pro player. That is unfathomable today, yet it was common then. Pro football's salaries were far closer to those of other jobs, and players often took other offers when they became available.

Note: Stanfel served in the United States Army in the Pacific Theater during the war, according to the Detroit Lions 1953 Media Guide.

Gene Brito
End, Redskins, Los Angeles Rams 1951–53, 1955–60

After graduating from high school, Gene Brito spent four years in the service. He enrolled at Loyola Marymount University in his native Los Angeles, graduating in 1951. When he played his first game in the NFL, Brito was just one month shy of his 26th birthday.

After spending his first two seasons with the Redskins as an offensive end, Brito's talents really came to the fore when head coach Curly Lambeau switched him to defense in 1953. Although relatively light for an end at 225 lbs., Brito was extremely quick and he earned the first of five Pro Bowl berths that year. Brito jumped to Canada in 1954, but Washington coaxed him back the following year. From 1955–58 he was a first-team All-Pro and Pro Bowler.

Traded to the Rams in 1959, Brito was injured and missed most of that season. He bounced back in 1960 and made second-team All-Pro. But the following year in training camp, Brito was struck down by Amyotrophic Lateral Sclerosis (ALS, or Lou Gehrig's Disease), which forced him to retire at 35 and ultimately took his life in 1965.

Had Brito played exclusively on defense beginning in 1951, his Hall of Fame credentials might be overwhelming. The long military stint that pushed back the start of his career also cut into the period in which he was one of the game's best players.

Brito's chances for the Hall of Fame have probably also been hurt by the weak teams he played on. He did not play in a single postseason game, and the Redskins and Rams posted a combined 44–60–4 record during his tenure. His teams only finished above .500 twice and only finished as high as second place once.

Like Speedie, Brito jumped to Canada for a much higher salary than he earned in the NFL. Before free agency and the players union, that was one of the only options available to players seeking better salaries. Had they played those years in the NFL instead of Canada, Brito and Mac Speedie might have made the Pro Football Hall of Fame a long time ago.

Note: Brito was a staff sergeant in the army and served as a paratrooper during the war in the Pacific, including a combat jump in the Negros Islands, according to the Redskins 1956 Media Guide.

Lou Rymkus
Tackle, Redskins, Browns 1943, 1946–51

As a rookie, Lou Rymkus was named first-team All-Pro and played in the NFL title game. That set a pattern that repeated itself in every year of his career. In each of his seven seasons, Rymkus was named as at least a second-team All-Pro and his team made it to its league Championship Game, winning five times.

After his outstanding rookie season, Rymkus went into the U.S. Navy. During his two-year stint, he signed with the Browns for their inaugural season in 1946. Rymkus was a first-team All-League selection in 1947–49, and he was a first-team All-AAFC/NFL selection in 1946 and 1949 and a second-team choice in 1948.

Although Rymkus went both ways in the first part of his career, it was on offense that he really established himself as an outstanding player. The pass pocket was a new idea in 1946, and it was one of the keys to Cleveland's great passing attack. Rymkus was widely recognized as one of the game's best pass blockers, if not the best. He earned second-team All-Pro honors in 1950–51 as the Browns posted a 21–3 record in their first two NFL seasons.

Like Speedie and Stanfel, Rymkus has been overshadowed by a large number of Hall of Fame teammates. Seven of his Cleveland teammates are in the Pro Football Hall of Fame. And like Speedie and Barwegan, Rymkus' stature as a player has been affected by misperceptions about the AAFC.

In fact, Rymkus' career illustrates the absurdity of the notion that the AAFC was anything but a major league. He was an All-Pro in the NFL as a rookie, continued as an All-Pro for four AAFC seasons, and then was an All-Pro in the NFL again in 1950–51. Unless Rymkus was a dramatically better player in 1943 and 1950–51 than in 1946–49, that trajectory points to the two leagues being about equal.

Lou Rymkus, formerly of the Houston Oilers coaching staff, was hired as a coach by the Detroit Lions in 1966. This is a 1961 photo. (AP Photo)

Rymkus retired at 32 while still one of the game's best linemen. Like Stanfel, that was partly because of injuries but mostly because he wanted to coach and an opportunity was available. And just as Rymkus' playing career was a rousing success, so was his brief tenure as a head coach. In his only full season, he guided the Oilers to the 1960 AFL Championship.

Note: Rymkus was inducted into the navy at the Great Lakes facility in late March 1944. He was stationed at Bainbridge where he played on the base's crack team, and in December that year he was transferred to Pearl Harbor. Seaman 1st Class Rymkus was signed to the Browns in August 1945, anticipating his discharge from the service.

* * * *

Whether or not any of these five players makes it to the Hall of Fame, all have credentials and extenuating circumstances because of the war and the era they played in that call for a re-examination from selectors. Any one of them would have been a better choice than Canadeo, Dudley, McAfee, Parker, and Trippi—and Barwegan, Stanfel, and especially Speedie had better careers than a whole lot of other Hall of Famers, as well. In the most extreme inconsistency in the World War II standard, Speedie has credentials that are vastly superior to Canadeo's (four receiving titles to zero rushing titles, six years as a first-team All-Pro to two,

five championship rings to one) and he missed four seasons to military service, while Canadeo missed one.

Again, by no means is that to suggest that the selectors erred in respecting the time lost to military service of those who were inducted. However, there is no getting around the fact that there are considerable inconsistencies in how the World War II standard was applied and to whom that respect was accorded. Should the selectors review and perhaps induct some of the wartime players profiled here who have thus far been bypassed, then the Pro Football Hall of Fame would be an even greater institution for it.

A version of this article was originally published in *The Coffin Corner*, Volume 27, Number 4 (2005). Reprinted with permission of the Professional Football Researchers Association.

Section 4

The Spirit of Football: Legends, Men, Valor, Legacy

THE NFL SUPPORTS THE WAR EFFORT

Just as America's general population rallied behind the United States' World War II effort, so too did the National Football League. Hundreds of players joined the effort through enlistment, as the NFL organizationally looked for additional ways to make a difference.

One such endeavor was the selling of War Bonds, an activity that generated $4,000,000 worth of sales in 1942 alone. Treasury citations were given to three Green Bay Packers—future Hall of Fame coach Curly Lambeau, quarterback Cecil Isbell, and future Hall of Fame end Don Hutson, who were credited with selling $2,100,000 worth in a single night during a rally held in Milwaukee.

The NFL also donated the revenues from 15 exhibition games to service charities. The games produced a total purse of $680,384.07. It was reported to be the largest amount raised by a single athletic organization.

Included in the exhibition games were the Army Emergency Relief Series games between NFL teams and military All-Star aggregations. Eight games were played at eight different locations. The All-Star teams, billed as West Army and East Army All-Stars, faced the Detroit Lions, Brooklyn Dodgers, Green Bay Packers, Chicago Cardinals, Washington Redskins, and the Chicago Bears. The series ended with the All-Stars winning four games and the NFL winning four games.

August 30 at Los Angeles:
Washington Redskins 26, West Army All-Stars 7

September 6 at Denver:
West Army All-Stars 16, Chicago Cardinals 10

September 9 at Detroit:
West Army All-Stars 12, Detroit Lions 0

September 12 at New York:
East Army All-Stars 16, New York Giants 0

September 13 at Milwaukee:
Green Bay Packers 36, West Army All-Stars 21

September 16 at Baltimore:
East Army All-Stars 13, Brooklyn Dodgers 7

September 19 at Syracuse:
New York Giants 10, West Army All-Stars 7

September 20 at Boston:
Chicago Bears 14, East Army All-Stars 7[366]

THE STARS AND STRIPES 1943

The October 27, 1943, edition of the Armed Forces newspaper *Stars and Stripes* recognized the tremendous impact and influence football had on American military tactics and strategy during World War II:

"Football strategy is being used all over the world today in tactics designed to outsmart the enemy—so football training should be invaluable in the training of our armed forces. That's the opinion of Lieutenant Commander Mal Stevens, former football coach of Yale and New York University and now mentor of the Naval Training Station team at Sampson, New York. Most of our great admirals and generals—Halsey, Eisenhower, and MacArthur—were football players. The individual strategy and thinking as a result of football training and

Generals Eisenhower and Bradley in Normandy. Eisenhower is talking with paratroopers from the 101ˢᵗ before the invasion. (Photo courtesy of the National World War II Museum)

conditioning make for faster and clearer decisions. The Russians have been using the old mousetrap play right along drawing the enemy in then encircling and sideswiping. Our navy 'did an end run around Sicily' and the old wedge play 'is the split and divide German method.' The air barrage 'helps soften up defenses in battle' the same as in football, disorganizing the secondary defenses. All in all, war and football demand highly organized team play in addition to raw physical courage."[367]

THE MEN

The NFL had its share of men who served in WWII. However, there are some whose stories really need to be told. Some of these men we strictly think of as just football players. That is *not* true. They were also flyers, soldiers, sailors, and Marines.

Tom Harmon, U.S. Army Air Corps-WWII

By Frederic Allen Maxwell[368]

The odds were against him 6–1, but if Tom Harmon didn't do something, they would all die.

On football fields in the late 1930s, Tom had pioneered a risky technique called "running the rapids," turning directly into trailing defensemen, stopping them in their tracks, then racing by. Now, piloting his P-38 fighter over China, he reacted the same way. His famed commander, General Claire Chennault, later wrote that "oblivious to his personal safety," Harmon turned his craft directly into the half-dozen Japanese Zeros that had suddenly appeared above him. He raced into their midst,

firing away. It worked. The group split up as this crazed plane spewed bullets at them.

Harmon's was one of four P-38s protecting a flight of American bombers. It was October 30, 1943—the middle of World War II. Harmon was one of the bold American pilots who took on the Japanese in the skies over occupied China. The skill and bravado of a fighter pilot came naturally to Harmon. On the ground, the University of Michigan football star was fast, brave, and strong—and quite possibly the best college football player ever.

His talent was so overwhelming (and he was so handsome) that he earned the adoration of people who'd never watched a down of football in their lives. In 1940, Harmon appeared on the cover of *Life* magazine over the caption "Michigan's Great Harmon." *Time* magazine had put him on its cover the year before. After graduating, he starred in a Hollywood movie, *Harmon of Michigan*, about himself. His fans couldn't get enough of him.

When he enlisted in the Army Air Corps, his exploits made for inspiring stories back home. But fame also made him a target—killing or capturing him would be a Japanese propaganda coup, hence their placing a reward on his head.

In any case, his celebrity couldn't help Harmon now. Three of the Zeros were headed toward the American bombers. Meanwhile, he snuck up under a Zero and opened up his guns. The canopy of the Japanese fighter sheered away, its engine burst into flames. The Zero spun out of control, free falling toward the ground, trailing fire and smoke. Harmon pulled up, looking for another target. The dogfight was

Tom Harmon in his flight jacket. (Photo courtesy of the Bentley Historical Library, University of Michigan)

roaring some 8,000' above the Yangtze River, about 350 miles into Japanese-occupied China. It was a cool, clear Saturday morning with good visibility. He soon found another target.

As a Zero climbed from a lake below, Harmon plunged in on it and fired. A chunk tore out of the Zero's left wing then—boom!—it blew up. It was Harmon's third kill of the war.

He had no time to celebrate. From nowhere, three shots tore into his P-38. One clanged off the armor plating behind him. Another banged off the armor under his seat. The third bullet

shot between his legs, igniting the gas line, blowing his famously fleet feet off the pedals and ripping off most of his pants. He reached down, frantically patting with his hands to exterminate the flames searing his legs. The console exploded. His cockpit instantly became an inferno. Harmon was on fire, his plane free-falling earthward. With his left hand he painfully loosened his seat belt, jettisoned his canopy, and was immediately sucked out into the open air, into the dogfight.

Harmon panicked. He yanked his ripcord, and the parachute jerked open—far too soon. He was 5,000' in the air, in the middle of a 10-plane dogfight, a free-floating, defenseless target under a billowing white bullseye. Zeros strafed his chute. He hung his head down over his chest and played dead. And he prayed. Oh, did he pray.

Years later, Thomas Dudley Harmon would recall those harrowing moments in his autobiography, *Pilots Also Pray*. Harmon grew up in Gary, Indiana, the youngest son of a steel mill security guard. He worked his way through Michigan in the late 1930s while building his outstanding football career.

By his junior season in 1939, he appeared on the cover of *Time*, which reported he was a "gregarious, lantern-jawed six footer with a Tarzan physique" who runs "with the power of a wild buffalo and the cunning of a hounded fox." He was touted by sportswriters as "the Michigan maestro," "the wily Wolverine," and "triple threat Tommy." The 6', 195-lb. running and defensive back, passer, and kicker actually exceeded the hype.

Launching his senior season against California at Berkeley, he caught the opening kickoff and ran it back 94 yards for a touchdown. On his first carry from scrimmage he scored on a run of 86 yards then twice more from 70 and 65 yards. One Memorial Stadium spectator, a fellow Irish Catholic football enthusiast, John F. Kennedy, later said that one of his top sports experiences was when "I saw Tom Harmon score 21 points...in the first half against California." Harmon was so unstoppable that *Life* devoted a full page to pictures of an inebriated Cal fan who, frustrated that no player could take Harmon down, jumped onto the field and tried to tackle him. Like Cal, he failed. Footage of the incident led newsreels worldwide, making him internationally famous.

But it was in his last game as a Wolverine that Harmon gave the most extraordinary all-around college gridiron performance ever. Against Ohio State. In Columbus.

Playing on a rainy day and a muddy field, Harmon scored two rushing touchdowns, threw for two passing touchdowns, kicked four extra points, intercepted three passes and ran one of them back for yet another touchdown, returned three kickoffs for a total of 81 yards, and punted three times for a still-record average of 50 yards. In the process, he broke the all-time college scoring tally of Illinois' fabled "Galloping Ghost," Red Grange. As he came off the field with 38 seconds left, the 73,648 rain-drenched Ohio State fans made a remarkable gesture that would be impossible to imagine today—they put aside their partisanship and gave the man who'd scored 34 points of the 40–0 score, the

Harmon jumps the line. (Photo courtesy of the Bentley Historical Library, University of Michigan)

worst-ever trouncing of their beloved Buckeyes, a shouting, screaming, and standing ovation, and then mobbed him, shredding his jersey. That year Harmon won the Camp, Rockne, and Maxwell awards and the sixth Heisman trophy.

And as he floated down into China, Zeros were trying to shred his parachute. The lake below came closer, and then he stopped. His chute had caught in a tree.

Despite facing a death sentence ever since helping Doolittle's Raiders survive after bombing Tokyo the year before, Chinese guerrillas cut down and rescued the severely injured Harmon.

Harmon had already survived a plane crash earlier that same year when he ditched the bomber he was piloting during a tropical storm over South America. The only survivor, Harmon dragged himself for four days through the forest to safety, refusing to let himself drink a drop of water for fear that contaminants would sicken him when he needed his strength. It had been an astonishing display of will.

What happened in China was even harder. In what Harmon would call the Chinese version of the American Underground Railroad, during the next 34 days he was stealthily carried back to Allied lines. His physical exam told the tale. In it, Flight Surgeon Major John Burns concluded by saying, "Thus, injured, with extensive burns which had become infected, at times delirious, suffering from shock and the weakening effects of loose bloody bowel movements, without adequate clothing or food, having no medical attention and traversing the expanse of the vast interior of China in unsanitary conditions where disease is rampant, Lieutenant Harmon managed, with his magnificent fortitude and what must have been prodigious stamina, to carry on until he was at long last delivered into the hands of his Commanding Officer at base."

He was awarded the Silver Star and a Purple Heart.

After the war, Harmon played briefly for the Los Angeles Rams, but his injuries had robbed him of his speed and power. He soon entered the career he'd always wanted as a sportscaster, and he married his movie star wife, Elyse Knox, in Ann Arbor's Grace Chapel. In a stylish tribute to her war-hero husband, she wove part of the parachute that saved him into her wedding dress.

When Harmon died in 1990, a *Los Angeles Times* reporter noted that Harmon had "married a gorgeous movie star and they had the most beautiful children this side of *The Sound of Music* cast." Given Harmon's devotion to his family, it's a fitting tribute that most people know him today because of his accomplished children and grandchildren. Harmon's son, Mark, quarterbacked at UCLA before becoming an actor; he stars in CBS' *NCIS: Naval Criminal Investigative Service*. Tom's oldest daughter, Kris, married teen idol and singer Ricky Nelson and appeared with him on his parent's long-running 1960s family sitcom, *The Adventures of Ozzie and Harriet*. His youngest daughter, Kelly, was the WRIF girl, the photogenic face of the popular Detroit rock station. His sons-in-law included renegade automaker John DeLorean, and among his grandkids are actress Tracy Nelson and the singing duo The Nelsons.

Bill Pennington of *The New York Times* called Harmon an "All-American football player, magazine cover boy, newsreel idol, Heisman trophy winner, war hero, author, broadcaster, and movie star. He was a man for his times—all of them." The *L.A. Times* eulogy mourned that "he takes an era with him" and "helped football become the big time that it is" and that "his habits were beyond reproach. He radiated dignity and reserve."

MEN OF VALOR

No professional sport has as many Medal of Honor recipients as football. Valor, however, is not just measured in medals alone. Although most of the veterans earned their medals in World War II, that is only part of the story.

Maurice "Footsie" Britt

U.S. Army, World War II

They say he chased the German "Desert Fox," Field Marshall Erwin Rommel, out of North Africa. They said his courage under combat was astounding. He was the perfect embodiment of the American spirit: high school class president, class valedictorian, good-looking, brave, a sports star in football and basketball, and eventually an officer in the U.S. Army. Performance was always at the heart of Maurice Britt. His talent earned him a scholarship to the University of Arkansas in Fayetteville for both sports. He was drafted by the NFL's Detroit Lions on December 10, 1940. On June 8, 1941, Britt married the

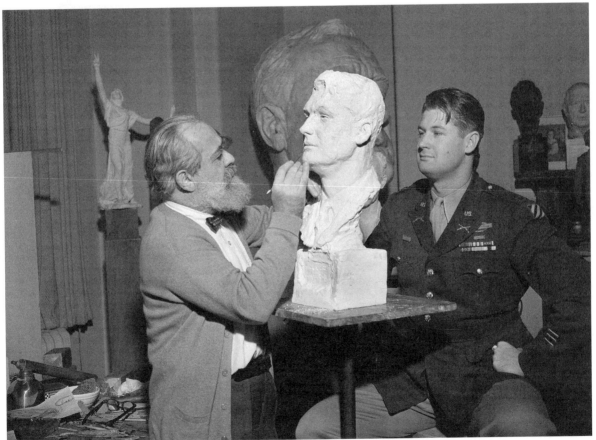

Jo Davidson (left) puts the finishing touches on his bust of Captain Maurice L. Britt—the first army man in the nation's history to receive his country's three highest combat awards in a single war—at Davidson's studio in New York City on December 14, 1944. The Lonoke, Arkansas, hero wears the Distinguished Service Cross, the Medal of Honor, and the Silver Star. (AP Photo/Anthony Camerano)

love of his life, Nancy Mitchell, and the next day he graduated with a degree in journalism.

There was one game Maurice Britt said he always remembered. On November 16, 1941, in front of 16,000 fans at Detroit's Briggs Stadium, the Lions and Philadelphia Eagles were playing for pride—there were no playoff implications. It seemed at first that the Eagles were the only ones who cared that day, taking their biggest lead at 17–7 and seemingly pushing the Lions around for three quarters. Then a furious Lions comeback began in the fourth quarter with 8:00 minutes left in the game. Lions quarterback Dick Booth's short pass to running back Bryon "Whizzer" White and his 69-yard four-broken-tackle sprint to the end zone brought the Lions closer at 17–14 and the crowd to its feet. That score awoke Detroit's stubborn defense, and they held the Eagles to just three plays and forced a punt in the next series. The Lions' drive began deceptively enough when fullback Steve Belichick's[369] 12-yard pass to White set up great field position and a memory that would last a lifetime. Entering the game for the first time that day was Maurice Britt, the rookie All-American end from the University of Arkansas.[370]

The Eagles seemed confused from the previous trick play as the Lions' next play went into action. They played a zone defense and didn't notice as Britt sprinted down the field. All eyes were on White. Lions quarterback Dick Booth spotted Britt and threw a 30-yard pass to the sure-handed end who caught it and ran the remaining 15 yards into the end zone. The Lions won, 21–17. Bryon White, who would

later become a Supreme Court Justice, and Maurice Britt were the celebrated local heroes of what became "the comeback of '41." The Lions finished the season with a 4–6–1 record.

Three weeks later America was at war. The Japanese bombed Pearl Harbor.

Maurice Britt played all of the 1942 season for the pathetic Lions who not only lost every game they played but also lost many players such as White and Belichick to the war. November 29, 1942, would be the last NFL game Maurice Britt would ever play. Of course, Britt didn't know that at the time.

Shortly after the season he reported to the army for duty. The fact he was a college graduate and ROTC cadet at Arkansas earned him the rank of second lieutenant. Lt. Britt was assigned to Company L, 30th Infantry Regiment, 3rd Infantry Division. He would stay with this unit for his entire tenure in the army.[371]

Britt's exposure to combat began in North Africa when Company L landed at Casablanca and then silenced Fort Blondin, a French artillery position that threatened the left flank of the 3rd Infantry Division's beachhead. Maurice Britt's battalion was assigned not long thereafter as the personal bodyguard to President Franklin D. Roosevelt and Prime Minister Winston Churchill for the Casablanca Conference. Once guard duty was over, Britt's unit rejoined the 3rd Infantry for the invasion of Sicily.

Lt. Britt's 3rd Battalion, 30th Infantry Regiment landed on Sicily's coast on July 10, 1943. Beginning from "Blue Beach," which was located between Licata and Gela, the Allied goal was to drive north to Palermo. Under

Britt's leadership, Company L's tactical march covered 54 miles in 33 hours over difficult terrain without food or water resupply for the successful assault on the town of San Stefano.[372] The Sicilian Campaign ended not long thereafter, and Britt earned a short rest before his "rendezvous with destiny" in the horrible, bloody Italian Campaign.

Britt's third assault landing took place on September 19, 1943, at Salerno. With his company commander wounded and evacuated, Britt assumed command and led his men in the attack on Acerno, which was about 10 miles east of Salerno. The Germans were dug in at Acerno, placing heavy-duty machine guns at strategic locations using the large chestnut trees as cover. They were holding up the advance of Company L.

Lt. Maurice Britt, who was not one for waiting around, grabbed a rifle grenade and crawled forward toward the German position and came under intense German machine gun and mortar fire. He finally got close enough to fire his grenades into the German machine gun position, killing the two gunners, driving away the mortar squad, and opening up the way for the regiment to advance even further. Once back behind the lines, Britt noticed his arm was bleeding; projecting from it was a piece of shrapnel that was removed and bandaged up. For his heroic actions and aggressive leadership, Lt. Britt was awarded the Silver Star, and for his wounds he was awarded the Purple Heart.[373]

On October 29, 1943, Britt was ordered to take his company to neutralize the German position on Monterotondo that controlled a major highway leading in to Rome. Under Britt's command, his battalion fought their way through the cold, mud, sleet, and the Germans for nearly two weeks. One of Britt's men was wounded and fell down the side of the mountain as they ascended. Not waiting for the cover of darkness, Britt quickly scooted down the hill and carried the man to safety. The battalion was running out of food and water, and they didn't have winter clothing. For two days no supplies came. They were all soaked to the skin, and although they had every reason to quit, they didn't. They advanced, took the hill on November 8, and earned the Presidential Unit Citation for the battalion. This high ground of Monte Rotundo was the scene of ferocious German counterattacks that would take the lives of the American defenders little by little. Replacements did not arrive. Britt's unit was cut off.

It was November 10, 1943. With just 55 men, Britt's company was protecting the eastern slope of the wooded mountain in what is called an "extended position."[374] Battalion Commander Lt. Col. Edgar Doleman said, "Contact was maintained only by patrols and listening posts."[375] Somehow the Germans were able to get between Britt's L Company and nearby K Company where they took some American prisoners and used them as a "human shield." As the Germans forced the Americans to walk ahead of them toward Britt's lines, they were ordered to shout, "We are Americans! Let us through!" At about 50 yards out, Britt spotted the German ruse, and according to Cpl. John Syc, Britt said to the American POWs, "Take off! They can't hurt you! We're going to fire anyway!" The American POWs scattered, and Britt's men opened fire. The German response was furious—mortar fire and nearly 100 of their men descended on the thinly held American lines. Cpl. Syc heard Britt yell, "Ow!" and grab his side but ordered Syc to just "fire faster."[376] Britt kept moving from one end of the line to the other inspiring his men and, according to an eyewitness, PFC Fred Marshall,

"He [Britt] fired about 75 rounds from his carbine, changing clips five times before running out of ammunition...he ran from side to side of our machine gun, firing at every sound and sight of Germans; later I saw Lt. Britt, slightly bleeding from his face, having run out of carbine ammo, grab the M1 rifle from a badly wounded man lying near me and continue to fire with it. He also grabbed some hand grenades and went ahead into a wooded area ahead of our position, looking for Germans. A few minutes later, I saw him throwing grenades, disregarding machine-pistol bursts hitting all around him. I marveled that he wasn't hit. Concussion grenades were bursting all around him."[377]

Britt was hit. He had a half-inch-wide gash down his left side slightly above his hip. His uniform top was stained with his blood. He was ordered to go to the aid station by Col. Doleman. Britt reported to the aid station, and as he sat on the end of an empty K-Ration box, those around him stared at him in amazement. According to witnesses as he waited for help, his canteen was pierced with bullet holes and his shirt was covered with sweat and blood. His field glass case, which was pierced with bullet holes, was swinging back and forth from his

neck. His men were in awe. Battalion medical officer Captain Roy Hanford knew that Britt's wounds required him to go back to the hospital, but Britt wouldn't hear of it.

"I've got to get back up that hill and help my boys," Britt said.

Hanford said, "I applied bandages and sulfa powder and a multitude of bandages, and off he went. I totally missed the piece of shrapnel embedded in his chest muscle."[378]

For his actions Lt. Maurice Britt was awarded the Medal of Honor and promoted to captain. He would have to wait to actually get the medal. There was work to do. Britt's war was far from over. He was allowed a brief break for a few days of recovery and rest.

On January 22, 1944, Captain Britt and Company L and the 30th Infantry Regiment landed at Salerno's shores. In an attempt to expand the beachhead, two companies, one under the command of Cpt. Britt and the other under the command of Cpt. Burleigh Packwood, moved across the Mussolini Canal to seize two key road junctures. This area seemed free of German troops just the day before. As the American troops advanced, they came under devastating German machine gun and artillery fire. German tanks were also in the area, providing supporting fire. American units were driving the enemy back until a well-hidden machine gun nest opened up, killing many boys in L Company. Nobody could tell where the fire was coming from, so Britt stood up and performed two jumping jacks, clapped his hands and yelled as loud as he could, hoping to draw fire. It worked! He spotted the German position and directed mortar and artillery fire on the target. From that moment on, the road junction became famously known as "Britt's Junction."

Just two days later on January 24, Britt and two other junior officers of L Company moved ahead to scout the terrain and were shocked to observe nearly six German tanks approaching. Britt and his men went in to a nearby stone farmhouse and used it as an observation post to direct artillery fire on the German Panzers. One German tank got to within 300 yards of the farmhouse and fired its shell into the house and blew it apart, sending stones and shrapnel everywhere. The blast tore off Britt's right arm at the elbow and broke his leg and three toes. As he sat there in the debris, he picked up his severed arm and said, "I always figured it would happen this way."[379]

Britt was rescued, evacuated, and sent home on a hospital ship. Arriving in Atlanta's Lawson General Hospital for treatment and rehabilitation, his wife met him and his recovery began. On June 5, 1944, at the University of Arkansas graduation ceremony, Maurice Britt was awarded the Congressional Medal of Honor in an emotional ceremony. Interestingly enough, on this same day halfway across the world, Rome fell to Allied forces.

Medal of Honor Citation:

For conspicuous gallantry and intrepidity at the risk of his life above and beyond the call of duty. Disdaining enemy hand grenades and close-range machine pistol, machinegun, and rifle, Lt. Britt inspired and led a handful of

his men in repelling a bitter counterattack by approximately 100 Germans against his company positions north of Mignano, Italy, the morning of 10 November 1943. During the intense firefight, Lt. Britt's canteen and field glasses were shattered; a bullet pierced his side; his chest, face, and hands were covered with grenade wounds. Despite his wounds, for which he refused to accept medical attention until ordered to do so by his battalion commander following the battle, he personally killed 5 and wounded an unknown number of Germans, wiped out one enemy machinegun crew, fired 5 clips of carbine and an undetermined amount of Ml rifle ammunition, and threw 32 fragmentation grenades. His bold, aggressive actions, utterly disregarding superior enemy numbers, resulted in capture of 4 Germans, 2 of them wounded, and enabled several captured Americans to escape. Lt. Britt's undaunted courage and prowess in arms were largely responsible for repulsing a German counterattack, which, if successful, would have isolated his battalion and destroyed his company.

Joe Foss
USMC, World War II

He was a war hero, an inspiration to millions. He was a politician and an innovator in professional sports as the first commissioner of the American Football League. Foss became Governor of South Dakota. He also gave a young kid from the Dakotas his start. We know that kid today as Tom Brokaw, the NBC news legend and author of *The Greatest Generation*. Foss was also president of the National Rifle

Association (NRA). He was a man's man. He was Joe Foss.

Todd Anton Met Joe Foss

I met Joe Foss at the dedication of the National D-Day Museum (now known as the National World War II Museum) back in 2000 and 2001 for the grand opening of the museum and also for the dedication of the Pacific Wing of the museum. Joe Foss was not just a man, but also a force of nature to anyone who met him. As countless people sought his autograph or a quick word, he actually engaged me in a conversation as we walked into the museum for a private event, leaving the congestion of the crowd for the inner peace of the Museum's Louisiana Memorial Pavilion. Inside, Mr. Foss, who asked me to call him Joe, wanted to know who I was and what I had done to be invited. I told him I was a public school history teacher who interviewed veterans, son of a WWII veteran and a guest of Stephen Ambrose who was the museum's founder.

"A teacher, huh?" he said.

Oh God! I thought. *Here it comes.*

The teaching profession is often not respected anymore; it's become so politicized and so disrespected that I feared a lecture on what teachers do wrong. I've grown used to it.

"Well, let me shake your hand, Todd. You're a real soldier of democracy."

I was dumbstruck. Being called a soldier of democracy by a man wearing the Medal of Honor—a Marine legend calling me a "hero?"

"No way, sir. You and these veterans are the heroes," I said.

Joe Foss. (Photo courtesy of the National World War II Museum)

"Well, Todd, let me share this with you from General of the Army Omar Bradley."

He took off his cowboy hat and tried to remember it and started speaking.

"Teachers are the real soldiers of democracy. Others defend democracy, but teachers make it work. Something like that, Todd"

I had heard that before, but to be told that from Joe Foss is something special.

Military Career:

Upon graduation, Foss enlisted in the Marine Corps Reserve. He earned his wings at Pensacola

216

and was commissioned a second lieutenant. After Pearl Harbor he was ordered to report to an aerial reconnaissance squadron but held out for fighter duty despite being told he was "too old" at age 27. He won the argument, and after training in an F-4F Wildcat, he was sent to the South Pacific.

On October 9, 1942, Foss and his fighter wing found themselves at Henderson Field on Guadalcanal. His two four-plane group would eventually come to be called "Foss' Flying Circus" and would fly more than 60 missions. On October 16, he shot down two Japanese Zeros and a bomber to bring his total of kills to five, making him an ace in just a week. By mid-November, Foss' personal total of downed Japanese planes stood at 19, and he had been shot down once himself. During these first six weeks at Guadalcanal, he received the Distinguished Flying Cross.

After being hospitalized with a wound and a bout of malaria, he returned to Guadalcanal and picked up where he left off. He eventually racked up 26 confirmed enemy aircraft shot down and 16 probable kills, equaling famed ace Eddie Rickenbacker's World War I record.

Henderson Field, Guadalcanal. (Photo courtesy of the National World War II Museum)

On what would be his last Guadalcanal mission, his group scrambled to intercept nearly 100 Japanese warplanes. Spotting the enemy, Foss signaled his outnumbered men not to attack but to circle above the Japanese planes in tight formation. The Japanese believed his group was a decoy for a huge American air armada and they turned and ran. Foss had accomplished one of the greatest bluffs in the history of aerial combat. Many historians call that a turning point in the war.

Congressional Medal of Honor:

Foss was called back to Washington in May 1943 to help lead the campaign for U.S. War Bonds. He found himself on the cover of *Life* magazine when President Franklin Roosevelt presented him with the nation's highest award, the Congressional Medal of Honor for outstanding heroism above and beyond the call of duty during his entire time on Guadalcanal. In part his citation read: "His remarkable flying skill, inspiring leadership, and indomitable fighting spirit were distinctive factors in the defense of strategic American positions on Guadalcanal."

After the war, Foss returned to South Dakota where he helped organize the state's Air National Guard unit. He was elected to the South Dakota House of Representatives.

He was recalled to active duty in the Air Force during the Korean War, and after the war ended, he became the commander of the South Dakota Air National Guard—retiring with the rank of Brigadier General.

Political & Business Career:

In 1954, he was overwhelmingly elected governor of South Dakota and then re-elected to a second term. He went on to become the first commissioner of the American Football League (AFL). He continued until 1966 and helped conceive of the Super Bowl with Pete Rozelle.

Medal of Honor Citation:[380]

For outstanding heroism and courage above and beyond the call of duty as executive officer of Marine Fighting Squadron 121, 1st Marine Aircraft Wing, at Guadalcanal. Engaging in almost daily combat with the enemy from 9 October to 19 November 1942, Capt. Foss personally shot down 23 Japanese planes and damaged others so severely that their destruction was extremely probable. In addition, during this period, he successfully led a large number of escort missions, skillfully covering reconnaissance, bombing, and photographic planes as well as surface craft. On 15 January 1943, he added 3 more enemy planes to his already brilliant successes for a record of aerial combat achievement unsurpassed in this war. Boldly searching out an approaching enemy force on 25 January, Capt. Foss led his 8 F-4F Marine planes and 4 Army P-38's into action and, undaunted by tremendously superior numbers, intercepted and struck with such force that 4 Japanese fighters were shot down and the bombers were turned back without releasing a single bomb. His remarkable flying skill, inspiring leadership, and indomitable fighting spirit were distinctive factors in the defense of strategic American positions on Guadalcanal.

THREE TIMES FOR UNCLE SAM

There are two football players who participated in three wars: Ralph Heywood and Harry J. Marker.

Ralph Heywood

Chicago Rockets, Detroit Lions, Boston Yanks, New York Bulldogs / United States Marine Corps

Born: September 11, 1921, in Los Angeles, California
Died: April 10, 2007, in Bandera, Texas
Position: E-DE

Not too many people know about Ralph Heywood. His career wasn't long enough for anyone to really notice. However, from 1946–49 Ralph Heywood played for one team in the All-America Football Conference—the Chicago Rockets (1946)—and three NFL teams: Detroit Lions (1947–48), Boston Yanks (1948), and New York Bulldogs (1949). The former USC All-American of 1943 was also not only part of three different NFL teams, but he also served in three different wars: World War II, Korea, and Vietnam; eventually becoming a colonel. Other than Harry J. Marker, he is the only NFL player to serve in World War II, Korea, and Vietnam. Col. Ralph Heywood was in the Marines for 32 years. He was amazing in his service, even doing duty as the United States Naval Attaché in the Dominican Republic and as commandant of the Marine Military Academy in Harlingen, Texas.

As a USC Trojan, Heywood—a two-way end and punter, was team captain of the '43 team that made the Rose Bowl. He played just five games for USC that year but still earned All-American honors before being drafted and sent to the South Pacific to serve aboard the USS *Iowa*. Heywood saw action at Kwajalein and Enewetak. The *Iowa* suffered a few hits from Japanese shore batteries at Mili Atoll in the Marshall Islands but sustained no real damage.

As part of the famed Task Force 58, Heywood saw further action in supporting the liberation of Wake Island, also fending off Japanese kamikaze attacks on November 25, 1944.

One would think facing the Japanese would be enough—but upon the sea, Nature rules and not the navy. One of the largest typhoons in 30 years came upon the fleet even as the *Iowa* was in drydock for routine maintenance. As a shipmate recounted, "It was a very scary night, the *Iowa* rolled to about a 45-degree angle at one point, and we all held our breaths that it wouldn't happen again. As our luck went, it happened at meal time so you can imagine the condition of the deck in the mess hall."[381]

Eventually they rode out the typhoon, and the USS *Iowa* sailed off the coast of Japan where she helped finish off what the B-29s couldn't from the air. With their constant shelling and use of her 16" guns, the surrender of the Yokosuka Naval District was assured. The *Iowa* sailed into Tokyo Bay along with the USS *Missouri* to land American Occupation Forces, and Ralph Heywood was there for all of it.

Finally arriving home, Heywood picked right up where he left off at USC. He didn't play for the Trojans this time. Instead, he played in the

NFL and earned his degree in cinematography at USC. He acted in a few movies, one with Charlton Heston, and he golfed with Bob Hope.

The war in Korea escalated in 1952, and Heywood returned to active duty for the Marines. This time he stayed in the Corps for a while and eventually commanded the 26th Marine regiment in Vietnam, seeing multiple engagements. His military medals and awards include the Vietnam Service Medal with one Bronze Star, Vietnam's Cross of Gallantry with Gold Star, and the Republic of Vietnam Campaign Medal with Device.[382] He never said much about his time in the service. For that generation it was unseemly to talk about your accomplishments when you knew those who were killed did so much more.

Ralph Heywood struggled with Alzheimer's later in his life. His wife, Suzie, gave up nearly everything to care for him. "I am not a martyr... he would have done the same for me and he deserved it," she said.

Ralph Heywood died in his wife's arms on April 10, 2007, as she gently and lovingly caressed him and sang the "Marine Corps Hymn" over and over.[383]

Harry Marker

Pittsburgh Pirates / United States Army
Born: September 17, 1910, in Ligonier, Pennsylvania
Died: April 19, 1989, in Patrick AFB, Florida
Position: B

Harry Marker played just one game for the 1934 Pittsburgh Pirates, but that established him forever as a professional football player in the National Football League. The Pirates were 2–10 that season under coach Luby DiMeolo, winning their first game of the season against the Cincinnati Reds and then winning one of the two games they played against the Philadelphia Eagles.

Harry was the son of James and Mary Marker of Ligonier, Pennsylvania. James was a truck driver with a milk route in the area. Harry had an older brother, Lewis, who worked in highway construction, and an older sister, Katherine.

He played halfback for West Virginia University with one of his more notable moments being a 98-yard return on an interception against West Virginia Wesleyan in the fourth quarter of the October 15, 1932, game in Morgantown. He'd also recorded an 83-yard touchdown run in the fourth quarter of the game against Georgetown. He substituted into the North-South game on December 10, playing as right halfback for the North. The South won, 7–6.

Signed by Art Rooney of the Pittsburgh Pirates, Marker played as a substitute in the team's first game of the season on September 9. It was a 13–0 win in Pittsburgh. It was the only game in which he ever played, and he is not credited with any yardage. That was the one and only game he played in the pros. In 1940 he was living in Ligonier with his wife, Emma, and working as a salesman in a retail clothing store. He enlisted in the U.S. Army just a few months after Pearl Harbor (March 25, 1942) and embarked on a long career of military service that saw him in the army during World War II, the Korean War, and Vietnam. After Colonel Marker retired from the army on November 30, 1965, he moved to Satellite Beach, Florida, in 1972. He was a member of Patrick Air Force Base Chapel, the Retired Officers Association, Air Force Association, Honor America Inc., and Disabled American Veterans. He was survived by his sister, Katherine.[384]

COLLEGIATE GRIDIRON VALOR FROM 1896–WORLD WAR II

A note about college football players killed during wartime.

In addition to the pro players who were killed during their time in the service, there is a large number of college football players who also gave their lives while serving. Author Jim Koger devoted considerable time to compiling a listing of more than 2,000 college players who were killed, died, or missing in action. He has presented them in his 1991 book, *Upon Other Fields on Other Days*. The earliest player he lists is Winchester Osgood, a former University of Pennsylvania player killed in action in 1896 at the age of 26. He was in Cuba "leading an insurrection against the Spaniards" at the time. Osgood had played for the Quakers in their unbeaten season of 1894.

When the USS *Maine* was blown up in Havana Harbor in February 1898, lost was former Annapolis (Class of 1890) player Darwin R. Merritt. That same year, losses included Sgt. Hamilton Fish Jr. of Columbia University, serving with Teddy Roosevelt's Rough Riders and shot in the stomach by a sniper. Seven days later, during the charge up

San Juan Hill, Lt. Dennis Michie (captain and quarterback of the first West Point football team, 1890) was killed while leading his men of the 17th Infantry. Koger lists five other players killed that year and a total of 18 killed during the Spanish-American War.

There were two killed in the Philippine Insurrection and one in the Mexican Revolution when Pancho Villa's men crossed the border at Columbus, New Mexico. Koger names 199 killed during World War I with many of the most important battles represented: the Argonne Forest, Belleau Wood, Chateau Thierry, Flanders Field, and the battle for the Somme. Some were more accidental than others and not in actual combat; Lt. Warren McLean (Princeton 1912) was killed when thrown from his horse at Fort Oglethorpe in October 1917.

Five men were awarded both the Distinguished Service Cross and the Croix de Guerre: 1st Lt. Clarence Allen Jr. (Yale, Stanford); Lt. Fred Becker (Iowa); Lt. Fred Norton (Ohio State); David E. Putnam (Harvard); and Neilson Poe (Princeton).

Two were awarded the Congressional Medal of Honor. First Lt. William Bradford Turner (Williams 1914) was killed on September 27, 1918, while leading his men of the 105th Infantry near Ronssoy, France. Koger explains, "He was wounded three times during the advance, all the while taking the lives of a number of the enemy in hand-to-hand combat as he and his charges overran three lines of trenches. When his pistol rounds were expended, Turner bayonets four members of a machine-gun crew with a captured rifle. Minutes after the loss of their positions, the Germans mounted a counter-attack, surrounding Turner's post and inflicting a fourth, and mortal, wound."[385]

In October 1918, Lt. Harold Ernest Goettler of the 50th Aero Squadron was "mortally wounded by German groundfire as he daringly flew his two-seater observation plane into a valley near Binarville, France, to drop needed supplies to the much-publicized 'Lost Batallion,' which was completely surrounded by the enemy. He managed to return to his base, landing his plane safely, but by the time the attending ground crew had reached his plane, his life's breath was gone."[386] Goettler had played for the University of Chicago and was a lineman for the 1913 co-national championship Maroons (Knute Rockne's Notre Dame squad shared the title).

During World War II, in addition to Jack Lummus (profiled elsewhere in this book), there were five other men awarded the Medal of Honor.

On December 23, 1941, Marine Capt. Henry T. Elrod (University of Georgia), a fighter pilot for VMF–211, sank a Japanese destroyer and shot down two Japanese bombers before his own Wildcat was hit. He crash-landed his plane on Wake Island and then joined the men on the ground fighting off the invaders. He was just starting to lob a hand grenade in close fighting when he was killed by a Japanese soldier who had been playing dead by lying in the sand.

Marine Corps Major Kenneth D. Bailey lost his life on September 23, 1942, on Guadalcanal. The former University of Illinois end was now a member of Carlson's Raiders and suffering a head wound, then he was killed by machine-gun

fire while leading his company in hand-to-hand combat.

On November 23, 1943, 1st Lt. Alexander Bonnyman (Princeton) was killed in bloody fighting with the 8th Marines at the Betio airstrip on Tarawa.

One of the leading aces of the war, USMC 1st Lt. Robert M. Hanson (Hamline University) was probably living on borrowed time. He is credited with shooting down 25 Japanese planes but had downed 20 of them in a 17-day period as American forces (and his VMF-215 squadron) were preparing to take Rabaul. His plane was shot down on February 3, 1944.

Montana State's U.S. Army Capt. William W. Galt was killed on May 29, 1944. "He was credited with killing more than 40 Germans from his position in the gun turret of a tank before being stopped by enemy fire." He was killed on the Villa Crocetta in Italy.[387]

The Medal of Honor Citations:

William B. Turner: He led a small group of men to the attack, under terrific artillery and machinegun fire, after they had become separated from the rest of the company in the darkness. Single-handed he rushed an enemy machinegun which had suddenly opened fire on his group and killed the crew with his pistol. He then pressed forward to another machinegun post 25 yards away and had killed 1 gunner himself by the time the remainder of his detachment arrived and put the gun out of action. With the utmost bravery he continued to lead his men over 3 lines of hostile trenches, cleaning up each one as they advanced, regardless of the fact that he had been wounded 3 times, and killed several of the enemy in hand-to-hand encounters. After his pistol ammunition was exhausted, this gallant officer seized the rifle of a dead soldier, bayoneted several members of a machinegun crew, and shot the other. Upon reaching the fourth-line trench, which was his objective, 1st Lt. Turner captured it with the 9 men remaining in his group and resisted a hostile counterattack until he was finally surrounded and killed.

Harold E. Goettler: 1st Lt. Goettler, with his observer, 2nd Lt. Erwin R. Bleckley, 130th Field Artillery, left the airdrome late in the afternoon on their second trip to drop supplies to a battalion of the 77th Division which had been cut off by the enemy in the Argonne Forest. Having been subjected on the first trip to violent fire from the enemy, they attempted on the second trip to come still lower in order to get the packages even more precisely on the designated spot. In the course of this mission the plane was brought down by enemy rifle and machinegun fire from the ground, resulting in the instant death of 1st Lt. Goettler. In attempting and performing this mission 1st Lt. Goettler showed the highest possible contempt of personal danger, devotion to duty, courage, and valor.

Henry T. Elrod: For conspicuous gallantry and intrepidity at the risk of his life above and beyond the call of duty while attached to Marine Fighting Squadron 211, during action against enemy Japanese land, surface, and aerial units at Wake Island, 8 to 23 December 1941. Engaging

vastly superior forces of enemy bombers and warships on 9 and 12 December, Capt. Elrod shot down two of a flight of 22 hostile planes and, executing repeated bombing and strafing runs at extremely low altitude and close range, succeeded in inflicting deadly damage upon a large Japanese vessel, thereby sinking the first major warship to be destroyed by small caliber bombs delivered from a fighter-type aircraft. When his plane was disabled by hostile fire and no other ships were operative, Capt. Elrod assumed command of one flank of the line set up in defiance of the enemy landing and, conducting a brilliant defense, enabled his men to hold their positions and repulse intense hostile fusillades to provide covering fire for unarmed ammunition carriers. Capturing an automatic weapon during one enemy rush in force, he gave his own firearm to one of his men and fought on vigorously against the Japanese. Responsible in a large measure for the strength of his sector's gallant resistance, on 23 December, Capt. Elrod led his men with bold aggressiveness until he fell, mortally wounded. His superb skill as a pilot, daring leadership, and unswerving devotion to duty distinguished him among the defenders of Wake Island, and his valiant conduct reflects the highest credit upon himself and the U.S. Naval Service. He gallantly gave his life for his country.

Kenneth D. Bailey: For extraordinary courage and heroic conduct above and beyond the call of duty as Commanding Officer of Company C, 1st Marine Raider Battalion, during the enemy Japanese attack on Henderson Field,

Guadalcanal, Solomon Islands, on 12–13 September 1942. Completely reorganized following the severe engagement of the night before, Maj. Bailey's company, within an hour after taking its assigned position as reserve battalion between the main line and the coveted airport, was threatened on the right flank by the penetration of the enemy into a gap in the main line. In addition to repulsing this threat, while steadily improving his own desperately held position, he used every weapon at his command to cover the forced withdrawal of the main line before a hammering assault by superior enemy forces. After rendering invaluable service to the battalion commander in stemming the retreat, reorganizing the troops, and extending the reverse position to the left, Maj. Bailey, despite a severe head wound, repeatedly led his troops in fierce hand-to-hand combat for a period of 10 hours. His great personal valor while exposed to constant and merciless enemy fire, and his indomitable fighting spirit inspired his troops to heights of heroic endeavor which enabled them to repulse the enemy and hold Henderson Field. He gallantly gave his life in the service of his country.

Alexander Bonnyman: For conspicuous gallantry and intrepidity at the risk of his life above and beyond the call of duty as Executive Officer of the 2nd Battalion Shore Party, 8th Marines, 2nd Marine Division, during the assault against enemy Japanese-held Tarawa in the Gilbert Islands, 20–22 November 1943. Acting on his own initiative when assault troops were pinned down at the far end of Betio Pier by the overwhelming fire of Japanese shore batteries, 1st Lt. Bonnyman repeatedly defied the blasting fury of the enemy bombardment to organize and lead the besieged men over the long, open pier to the beach and then, voluntarily obtaining flame throwers and demolitions, organized his pioneer shore party into assault demolitionists and directed the blowing of several hostile installations before the close of D-Day. Determined to effect an opening in the enemy's strongly organized defense line the following day, he voluntarily crawled approximately 40 yards forward of our lines and placed demolitions in the entrance of a large Japanese emplacement as the initial move in his planned attack against the heavily garrisoned, bombproof installation which was stubbornly resisting despite the destruction early in the action of a large number of Japanese who had been inflicting heavy casualties on our forces and holding up our advance. Withdrawing only to replenish his ammunition, he led his men in a renewed assault, fearlessly exposing himself to the merciless slash of hostile fire as he stormed the formidable bastion, directed the placement of demolition charges in both entrances and seized the top of the bombproof position, flushing more than 100 of the enemy who were instantly cut down, and effecting the annihilation of approximately 150 troops inside the emplacement. Assailed by additional Japanese after he had gained his objective, he made a heroic stand on the edge of the structure, defending his strategic position with indomitable determination in the face of the desperate charge and killing three of the enemy before he fell, mortally wounded. By his dauntless fighting spirit, unrelenting aggressiveness, and forceful leadership throughout three days of unremitting, violent battle, 1st Lt. Bonnyman had inspired his men to heroic effort, enabling them to beat off the counterattack and break the back of hostile resistance in that sector for an immediate gain of 400 yards with no further casualties to our forces in this zone. He gallantly gave his life for his country.

Robert M. Hanson: For conspicuous gallantry and intrepidity at the risk of his life and above and beyond the call of duty as fighter pilot attached to Marine Fighting Squadron 215 in action against enemy Japanese forces at Bougainville Island, 1 November 1943; and New Britain Island, 24 January 1944. Undeterred by fierce opposition, and fearless in the face of overwhelming odds, 1st Lt. Hanson fought the Japanese boldly and with daring aggressiveness. On 1 November, while flying cover for our landing operations at Empress Augusta Bay, he dauntlessly attacked 6 enemy torpedo bombers, forcing them to jettison their bombs and destroying one Japanese plane during the action. Cut off from his division while deep in enemy territory during a high cover flight over Simpson Harbor on 24 January, 1st Lt. Hanson waged a lone and gallant battle against hostile interceptors as they were orbiting to attack our bombers and, striking with devastating fury, brought down four Zeroes and probably a fifth. Handling his plane superbly in both pursuit and attack measures, he was a master of individual air combat, accounting

for a total of 25 Japanese aircraft in this theater of war. His great personal valor and invincible fighting spirit were in keeping with the highest traditions of the U.S. Naval Service.

William W. Galt: For conspicuous gallantry and intrepidity above and beyond the call of duty. Capt. Galt, Battalion S3, at a particularly critical period following 2 unsuccessful attacks by his battalion, of his own volition went forward and ascertained just how critical the situation was. He volunteered, at the risk of his life, personally to lead the battalion against the objective. When the lone remaining tank destroyer refused to go forward, Capt. Galt jumped on the tank destroyer and ordered it to precede the attack. As the tank destroyer moved forward, followed by a company of riflemen, Capt. Galt manned the .30-caliber machinegun in the turret of the tank destroyer, located and directed fire on an enemy 77mm anti-tank gun, and destroyed it. Nearing the enemy positions, Capt. Galt stood fully exposed in the turret, ceaselessly firing his machinegun and tossing hand grenades into the enemy zigzag series of trenches despite the hail of sniper and machinegun bullets ricocheting off the tank destroyer. As the tank destroyer moved, Capt. Galt so maneuvered it that 40 of the enemy were trapped in one trench. When they refused to surrender, Capt. Galt pressed the trigger of the machinegun and dispatched every one of them. A few minutes later an 88mm shell struck the tank destroyer and Capt. Galt fell mortally wounded across his machinegun. He had personally killed 40 Germans and wounded many more. Capt. Galt pitted his judgment and superb courage against overwhelming odds, exemplifying the highest measure of devotion to his country and the finest traditions of the U.S. Army.

EUGENE EVANS AND TIM HOWARD
By Ken Kraetzer

Eugene "Dippy" Evans and Tim Howard were teammates, the pride of Pelham High School just outside New York City and later at Morgan State in Baltimore. They led their college team to a national title, joined the Marines, and gave their lives for their country.

Evans was possibly the best athlete in Pelham High history. Secretary of his 1945 graduating class, he batted .444 for the baseball team, was the star high jumper for the track team, was All-County at basketball, and was a three-year letterman at football and captain of the team his final year. Eli Page Howard Jr.—"Tim" as he was called growing up—was a year behind Evans in high school, where he co-captained the undefeated 1945 PMHS football team. Howard was known in football as the "Touchdown King." Both he and Evans went on to serve in the U.S. Marine Corps during an era when African Americans trained in different camps and served in segregated units.

Both enrolled at Morgan State in Baltimore where the football team was coached by the legendary Edward P. "Eddie" Hurt. Evans and Howard led Morgan to a CIAA title in 1949, which was considered the national championship of "Historical Black Colleges." Two players of that era at Morgan, Len Ford and Rosey Brown, were elected into the Pro Football Hall of Fame.

Evans and Howard were both cadets in the new ROTC program at Morgan State, and Howard was named the first Cadet Commander of the program.

Just a year after graduation from college, Lt. Evans was sent to Korea, a member of the 32nd Infantry Regiment, Seventh Infantry Division. On the night of July 19, 1952, Lt. Evans led a scout mission across enemy lines, testing enemy positions before an anticipated battle. The small group of soldiers was ambushed, one soldier was taken prisoner, and several escaped. Lt. Evans was killed. Leon Sparks, one of the soldiers who survived the mission, called to tell the story of his last mission and how much Evans was respected by the mostly white soldiers who served under him.

Howard also served in Korea, later in Europe, in Vietnam, and at the Pentagon in Washington, rising to the level of Lieutenant Colonel. For his second tour to Vietnam, Col. Howard was named commander of the Third Battalion of the 196th Light Infantry Brigade. On August 19, 1969, less than a month after the first manned landing on the moon, Col. Howard was leading his unit from a helicopter during a fierce battle. The helo was shot down amidst fighting so intense that American forces could not get to the crash site for five days. Col. Howard's internment site is the last grave site at the top of Arlington's section 39. His father, a World War I veteran, is interred in the row ahead.

LEGACY: ROCKY BLEIER, U.S. ARMY, VIETNAM, "WE NEED YOU"

World War II was called by historian and commentator Studs Turkel "The Good War." There were clear objectives: unconditional surrender and absolute victory. The enemy was obvious, and for the most part the battlefield was clearly definable. America was united, passionate, and committed as "nothing was too good for our boys." In 1945 those going to war knew no matter what that there was a nation behind them and awaiting their return. Indeed Sinatra's "I'll Be Seeing You" fostered a romantic calling of awaiting romance and love that awaited the returning soldier.

However, just 23 years later, things had dramatically changed in America.

As it was in 1945, America was at war in 1968. This time it was fighting a war in Southeast Asia in Vietnam and also fighting amongst itself at home over a war very few could understand or even explain. Two of America's political leaders were dead. America tried to cope with the senseless murders of Dr. Martin Luther King Jr. and Robert F. Kennedy. While Frank was still singing about love and appealing to nostalgia for the good old days in 1968, Jim Morrison and The Doors were singing about the insanity of both butter and guns, TV death on the news, and the senselessness of it all in their anti-war song, "Unknown Soldier." Some soldiers were known, however, and they set aside everything for a cause greater than themselves.

One such soldier was Rocky Bleier, U.S. Army.

Rocky Bleier

Pittsburgh Steelers / United States Army

Born: March 5, 1946, in Appleton, Wisconsin

Position: RB

It turned out that 1968 was quite a year for Bleier. He was drafted twice—as the 16th-round draft pick of the Pittsburgh Steelers and as an

After taking a handoff from quarterback Terry Bradshaw (rear), Pittsburgh Steelers running back Rocky Bleier (20) looks for running room in a 1975 game.

infantryman for the U.S. Army. Bleier set aside football to change uniforms from the Steelers' Black and Gold to Army green. On patrol outside of Chu Lai, Vietnam, while carrying a grenade launcher in August 1969, Bleier's unit came under attack in a firefight in which a bullet pierced Bleier's left leg and moments later a VietCong grenade ripped his right leg. Rocky Bleier was transferred to Tokyo where he was told he would never play football again.

"I didn't buy that," he said.

Still, three weeks in a hospital had to take an emotional toll.

Then an improbable gesture arrived. Steelers owner Art Rooney sent Bleier a postcard which read, "Rock—the team's not doing well. We need you. Art Rooney."

That started the long road back to the field. Bleier was obligated. "When you have somebody take the time and interest to send you a postcard, something that they didn't have to do, you have a special place for those kind of people."

Making it back to the field was going to take time, dedication, rehab, and commitment. There was an intrinsic duty in the soul of this man that drove him to finally make the team in 1972 and become a member of one of the most feared NFL teams in history. In his 11-year career with the Steelers, Bleier won four Super Bowl rings.

However, Bleier's true character is seen in his many trips to visit the troops and Wounded Warriors. There is an immediate connection with them, many who never saw him play or even know who he is. There exists among veterans, regardless of age, a brotherhood that can never be explained and to attempt it is futile.

Bleier said it better: "The military infused me with some lessons that you couldn't learn as quickly anywhere else. You were thrown together with people from such different backgrounds that it was an eye-opener for everybody—for kids from the South, from farm families in the Midwest, from the big cities such as New York and Chicago.

"The army showed me a lot about leadership that I've carried with me in business after retiring from football. As an acting platoon leader in basic training, I let a bunch of guys disobey orders by going into town to get ice cream, but I didn't stick up for my men after they got caught. My platoon sergeant made sure it would be a lesson I'd remember.

"I learned that sometimes you had to take on more responsibility than you wanted to, and did things you didn't like in order to get the job done; that you couldn't shirk your duty when it fell to you to take the lead; and that if you had the training and the inner character, you'd always react properly when a crisis arose."[388]

Art Rooney was right in 1969 when he said, "We still need you Rocky," and that is true even today.

Rocky, America still needs you.

INDOMITABLE: COLONEL GREGORY D. GADSON

Colonel Gregory D. Gadson is Garrison Commander at Fort Belvoir in Virginia outside of Washington, D.C., and is the former director of the U.S. Army Wounded Warrior program. A

1989 graduate of West Point, he was a four-year letterman on the Army football team during the 1985–88 seasons.

Colonel Gadson has served in the U.S. Army for more than 20 years as a field artillery officer. He has served in major conflicts and contingencies of the last two decades, including Operation Desert Shield/Desert Storm in Kuwait, Operation Joint Forge in Bosnia-Herzegovina, Operation Enduring Freedom in Afghanistan, and Operation Iraqi Freedom.

Ken Kraetzer interviewed Colonel Gadson in May 2013 with some questions about what he learned from playing football that helped him in the military and through the aftermath of the severe injuries he suffered from a roadside bomb in Baghdad that rendered him a bilateral amputee.

KK: From all of us at the Sons of the American Legion, thank you for your service. Colonel, you enrolled at West Point in 1985 and began your career of service to our country. What attracted you to the military?

GG: I spent my formative years through high school in Chesapeake, Virginia. I was a jock athlete in high school, and football was my favorite sport, and like many kids probably had dreams of playing college football and maybe the pros. I really wanted to play Division 1 football, quite honestly; I wanted to play at what I thought was the top level. And for me West Point was the only opportunity I had to do that. That's how my dreams of playing Division 1 football drew me into the army.

KK: Under Coach Jim Young, you were part of three Army teams that defeated Annapolis in

Gregory Gadson is a 1989 graduate of West Point. (Photo courtesy of the United States Military Academy at West Point)

the Army-Navy game. Why is the Army-Navy game still considered one of the best rivalries in football?

GG: It is a rivalry, yes—for a few hours on a Saturday we battle each other. It is a hard-fought game, and we play the game the way it is supposed to be played—with dignity and respect. At the end of the game we have tremendous respect for each other. We all recognize the word "rivalry," but for 364 days out of 365 days we are allies, brothers and sisters in arms, and we have more in common with each other. Later we may see these guys on the battlefield, so it is really profound.

KK: You played defense on the Army Black Knight football team wearing No. 98. What did football teach you that helped you in the army and with overcoming injury?

GG: It has taught me so much. Metaphorically or cliche, we say that when you get knocked down, you get up in football, and that is what the sport is about. That is part of it, but I think it is a lot deeper than that, because anybody can get knocked down and anybody can get up. But one day I heard Marshall Faulk say, "Not everyone can stand up." And it is really about not just about getting up, but standing up, and fighting, and giving your best at every opportunity you have. That is what it has really taught me—whether you have a good play or a bad play, that is in the past. You've got to get up and prove yourself again on every down.

It has influenced how I've tried to lead—in terms of never resting, never quite being so comfortable that you are not trying to improve yourself, and so building those kinds of habits, having that become part of your character. I was fortunate that being injured at age 41, it had become part of my character, and ultimately when the dust settled, I knew what I needed to do to get my life back together.

KK: You were commissioned in 1989 and served all over the world, then in May 2007 you were severely injured in Iraq, What can you tell us about what happened and how you were able to recover from that terrible injury?

GG: On May 7th of 2007, my vehicle was struck by a roadside bomb, and ultimately those injuries cost me both of my legs—amputated

While at West Point, Gregory Gadson played defense for Coach Jim Young. (Photo courtesy of the United States Military Academy at West Point)

above the knee—as well as a pretty severely damaged right arm. It was a life-changing moment. I will share that you don't imagine your life like this, it was not one I was very optimistic about. That was my knockdown; I was knocked down literally and figuratively. I just believed that part of my character was that I was going to fight.

Coach Young often read us a couple of lines from a poem: "I lay me down to bleed a while, and I rise with you and fight again." That was the spirit of Army football. We knew that was the kind of attitude, the kind of energy, the determination we needed to have to be successful, to be victorious. It has been a big part of how I approach things.

KK: After what must have been a grueling rehabilitation, you were able to recover and resume some activities. Later that year one of your former teammates, Mike Sullivan—then a New York Giants coach—invited you to speak to the team. How did it feel to spend time with an NFL team, and what did you say to the team for them to take to heart?

GG: The New York Giants are a class organization. Mike Sullivan is no longer with them, but Mike Sullivan, Tom Coughlin, Jerry Reese, the Giants ownership, Mr. Mara, Mr. Tisch, and all the players—that was a team, a family, and they welcomed me into their organization. I still consider myself a Giant.

I talked about the power of sports in people's lives and how many times I'd watched soldiers get up in the middle of the night, even after a 12-hour shift, how soldiers would do anything to watch a game.

I shared my story. I shared that life is fragile. We have to play every down like it is our last.

Gregory Gadson in action with Army versus Washington. He played for Army from 1985–88. (Photo courtesy of the United States Military Academy at West Point)

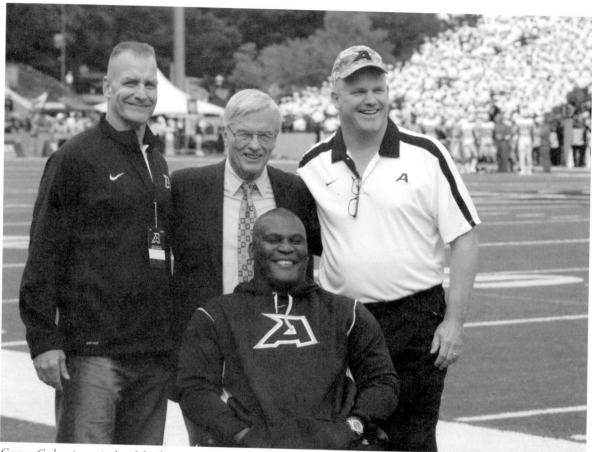

Gregory Gadson is reunited with his former coach, Jim Young (center). Flanking Young are LTC Chuck Schretzman (left) and LTC(P) Steve Svoboda (Army Team Doc) (right). (Photo courtesy of Ken Kraetzer)

We have to play with that kind of conviction. You never know when your life is going to change, you never know when you are going to have a season or a career-ending injury, or some other kind of accident that can change your life. You need to live your life not in fear of something bad happening to you, but living and making the most of it because there is never a guarantee of a tomorrow.

KK: Before your current command at Ft. Belvoir, you served as director of the U.S. Army Wounded Warrior program. What are some of the points you offered to other injured military members to help them recover from serious injury?

GG: A lot can be said by not saying anything. What I mean by that is, just like many of the service members who were wounded before me, just seeing them function, seeing them live their lives, seeing them two and three years after they were wounded, shows you that there is light at the end of the tunnel, that in a very subtle way, that is one of the messages you can send just by being present, being an example, continuing to lead your life, and for me continuing to wear the uniform and serve puts on notice that you can overcome these injuries.

On a more personal level, one of the things that I say to someone I am just meeting for the first time, or someone who is newly wounded— when I am visiting at the hospital, for instance—is that the worst is over. The fact we are sitting here talking right now means that the worst is behind you. Let's talk about the future. Let's talk about what you want to do. Most of your dreams are still intact, we just have to find a way to achieve them.

KK: We attended the seminar at West Point at which NFL Commissioner Roger Goodell and Army Chief of Staff Ray Odierno spoke about the need for both football players and soldiers to seek proper treatment for concussion injuries. Why is treatment for concussion injuries so important for both football players and soldiers?

GG: Because your long-term health is at stake, and because the quality of your play, the quality of your performance if you are a soldier, is, too. It's not really about how tough you are. You can be putting other people at risk if you are not performing at your best. There is a difference between being hurt and being injured. Certainly after being involved in an explosion, it is only prudent, if not required, that

you get yourself checked out. For football players it is a lot more subtle and so as a player you need to exercise good judgment and know yourself and know when you need to be checked out. If you are being tough over smart, you are quite honestly jeopardizing yourself and potentially your fellow players because you are not at your optimum.

KK: You were featured in 2012 in the military science fiction movie *Battleship*. Your character is that of an army officer who leads the fight, charging up a mountain on prosthesis and hiking boots and going toe to toe with an alien. You actually have on an army T-shirt and a Giants cap. What has been the reaction to your role from the veterans and Wounded Warrior community?

GG: It has all been very positive. I am just in awe that my role has garnered that much attention and that it has an impact on so many different communities. Folks with disabilities, not just soldiers, not just veterans, not just wounded warriors, but anyone. I don't wake up with the mission of inspiring anyone. I am just trying my best to do my duty. I just try to do my part, live my life, do my part. I often say that I am blessed for sure.

KK: A question from Sons of the America Legion member Todd Anton. For students in schools today, what do you want them to know about you and the soldiers you served with and what they did for our nation?

GG: Not everyone is going to be able to serve in the uniform. The challenge is to find a way to serve your community, to serve mankind—to understand that our lives are about something greater than us as individuals. Whether it is about coaching or volunteering, or serving our country, it is the idea that we are willing to serve mankind, put more into it than what we take out of the system, what we take from our country. It is the spirit of service that I would want to impart to them.

Colonel Gadson's awards include Legion of Merit, three Bronze Star Medals, a Purple Heart, Meritorious Service Medal (three Oak Leaf Clusters), Army Commendation Medal (three OLC), Army Achievement Medal (two OLC), National Defense Service Medal (two OLC), Southwest Asia Service Medal with two Bronze Stars, two Armed Forces Expeditionary Medals, Global War on Terrorism Expeditionary Medal, Global War on Terrorism Service Medal, the Saudi Arabian Liberation Medal, Kuwaiti Liberation Medal, Afghanistan Campaign Medal, and the Iraq Campaign Medal. He is also authorized to wear the Combat Action Badge and the Master Parachutist Badge.

A 1989 graduate of the United States Military Academy at West Point, Colonel Gadson holds master's degrees in information systems from Webster University and policy management from Georgetown University. In 2010, he was an Army War College Fellow at the Institute of World Politics in Washington, D.C. He is also a graduate of the Command and General Staff College and the Field Artillery Officers Advanced Course.

Section 5

NFL Owners Who Served

Within a year after the attack on Pearl Harbor, something happened that one can barely imagine today—six of the men who owned NFL professional football teams had enlisted in the armed services. These were multimillionaires all, men who were often older than those who would have been called, men who need not have enlisted—but did.

They were:

- George Halas, owner/coach of the Chicago Bears, who enlisted in the navy. For Halas, it was his second enlistment. He had also served during World War I.[389]
- Fred Levy, Jr., co-owner of the Cleveland Rams, who enlisted in the Army Air Corps.
- Wellington Mara, co-owner of the New York Giants, who enlisted in the navy.
- Dan Reeves, co-owner of the Cleveland Rams, who enlisted in the Army Air Corps;
- Alexis Thompson, owner of the Philadelphia Eagles, who enlisted in the army.
- Dan Topping, owner of the Brooklyn Dodgers, who enlisted in the Marines.

Bud Adams

Kenneth Stanley "Bud" Adams Jr.

Born: January 3, 1923

Owner: Tennessee Titans

Kenneth Stanley "Bud" Adams Jr. was—like Ralph Wilson—among the founders of the American Football League. Adams was one of the original owners of the Houston Oilers and is currently the senior owner in the NFL. Born in Bartlesville, Oklahoma, on January 3, 1923, Adams is the only Native American among the owners. He is on the rolls of the Cherokee Nation—for which his uncle William served as chief from 1949–71. Bud built on his father's work in the oil business; "Boots" Adams was president of Phillips Petroleum beginning in 1939. Adams is chairman and CEO of Adams Resources & Energy Inc., a wholesale supplier of oil and natural gas. He also owns a number of Lincoln-Mercury automobile franchises, which likely pleases Detroit Lions owner William Clay Ford. He also has extensive ranching and farming interests in Texas and California.

Bud Adams is currently the owner of the Tennessee Titans, as the 1997 move to Nashville (though the team played in Memphis for two years while its stadium was being built) made the Titans the current incarnation of the original Oilers.

Adams attended Culver Military Academy where he lettered in football, basketball, and baseball, and graduated in 1940, later graduating from the University of Kansas with an engineering degree—but not until after service during World War II as a lieutenant in the United States Navy, serving in the Pacific. Still in college at Kansas, Adams signed up in 1942 with the U.S. Naval Reserve and was called to active duty in July 1943 in the V-12 program. He earned his commission as an ensign at Midshipman Officer Specialty School at Notre Dame. He served as an aviation engineering officer in a PAC-Fleet carrier unit until returning Stateside about three months after the end of hostilities in 1945. He served as an aide in the U.S. Navy's Congressional Liaison Office in Washington, D.C., prior to his discharge in 1946.

At KU he earned a letter in football, and he is one of the few owners who has played the game at any advanced level. His interest in sports has also seen him as a part-owner in professional baseball, basketball, and boxing enterprises.

Tom Benson

Born: July 12, 1927, in New Orleans, Louisiana
Owner: New Orleans Saints

Tom Benson, owner of the New Orleans Saints, enlisted in the United States Navy at age 17 and served in the Pacific Theater in 1945 aboard the battleship the USS *South Dakota*. A native of New Orleans (born in the Crescent City in 1927), he was very successful in business and was in a position that he was able to step in and buy the struggling franchise in 1985 in order to forestall a planned sale that would have moved the team to Jacksonville. His success in business came from the automobile business, and he continues to own several dealerships in and around both New Orleans and San Antonio.

Some of the profits from the dealerships led him to invest in local banks, purchasing some of them and building a holding company called Benson Financial, which was sold in turn to Wells Fargo in the mid-1990s.

A private man, he has continued to support efforts to honor the United States Navy and holds the distinction of being the only enlisted man to serve on the board of trustees of the Pensacola National Naval Aviation Museum.

Benson was a leading advocate for the National World War II Memorial in Washington, D.C., and a major contributor and past director of The National World War II Museum in New Orleans, where his pledges helped fund the Pacific Exhibit grand opening and the Midway Theater.

In 2007, Benson was honored by the U.S. Navy Memorial Foundation with its Lone Sailor Award, presented to those who "exemplify the core values of honor, courage, and commitment." And in early 2010, his Saints became Super Bowl Champions.

William Clay Ford

Born: March 14, 1925, in Detroit, Michigan
Owner: Detroit Lions

William Clay Ford is the sole owner of the Detroit Lions franchise, as he has been since

1964. Grandson to Henry Ford, he served as chairman of the executive committee of the Ford Motor Company board of directors for 57 years until his retirement in 2005. Born on March 14, 1925, Ford joined the U.S. Navy Air Corps as an 18-year-old air cadet in 1943 during the heart of World War II. He underwent 25 weeks of pre-flight training with its requisite physical conditioning including swimming, running, boxing, wrestling, and obstacle course work—testing strength and speed and endurance. Of all the men in his class, Bill Ford finished first.[390]

He was still an aviation cadet at the time of his discharge in 1945. After departing his service in the navy, he enrolled at Yale where he became captain of both the tennis team and the soccer team, and he was a nationally ranked tennis player until two Achilles tendon surgeries.

Ford went on to attend Yale University in the postwar era, graduating in Economics in 1949. He married in midstream to another offspring of an automotive pioneer, Martha Firestone, granddaughter to tire magnate Harvey Firestone. The couple enjoyed a June 1947 wedding. Their son William Clay Ford Jr. has served as Chairman of Ford since 1999.

Bill Ford remembered in a 1962 press release, "Professional football in Detroit goes back…to 1925, when Jimmy Conzelman paid all of $25 for a franchise. The price has gone up a bit." The original franchise only lasted two years, was then reinstated after a year, but once again became inactive. Finally, a local radio station owner, George Richards, was determined to see

William C. Ford. (Photo courtesy of the Detroit Lions)

a team in Detroit once more so he bought one—the Portsmouth (Ohio) Spartans—and moved it to Detroit in 1934. Ford became a member of the Lions' board in 1956; he was elected president in 1961.

He has remained a devoted Detroiter, committed to the city as witnessed by his decision to fund construction of Ford Field in downtown Detroit in 2002, which led to the hosting of Super Bowl XL in 2006. His interest in the team dated back to the first year the Lions fielded a team, 1934, when his father—Edsel Ford—took him as a young boy to see the team play.

He has been active in charity work and among other honors has been a life trustee of the Eisenhower Medical Center, a national trustee for the Boys' and Girls' Clubs of America, and honorary chair of the United Way Community Services. In September 2005, he was inducted into the Michigan Sports Hall of Fame.

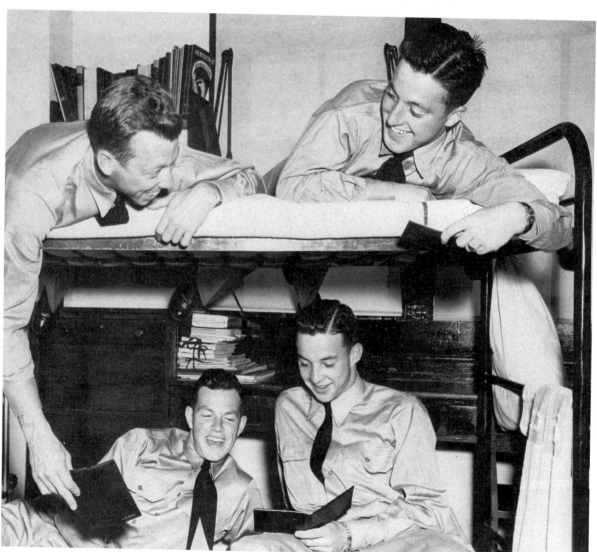

Relaxing during the evening rest period at St. Mary's Pre-Flight School in Oakland, California, William Clay Ford (right, in lower bunk) compares girlfriend pictures with his bunkmates, Cadets Robert Calhous (lower left), James Easton (upper left), and Bryce Eastburn on April 23, 1945. (AP Photo)

Alex Spanos

Born: September 28, 1923, in Stockton, California

Owner: San Diego Chargers

In 1984, the hard-working Alex Spanos became owner of the San Diego Chargers—something he declared was the culmination of a lifelong dream. He had been raised in the family business, starting to work at age eight preparing pastries in his father's restaurant seven days a week, day and night. Constantinos "Gus" Spanos had come to America in late 1912.

A native of Stockton, California, who was born in 1923, Alex saved up $800 and bought his own truck, setting out to start his own catering business even as he pursued his degree at the University of the Pacific in Stockton. From catering, he expanded into real estate and eventually construction, building that business into A.G. Spanos Companies, which has been described as one of the nation's largest family-owned construction companies.

His college career was interrupted, however, by the Second World War. He began at Cal Poly in 1941, studying aeronautical engineering. The attack on Pearl Harbor came before he completed his first semester. Spanos enlisted in the Army Air Forces on February 9, 1942, and served three years and three months. Spanos was made a flight lieutenant and initially trained as a pilot during the war but transferred out of flight school to become a gunner in B-29s. He was given the rank of sergeant. Interestingly, his father, Gus, had also signed up to become a pilot in World War I but was not accepted into the air program, serving instead in the regular army from 1918 to 1919, thereby earning his citizenship papers.

Alex resumed his studies after the war and earned his degree while lettering in swimming and diving in 1946 and serving as the drum major for the Mustang Marching Band. Then he threw himself into his company's work. As the firm became increasingly successful, Spanos became more active in civic and charitable efforts. His work was key in bringing the Super Bowl to San Diego, helping build the San Diego Hall of Champions, and projects at Children's Hospital and the like. He personally funded the

Alex Spanos with his mother, Evanthia Spanos. (Photo courtesy of the San Diego Chargers)

cost to transport more than 145 World War II veterans and their families to Washington to enjoy a visit to the newly constructed National World War II Memorial. He served on George W. Bush's Presidential Delegation to the 2004 Olympic Games in Athens and even funded the making of a 2006 dramatized documentary film, *The 11th Day*, which is a tribute to the Greek resistance who dealt the Germans their first major defeat of the war, killing or injuring almost 50 percent of the 8,000 elite airborne assault troops, and then fighting the Nazi attempt to occupy Crete for four years despite the execution of thousands of Cretans.

Spanos has written an autobiography, *Sharing the Wealth: My Story*. In his book, with every opportunity to tell his story and elaborate on his service, he was as humble as could be—not an unusual characteristic for the men and women of this generation. Spanos wrote, "World War II interrupted my plans. I became a sergeant in the air force. I returned home to Stockton with my lovely wife, Faye, who would become the bedrock of my world." Was that it? Eight words in a 254-page book? Fortunately, more than 30 pages later, he offered just a little more information.

Spanos had been in college but left two months after Pearl Harbor. On February 9, 1942, he enlisted in the Army Air Forces and—just barely—passed the examination to become an aviation cadet; he hoped to become a pilot. During training, a false claim of paternity led to him being transferred. "Instead, they sent me to the B-29s, where I became a gunner." He was stationed in Colorado, then at Shreveport,

and then to Drew Field in Tampa. At the end of 1945, he was transferred to Albany, Georgia, and ultimately posted to Santa Ana, California, where he was discharged in February 1946 with the rank of staff sergeant.[391]

Ralph C. Wilson Jr.

Born: October 17, 1918, in Columbus, Ohio
Owner: Buffalo Bills

Ralph C. Wilson Jr. is the founder of the Buffalo Bills and one of the founding owners of the American Football League. Wilson was justly recognized with induction into the Pro Football Hall of Fame on August 8, 2009. Born on October 17, 1918, in Columbus, Ohio, Wilson grew up in Detroit and attended both the University of Virginia and the University of Michigan Law School—but, as with many of his generation, World War II interrupted his studies. Wilson enlisted in the United States Navy and served five years, most of which was at sea.

While in the war, Lt. Wilson was involved in some of the most dangerous service of all—working aboard a minesweeper. Needless to say, German forces were well aware of the importance of trying to disrupt or sever Allied supply lines. If they could sufficiently inhibit the massive flow of both personnel and materiel from the United States to the Allied powers, it could make all the difference in the war. The use of mines to protect beachfronts and ports was extensive. Even if the Allies had taken a port, new mines could be sown by air drops during the night and mines were sometimes

On D-Day men ride in an LCVP toward Omaha Beach. (Photo courtesy of the National World War II Museum)

dropped by parachute into shipping lanes. George Sessions Perry of *The Saturday Evening Post* spent some time aboard Yard Mine Sweeper No. 29 off the coast of France in 1944. The YMS was a fairly small wooden ship (which frustrated magnetic mines), and No. 29 was just 136' in length. This largely unheralded minesweeping craft was originally intended for home defense but proved invaluable in advance of invasion landings. YMS 29 was active both at Anzio beachhead and on D-Day.

Lt. Ralph Wilson was the skipper of No. 29 (YMS craft did not have names) and had experience with the patience and the courage it took to perform his duties. As Perry wrote, "It takes time and guts to clear a mine field, and especially the latter. The men who do it live on the brink of sudden death and know it."[392] The craft Wilson captained was at that point the last one of the first group of YMSs to come over from America. It had swept most of the North African coast and had led the fleet into Salerno and Anzio and Provence.

Perry asked Wilson if he'd ever seen any of his friends strike a mine. "Yes," Wilson replied, "That was at Anzio. It was a ship we'd worked with for a year. We'd gone on liberties together a lot, and the officers and crew of both ships had more or less been neighbors throughout the war. Both of us were sweeping, and suddenly there was a terrific explosion. Black smoke and black water rose a hundred feet in the air. Then we felt the blast of the explosion. Felt it, knowing that this was just a faint echo of the thing that had pulverized our friends. It was horrible. These men in my crew had fought a lot more war than most people ever will. But that night took the starch out of 'em."

Wilson also served in the Pacific. He'd first arrived in Pearl Harbor and wound up in Okinawa. He was the captain of a ship that carried a flag officer who was in charge of about 24 smaller minesweepers. He told Joe Horrigan of the Pro Football Hall of Fame, "Our ship, we were the first non-minesweeper to enter Tokyo Bay." He then sailed south and went to Hiroshima. "On the outskirts of Hiroshima, it was complete wasteland. There was only one building standing in Hiroshima, and that was right in the middle of town. It was tilted one way, all the windows were blown out, of course…. I can say I was the first American to see Hiroshima."[393]

Wilson was back in Tokyo Bay in time for the Japanese surrender and watched the ceremonies on the USS *Missouri* from a distance.

Following the war, he went into the insurance business his father had begun and developed that further while expanding investments into mines and factories in Michigan, buying a number of manufacturing enterprises, construction firms, and even some radio stations. He was a minority owner of the Detroit Lions but jumped in with both feet when the American Football League was founded, becoming the owner of the Buffalo Bills. Later, he made loans to save the shaky operations of the Oakland Raiders and Boston (later New England) Patriots. The Bills currently play at the appropriately named Ralph Wilson Stadium.

Two of his three daughters are also involved with the Bills. His daughter Linda Bogdan served as the first female scout in professional football and then served as vice president of the Bills until her passing in 2009. Daughter Christy Wilson Hofmann serves as a consultant in the team's merchandising department.

Appendix 1

NFL Personnel Who Served in World War II

From Abbey to Zuzzio, the following NFL honor roll includes 1,002 NFL personnel who served in the military during World War II:

Hall of Famers in bold

Joe Abbey
Chet Adams
K.S. (Bud) Adams
Neal Adams
Robert Adkins
Ben Agajanian
Alex Agase
Robert Agler
Joe Aguirre
Leonard Akin
Frankie Albert
Art Albrecht
Charles Aldrich
Bruce Alford
Warren Alfson
Joseph Allton
Dr. Eddie Anderson
Stan Andersen
Steve Andrako
Ray Apolskis
Tony Arena
Loyd Arms
Graham Armstrong
Lee Artoe
Earl Audet
Charles Avedisian
Don Avery

John Badaczewski
Steve Bagarus
E.L. Bailey
Al Baisi
Jon Baker
Frank Balasz
Bob Balog
Emil Banjavic
Vince Banonis
Jack Banta
Jim Barber
Walter Barnes
Len Barnum
Emmett Barrett
Sam Bartholomew
Francis Barzilauskas
Nick Basca
Stan Batinski
Cliff Battles
Burt Baumgartner
Lloyd Baxter
Alyn Beals
Weyland Becker
Chuck Bednarik
Charles Behan
J. Edward Beinor
Steve Belichick

Edward Bell
Tom Benson
Edward Berrang
Rex Berry
Libero Bertagnolli
Frank Binotto
Keith Birlem
Del Bjork
Robert Bjorklund
William Blackburn Jr.
Al Blozis
Frederick Boensch
Jack Boone
Dick Booth
Gil Bouley
Tony Bova
Cloyce Box
Ray Bray
Leo Brennan
Paul Briggs
Lawrence Brink
Maurice Britt
Dave Brown
George Brown
Hardy Brown
Howard Brown
Paul Brown

Thomas Brown
Phil Bucklew
Harry Buffington
Ray Buivid
Joe Bukant
George Buksar
Rex Bumgardner
Jefferson Davis
Burkett
Dale Burnett
Paul Burris
Sherill Busby
Ray Busler
Young Bussey
Carl Butkus
Joe Byler
Larry Cabrelli
George Cafego
Ronald Cahill
Ralph Calcagni
James Callahan
William Campbell
Tony Canadeo
Rocco Canale
John Cannella
Leo Cantor
Don Carlos

243

Eddie Casey
Dick Cassiano
Jim Castiglia
Tony Cemore
Edward Champagne
Jim Champion
Ben Chase
Lloyd Cheatham
Charles Cherundolo
Chet Chesney
John Chickerneo
William Chipley
Andrew Chisick
Paul Joseph
Christman
August Cifelli
Edward Cifers
Robert Cifers
Frank Clair
Stewart Clancy
Harry Clark
Potsy Clark
Stuart Clarkson
Corwin Clatt
Boyd Clay
Cal Clemens
John Clement
Jack Cloud
John Clowes
Leon Cochran
John Cochran Jr.
Homer Cole
Pete Cole
Thomas Colella
William Collins
Don Colo
William Combs
Merlyn Condit
Charley Conerly
Gerry Conlee

George Conner
Ted Cook
Joseph Coomer
Edward Coon
Atlon Coppage
George Corbett
Olie Cordill
Michael Corgan
Russell Cotton
Albert Coupee
Gerald Courtney
Gerard Cowhig
Clem Crabtree
Lou Creekmur
Theodore Cremer
Harold Crisler
Jim Crowley
Ward Cuff
Jim Cullom
Louis Daddio
Frank Damiani
Jim Daniell
Ed Danowski
Bob Davis
Corby Davis
Fred Davis
Jerome Davis
Ralph Davis
William Davis
Rufus Deal
Hal Dean
Thomas Dean
William John
deCorrevont
Louis DeFilippo
Robert DeFruiter
Bob deLauer
Albert Demao
Vincent Dennery
Arthur Deremer

Bob Derleth
Dan DeSantis
Versil Deskin
William Dewell
David diFilippo
Don Doll
Joe Doller
Dick Dolly
Joseph Domnanovich
Allen Donelli
Art Donovan
John Doolan
Otis Douglas
Elwood Dow
Harley Dow
Kenneth Dow
Harry Dowda
Dorland Doyle
Ed Doyle
Charles Drulis
John Druze
Walter Dubzinski
Joseph Duckworth
Andrew Dudish
Bill Dudley
Kay Eakin
Ralph Earhart
Roger Eason
Ray Ebli
Brad Ecklund
Weldon Edwards
William Edwards
Clyde Ehrhardt
John Eibner
Charles Eikenberg
Don Eliason
Everett Elkins
Carlton Elliott Jr.
Drew Ellis
Lawrence Ellis

Mush Elser
Ox Emerson Jr.
Frank Emmons
Fred Enke Jr.
Rex Enright
Dick Erdlitz
Len Eshmont
Clarence Esser
Fred Evans
Murray Evans
Ray L. Evans
Richard Evans
Weeb Ewbank
Arthur Faircloth
Nello Falaschi
Tony Falkenstein
Tom Farmer
Jake Fawcett
Tom Fears
Walter Fedora
Charles Fenenbock
Ralph Fife
Frank Filchock
Jack Finlay
Edward Fiorentino
Dr. Paul Fitzgibbon
Ray Flaherty
Richard Flanagan
Dick Flatley
Vernon Foltz
Len Ford
William Clay Ford
George Forester
Aldo Forte
Robert Forte
Dan Fortmann
Ralph Foster Jr.
Terry Fox
Sam Francis
George Franck

Joseph Frank
Paul Franklin
Ray Frankowski
Ray Frick
Benny Friedman
Sherwood Fries
William (Red)
Friesell
Ralph Fritz
Andrew Fronzcek
Edward Frutig
Tony Furst
James Gaffney
Hugh Gallarneau
Milt Gantenbein
Don Garlin
Lester Gatewood
Frank Gatski
Charles Gelatka
Lee Gentry
Ray George
Elwood Gerber
William Geyer
Louis Ghecas
Joe Gibson
Robert Gifford
Sloko Gill
James Gillette
Earl Girard
Chester Gladchuk
Fred Gloden
Ed Goddard
Tod Godwin
William Godwin
Paul Goebel
Clark Goff
Marshall Goldberg
Joseph Golding Jr.
Sam Goldman
George Gonda

Henry Goodman
Owen Goodnight
William Goodwin
John Goodyear
Paul Governalli
Lyle Graham
Otto Graham
Bud Grant
William Gray
John Greene
Tom Greenfield
Don Greenwood
Visco Grgich
Frank Grigonis
Billy Grimes
Roger Grove
Lou Groza
George Gulyanics
Mike Gussie
Ace Gutowsky
William Hachten
John Hackenbruck
Banard Hafen
George Halas
Irving Hall
L. Parker Hall
Robert Halperin
William Halverson
John Haman
Ray Hamilton
Robert Hanlon
Merle Hapes
Pat Harder
Roger Harding
James Hardy
Cecil Hare
Tom Harmon
Maurice Harper
Henry Harris
Granville Harrison

Richard Harrison
Howard Hartley
Ken Hayden
Tom Hearnden
Ken Heineman
George Hekkers
William Hempel
Robert Hendren
Kirk Hershey
Ralph Heywood
Howard Hickey
Edward Hiemstra
John Higgins
Ben Hightower
Bill Hillman
Clarke Hinkle
Jack Hinkle
Elroy Hirsch
Joseph Hoague
Herman Hodges
Lester (Dick)
Hoerner
Wayne Hoffman
John Hollar
Tony Holm
Mike Holovak
Harry Hopp
Richard Horne
Les Horvath
Lin Houston
Sherman Howard
Jim Lee Howell
John Howell
Frank Hrabetin
Frank Hubbell
Dick Huffman
Frank Huffman
Bill Hughes
Fred Vant Hull
Dick Humbert

Robert Ingalls
Burt Ingwersen
Dr. A. Ippolito
Tex Irwin
Chris Iverson
Bob Ivory
Frank Ivy
Jack Jacobs
Marvin Jacobs
Harry Jacunski
Tommy James
Ben Janiak
Edward Jankowski
Mike Jarmoluk
Floyd Jaszewski
Robert Jeffries
Jack Jenkins
Arthur Jocher
Cecil Johnson
Clyde Johnson
Don Johnson
Glenn Johnson
Howard Johnson
Nathan Johnson
William Johnson
William L. Johnson
William O. Johnson
James Johnston
Arthur Jones
Edgar Jones
Elmer Jones
Harvey Jones
James Jones
James (Casey) Jones
Lewis Jones
Thurman Jones
Michael Jurich
Walter Jurkiewicz
Ed Justice
Steve Juzwik

Robert Kahler
Eddie Kahn
Tommy Kalmanir
Bernard Kapitansky
Jack Karwales
Edward Kasky
Leo Katalinas
William Katrishen
Ken Kavanaugh
E.J. Kawal
Eulis Keahey
Jim Keane
Thomas Keane
William Kennedy
Nick Kerasiotis
Ralph Kercheval
Bill Kern
Alex Ketzko
Walter Kichefski
George Kiick
Warren Kilbourne
Glenn Killinger
Frank Kilroy
Frank Kinard
George Kinard
Edward King
Jack Kirby
Ben Kish
Adolph Kissell
John Kissell
Lee Kizzire
Harry Kline
John Knolla
Larry Knorr
Mike Koken
Edward Kolman
John Koniszewski
Joe Koons
Dr. Joe Kopcha
Jules Koshlap

John Kovatch
George Kracum
Kenneth Kranz
Max Krause
Al Kreuger
Bob Krieger
Frank Kristufek
John Ksionzyk
Bert Kuczynski
Joe Kuharich
John Kuzman
Steve Lach
W.S. Lafitte
Harold Lahar
Jospeh Lamas
Walter Lamb
Tom Landry
Mort Landsberg
James Lankas
Grenville Lansdell
Ted Lapka
John Lascari
Lindy Lauro
Dante Lavelli
Hubbard Law
Jimmy Lawrence
Peter Layden
Milan Lazetich
William Lazetich
Edgar Lechner
William Leckonby
William Lee
Clyde LeForce
Darrell Lester
Russ Letlow
Steve Levanitis
Howard Levitas
Fred Levy
Leonard Levy
Marv Levy

Art Lewis
Cliff Lewis
Frank Liebel
Don Lieberum
R. Jack Lininger
James Lipinski
Joe Litzenich
Howard Livingston
Pat Livingston
Robert Livingston
Ted Livingston
Richard Loepfe
Andy Logan
Dr. James Logan
Joe Lokanc
Robert Long
John Lookabaugh
Don Looney
Sid Luckman
Jack Lummus
Ken Lunday
Jay MacDowell
Art Macioszczyk
Bill Mackrides
Elmer Madarik
Lloyd Madden
Robert Maddock
John Magee
Dante Magnani
Francis Maher
Ray Mallouf
Charles Malone
Joe Maniaci
Robert Mann
Eggs Manske
Joseph Manzo
Jack Mara
Wellington Mara
Gino Marchetti
Basilio Marchi

Andy Marefos
Joe Margucci
John Martin
Vernon Martin
Bernie Masterson
Ned Mathews
John Mattiford
Albert Matuza
Stanley Mauldin
Frank Maznicki
George McAfee
Wes McAfee
Jack McAuliffe
John McBride
Mike McCaskey
Bob McChesney
Clint McClain
Frank McCormick
Joel McCoy Jr.
Hugh McCullough
Coley McDonough
Paul McDonough
Robert McDougal
Banks McFadden
Barney McGarry
Clarence McGeary
Jack McGinley
Paul McKee
Lee McLaughlin
James McMillen
Johnny (Blood)
McNally
Ed McNamara
Jim Meade
Jack Meagher
Curtis Mecham
James Mello
John Mellus
Art Mergenthal
Monte Merkel

Ed Merkle
Walter Merrill
Fred Meyer
John Michelosen
Lou Midler
Joe Mihal
Mike Mikulak
Don Miller
Eddie Miller
Wayne Millner
Paul Mitchell
Art Modell
Dr. John Mohardt
Bo Molenda
Avery Monfort
Thomas Mont
James Montgomery
Jim Mooney
Allen Moore
Paul Moore
Wilbur Moore
William R. Moore
Gonzalo Morales
Boyd Morgan
Francis Morris
George Morris
Robert Morrow
Raymond Morse
Clure Mosher
Perry Moss
Kelley Mote
Marion Motley
Tim Moynihan
Rudy Mucha
Garvin Mugg
Joe Muha
Carl Mulleneaux
Noah Mullins
William Murphy
Chet Mutryn

R.L. Nardi
Andy Natowich
Fred Naumetz
Walter Neilsen
Bob Nelson
Steven Nemeth
Carl Nery
Ernie Nevers
Hamilton James
Nichols Jr.
Emery Nix
Jack L. Nix
Leo Nobile
Leo Nomellini
Bob Nowaskey
Robert Nussbaumer
Jerry Nuzum
Bill O'Brien
John O'Keefe
Charles O'Rourke
Duncan Obee
Urban Odson
Doug Oldershaw
Mitchell Olenski
Lawrence Olsonoski
Daniel Orlich
Joe Osmanski
Dr. William
Osmanski
Al Owen
Vincent Pacewic
Lou Palazzi
Mike Palm
Derrell Palmer
Ernie Pannell
Dave Parker
Joe Parker
Clarence (Ace)
Parker
Mickey Parks

Lloyd Parsons
William Paschal
George Paskvan
Joe Pasqua
Rupert Pate
Frank Patrick
John Patrick
Maurice Patt
Billy Patterson
Ted Pavelec
Stanke Pavkov
Larry Peace
James Pearcy
Win Pedersen
James Peebles
Claude Perry
Joe Perry
William Petrilas
Steve Petro
George Petrovich Jr.
John Petty
Alex Piasecky
Robert Pifferini
Pete Pihos
John Pingle
Henry Piro
Rocco Pirro
Dick Plasman
George Platukis
Warren Plunkett
Dick Poillon
John Polanski
Francis Polsfoot
Hampton Pool
Jim Poole
John Poto
John Prchlik
Mervin Pregulman
Pat Preston
Charles Price

Robert Priestly
Dom Principe
Abisha Pritchard
Ray Prochaska
Frederick Provo
Marion Pugh
Andy Puplis
Calvin Purdin
Chuck Quilter
Ed Quirk
George Rado
William Radovich
Norbert Raemer
Phil Ragazzo
Garrard Ramsey
Walter Rankin
John Rapacz
Robert Ravensberg
Frank Reagan
C.L. Reese
Hank Reese
Kenneth Reese
Dan Reeves
Bob Reinhard
Pug Rentner
Hank Ress
Joe Restic
James Reynolds
William Reynolds
Jay Rhodemyre
Frank Ribar
Ray Riddick
Richard Rifenburg
Charles Riffle
Thron Riggs
Jack Riley
Thomas Roberts
Robert Robertson
Tom Robertson
Andy Robustelli

Lyle Rockenbach
Henry Rockwell
Mike Rodak
Thomas Rodgers
Cullen Rogers
Herman Rohrig
Rudolph Romboli
Salvatore Rosato
Ted Rosequist
Kenneth Roskie
Stillman Rouse
Harmon Rowe
Robert Rowe
Ed Royston
Pete Rozelle
Tony Rubino
Martin Ruby
Al Russas
Bo Russell
Dougal Russell
Jack Russell
Ralph Ruthstrom
Dave Ryan
Kent Ryan
Julius Rykovich
Lou Rymkus
Joseph Sabasteanski
Edwin Saenz
Charles Sample
John Sanchez
Jack Sanders
Orban (Spec) Sanders
Curt Sandig
John Sandusky
Sandy Sanford
Ollie Sansen
Frank Santora
Dominic Sanzotta
Tony Sarausky
Paul Sarringhaus

Larry Sartori
George Sauer
Joe Savoldi
Mike (Mo) Scarry
Bernie Scherer
Alex Schibanoff
John Schiechl
Paul Schissler
Herman Schneidman
John Schneller
Ivan Schottel
Tex Schramm
Bill Schroll
Carl Schuette
Charles Schultz
Victor Schwall
Perry Schwartz
Richard Schweidler
Wilson Schwenk
Perry Scott
Charles Seabright
Earl Seick
Clarence Self
Harry Seltzer
Bob Shaw
Charles Shaw
Alec Shellogg
Rhoten Shetley
John Shirk
Bunny Shoemann
Hal Shoener
Herbert Shoener
John Shonk
Fred Shook
Alexander Sidorik
Dr. John Siegal
Herbert Siegert
Stephen Sierocinski
Joseph Signaigo
Rudolph Sikich

Jack Simmons
Walt Singer
Steve Sinko
Frank Sinkwich
Emil Sitko
James Sivell
Joe Skladany
Robert Skoglund
Dwight Sloan
Marty Slovak
Bruce Smith
Ernie Smith
Gaylon Smith
George Smith
Graham Smith
J. Robert Smith
Jack Smith
O. Edwin Smith
V.T. Smith
Dave Smukler
Bill Smyth
Hank Soar
Ben Sohn
Jack Sommers
Gus Sonnenberg
Vic Spadaccini
Eugene Spangler
Alex Spanos
Al Sparkman
Mac Speedie
Joseph Spencer
George Speth
Ed Stacco
Jack Stackpool
James Stacy
Norman Standlee
Leo Stasica
Arthur Statuto
Ernie Stautner
John Steber

Gilbert Steinke
William Steinkemper
Paul Stenn
Dave Stephenson
Robert Steuber
Ralph Stevenson
Dean Steward
Walter Stickel
J.P. Stout
Richard Stovall
Clem Stralka
Joe Stringfellow
Woody Strode
John Strzykalski
Roy Stuart
Joe Stydahar
Steve Sucic
Bob Sufferidge
Bob Sullivan
Leonard Supulski
D. John Sutherland
Joe Sutton
Earl Svendsen
George Svendsen
Robert Swisher
Paul Szakash
Walter Szot
Bob Tanner
Hugh Taylor
Dan Tehan
Alexis Thompson
Tommy Thompson
Wilfred Thorpe
Owen Thuerk
Robert Thurbon
Pete Tinsley
Bob Titchenal
Silus Titus
Dick Todd
Joseph Tofil

Lou Tomasetti
Andrew Tomasic
Mario Tonelli
Dan Topping
Henry Topping
Zollie Toth
John Treadaway
Charley Trippi
John Tripson
Robert Trocolor
Clyde Turner
Orville Tuttle
Enrico Uguccioni
Harry Ulinski
Andrew Uram
Alex Urban
Emil Uremovich
Norm Van Brocklin
Hal Van Every
Fred Vanzo
Jack Vetter
Walter Vezmar
Joe Vodicka
Evans Vogds
Carroll Vogelaar
Don Vosberg

James Wade
Wiliam B. Walker
Will Walls
William Ward
Buist Warren
Bob Waterfield
Foster Watkins
Joseph Watson
Joseph Watt
George Watts
Charles Weaver
Don Weedon
Ray Wehba
Art Weiner
Bernard Weiner
Arnie Weinmeister
Isadore Weinstock
Dick Weisgerber
Howie Weiss
Don Wemple
Ralph Wenzel
Hodges West
Pat West
Stanley West
Robert Westfall
Chet Wetterlund

Thomas Wham
Ernie Wheeler
J.J. Whire
Arthur White
Byron White
Paul White
Marvin Whited
Lloyd Wickett
Bob Wiese
George Wilde
Richard Wildung
Wilbur Wilkin
Boyd Williams
Don Williams
Ellery Williams
Frank Williams
Jerry Williams
Walter Williams
Ernest Williamson
Jack Wilson
John Wilson
Ralph Wilson Jr.
Warren Camp
Wilson
Abner Wimberly
Pete Wissman

Robert Wood
Dick Woodard
John Woudenberg
John Wozniak
Frank Wydo
John Wyhonic
Ventan Yablonski
Ray Yageillo
Howard Yeager
John Yonakor
James Youel
Len Younce
Claude Young
George Young
Roland Young
William Young
Frank Zadworney
Gust Zarnas
Joe Zeller
Joseph Zeno
Frank Ziegler
John Zilly
Robert Zimny
Louis Zontini
Frank Zoppetti
Tony Zuzzio

NFL Personnel Who Served in the Korean War

The following NFL honor roll is of 226 NFL personnel who served in the military during The Korean War:

Hall of Famers in bold

Nicholas Adduci
John Amberg
Rudolph Andabaker
Elmer Arterburn Jr.
Dale Atkeson
Bill Austin
Ed Bagdon
Kenneth Barfield
Paul Barry
Joe Bartos
Maurice Bassett
Edward Bawel
Lloyd Baxter
Ray Beck
Edward Bell
Marvin Berschet
Jack Bighead
Don Boll
Bill Bowers
Cloyce Box
Bob Boyd
Harold Bradley
Ed Brown
James Cain
Joe Campanella
Marion Campbell
Stanley Campbell

Pat Cannamela
Camillo Capuzzi
Bob Carey
Ken Carpenter
Russ Carroccio
Bud Carson
Rick Casares
Frank Cassara
Tom Catlin
Lynn Chandnois
Earnest Cheatham
Herman Clark
Randall Clay
Bill Collins
Larry Coutre
John Cox
Jim Cullom
Al Davis
Art Davis
Ameleto Del Bello
Dick Deschaine
Dorne Dibble
Al Dorow
Dick Doyle
Dick Dugan
Doug Eggers
Leo Elter

Dick Evans
Hal Faverty
Howard Ferguson
Tom Finnin
Bernie Flowers
Dick Flowers
Herschel Forester
Bob Forte
Joe Fortunato
Dominic Fucci
Bob Gain
Arnie Galiffa
Ray Gene Smith
Hal Giancanelli
George Gilchrist
Gary Glick
Robert Goode
Ken Gorgal
Everet Grandelius
Bob Griffin
Forrest Griffith
Roscoe Hansen
John Hatley
Hall Haynes
Don Heinrich
John Helwig
Ed Henke

Ralph Heywood
John Hock
Jack Hoffman
Al Hoisington
Glenn Holtzman
William Horrell
Harry Hugasian
Weldon Humble
Charlie Hunsinger
Kenneth Huxhold
John Huzvar
George Idzik
Ken Jackson
Vic Janowicz
Bill Jessup
Herb Johnson
Charles Jones
Charlie Justice
Johnny Karras
Bob Kelley
J.D. Kimmel
Jim Kincaid
George Kinek
Don King
Edward Kissell
Don Klosterman
Pat Knight

Ken Konz
Eldred Kraemer
John Kreamcheck
Ray Krouse
Jim Landrigan
Dick (Night Train) Lane
Robert Langas
Bud Laughlin
Eddie LeBaron
Toy Ledbetter
Jack Lee
Robert Lee Smith
Jimmy Lesane
Veryl Lillywhite
Gene (Big Daddy) Lipscomb
Cliff Livingston
Lloyd Lowe
Ken MacAfee
John Macerelli
Gilbert Mains
Leon Manley
Dave Mann
Joe Matesic
Ollie Matson
Clay Matthews Sr.
John Mazur
Art McCaffray
Willie McClung
Dewey McConnell

Mike McCormack
Len McCormick
Lewis McFadin
Bob Meyers
Art Michalik
Andrew Miketa
Fred Miller
Paul Miller
Bill Milner
Billy Mixon
Edward Modzelewski
James Monachino
George Morris
Art Murakowski
Jim Mutscheller
Bob Myers
Jack Nix
James Norman
Pat O'Donahue
Chester Ostrowski
Don Owens
Jim Owens
Bob Perina
Pete Perini
Volney Peters
John Petibon
Earl Putnam
Volney (Skeets) Quinlan
George Radosevich
Rex Reed Boggan

Ken Reese
John Reger
Les Richter
Fred Robinson
Ben Roderick
William Roffler
Ray Romero
Brad Rowland
Pete Schabarum
Bob Schnelker
Gene Schroeder
Ed Sharkey
Billy Shipp
Don Shula
Joe Signaigo
George Sims
Emil Sitko
Joseph Skibinski
Gordy Soltau
Julian Spence
Art Spinney
John Steber
Dick Steere
Majure Stribling
Breck Stroschein
Jack Stroud
Leo Sugar
Leonard Szafaryn
Walt Szot
Jesse Thomas
Ralph Thomas

Billy Tidwell
Travis Tidwell
Bob Toneff
Frank Tonnemaker
Ted Topor
Wally Triplett
Harold Turner
Edward Tyrrell
Chuck Ulrich
Teddy Vaught
Bill Wade
Fred Wallner
James Weatherall Jr.
Gerald Weatherly
Larrye Weaver
Charles Weber Jr.
Ted Wegert
Stan West
Bob White
Ray Wietecha
Bob Williams
Wally Williams
Tom Wilson
Elmer Wingate
Casimir Witucki
Junior Wren
Walter Yowarsky
Caroll Zaruba
Ronald Zatkoff

Appendix 3

NFL Personnel Who Served in the Vietnam War

The following NFL honor roll is of 28 NFL personnel who served in the military during the Vietnam War:

Hall of Famers in bold

Joe Bellino
Willie Betlon
Rocky Bleier
Gary Bugenhagen
John Butler
Woody Campbell
Ernie Cheatham

Jim Clack
Moses Denson
Glen Ellison
Joe Haering
Alvin Hall
Cliff Harris
Ralph Heywood

Cornelius Johnson
Charlie Joiner
Bob Kalsu
Howard Kindig
MacArthur Lane
Gary Larsen
Joe Don Looney

Mike Montler
Ray Nitschke
Roger Staubach
Les Steckel
Don Steinbrunner
Don Talbert
Herb Travenio

Lists as presented by the Pro Football Hall of Fame.

Appendix 4

NFL Players and Coaches with Ties to the Military

Note: The following list was updated from its original source (listed at the end of this appendix) to reflect status changes through June 2013.

Ties to the military:

DB Phillip Adams, Oakland Raiders—Father served in the army.

DE Jared Allen, Minnesota—Grandfather, Ray, served in the Marine Corps and his brother, Scot, is currently serving in the Marine Corps.

G/C Eugene Amano, Tennessee—Father served in the navy for 25 years. Eugene was just released by the Titans.

OT Shawn Andrews, New York Giants—Brother, Derrick, is a sergeant in the army and recently finished a term in Kuwait. Shawn was an unsigned free agent as of 2010.

G/OT Stacy Andrews, Seattle—Brother, Derrick, is a sergeant in the army and recently finished a term in Kuwait. Stacy is currently an unsigned free agent.

DE Kentwan Balmer, Washington—Cousin is in the Marine Corps. Kentwan is currently an unsigned free agent.

LB Tully Banta-Cain, New England—Father, Adam, played football for the Naval Academy.

WR Hank Baskett, Minnesota—Father spent more than 30 years in the air force; mother served as CFO at air force base in Clovis, New Mexico; brother served in the army for more than 10 years.

Offensive assistant Chris Beake, Cleveland—Served in the air force as a civil engineer officer from 1995–98.

WR Bernard Berrian, Minnesota—Parents, Sallie and Joseph, are retired air force mechanics. Bernard no longer plays football.

LB Michael Boley, New York Giants—Brother was an army specialist who served in Afghanistan. Michael was released by the Giants in 2012.

DB Zack Bowman, Chicago—Father, Zackary, is a master sergeant in the air force.

QB Drew Brees, New Orleans—Grandfather served in World War II.

WR Kenny Britt, Tennessee—Sister, Specialist Laura Johnson, serves at Victory Base Camp in Iraq.

S C.C. Brown, Detroit—Currently in the National Guard; unit is prepared for Afghanistan if needed. C.C. is an unsigned free agent.

OT Jammal Brown, Washington—Father, Charles, is retired from the army. Jammal is currently an unsigned free agent.

C Jason Brown, St. Louis—Brother, Lunsford, served in Iraq and was killed in 2003. Jason is currently an unsigned free agent.

Offensive coordinator Jim Caldwell, Baltimore—Uncle, John, served in the air force; cousins, Sean and Letha, served in the navy and the army, respectively.

LB Caleb Campbell, Kansas City—Served in the army.

QB David Carr, New York Giants—Grandfather served in the air force; Brother-in-law is in the Marine Corps.

CB Nolan Carroll, Miami—Father, Nolan Sr. was a senior master sergeant in the United States Air Force; mother, Jennifer, retired from the navy in 1999 as a lieutenant commander and is now the current Florida lieutenant governor.

LB Danny Clark, New Orleans—Has twin brothers in the armed forces—Jason (air force) and Joshua (Marine Corps).

RB Thomas Clayton, Cleveland—Father was a sergeant first class in the army for 25 years. Thomas is currently an unsigned free agent.

CB Nate Clements, Cincinnati—Father served in the army. Nate is currently an unsigned free agent.

Offensive assistant Jim Bob Cooter, Denver—Grandfathers Ted and Bobby served in the army.

Defensive coordinator Gunther Cunningham, Detroit—Father was a sergeant in the air force.

OT Anthony Davis, San Francisco—Grandfather served in the army.

G Kris Dielman, San Diego—Father served in the army and has cousins in both the army and navy.

OL Evan Dietrich-Smith, Green Bay—Brother, Alex, is a specialist-team leader in 10th Mountain Division of the army.

General manager Mark Dominik, Tampa Bay—Father, Glenn, was in the navy; Brother, Todd, was in the navy; grandfather, Edward, was in the army during WWII; father-in-law, Forrest, was in the army.

QB Trent Edwards, Philadelphia (released in 2013)—Father, Andy, flew reconnaissance missions during Vietnam War. Maternal grandfather was awarded Navy Cross for Valor during bombing of Pearl Harbor.

DE Chris Ellis, Pittsburgh (until 2011)—Father and mother served in the army and navy, respectively.

DE Demetric Evans, San Francisco—Has cousins in both the army and navy.

FB Jerome Felton, Minnesota—Brother, Simon, is in the army and currently serving in Afghanistan.

CB Cortland Finnegan, St. Louis—Mother served 20 years in the army.

WR Larry Fitzgerald, Arizona—Attended Valley Forge (PA) Military Academy after high school; his grandfather was a lieutenant in the army who won a Purple Heart for his service in Korea; aunt and uncle, Paul and Sam Jones, are both lieutenant colonels in the army.

CB Drayton Florence, Carolina—Father, Drayton Sr., is a retired army medic; sister, Lakisha, is currently serving in the army.

Head coach John Fox, Denver—Father was a member of one of the original Navy SEAL teams created by President John F. Kennedy in the early 1960s.

C Hank Fraley, St. Louis—Brother was stationed with the army in Iraq; father is a Vietnam veteran.

LB Marcus Freeman, Houston—Father, Michael, served 26 years in the air force.

Head coach Chan Gailey, Buffalo—Father, Tom, was in the Marine Corps. Chan was fired in 2010.

K Graham Gano, Carolina—Has two brothers in the navy and his father was in the Marines.

DE Ben Garland, Denver—Currently on the club's reserve/military list and is now a strength and conditioning coach at the Air Force Academy.

K Shayne Graham, Cleveland—Father served in the army in Vietnam.

Linebackers coach Kevin Greene, Green Bay—Served as a captain for 16 years in the Army Reserve during the off-seasons when he was an NFL player.

S Cedric Griffin, Washington—Mother served in the navy; father served in the air force.

S Michael Griffin, Tennessee—Mother served in the navy; father served in the air force.

FB Ahmard Hall, Tennessee (as of 2012)—Served four years in the Marines (3rd Battalion, 8th Marines out of Camp Lejeune, North Carolina), including missions in Kosovo (1999) and Afghanistan (2002).

WR Chad Hall, San Francisco—Attended the Air Force Academy and was a second lieutenant at Hill Air Force Base in Salt Lake City, Utah.

LB Parys Haralson, San Francisco—Grandfather served in the army.

LB Adam Hayward, Tampa Bay—Brother and sister served in the army and cousin was in the Marine Corps.

CB Ellis Hobbs, Philadelphia—Father, Ellis Hobbs Jr., served for over 30 years and graduated as a sergeant major before retiring from the military. Ellis has not played football since 2011).

DE Jason Hunter, Oakland—Father, James, served 25 years in the 82nd Airborne Division in the army.

G Mike Iupati, San Francisco—Brother-in-law is currently serving in the army.

RB Steven Jackson, Atlanta—Father served in the Marines.

WR Vincent Jackson, Tampa Bay—Father, Terrence, was an army medic.

LB Dhani Jones, Cincinnati—Both parents served in the military.

Special teams assistant Ben Kotwica, New York Jets—Served in the army as an Apache helicopter pilot in Iraq.

LB Manny Lawson, Buffalo—Father, Donald, served in the air force.

Head coach Marvin Lewis, Cincinnati—Father was in the army, was stationed in Germany.

DT Roy Miller, Jacksonville—Father and cousin served in the army.

Linebacker coach Mike Murphy, Indianapolis—Father, George, served in the navy; cousins William B. and William M. served in the army and navy, respectively.

LB Ben Leber, St. Louis—Father, Al, was stationed in Korea with the army when he met Ben's mother, Han.

WR Brandon Lloyd, New England—Nephew is serving in Iraq and brother is a retired member of the air force. Brandon is an unsigned free agent as of 2012.

OT Phil Loadholt, Minnesota—Father was a sergeant first class in the army.

Assistant head coach/Defensive line coach Rod Marinelli, Dallas—Served a one-year tour of duty in Vietnam.

QB Ingle Martin, Denver—Uncle, Chris, is a lieutenant commander and pilot for the navy. Ingle was released.

FB Jason McKie, Baltimore—Father spent 23 years in the air force. Jason was released in 2011.

OT Marcus McNeill, San Diego—Mother, Leola, is a colonel in the air force, stationed at Dobbins Air Force Base in Marietta, Georgia.

OT Pat McQuistan, Arizona—Brother is in the air force. Pat is an unsigned free agent since 2012.

CB Will Middleton, Jacksonville—Brother, Wyatt, started at safety for Navy for four years and graduated from the U.S. Naval Academy. Will is currently a free agent.

DT Roy Miller, Jacksonville—Father and cousin served in the army.

DE/DT Kyle Moore, Chicago—Father, Joseph, served in the army for 22 years.

RB Sammy Morris, Dallas—Father, Sammy, was an air force staff sergeant; brother, Brien, serves in the air force. Sammy is currently an unsigned free agent.

DE C.J. Mosley, Detroit—Father, Calvin Mosley Sr., is a retired first master sergeant with the United States Army.

G Jamar Nesbit, New Orleans—Father, Ronald, works for the Army Corps of Engineers.

DE Igor Olshansky, Miami—Father was in the Russian Army; grandfather fought for the Russian Red Army in World War II.

DT Mike Patterson, New York Giants—Uncle was a sergeant at Los Alamitos Army Base.

Tight End Coach Justin Peelle, Philadelphia—Grandfather is a retired navy captain.

Special Teams Coordinator Mike Priefer, Minnesota—Served in the navy (1991–94) as a helicopter pilot and was stationed in the Persian Gulf.

DE Melila Purcell, Cleveland—Father is an active reservist in the army. Melila was waived in 2012.

WR Josh Reed, San Diego—Brother (army) and cousin (navy) recently served in Iraq.

G Tyler Reed, Chicago—Father, Gary, played football for the Naval Academy from 1971–75.

Quarterbacks coach Frank Reich, San Diego—Father, Frank, served in the Marines.

Head coach Andy Reid, Kansas City—Father served in the navy in World War II.

FB Tony Richardson, New York Jets—Father was a sergeant major in the army; sister, part of Desert Storm, is serving in the army at Fort Bragg, North Carolina.

Head coach Ron Rivera, Carolina—Father was an army officer; Ron lived in three countries as a child.

S Mark Roman, San Francisco—Five of his six brothers served in the army.

WR Eddie Royal, San Diego—Sister, Christina, served in Iraq as a member of the Air Force Office of Special Investigations Detachment 104.

CB Lydell Sargeant, Buffalo—Father, Drew, served in the air force for more than 20 years. Lydell was cut in 2010.

LB Cody Spencer, Detroit—Brother serves in the army, currently stationed in Iraq. Cody is no longer playing.

OT Joe Staley, San Francisco—Grandfather was in the navy during the Korean War; uncle was in the navy.

DT Randy Starks, Miami—Father served in the army for more than 20 years, mostly in Germany.

TE Tony Stewart, Oakland—Father, Malcolm, was in the army and stationed in Germany when Tony was born. Tony was released in 2010.

Offensive coordinator Mike Sullivan, Tampa Bay—Graduate of Army Airborne, Ranger, and Air Assault schools.

CB Charles Tillman, Chicago—Father was an army sergeant; Charles attended 11 schools in 13 years.

LB Pat Thomas, Buffalo—Father was a chief petty officer in the navy.

Tight ends coach Ricky Thomas, Indianapolis—Father, John, served in the air force.

DE Dave Tollefson, New York Giants—Brother is serving in the Marine Corps.

Head coach Norv Turner, San Diego—Father served in the Marines.

Former quarterbacks coach Ron Turner, Indianapolis—Father, Richard, served in the Marines. Ron is now the head coach at Florida International University.

K Lawrence Tynes, New York Giants—Father served in the navy as a master chief. Lawrence is now a free agent.

WR Roberto Wallace, Tennessee—Father, Roberto, is retired from the U.S. military.

LB DeMarcus Ware, Dallas—Wife, Taniqua, served in the air force.

Defensive line coach Mike Waufle, St. Louis—Served in the Marine Corps from 1972–75.

DE Mario Williams, Houston—Brother-in-law served in the army and was killed in Iraq.

WR Troy Williamson, Jacksonville—Brother is a career Marine, who just returned from Iraq; sister serves in the navy.

LB Patrick Willis, San Francisco—Father was in the National Guard.

Owner/President Ralph Wilson Jr., Buffalo—Navy veteran, served in WWII.

LB Will Witherspoon, Tennessee—Father was in the air force. Will is an unsigned free agent as of 2012.

DB Dexter Wynn, Detroit—Mother is a retired air force civil engineer who served in the Gulf War. Dexter is currently a free agent.

DT Bryant Young, San Francisco—Father served in the army; brother served four years in Desert Storm; wife was the daughter of a career military man (retired).

Offensive line coach Larry Zierlein, Phoenix—Served in the Marines for two years, including a one-year tour of duty in Vietnam.

Source: http://www.nfl.com/news/story/09000d5d8237c5f6/article/nfl-players-and-coaches-with-ties-to-the-military

Notes

1. Brian Cronin. "Sports Legends Revealed: Did the owners of the Pittsburgh Eagles trade teams?" *Los Angeles Times,* http://latimesblogs.latimes.com/sports_blog/2010/04/sports-legends-revealed-did-the-owners-of-the-pittsburgh-steelers-and-philadelphia-eagles-trade-team.html.

2. Pro Football Hall of Fame. (n.d.). "Football and America: World War II." Retrieved from http://www.profootballhof.com/history/general/war/worldwar2/page2.aspx.

3. Sports Then and Now "Remembering the NFL on December 7, 1941" http://www.sportsthenandnow.com/2011/12/06.

4. Frank Graham Jr., "The Day the War Came to the Polo Grounds," *Sports Illustrated,* http://sportsillustrated.cnn.com/vault/article/magazine/MAG1079199/index.htm.

5. Pro Football Hall of Fame, Leemans, "Tuffy" http://www.profootballhof.com/hof/member.aspx?PLAYER_ID=127.

6. Will McDonough. (1999). *The History of the NFL: The Complete Story of the National Football League, 1920–2000.* (New York: Smithmark Publishers, 1999).

7. Todd Anton, *No Greater Love.* (Burlington, MA: Rounder Books, 2007), 205.

8. S.L. Price, "The Second World War Kicks Off—December 7, 1941: Redskins Versus Eagles on Pearl Harbor Day," *Sports Illustrated,* November 29, 1999. http://sportsillustrated.cnn.com/vault/article/magazine/MAG1017830/index.htm

9. Ibid.

10. Ibid.

11. Cindy Boren. "The Early Lead: On December 7, 1941, Crowd at Redskins Game Was Kept in the Dark About Attack," *The Washington Post,* December 7, 2010. Retrieved from http://voices.washingtonpost.com/early lead/2010/12/on_dec_7_1941_crowd_at_redskin.html.

12. Ibid.

13. Bob Cunningham. "The most forgotten game ever played: Dec. 7, 1941," *Bleacher Report,* December 8, 2008. Retrieved from http://bleacherreport.com/articles/90449-the-most-forgotten-game-ever-played-dec–7–1941.

14. Price, op. cit.

15. Will McDonough, op. cit.

16. Cronin, op. cit.

17. "NFL History by Decade," http://www.nfl.com/history/chronology/1941–1950.

18. *Pearl Harbor Two Hours that Changed America,* ABC News Specials. ABC News with NHK Japan. Compact disc. 1991.

19. Will McDonough, op. cit.

20. Cronin, op. cit.

21. Ibid.

22. http://www.jacklummus.com.

23. Theodore Hull. "The World War II Army Enlistment Records." National Archives. http://www.archives.gov/publications/prologue/2006/spring/aad-ww2.html.

24. James H. Doolittle. "Individual Report on Tokyo Raid" http://www.doolittleraider.com/interviews#James H. Doolittle Individual Report on Tokyo Raid.

25. *The War Times Journal,* "The Guadalcanal Campaign: Turning Point in the South Pacific–1942," http://www.wtj.com/articles/guadalcanal.

26. Pro Football Hall of Fame, "FOOTBALL AND AMERICA: World War II." http://www.profootballhof.com/history/release.aspx?RELEASE_ID=1178.

27. Washington Redskins, "Ghosts of DC", http://www.ghostsofdc.org/2012/09/07/redskins–1942-championship.

28. Dave Blevins. *The Sports Hall of Fame Encyclopedia: Baseball, Basketball, Football, Hockey, Soccer.* (Google e-book, 2011). Retrieved from http://books.google.com/books/about/The_Sports_Hall_of_Fame_Encyclopedia.html?id=a7CnkH2HIsQC.

29. Keith Yowell. "Today in Pro Football History: 1943 NFL Approves Merger of Eagles and Steelers for '43." (June 19, 2010). Retrieved from http://fs64sports.blogspot.com/2010/06/1943-nfl-approves-merger-of-eagles.html.

30. Hull, op. cit.

31. Yowell, op. cit.

32. NFL History 1941–1950 http:www.nfl.com/history/chronology/1941-1950, 2005. http://www.nfl.com/history/chronology/1941–1950.

33. Yowell, op. cit.

34. NFL History 1941–1950, op. cit.

35. For more on Nagurski, see Jim Dent. *Monster of the Midway* (New York: St. Martin Press, 2004).

36. Bryn Swartz. "One for the ages: Sid Luckman's 1943 NFL Championship Game," *Bleacher Report*, March 5, 2010. Retrieved from http://bleacherreport.com/articles/357519-one-for-the-ages-sid-luckmans-1943-nfl-championship-game.

37. NFL History 1941–1950, op. cit.

38. ABC News, *The 20ᵗʰ Century America's Time with Peter Jennings.* Episode 2: "Over the Edge," 1999. http://www.youtube.com/watch?v=KgjG9BAi_RU.

39. Yowell, op. cit.

40. Bob Carroll, John Thorn, and Michael Gershman. *Total Football: The Official Encyclopedia of the National Football League.* (New York, NY: HarperResource, 1997).

41. Joseph S. Page. *Pro Football Championships before the Super Bowl: A Year by Year History* (Jefferson, NC: McFarland and Co., 2011).

42. The Office of Strategic Services was the precursor to the Central Intelligence Agency, more commonly known as the CIA.

43. Much of that information came from Major League Baseball catcher Moe Berg who was in the service of the OSS in Europe. See Linda McCarthy's essay on Berg in Todd Anton and Bill Nowlin, eds., *When Baseball Went to War.* (Chicago: Triumph Books, 2008).

44. Cronin, op. cit.

45. James Quirk and Rodney D. Fort. *Pay Dirt: The Business of Professional Team Sports.* (Princeton, NJ: Princeton University Press, 1992).

46. Griffith, op. cit.

47. Will McDonough, op. cit.

48. Pete Dymeck. "The Year America Stood Still: Army's Dream Season of 1945," *Bleacher Report*, October 26, 2008. Retrieved from http://bleacherreport.com/articles/73648-the-year-america-stood-still-armys-dream-season-of–1945.

49. http://www.oberlin.edu/archive/WWI.html.

50. Kevin Quinn. *Sports and Their Fans: The History, Economics, and Culture of the Relationship between Spectator and Sports.* (Jefferson, NC: McFarland and Co., 2009), 64.

51. Robert Janis. "Whatever happened to…Eddie LeBaron," *Washington Times*, May 29, 2008. Retrieved from http://www.washingtontimes.com/blog/redskins-fan-forum/2008/may/29/whatever-happened-to-eddie-lebaron.

52. William Nak. "A True American," *Sports Illustrated*, July 23, 2001.

53. Ibid.

54. *New York Times*, December 29, 1940.

55. *New York Times*, November 25, 1941.

56. Chester County Hall of Heroes, http://dsf.chesco.org/heroes/basca/basca.htm. We acknowledge that this site shows Basca as born in 1917, but have presented his birth year as 1916 per Pro-Football-Reference.com.

57. *Boston Globe*, September 9, 1942. Some 38,000 attended the game at Fenway, a 14–7 win for the Bears. Basca kicked the ball for the extra point after the Army team scored its lone touchdown.

58. Ibid.

59. Chester County Hall of Heroes, http://dsf.chesco.org/heroes/basca/basca.htm

60. http://www.findagrave.com/cgi-bin/ fg.cgi?page=gr&GRid=33808923

61. Hulek's account is provided in Terry Frei's May 31, 2010, *Denver Post* column.

62. *Washington Post*, November 4, 1940.

63. Vasak's article appears in the January 2006 issue of *Elysian Fields* (the "Official Paradise Valley Estates Residents' Newsletter"), Fairfield, California.

64. http://www.guhoyas.com/genrel/121505aaj.html. An article in *Coffin Corner*, Vol. VIII, #6 by Victor Mastro, Frank Alkyer, and others says Blozis was killed during the Battle of Black Mountain, near Colmar, France.

65. *New York Times*, January 26, 1991.

66. *New York Daily News*, February 25, 2003.

67. Ibid.

68. Patrick McArdle, "A Tale of Two Hoyas," *Georgetown Magazine*, Fall/Winter 1994–95.

69. *New York Times*, February 20, 1944.

70. *New York Times*, December 18, 1944.

71. http://www.redcross.org/museum/history/ww2a.asp

72. Thanks to Jay Blackman, University of Tennessee—Chattanooga.

73. The website www.oldestlivingprofootball.com/ charleschuckbraidwood.htm also says that Braidwood was born in Illinois, citing the *Portsmouth Times* of January 23, 1945.

74. Ralph B. Cushman. *Young Bussey Young Stud: An All-American Legend* (Houston: Bigco Press, 1993).

75. Ibid., 5–13.

76. Ibid., 161.

77. Ibid., 174.

78. The ship's captain was W.A. McHale—so Bussey truly served in "McHale's Navy."

79. Cushman, *Young Bussey*, 195.

80. "Bears Honor Roll" reproduced on the first page of the photo insert in Cushman's book, following page 80.

81. Martin Dreyer, "Mom Believes Son Still Alive," *Houston Chronicle*, November 11, 1956.

82. *Los Angeles Times*, March 30, 1945.

83. Jeff Walker, "For the Boys," *Leatherneck*, August 2008.

84. *New York Times*, June 3, 1945. Franck later told Arthur Daley that Chevigny had exuded excitement during the shelling, saying, "Gee, this is fun." He urged Franck to run for the post with him, but Franck declined—and survived. See the November 30, 1945, *Times*.

85. Walker, *Leatherneck*, op. cit. *Note: Pro-Football-Reference.com has Chevigny born in Hammond, Indiana, but we believe his correct town of birth was Dyer.*

86. Vinny DiTrani. "The Dayton Triangles" *Bergen County Record*, August 24, 2003.

87. *Chicago Tribune*, December 7, 1925.

88. See article on Operation Torch by David H. Lippman at http://usswashington.com/worldwar2plus55/dl08no42. htm.

89. http://schuylkillcountymilitaryhistory.blogspot.com/ search?q=doyle.

90. E-mail from Mark Cohen to Bill Nowlin on July 3, 2010. Thanks also to Brenda Barnes, Karen Tjarks, and Roger Rainwater of Texas Christian University.

91. http://www.pacificwrecks.com/aircraft/b-24/44-40929. html

92. Dan Magill. "Former Dog died a Hero at Iwo Jima." OnlineAthens, *Athens Banner-Herald, February 18, 2001.*

93. Ibid.

94. Jeffrey S. Williams. "Remembering Smiley: Bulldog, Packer, and Maui Marine," UGA Sports Communications. February 22, 2010. Accessed at: http://www.nmnathletics.com/ViewArticle. dbml?DB_OEM_ID=8800&ATCLID=204892993

95. Ibid.

96. *Washington Post*, March 18, 1945.

97. http://www.thecolumnists.com/isaacs/isaacs216.html

98. Pro-Football-Reference.com shows his birthdate as November 21, but his gravestone says it was November 23.

99. *Los Angeles Times*, September 22, 1943.

100. *Los Angeles Times*, September 30, 1943.

101. *Laramie Republican*, October 28, 1943.

102. *Laramie Republican*, December 27, 1943.

103. www.pacificwrecks.com/aircraft/b-25/41-30046.html

104. Reported in both the *Riverton Review* and the *Greybull Standard*, March 2, 1944.

105. From the Baylor Bears website: "Baylor University is believed to be the only school in America to have two former athletes win the Congressional Medal of Honor. Both men, Jack Lummus and John (Killer) Kane, won the nation's highest military honor for heroics in World War II:

"Kane played football and basketball at Baylor and was a member of the ill-fated 1927 basketball team that lost 10 of its members in a bus-train wreck. Kane was one of 12 survivors.

"Kane joined the Army Air Corps in 1932 and soon became a bomber commander of legendary proportions. It was said he was the best pilot and toughest commander in the Air Corps. It was often debated who feared him more–the Germans or his own men.

"On August 1, 1943, Kane led what at the time was the deadliest air battle in history—a low-level, long-range bombing raid on Hitler's oil-refining complex in Ploesti, Romania. The site produced a major part of the Axis' fuel and was one of the most heavily guarded locations in history."
--http://www.baylorbears.com/trads/bay-medalhonor.html

106. www.jacklummus.com

107. http://www.findagrave.com/cgi-bin/fg.cgi?page=gr&GRid=5796720

108. Richard F. Newcomb, *Iwo Jima* (New York: Holt Paperbacks, 2002). Thanks also to Gary Bedingfield.

109. *Rockford Register-Republic*, Rockford, Illinois, April 20, 1942.

110. Thanks to Jeff Keag, Alison Reynolds, and Carrie Schwier of Indiana University who tracked down materials which were important in documenting McCaw's connections with I.U.

111. *Indiana Daily Student*, September 6, 1922.

112. Letter on file in Indiana University Archives.

113. *Washington Post*, September 21, 1930. Some of his heroics are detailed in an October 6, 1931 article in the *Post*, at a time Georgetown was seeking "another Mooney."

114. *New York Times*, November 4, 1928.

115. *New York Times*, October 3, 1944.

116. *New York Times*, November 1, 1945.

117. *Chicago Tribune*, October 1, 1934, and October 16, 1934. The latter news story added, "His long distance booting had been an outstanding feature in all of his team's games."

118. *Chicago Tribune*, November 27, 1938, and August 31, 1939.

119. *Chicago Tribune*, August 25, 1940.

120. *New York Times*, October 3, 1944. The *Times* incorrectly cited his age as 39, but we have corrected that in the quotation.

121. *The Stars and Stripes*, September 15, 1944. Other sources variously provide his date of death as September 9 and 13.

122. http://chronicles.dickinson.edu/encyclo/s/ed_supulskiL.htm.

123. *New York Times*, September 30, 1937.

124. *Hartford Courant*, January 4, 1939.

125. *Chicago Tribune*, August 30, 1939.

126. *New York Times*, October 30, 1941.

127. *Washington Post*, November 10, 1941.

128. E-mail from David Wemple to Bill Nowlin, July 24, 2010. Thanks also to Ray Wemple.

129. *Chicago Tribune*, August 20, 1943.

130. *The Argus*, Illinois Wesleyan, September 13, 1944.

131. *Chicago Tribune*, November 16, 1941.

132. Address in Young's honor during halftime at a 1986 University of Oklahoma football game. http://www.cfb-history.com/2012/09/04/this-day-in-college-football-history-september-4th/

133. Berry Tramel. "Young a war hero, kind man. Ex-Sooner, killed near Tokyo in 1945, has been gone 62 years but never forgotten," *NewsOK*, August 6, modified August 30, 2007.

134. *Remembering Bob Kalsu*, NFL Films, 1999. It is available for viewing at http://nflfilms.nfl.com/2012/05/28/this-memorial-day-in-football-remembering-bob-kalsu/

135. http://www.findagrave.com/cgi-bin/fg.cgi?page=gr&GRid=6140788

136. William Nack, "A Name on the Wall," *Sports Illustrated*, July 23, 2001.

137. Jason Krump, "A Hall of Famer In Every Way," Washington State University Athletics, May 23, 2007. Retrieved from http://www.wsucougars.com/genrel/052307aae.html

138. *Farm and Dairy*, Salem, Ohio, December 13, 2001.

139. http://www.profootballhof.com/history/general/war/vietnam/page1.aspx

140. http://www.virtualwall.org/ds/SteinbrunnerDT01a.htm

141. *Bellingham* (WA) *Herald*, July 21, 1967.

142. http://aol.sportingnews.com/sport/story/2011–05–02/what-pat-tillman-set-out-to-do-finally comes-to-pass

143. http://www.thedailybeast.com/articles/2009/09/13/pat-tillman-anti-war-hero.html

144. aol.sportingnews.com, op. cit.

145. http://www.youtube.com/watch?v=vhwInUN8UY0

146. http://www.youtube.com/watch?v=aUCyr3B3IlM

147. aol.sportingnews.com, op. cit.

148. See, for instance, the *Los Angeles Times*, August 6, 1942. For more on Battles, see also "Cliff Battles" in *The Coffin Corner*, Vol. 22, #3 (2000). By John Seaburn (originally published in the Akron, Ohio, *Beacon Journal*) and "Cliff Battles" by Michael Richman in the Vol. 23, #2 (2004) *Coffin Corner*.

149. *Washington Post*, October 15, 1944. He also played in the 14–0 win over the Fleet City Bluejackets on October 28.

150. *Chicago Tribune*, May 14, 1945, and November 2, 1946.

151. *Washington Post*, May 3, 1981.

152. http://www.liberatorcrew.com/15_Gunnery/06_waist.htm

153. *New York Times*, November 30, 1948, reported the two crash landings.

154. http://www.8thafhs-pa.org/member-profiles/chuck-bednarik–467th-bg/

155. *Cleveland Plain Dealer*, March 31, 1942.

156. *Green Bay Packer Football News*, January 12, 1944, and *Italian Tribune News*, November 21, 1975.

157. *New York Times*, April 4, 2003.

158. *New York Times*, April 4, 2003.

159. *Sports Illustrated*, September 20, 2006.

160. *Sports Illustrated*, September 20, 2006.

161. *New York Times*, July 28, 1996.

162. *Chicago Tribune*, August 8, 1950.

163. *Baltimore News-American*, December 8, 1974.

164. Jim Sargent, "Bullet Bill Dudley," *The Coffin Corner*, Vol. 18, No. 4 (1996).

165. Robert Cannon, *Sports Collectors Digest*, August 19, 1994.

166. http://www.cmgww.com/football/dudley/biography_2.htm

167. John Harris, *Pittsburgh Tribune-Review*, February 5, 2010.

168. Milton Gross, *Sport*, November 1948.

169. *Cleveland Plain Dealer*, December 28, 1959.

170. *Chicago Tribune*, December 1, 1945.

171. http://www.coldhardfootballfacts.com/content/happy-birthday-weeb-we-hardly knew-ya/5807/ May 2007.

172. *Los Angeles Times*, January 6, 2000.

173. Ibid.

174. *Los Angeles Times*, November 4, 1947.

175. *Los Angeles Times*, January 6, 2000.

176. *New York Times*, January 8, 2000.

177. *Boston Globe*, November 27, 1942.

178. *Washington Post*, December 13, 1942. The Bears victory streak was reported in the December 14 *Christian Science Monitor*.

179. *Chicago Tribune*, December 14, 1942.

180. *New York Times*, December 6, 1945.

181. *Washington Post*, March 14, 1972.

182. Press release by Don Smith, Pro Football Hall of Fame. May 6, 1976.

183. *Sports Illustrated*, September 22, 2003.

184. *New York Times*, November 26, 2005.

185. http://www.clevelandbrowns.com/team/history/legends.html

186. *New York Times,* November 26, 2005.
187. Bob Barnett and Bob Carroll, *The Coffin Corner,* Vol. 6, Nos. 10 & 11 (1984).
188. *New York Times,* November 26, 2005.
189. *New York Times,* November 26, 2005.
190. http://www.ottograham.net/bio.html
191. *Chicago Tribune,* April 1, 1945.
192. Bob Oates, *Los Angeles Times,* April 10, 1985.
193. http://www.uscg.mil/history/people/ottograham.asp
194. *Boston Globe,* January 7, 1977.
195. *Los Angeles Times,* September 17, 1971.
196. *Christian Science Monitor,* November 29, 1947.
197. *New York Times,* December 20, 1951.
198. *Cleveland Plain Dealer,* December 18, 1983.
199. *New York Times,* December 20, 1951.
200. grozacharitygolf.org/aboutus.htm
201. *Boston Globe,* December 25, 1953.
202. The 1900 census has him as a grocer; George Halas' obituary in the November 1, 1983, *Chicago Tribune* says he was a tailor.
203. *Cleveland Plain Dealer,* October 22, 1942.
204. http://www.bearshistory.com/lore/georgehalas.aspx
205. *New York Times,* November 14, 1945.
206. *Chicago Tribune,* May 10, 1946.
207. *Chicago Tribune,* November 1, 1983.
208. http://www.uwbadgers.com/history/hirsch-era.html
209. *Denver Post,* January 29, 2004.
210. *New York Times,* November 14, 1943.
211. Ibid.
212. *Los Angeles Times,* May 14, 1946.
213. *Hartford Courant,* January 22, 1971.
214. *Pittsburgh Courier,* January 5, 1946.
215. *Pittsburgh Courier,* April 12, 1947.
216. *Hartford Courant,* January 22, 1971.
217. *San Diego Union,* July 23, 1965.
218. *Washington Post,* December 8, 1983.
219. *Los Angeles Times,* July 21, 1967.
220. Tom Landry with Gregg Lewis. *Tom Landry: An Autobiography* (New York: Harper Paperbacks, 1991).
221. *Chicago Tribune,* July 30, 1986.
222. Ibid.
223. *Los Angeles Times,* July 20, 1986.
224. *Chicago Tribune,* July 30, 1966.
225. *Cleveland Plain Dealer,* October 25, 1946, and *Atlanta Daily World,* July 24, 1975.
226. *Cleveland Plain Dealer,* October 25, 1946.
227. *Chicago Tribune,* July 30, 1966.
228. *New York Times,* January 22, 2009.
229. *New York Times,* January 22, 2009.
230. Levy's enshrinement speech at the Pro Football Hall of Fame, August 4, 2001.
231. Rick Telander. "No Joke," *Sports Illustrated,* October 17, 2004.
232. Joe Horrigan, "Marv Levy," *The Coffin Corner,* Vol. 23, No. 3 (2001).
233. *New York Times,* July 6, 1998.
234. *Chicago Tribune,* November 11, 1943.
235. *New York Times,* January 4, 1944, and *Chicago Tribune,* February 3, 1944.
236. *Chicago Tribune,* March 13, 1944.
237. *New York Times,* September 23, 1944.
238. *Chicago Tribune,* October 5, 1944, and *New York Times,* October 24, 1944.
239. *Washington Post,* March 31, 1945.
240. *New York Times,* October 26, 1005.
241. *New York Daily News,* January 24, 2008.
242. *Sports Illustrated,* September 25, 1972.
243. *Sports Illustrated,* September 25, 1972. Joe Horrigan's article is "Wellington Mara—A Giant" in the *Coffin Corner* Vol. 19, No. 2 (1997.)
244. *Canton Repository* (Canton, Ohio), May 13, 1942.
245. *Hartford Courant,* June 10, 1963 and Barry Maisel, *New York Daily News,* August 14, 1996.
246. United States Congress, March 28, 2006.
247. Gino Marchetti, as told to Maria Burns Ortiz. "My Army experience was life-altering," ESPN.com, November 11, 2009.
248. *New York Times,* February 12, 1972.
249. *Boston Globe,* January 5, 1942.
250. Bob Barnett and Bob Carroll, "George McAfee: 'One Play,'" *The Coffin Corner,* Vol. 1, No. 10 (1979).
251. *New York Times,* March 6, 2009.

252. http://www.pattillmanfoundation.org/years/2011/

253. http://www.foxsportsarizona.com/09/08/11/Tillman-McAfees-message-lives-on/landing_azcardinals.html?blockID=561106&feedID=3702

254. *New York Times*, February 29, 1944, and November 30, 1985.

255. *CBI Roundup*, Vol. II, No. 34, Reg. No. L5015, Delhi, May 4, 1944, and the *New York Times*, November 23, 1945.

256. *New York Times*, February 29, 1944.

257. *New York Times*, April 2, 1945.

258. *New York Times*, November 23, 1945. Daley repeated the story at least once more, in the November 7, 1954, *Times*.

259. http://packershalloffame.com/players/john-mcnally/

260. *New York Times*, November 7, 1954, and http://johnnyblood.packershalloffame.com/biography/

261. http://www.pressboxonline.com/story.cfm?ID=4789. Issue #135, March 2009.

262. *Washington Post*, December 26, 1948.

263. *Washington Post*, November 20, 1976.

264. *Chicago Tribune*, September 2, 1945.

265. Andy Piascik, "Marion Motley," *The Coffin Corner*, Vol. 24, No. 4 (2002).

266. *New York Times*, February 26, 1982.

267. *New York Times*, June 28, 1999.

268. *The Sporting News*, May 22, 1976.

269. *San Francisco Chronicle*, May 4, 1965.

270. Minnesota Historical Society, *The History of Minnesota Vol. III* (Lewis Historical Publishing Company, West Palm Beach, Florida, date unknown), 127. See also the *Chicago Tribune* of May 30, 1945, regarding the recurrence of a back injury from football that brought him back to the States to begin leading physical training programs.

271. http://www.jcs-group.com/military/war1941patriots/sports.html

272. http://www.collegefootball.org/famer_selected.php?id=40079 and *Los Angeles Times*, January 9, 1953.

273. *Los Angeles Times*, January 9, 1953.

274. *New York Times*, November 30, 1957.

275. *Chicago Tribune*, October 30, 1963, and an unidentified clipping by Dick Gordon found in Nomellini's player file at the Pro Football Hall of Fame in Canton.

276. *Los Angeles Times*, October 19, 2000.

277. *New York Times*, May 17, 2012.

278. Pro Football Hall of Fame press release found in Parker's player file at the Hall of Fame.

279. Press release from Pro Football Hall of Fame from Perry's player file.

280. *San Francisco Chronicle*, April 16, 1965.

281. *San Francisco Chronicle*, April 16, 1965.

282. Joseph Hession, *Forty Niners: Looking Back* (Foghorn Press, 1985), excerpted in *The Coffin Corner*, Vol. 18, No. 5 (1996).

283. *Washington Post*, August 16, 2011.

284. Ralph Bernstein, "Jack of All Trades," Philadelphia Eagles program, November 16, 1952, and *Chicago Daily News*, February 4, 1970.

285. Pro Football Hall of Fame press release.

286. Among other places, it's possible to see the film by search on YouTube on Dear Dad Melissa Pihos.

287. *New York Times*, April 16, 1971.

288. Bill Livingston, *Cleveland Plain Dealer*, September 4, 2012. Explanation of how arrangements were made may be found in the April 7, 1943, *Plain Dealer*.

289. Michael MacCambridge, *America's Game: The Epic Story of how Pro Football Captured a Nation.* (NY: Random House, 2004).

290. http://www.stamfordadvocate.com/default/article/Robustelli-still-bleeds-Big-Blue-109743.php

291. *USA Today*, March 23, 1989.

292. *Los Angeles Times*, July 30, 1959.

293. *New York Times*, December 8, 1996.

294. http://www.achievement.org/autodoc/printmember/roz0int-1

295. Ibid.

296. http://www.encyclopedia.com/topic/Tex_Schramm.aspx

297. *Los Angeles Times*, February 26, 1947.

298. *New York Times*, July 16, 2003.

299. *Pittsburgh Post-Gazette*, September 23, 2007.

300. *Springfield* (MA) *Union*, November 27, 1949.

301. Press release found in Stautner's Hall of Fame player file.
302. The August 29, 1941, *Chicago Tribune* provides play-by-play of the game, a 37–13 win for the Bears.
303. *Chicago Tribune*, February 23, 1943.
304. *Chicago Tribune*, December 12, 1944.
305. *Chicago Tribune*, May 26, 1946.
306. See, for instance, Arthur Daley's column in the *New York Times* of August 15, 1945.
307. *Springfield* (MA) *Union*, March 25, 1977.
308. Program for 1968 enshrinement at the Pro Football Hall of Fame, located in Trippi's player file at the Hall of Fame.
309. *New York Times*, January 3, 1943.
310. Bob Barnett and Bob Carroll, "Charley Trippi: A Success Story," *The Coffin Corner*, Vol. 11. No. 1 (1989).
311. *New York Times*, October 14, 1945.
312. *New York Times*, October 17, 1945.
313. http://www.newgeorgiaencyclopedia.org/nge/Article.jsp?id=h–832
314. *Atlanta Journal*, February 20, 1968. See also the *New York Times*, January 10 and 12, 1947.
315. http://www.chicagobears.com/tradition/hof-turner.asp
316. Undated interview transcription located in Turner's Hall of Fame player file.
317. *Texas Sportsworld*, January 1966, 58.
318. *Los Angeles Times*, October 22, 1945.
319. Al Thomy, "Ordinary Halfback Gets Big Chance," unattributed newspaper story from Van Brocklin's player file at the Pro Football Hall of Fame.
320. Jim Hunter, "What Kind of a Guy is Dutch?" unattributed newspaper story from Van Brocklin's Hall of Fame player file.
321. Thomy article, op. cit.
322. *Los Angeles Times*, December 25, 1999.
323. *Los Angeles Times*, December 4, 1942.
324. See for instance the April 27 *Los Angeles Times*.
325. *Los Angeles Times*, November 15, 1943.
326. *Los Angeles Times*, December 25, 1999.
327. *New York Times*, July 7, 2000, and *The Sunday Oregonian Magazine*, undated clipping from Weinmeister's player file at the Hall of Fame.
328. Bob Braunwart and Bob Carroll, "Arnie Weinmeister," *The Coffin Corner*, Vol. 4, No. 3 (1982).
329. *Toronto Globe and Mail*, May 23, 1954, and *Chicago Tribune*, May 22, 1954.
330. *New York Times*, July 7, 2000.
331. *Philadelphia Inquirer*, February 19, 1984.
332. http://www.cmgww.com/football/lane/biography1.htm
333. *New York Times*, February 1, 2002.
334. Randy Snow, *Austin Chronicle*, February 6, 2010.
335. Randy Snow, *Austin Chronicle*, February 6, 2010.
336. *Omaha World Herald*, October 20, 1957.
337. *New York Times*, February 20, 2011.
338. *Sports Illustrated*, October 11, 2004.
339. *Los Angeles Times*, February 20, 2011.
340. *Seattle Times*, May 31, 1953.
341. *The Stars and Stripes*, December 8, 1953, and December 11, 1954.
342. *The Oregonian*, May 5, 1954. The Congressional committee was embarrassed from the start to have named Hank Bauer, who'd serve four years in the Marine Corps during World War II, when it had meant to name Hank Sauer, who had served in the Coast Guard in 1944 and 1945.
343. http://www.profootballhof.com/story/2011/2/21/ollie-matson-trade-telegram/
344. *Boston Globe*, February 20, 2011.
345. *USA Today*, December 3, 2012.
346. *San Francisco Chronicle*, February 20, 2011.
347. Dan Benbow, "Actions, Not Words," InsightNews.com, April 7, 2011.
348. *Dallas Morning News*, September 8, 1952.
349. Associated Press wire service story datelined March 25, 1953. It ran, for instance, in the *Boston Globe* of March 26.
350. Paul Zimmerman, *The New Thinking Man's Guide to Pro Football*. (New York: Simon & Schuster, 1984), 54.
351. The trade was, of course, widely reported. See, for instance, the *Los Angeles Times*, June 13, 1952.
352. *Los Angeles Times*, March 12, 1953.
353. *Los Angeles Times*, August 9, 1953.
354. *Fresno Bee*, June 15, 2010.

355. *USAToday,* February 1, 2012.

356. Greg Cote, "Shula goes from comfort to combat," StAugustine.com, August 10, 2009.

357. *Cleveland Plain Dealer,* January 26, 1952.

358. Charlie Joiner's remarks come from a January 13, 2013, interview with Bill Nowlin.

359. *New York Times,* March 9, 1998.

360. *Boston Traveler,* October 17, 1961.

361. *Aberdeen* (SD) *Daily News,* November 9, 1961.

362. Coach Wayne Hardin's quotation is widely circulated. See, for instance, http://www.heisman.com/winners/r-staubach63.php

363. John Ingoldsby, "Roger Staubach: An Interview with the Super Bowl XLV Chairman," *Armchair General,* January 2010.

364. Ibid.

365. This paragraph combines comments Staubach made for Armchair General with material from Robert F. Jones' article on Staubach, "A Do-gooder Who's Doing Good" in the September 4, 1978, issue of *Sports Illustrated.*

366. http://www.profootballhof.com/history/general/war/

367. Gary L. Bloomfield, *Duty, Honor, Victory: America's Athletes in World War II.* by Gary Bloomfield, 244. (Guilford, CT: Lyons Press, 2003)

368. Frederic Allen Maxwell, "The Late Great 98," *Michigan Today,* http://michigantoday.umich.edu/2008/09/harmon.php. Used with permission.

369. Steve Belichick's son Bill is the head coach of the New England Patriots

370. Mason, Lt. Col. Jack. "My Favorite Lion, Maurice Britt." *ARMY Magazine,* May 2008.

371. Mason, 2008.

372. Mason, 2008.

373. http://www.ausa.org/publications/armymagazine/archive/2008/5/Documents/Mason.pdf

374. This means the defensive line was very thinly defended.

375. Mason, 2008.

376. Mason, 2008.

377. Mason, 2008.

378. Mason, 2008.

379. Mason, 2008.

380. "Joe Foss Institute." joefossinstitute.org. http://www.joefossinstitute.org/. Used with permission.

381. http://www.ussiowa.org/general/html/detail.htm

382. http://www.bccourier.com/Archives/Obit_detail.php?contentId=3862

383. http://lubbockonline.com/stories/041707/sta_041707072.shtml

384. Thanks to Saleem Choudhry, who wrote about Marker in his blog at the Pro Football Hall of Fame website: http://www.profootballhof.com/blog/choudhrys-chronicles/2011/07/11/history-uncovered/

385. Jim Koger, *Upon Other Fields on Other Days.* (Marietta, Georgia: Longstreet Press, 1991), 28.

386. Koger, 34.

387. Koger, 157.

388. http://www.rockybleier.com/supporting-veterans/21-i-never-forget-my-days-in-uniform

389. This listing comes from the *Chicago Tribune* of October 21, 1942.

390. *Detroit Lions Media Guide,* 1985.

391. Alex Spanos, *Sharing the Wealth.* (Washington DC: Regnery, 2002), 12, 44–46, 48, 51.

392. George Sessions Perry, "They Fight the Axis Devilfish," *The Saturday Evening Post,* November 25, 1944, 100.

393. Joe Horrigan interview of Ralph Wilson.

Selected Bibliography

Much thanks to the librarians and libraries at California State University–San Bernardino, Crafton Hills and Victor Valley Colleges in California for locating many of the books.

Todd Anton also wished to thank the administration, faculty, and staff at American Military University for their help and support in this project.

**When Football Went to War; Introduction
The Seasons: 1941**

Baron, Scott. *They Also Served. Military Biographies of Uncommon Americans.* Spartanburg, SC: MIE Publishing, 1998.

Bloomfield, Gary L. *Duty, Honor, Victory: America's Athletes in World War II.* Guilford, CT: The Lyons Press, 2003.

Blum, John Morton. *V Was for Victory: Politics and American Culture During World War II.* New York City: Harcourt Brace Jovanovich, 1976.

Brokaw, Tom. *An Album of Memories.* New York City: Random House, 2001.

Carroll, Bob. *100 Greatest Running Backs.* New York City: Crescent Books, 1989.

Congdon, Don, ed. *The Thirties: A Time to Remember.* New York City: Simon and Schuster, 1962.

Graham, Frank. *A Farewell to Heroes.* New York City: Viking Press, 1981.

Liddell Hart, B.H. *History of the Second World War.* New York City: Putnam, 1970.

Lingemann, Richard B. *Don't You Know There's a War On? The American Home Front 1941–1945.* New York City: GP Putnam and Sons, 1970.

Lord, Walter. *Day of Infamy.* New York City: Henry Holt, 1957.

McCallum, John D. *Southeastern Conference Football.* New York City: Charles Scribner's Sons, 1980.

Dodd, Mike. "The Year the Rose Bowl Left Home." *USA Today* December 19, 2001.

Sports Encyclopedia. "1941 Chicago Bears," June 3, 1999. September 23, 2010 <www.sportsencyclopedia.com.1941.bears>.

The Seasons: 1942

Burns, James MacGregor. *John Kennedy: A Political Profile.* New York City: Harcourt Brace Jovanovich, 1960.

Curran. Bob. *Pro Football's Rag Days.* New York City: Bonanza Books, 1969.

Hand, Jack. *Heroes of the NFL.* New York City: Random House, 1965.

Harwell, Ernie. *Diamond Gems.* New York City: Avon Books, 1991.

McCann, Kevin. *Man From Abilene.* New York City: Doubleday & Company, 1952.

Perrett, Geoffrey. *Winged Victory: The Army Air Forces in World War II.* New York City: Random House, 1997.

Sullivan, George. *Pro Football's All-Time Greats.* New York City: Putnam & Sons, 1990.

Whittingham, Richard. *The Bears: A 75-Year Celebration.* Dallas: Taylor Publishing, 1994.

My Family History. 1942 Military Enlistment US Armed Services. August 12, 2010 <www.myfamilyhistory.org/sabella/militarywwii.asp>.

Pro Football Hall of Fame. "1942 Season: Impact of Draft." August 12, 2010 <www.profootballhof.com>.

The Seasons: 1943

Bradley, Omar. *A Soldier's Story.* New York City: Henry Holt, 1951.

Campbell, Jim. *Golden Years of Pro Football.* New York City: Crescent Books, 1993.

Dupuy, R. Ernest. *World War II: A Compact History.* New York City: Hawthorn, 1969.

Eisenhower, Dwight D. *At Ease: Stories I Tell to Friends.* New York City: Doubleday, 1967.

Gunther, Bill. *Hall of Famers: All-Time Greats of Four Major Sports.* New York City: Stadia Sports Publishing, 1973.

McGuane, Thomas, with Glenn Stout. *The Best Sports Writing 1992.* Boston: Houghton Mifflin Company, 1992.

Lister, Valerie. "Other Leagues Shared Spotlight." *USA Today,* June 7, 1994.

Rushin, Steve. "War and Remembrance," *Sports Illustrated,* July 16, 2001.

Timanus, Eddie. "Army-Navy: Century of drama," *USA Today,* December 1, 1999.

About.com. "History 1900s," September 23, 2010 <http://history1900s.about.com/library/photos/blywwiip179.htm>.

Watchdog.com. "Chicago Bears 1943," July 23, 2010 <www.watchdog.comgoogleimages.>.

Chicago Bears. World Championship Program NFL Bears vs. Redskins, July 23, 2010 <www.chicagobears.com/news/newsstory.asp?story_id=4848>.

The Seasons: 1944

Ambrose, Stephen E. *D-Day. June 6, 1944: The Climatic Battle of World War II.* New York City: Simon & Schuster, 1994.

Ambrose, Stephen E. *The Wild Blue: The Men and Boys Who Flew the B-24's Over Germany.* New York City: Simon & Schuster, 2001.

Carroll, Bob. *100 Greatest Running Backs.* New York City: Crescent Books, 1989.

Hymas, Joe. *Flight of the Avenger: George Bush at War.* San Diego: Harcourt Brace Jovanovich, 1991.

Landry, Tom, with Gregg Lewis. *Tom Landry.* New York City: HarperCollins, 1990.

Moss, Al. *Pac-10 Football.* New York City: Crescent Books, 1987.

Tregakis, Richard. *Guadalcanal Diary.* New York City: Random House, 1943.

Brady, Erik. "Pioneer found pain, not fame in pro football hall of fame," *USA Today,* September 20, 1995.

Schuman, Michael. "The football's halls of fame," *Kansas City Star,* January 26, 1996.

Digital History. "Invasion Extra," September 23, 2010 <www.digitalhistory.uh.edu/news/newspapers>.

The Seasons: 1945

Breuer, William B. *Geronimo! American Paratroopers in World War II.* New York City: St. Martin's Press, 1992.

Comer, John. *Combat Crew: A True Story of Flying and Fighting in World War II.* New York City: William Morrow and Company, 1976.

Henry, Mark R. *The U.S. Army in World War II.* Oxford, United Kingdom: Osprey, 2001.

Higdon, Hal. *Pro Football USA.* New York City: Putnam & Sons, 1968.

Leckie, Robert. *The Story of Football.* New York City: Random House, 1965.

Mauldin, Bill. *Back Home.* New York City: William Sloan, 1947.

Newcombe, Richard F. *Iwo Jima.* New York City: Holt, Rinehart and Winston, 1964.

Ward, Gene, and Dick Hyman. *Football Wit and Humor.* New York City: Grosset & Dunlap, 1970.

Smith, Alan. "Gerald Ford, Vice President," *Sports Illustrated,* July 8, 1974.

NFL Supports the War Effort

Pro Football Hall of Fame. "The NFL Supports the War Effort," October 1, 2010 <http://www.profootballhof.com/history/decades/1940s/1492.aspx>.

Section 2: The Last Full Measure: The KIA of the NFL

Fleming, David. *Breaker Boys: The NFL's Greatest Team and the Stolen 1925 Championship.* Bristol, CT: ESPN, 2007.

Hallas, James H. *Killing Ground on Okinawa: The Battle for Sugar Loaf Hill.* Westport, CT: Praeger Publishers, 1996.

Newcomb, Richard. *Iwo Jima.* New York: Holt Paperbacks, 2002.

Section 4: The Spirit of Football: Legends, Men, Valor, Legacy

Harmon, Tom. *Pilots Also Pray.* New York: Crowell, 1944.

Kroger, Jim. *Upon Other Fields on Other Days: College Football's Wartime Casualties.* Atlanta, GA: Longstreet Press, 1991.

Section 5: NFL Owners Who Served

Spanos, Alex. *Sharing the Wealth: My Story.* Washington, D.C.: Regnery Publishing, 2002.